This book is concerned not so much with the 'prima donna' as with *prime donne*: a group of working artists (sometimes famous but more often relatively unknown and now long forgotten) and the circumstances of their professional lives. It attempts to locate these singers within a broader history, including not only the specificities of operatic stage practice but the life beyond the opera house – the social, cultural and political framing that shaped individual experience, artistic endeavour and audience reception. Rutherford addresses questions such as the multiple discourses on the image of the singer and their impact on the changing profile of the professional artist from *figlia dell'arte* at the beginning of the era to middle-class woman at the end; the aspect of the 'stage mother' and patronage; issues of vocal training and tuition; professional life in the operatic market-place; and performance (both vocal and dramatic) conventions and practices.

SUSAN RUTHERFORD is Lecturer in Performance Studies in Drama, School of Arts, Histories and Cultures at the University of Manchester. She is co-editor of *The New Woman and Her Sisters: Feminism and Theatre, 1850–1914* and the author of several essays on opera and singers. In 2003, she was the recipient of the biennial *Premio Internazionale: 'Giuseppe Verdi'*, awarded by the Istituto Nazionale di Studi Verdiani, for her forthcoming monograph on Verdi's heroines.

CAMBRIDGE STUDIES IN OPERA

Series editor: Arthur Groos, Cornell University

Volumes for *Cambridge Studies in Opera* explore the cultural, political and social influences of the genre. As a cultural art form, opera is not produced in a vacuum. Rather, it is influenced, whether directly or in more subtle ways, by its social and political environment. In turn, opera leaves its mark on society and contributes to shaping the cultural climate. Studies to be included in the series will look at these various relationships including the politics and economics of opera, the operatic representation of women or the singers who portrayed them, the history of opera as theatre, and the evolution of the opera house.

Published titles

Opera Buffa in Mozart's Vienna
Edited by Mary Hunter and James Webster

Johann Strauss and Vienna: Operetta and the Politics of Popular Culture
Camille Crittenden

German Opera: From the Beginnings to Wagner
John Warrack

Opera and Drama in Eighteenth-Century London: The King's Theatre, Garrick and the Business of Performance
Ian Woodfield

Opera Liberalism, and Antisemitism in Nineteenth-Century France: The Politics of Halévy's *La Juive*
Diana R. Hallman

Aesthetics of Opera in the Ancien Régime, 1647–1785
Downing A. Thomas

Three Modes of Perception in Mozart: The Philosophical, Pastoral, and Comic in *Così fan tutte*
Edmund J. Goehring

Landscape and Gender in Italian Opera: The Alpine Virgin from Bellini to Puccini
Emanuele Senici

The Prima Donna and Opera, 1815–1930
Susan Rutherford

The Prima Donna and Opera, 1815–1930

Susan Rutherford
University of Manchester

CAMBRIDGE
UNIVERSITY PRESS
OCM 71018781

CAMBRIDGE UNIVERSITY PRESS

Cambridge, New York, Melbourne, Madrid, Cape Town, Singapore, São Paulo

CAMBRIDGE UNIVERSITY PRESS

The Edinburgh Building, Cambridge CB2 2RU, UK

Published in the United States of America by Cambridge University Press, New York

www.cambridge.org
Information on this title: www.cambridge.org/9780521851671

First published 2006

Printed in the United Kingdom at the University Press, Cambridge

A catalogue record for this book is available from the British Library

ISBN-13 978-0-521-85167-1 hardback
ISBN-10 0-521-85167-x hardback

CONTENTS

List of illustrations | viii
Preface | ix

Introduction | 1
1 Sirens and songbirds | 27
2 Superdivas and superwomen | 58
3 Tutors and tuition | 90
4 The supporting cast | 120
5 Professional life | 161
6 Vocal and theatrical landscapes | 205
7 The singing actress | 231
Postscript | 275

Notes | 277
Bibliography | 340
Index | 365

ILLUSTRATIONS

1   Maddalena Grassi, portrait (courtesy of the Istituzione Casa della Musica, Parma) | 41

2   Poster for the Teatro Regio in Parma, 1816 (courtesy of the Istituzione Casa della Musica, Parma) | 165

3   Lillian Nordica as Brünnhilde (courtesy of the Metropolitan Opera House Archive) | 219

4   Katharina Klafsky as Brünnhilde (courtesy of Dirk Körschenhausen and Marcelo T. Galvao de Castro) | 220

5   Adelina Patti as Amina in *La sonnambula* (courtesy of the National Portrait Gallery) | 242

6   Wilhelmine Schröder-Devrient as Leonore in *Fidelio* (courtesy of the Österreichische Nationalbibliothek, Vienna) | 246

7   Gilbert-Louis Duprez as Arnold in *Guillaume Tell* (courtesy of the Museo del Teatro alla Scala) | 247

8   Pauline Viardot as Orphée (courtesy of Paul Frecker) | 249

9   Katharina Klafsky as Leonore in *Fidelio* (courtesy of Dirk Körschenhausen and Marcelo T. Galvao de Castro) | 250

PREFACE

The support of many people contributed to the development of this book. My colleagues at the University of Manchester, led by Professor Viv Gardner, generously agreed to my absence on various trips: funding was made available to me from the Department of Drama's research allocation and the Prudhoe Fund for a number of smaller visits; the University's Research Support Fund awarded me a larger grant to sustain several valuable months in Italy.

Permissions to publish documents, illustrations and material from other sources have been granted by various bodies. I am pleased to acknowledge David Mayer and the Chicago Historical Society for the inclusion of extracts from the letters of Mary Garden; the Istituzione Casa della Musica, Parma, for illustrations and letters from the Archivio Storico del Teatro Regio; the Museo del Teatro alla Scala, the Metropolitan Opera House archive, the National Portrait Gallery and the Österreichische Nationalbibliothek for the illustrations of various singers. Paul Frecker generously supplied the photograph of Pauline Viardot; Dirk Körschenhausen and Marcelo T. Galvao de Castro did likewise for the photographs of Katharina Klafsky. Michael Turnbull shared his findings on Mary Garden with me. Myles Gleeson-White gave me access to documents pertaining to the career of Cicely Gleeson-White. The book includes extracts from three of my earlier essays published elsewhere: I am grateful for the permission to reprint them here.

The staff of a number of important institutions and libraries aided my research. Cristina Trombella, the director of the Casa della Musica, Parma, has been kindness itself and made me welcome in myriad ways (even finding a home for my beloved *bicicletta*); I am grateful also to Francesca Montresor and Olivia Cantarelli, librarians Tommaso Granelli and Federica Bianchieri, and especially to Rosaria

Ferrari, who aided my investigations into the rich archives of the Teatro Regio and provided much support and friendship. During my many visits to the Istituto Nazionale di Studi Verdiani (with its peerless library of books and other material on the history of opera), its renowned director Pierluigi Petrobelli has been an invaluable mentor; Marisa Di Gregorio Casati and Anna Zuccoli have courteously dealt with my endless requests. Staff at the Biblioteca Archiginnasio, the Civico Museo Bibliografico Musicale, the Bibliothèque Nationale de France, the British Library, the Henry Watson Library and the John Rylands University Library have all been instrumental in assisting me.

Writing this book has often brought to mind voices from the past: I recall particularly those of Frederic Cox, Sheila Barlow, Horst Günter and Rosemary Walton, all of whom played a vital role in developing my understanding of singing and music. I hope at least some of what is written here reflects their teaching.

Conversations (some lengthy and ruminative, others brief and perfunctory) with a number of scholars were helpful in clarifying my mind and suggesting new directions. David Mayer sparked my interest in Mary Garden by generously handing me a box of her letters to his grandmother, and supervised the development of a portion of the following material in its original form as my Ph.D. thesis; George Taylor elucidated aspects of performance and nineteenth-century theatre; the ever-supportive Viv Gardner was always ready to discuss gender issues and theatre, and provided warm sisterhood throughout the period of writing. Michael Holt's unique perspective on art and culture illuminated my knowledge of the processes of creativity and the realities of theatre-making; I miss greatly his presence at the university since his retirement. Both David Fallows and Pierluigi Petrobelli possess a similar knack of being able to enlighten my grasp of a particular topic in a few short words, and make me think again. Stephen Banfield kindly commented on early drafts of two chapters. Fabrizio Della Seta made available to me useful material on Marietta Piccolomini. Linda Hutcheon's appreciation of some of this research in its earlier forms as conference paper and essay was of inestimable kindness, and gave me much encouragement. Visits to various seminars in Cambridge introduced me to the work of Karen Henson; Paolo Russo eased my first visits to Bologna, taking me to the library of the Università di Bologna. Mary Ann Smart's keen eye and compassionate ear provided valuable advice when it was most needed.

Throughout the long years of writing, I have been fortunate to have the wise, stimulating and often witty advice of a special group of people. The sage comments of the late John Rosselli guided earlier drafts of this book. Marco Capra opened the door not only to the Centro Internazionale di Ricerca sui Periodici Musicali (CIRPeM) with its fascinating microfilm resources of the nineteenth-century musical press, but also to his own reserves of knowledge, patience and encouragement: what I comprehend now of Italy and her history, I owe in many ways to him. My debt to Roger Parker, who has read every word of the following pages and taught me much, is incalculable. I have benefited immeasurably from his scholarship on operatic history and his fineness of intellectual judgement; on a personal level, his generosity of spirit is quite simply extraordinary. If at times I have wilfully chosen to ignore the advice of these good friends and pursued my own path, I hope they will forgive me; all errors in this book are, of course, entirely of my own making.

My editor, Victoria Cooper, has shown exceptional patience in the development of this book; I cannot thank her enough for her counsel and support over the years. During the preparations for publication, I have had the additional guidance of her assistant, Rebecca Jones, the production editor Jackie Warren and the copy-editor Lucy Carolan, who have magically resolved so many practical difficulties. I am grateful too for the care and interest of the Cambridge University Press series editor, Art Groos.

My family, as families always do, has borne the brunt of the work of the past years. The presence of Ruth in our household during perhaps the lowest point of all, when my husband and I were beset by illness and operations, was a precious gift; unfailing support was provided by my dear parents, my sister Anne, my niece Helen, and my brothers Nigel and Ian. My husband James has been the incarnation of his other name, Peter: enduringly steadfast and resolute in even the most difficult hours; the one, true, good companion. This book is for him.

Introduction

In Italy, a woman who writes for the public is a strange thing. I will therefore make myself courageous in the silence of all, and I will speak of things that interest all Italian women: I mean Rossini and his music. I do not seek praise, nor am I ambitious for some prize; I write for the truth, I want to verify some facts that have been bizarrely expounded, or believed with excessive ease; and if I cannot cite other authors, and refer as all scholars do to the music of the Greeks and Egyptians, I will speak of modern operas, and I too will say things that might deserve some attention.[1]

These words begin another book: Geltrude Maria Giorgi Righetti's brief but passionate defence of Rossini, written in 1823. It is a remarkable document, not so much for what it says about Rossini, but because it represented a rare attempt by a female singer to intervene in the public discourses surrounding opera, to extend the voice that was welcomed and applauded on the lyric stage into another, potentially far more hostile arena. Conscious of the singularity of her stance as both woman and singer, Giorgi Righetti was nevertheless determined to venture into this other dimension: 'I too will say things that might deserve some attention'. In contrast, the voices of other female singers only occasionally found their way into published material until much later in the century, although some, as we shall see, have survived through letters, diaries and other documents.

The term 'female singer' suggests a whole range of personages: a working-class schoolgirl, a society *dilettante*, a middle-class student at a conservatoire, a member of an operatic chorus, a struggling *seconda donna*, or a *prima donna assoluta*. All these manifestations of the singer make their appearance, albeit fleetingly, within the following pages. But the focus of the book is on the singer who aspired to become a *prima donna*.

From a certain perspective, the prima donna is hardly a shadowy or indistinct figure in the panorama of opera history. Since her first entrance onto the operatic stage some four centuries ago, she has been eulogised in sonnets and debased in pornography, acclaimed by enthusiasts and castigated by critics, mocked in satires and immortalised as a goddess. And her life story – particularly if her name was Malibran or Callas – has been told and retold, in material ranging from cartoons to scurrilous memoirs to (more occasionally) scholarly monographs. Nevertheless, almost all such material, whether in the form of individual biographies or more general accounts, tends to be concerned with a single and somewhat limited question: the phenomenon of a particular singer's fascination and artistry. The most notable exception to this approach is John Rosselli's authoritative *Singers of Italian Opera: the History of a Profession* (1992), with its focus on social history and the economics of the operatic marketplace.

My emphasis in this book, although indebted both to Rosselli's work and much of the material mentioned above, is rather different. It is concerned firstly not so much with one solitary 'prima donna' as with *prime donne*: a group of working artists, some of whom might have been famous but more often were relatively unknown and are now long forgotten. It also attempts to locate these singers within a broader history: one which includes not only the specificities of operatic stage practice but the life beyond the opera house – the social, cultural and political framing that shaped individual experience, artistic endeavour and audience reception. And within the opera house, its primary focus is that 'mid-point of intersubjectivity' between stage and auditorium that Attilio Favorini advises as the most fruitful investigative site of the theatrical event.[2] Above all, I am interested in the degree to which the experiences of these singers (and especially the way in which those experiences have been recorded or interpreted) depended on issues of gender.

But this book does not claim to be a history of female singers *per se*: it is more precisely a history of the discourses surrounding them, and the ways in which such discourses articulated various aspects of their history. Three discrete but contiguous areas are considered: the idea of the singer and the female voice, the actual experience of real singers, and the collision/collusion between the singer and the representation of women in opera. I accordingly employ aspects of literary criticism, social and cultural history, dramaturgical and musical analysis to investigate the meaning of the prima donna and meanings constructed by the prima donna (both on and off the operatic stage).[3] My range is necessarily wide in both historical and geographical terms, based on a period (1815–1930) encompassing three important histories: of the operatic stage, of the female singer, and of women in general.

First, this era is often regarded as opera's 'golden age'. One of the richest in operatic history, it was characterised by both an exceptional stylistic diversity of composition and a growth in the number and type of venues where opera was performed, building a global audience and creating opportunities for singers, composers and impresarios alike. I do not mean to suggest that the development of the operatic marketplace during this time was one of steady, sustained growth – on the contrary, it fluctuated according to the vagaries of local economies and political circumstances. Italy, for example, suffered at least three major periods of instability: during the 1820s, when the gaming licences issued to many opera houses were rescinded; in the 1860s and 1870s following unification, when the financial management of those theatres (particularly in Turin, Milan, Parma and Naples) previously controlled by either court rule or the Austrian government passed to the new Italian state, resulting in smaller budgets and economic restrictions; and again in the late 1890s, when the left-wing government withdrew funding from a number of theatres, with the consequent closure of La Scala for almost two years.[4] Similar episodes of upheaval or stagnation can be found in virtually every other country during the period. Nevertheless, opera as a whole continued to prosper on the world stage, finding a seemingly never-ending supply of new audiences and new practitioners and reaching a peak of activity in the years just preceding the First World War.[5] Only in the 1920s did this productivity finally decline, when the depressed world economy brought opera houses under severe financial pressures, the wages of singers were cut substantially, and the already faltering production of new operatic works decreased sharply. By 1930 the 'golden age' had ended.

The years 1815–1930 are also significant as the period in which the prima donna came to dominate the operatic stage, assuming the position held by the castrati in the previous century. Bans imposed by various popes since opera's inception in 1597 had ensured that women's access to the stage had been only partial, limited either to countries or states of Protestant denomination or to those (such as Venice) where theatrical practice took precedence over Catholic condemnation. In 1798, the new Roman republic not only rescinded these bans, but also dispensed with the prima donna's main competitor by outlawing the training schools of the castrati, by then seen less as the epitome of artistry and more as the victims of a barbarous tradition. Women henceforth became the focus of most operatic works, and the most significant element at the box office. Their new prominence did not, however, remain unchallenged for long. The development of the tenor voice from the light, flexible timbre of early singers such as Adolphe Nourrit and Giovanni Battista Rubini into the more dramatic instrument capable of sustaining thrilling high Bs and Cs in the *voce di petto* (supposedly first exemplified by Gilbert-Louis Duprez)[6] found increasing favour with the audience; by the 1890s tenors such as Jean de Reszke, Enrico Caruso and Beniamino Gigli were as popular as their female colleagues, if not more so. Other factors affected the prima donna's status towards the end of this era. By 1931, Ernest Newman was claiming that the diva was no more: 'In these days we may admire our singers but we do not worship them; for a journalist even to speak of a soprano as a *diva* is to raise a smile.' He cited several reasons: the age was an 'unromantic' one, singers were 'too plentiful', and besides, there were now so many other female 'stars' from film and sport that competed with the prima donna in the public gaze. Above all, new methods of marketing and publicity had destroyed the mystique enjoyed by former singers:

The Press Agent and the gossipy journalist, without intending it, have made the singer a trifle ridiculous; the plain man finds it hard to take people seriously about whom so much vulgar nonsense is talked . . . The modern prima donna, for commercial reasons, has come down into the crowd; and too close contact with the crowd has meant the loss of a good deal of the crowd's respect for her.[7]

Newman's complaints are of course typical of the laments made throughout operatic history that singers of a previous era were more accomplished and glamorous than their modern successors. Nevertheless, he was accurate in his assessment: by the 1930s the prima donna's prominence as a unique (or almost) symbol of female endeavour had begun to decline, at least in the eyes of the wider public.[8]

As Newman implied, the cycle of the prima donna's success also coincides with an important era in women's social, cultural and political history. This history is now well known, thanks to the efforts of writers such as Simone de Beauvoir et al.,[9] and need not be repeated at length here. Suffice it to say that the dominant society's preferred image of womanhood was that of the 'feminine ideal' – a concept elucidated most influentially by Jean-Jacques Rousseau in 1762[10] and adopted with enthusiasm by the newly established bourgeoisie of western society during the following century. The precise configuration of the feminine ideal varied in detail according to different cultures (thus, North American women were often regarded as more outspoken than their European counterparts, whilst even relatively early in the period German women were permitted to attend functions and walk outside unaccompanied by a male companion),[11] but the essence of this image remained the same – woman's duty was to please man, not herself, and her proper place was in the home. This concept, as Peter Gay records, was repeated indiscriminately throughout western society, and was inviolable: 'To agitate for the emancipation of women from these sacred tasks was to offend against the laws of God and man.'[12]

Nonetheless, many women (and some men) prepared to make themselves offensive in the cause of emancipation, for whilst this era implemented some of the harshest repressions of women hitherto experienced, it also witnessed the most concerted and determined effort by women to overcome such obstacles and gain freedom and equality. Mary Wollstonecraft had begun the protesting in her *Vindication of the Rights of Women* (1792), and from the 1850s onwards suffrage movements were visible in nearly all the Western countries, most particularly in Britain, the USA and Scandinavia. The feminine ideal or the 'Angel in the House' (as Coventry Patmore dubbed her in 1854)[13] was increasingly challenged by other, more vigorous images, such as the doyenne of apocalyptic feminism, the 'Female Saviour', in the 1850s and 1860s, and the rationally dressed, politically aware 'New Woman' of the 1890s.[14] Even more influential, perhaps, was the vision of numerous real women seeking entry to male bastions such as the universities, medicine and law.

Emboldened by such displays of defiance, more and more women demanded enfranchisement, although their efforts across the international spectrum met with mixed fortunes. By the outbreak of the First World War, the only countries that had awarded universal suffrage to women were New Zealand, Finland and Norway, along with most of Australia and a handful of American states. During the war, Denmark, Russia and Iceland followed suit, to be joined in the 1920s by Germany, Austria, Netherlands, Czechoslovakia, the USA, Hungary, Poland, Sweden – and, finally, Great Britain in 1928. But there were some important exceptions. France, Belgium and Italy only awarded the vote to women after the Second World War, primarily because of the strong Catholic opposition. This religious dimension not only encouraged right-wing politicians in their more traditional view of women, but also led anti-clerical liberal politicians to believe that women's own allegiance to the Catholic church would result in a massively conservative vote if they were granted suffrage.[15] In Italy, a further factor was the growth of fascism: many feminist groups at first supported Mussolini, only to be rewarded with repression (as was the case with the *Unione femminile nazionale*) or even forcible dissolution (like the *Associazione per la donna* in 1925)[16] – a fate that awaited other feminists in

Germany, Austria and Spain. Thus the energy the women's movement had demonstrated during the first two decades of the twentieth
century seeped away, either because winning the vote left the feminists uncertain of their future goals and divided amongst themselves,
or because other factors (such as fascism or Catholicism) determined
a rigorous return to anti-feminist values.[17] By the 1930s, this first
great concerted effort of international feminism had reached a
close.[18]

Geographically, this book revolves around the most common
international circuit travelled by opera singers of that time: Europe,
Britain and the Americas. (Of course, some singers, such as Anna
Bishop, went much farther afield; others, such as Rosa Ponselle,
travelled hardly at all.) Whilst for the purposes of historical investigation the perimeters of this circuit may seem extended, they are
largely determined by the international nature of the operatic experience and the nomadic existence of many artists. About half
the singers considered here are from Britain, North America and
Australia; the other half are European. Snobbery and an innate belief
that the best singers were foreign often ensured that the artists
employed in Britain or America (North and South) were European,
whilst the greater employment opportunities on the continent attracted large numbers of British and American singers. I have attempted to explore something of both groups, although as European
singers have received more significant scholarly attention of late,
my emphasis has been rather more towards the experiences of
British, American and Australasian singers at home and abroad. My
research has tended therefore to follow the singer on her travels
through various countries, rather than concentrate on one particular
area. There are inevitable omissions owing to lack of space; even
more owing to lack of evidence.

With regard to both historical and geographical matters, however,
the coverage here is by no means equal in all chapters. Some of
this partiality is to do with focus: Chapters 3 and 4 centre on the
increasing move of women from non-professional backgrounds into
operatic careers, and therefore concentrate on the period 1850–1930;

Chapters 5 to 7, detailing practices within the opera house, are more evenly spread across 1815 to 1930. Other instances of limited coverage are a result of the availability of evidence. Material pertaining directly to the experiences of singers is often fragmentary in the first decades of the nineteenth century. Whilst singers figure frequently as subjects for reviews within the music periodicals throughout the period, they were rarely interviewed directly until the *fin-de-siècle*; equally, few women singers wrote autobiographies before the 1880s. And when they did so, the market for such literature was found primarily within the United States and Britain (Rosselli comments that 'biographies and memoirs' were a genre 'thought little of in Italy');[19] thus, most of the autobiographical sources consulted here, even when describing the experiences of mainland European singers such as Ernestine Schumann-Heink or Emma Calvé, were published in English. For this and other reasons there is a noticeable absence of the singers' own voices in the early part of the period, in contrast to the full flourishing of the publicity machine from the end of the century onwards.

The breadth of the historical and geographical areas covered undoubtedly invites criticisms. Similar problems were faced by historians Bonnie S. Anderson and Judith P. Zinsser in their series *A History of Their Own: Women in Europe from Prehistory to the Present* (1988). They argued that, in a world which has viewed women as 'a separate category of being', the similarities of gendered experience were more significant than 'differences of historical era, class and nationality'.[20] With respect to the present study, this is not to imply that substantial differences did not exist between, say, the experiences of Angelica Catalani (soprano, Italian, prima donna *assoluta* of international renown) at the beginning of the period, and those of Kathleen Howard (mezzo-soprano, American, middle-rank singer) towards the end. Nor is it to deny that many experiences of professional life were shared by male singers. On the contrary, this book explores various topics that were of equal importance to *both* genders: or rather, that were common to the enterprise of becoming and sustaining a career as a singer. Nevertheless, a number of themes connected directly to issues of gender recur with regularity and subtle variation in the history of opera. This study, without claiming to be either exhaustive or definitive, seeks to address some of these questions, and to establish a broad base from which other, more detailed investigations might emerge.

WOMEN AND OPERA

The question of women's involvement in opera has been of late rather vexed. Catherine Clément's *L'Opéra ou la défaite des femmes*, published in 1979 at the height of feminism's forays into all aspects of culture, was an impassioned polemic on the wrongs opera has done to women. Publication in English in 1988 confirmed its status as a provocative feminist exposé, and Clément's findings have been cited and supported by a number of scholars. Others, however, including Ellen Rosand, Katherine Bergeron, Anthony Arblaster, Paul Robinson, Ralph P. Locke, Mary Ann Smart and Carolyn Abbate, have pointed out the narrowness of Clément's ahistorical stance and emphasis on literary narrative, arguing above all on the primacy of music as the real source of gender delineation in opera.[21] It seems superfluous to add anything more to these weighty voices (especially to the elegant, lucid analyses of Rosand and Abbate); but in the present context, it is worth sketching in briefly some of the messier details Clément forgets in her retelling of opera's narrative in western society.

Clément undoubtedly made us think again about the portrayal of women in opera. But the sharpness of her focus on the single aspect of victimisation – the heroine's 'undoing' through either death or domestication – blurs our perspective of the broader panorama of operatic history. The most limiting dimension of her polemic is the implication of *intent* – that opera was merely 'a great masculine scheme surrounding a spectacle thought up to adore, and also to kill, the feminine character'.[22] It is difficult to imagine that a similarly sweeping statement made about 'theatre' or 'literature' or 'art' or 'music' would have exerted such sway in scholarly writing – there, at least, is a recognition that such artforms include a vast array of different works across centuries, and in consequence reflect multiple aspects of female representation. The notion that 'opera' can somehow be reduced to a clutch of compositions – and those only drawn from the tragic repertoire – is a glum misreading of the actual operatic experience for both the nineteenth-century artist and spectator.

A cluster of factors need consideration if we are to appreciate more fully the complexities of women's position in opera of this period. Certainly, opera was as tightly woven into the fabric of social customs as other cultural manifestations, and as equally subject to the dominant themes that pervaded artistic reflection. And Clément is right to identify its provenance as essentially masculine. Only a handful of women composers and librettists found their way into operatic composition; of those, even fewer successfully achieved public performance in élite opera houses (Louise Bertin and Ethel Smyth are perhaps the most notable exceptions in this era).[23] But this does not mean that all male composers were necessarily ignorant of the political issues of the Woman Question, or indeed opposed to change. Wagner's final essay, 'On the Feminine in the Human', advocated female emancipation, arguing that woman was a 'victim of power structures determined according to masculine principles and reproduction' (he died before completing it);[24] Alexander Borodin openly supported the movement for women's rights in Russia;[25] partial claims for developing more progressive images of women might be made for a host of other composers, including Rossini, Donizetti, Verdi, Tchaikovsky, Giordano, Strauss, Dukas and Janáček, to name but a few. Nor can we lay all the responsibility for the kinds of roles created for women on the shoulders of the composers. A letter by Donizetti, written in 1842 about his composition of *Le Duc d'Albe* for the mezzo-soprano Rosine Stoltz, reveals an almost modern understanding of the limitations of certain kinds of female representation:

> I too am of the opinion that there are some changes to make in the *Duca d'Alba*: the conspiracy less dominant, the love interest warmer. For the

rest, I would have imagined that it ought to be very effective. I had above all cherished the *rôle* of the heroine: perhaps a new *rôle* in the theatre, a *rôle* of action, where almost always the heroine is passive. Here she is young, enthusiastic, loving, a Joan of Arc. And I think Mme Stoltz would have been admirable for it, because there are many, many situations that seem to have inspired me, and I am sure that I have never written a more beautiful or more innovative female *rôle*.[26]

Stoltz, however, had obscurely refused the part – perhaps, according to Ashbrook, because she believed the opera would not afford her the 'desired prominence', perhaps because it had originally been composed for another singer, Julie Dorus-Gras,[27] perhaps because she preferred to play a more traditional kind of heroine – and the opera was never completed by Donizetti.[28] (The libretto by Scribe and Duvéyrier, a treatment of a sixteenth-century Flemish uprising, was subsequently refashioned and set in Sicily for use by Verdi in *Les Vêpres siciliennes*.) Even if male composers were willing to take risks with their portrayal of women, pioneering characterisation thus sometimes fell foul of the singers' own reluctance to undertake more daring roles.

But it is Clément's ire about the deaths of heroines that has most caught the public imagination. The kind of response it engendered is illustrated by Rebecca Meitlis' comment: 'What always rankles in me is that male composers and writers create women who are such gleaming ideals – who love, and are talented and beautiful – and who are then destroyed. It seems inevitable that Violetta and Tosca have to die.'[29] If such remarks reflect the expectations of contemporary feminism and our need to discover 'positive' images of womanhood, they also betray how far adrift we now are from understanding the nature of operatic experience in that era. Meitlis' sense of inevitability about the fate of Violetta and Tosca is a proper consequence of the conventions of tragedy – these heroines do not die simply because they are women but because they are tragic protagonists. To define the purpose and effect of such deaths, we need to determine whether they differ in any important sense from the male fatalities that similarly litter the operatic stage in this era.

The operatic death scene was essentially a nineteenth-century invention. Earlier operas were mostly – but not entirely – constructed around the *lieto fine* ('happy ending'). The move towards tragedy in the 1820s certainly coincided with a new emphasis on the heroine, but it is difficult to argue that this was a conscious (or even unconscious) misogynistic act. Tragedy was regarded as bringing a new, much-needed seriousness to the operatic stage. In 1831 the composer and organist William Crotch articulated a common belief about the purpose of tragedy and its capacity to touch and elevate its audience: 'The humorous incidents of a drama make men laugh; the tender and happy parts excite the smile of approbation; but the tragic scenes petrify them into silent, serious, breathless attention. The superiority of the tragedy over the comedy and of both over the farce, is therefore obvious.'[30] Even operas that had hitherto accorded with the *lieto fine* tradition found themselves subject to this new convention. The final sextet of Mozart's *Don Giovanni* was often omitted, the opera instead ending with Giovanni's descent into Hell; whilst Wagner described how he 'completely changed the ending, with its inevitable marriage' of Gluck's *Iphigénie en Aulide* in 1847, in order 'to make it more consonant with Euripides' play'.[31]

Who dies? Certainly, some women die alone: Violetta, Senta, Gioconda, Mimì, Butterfly. And so do some men: Arturo in *La straniera*, the title roles of *Ernani* and *Werther*, Riccardo in *Un ballo in maschera*, Federico in *L'arlesiana*. But lovers often die in company: Pollione joins Norma in her funeral pyre, as Aida will later join Radames in his tomb; Otello (at least in Verdi's version) kills himself when his blood-rage of jealousy is finally quenched by the certainty of Desdemona's innocence; José waits sullenly by Carmen's body for the inevitable arrest for her death; Tosca leaps to her death only after she herself has dispatched Scarpia and then watched her lover Cavaradossi die before her own eyes. Romeo and Juliet, Lucia and Edgardo, Tristan and Isolde, Pelléas and Mélisande all fulfil the convention of the 'delayed happy ending' and unity beyond the grave.

If women were not the only victims of the new focus on death, nor were they the only admired executors of its performative aspects. The Italian tenor Napoleone Moriani (?1808–78) was known as 'Moriani della bella morte' because of his superlative skills in dying onstage, arousing audiences to *fanatismo*; later he schooled Clara Novello in the secrets of theatrical demise.[32] This was an era in which death was perceived very differently from nowadays: instead of the modern taboo, the 'great silence' Philippe Ariès argues exists in contemporary society, death was the 'place for the realization of self'.[33] Likewise in nineteenth-century opera, the crisis of death often marked the crystallisation of the character's self-knowledge: Marguerite, lost in her mad despair and self-condemnation for her crimes, finds confirmation of her essential goodness as the angels lift her to heaven in *Faust*; Carmen's persona of good-time girl is transfigured into a serious proto-feminist as she holds fast to her ideals of independence; Butterfly, reclaiming her Japanese heritage and casting off her Americanised trappings, discovers in her act of hara-kiri that she is more her father's daughter than Pinkerton's plaything. To an audience whose perspective of death was so different to our own, such scenes were generally perceived less as brutal punishments and more as defining moments in the arc of the character's delineation. And the high mortality rates of the era in the world beyond the opera house gave a distinct context to some death scenes. The Russian diarist Marie Bashkirtseff, herself suffering from tuberculosis, experienced a kind of presentiment in the portrayal of the final moments of the consumptive Violetta in Verdi's *La traviata*, which she witnessed in Paris in 1878: 'in the last act I had not exactly the wish to die, but the idea that I should suffer and die just at the moment when all was about to end happily'.[34]

Death scenes also had radical implications in an era where censorship prevailed. Composers and librettists chafed against the restraints that forbade the use of suicide or explicit violence on stage. In the early performances of Rossini's *Otello* (1816), Otello's dispatch of his wife had to happen offstage in the discreet curtaining of

Desdemona's bed, thus necessitating the use of a knife – after all, the threat of menace was far better conveyed by the flash of gleaming steel in the preceding passages; Otello chasing Desdemona around the stage with a pillow would have seemed, even by operatic standards, more than faintly ridiculous. In such a policed environment, the manner of death often became a site for artistic challenge and defiance.

And it is worth remembering that the operatic repertoire of this era also provided plenty of feisty heroines 'who love, and are talented and beautiful' – and who *don't* die. Amongst the literally thousands upon thousands of operas written in the nineteenth century (many now lost completely; others available only as libretti within the opera house archives), there is a rather astonishing range of female portraits in both serious and comic opera. Any summarising of the era's operatic representation of women needs to take account of indomitable heroines such as the title-role of *Medea in Corinto* (Mayr), Leonora in *Fidelio* (Beethoven), Isabella in *L'italiana in Algeri* (Rossini), Marie in *La Fille du régiment* (Donizetti), Odabella in *Attila* (Verdi), Hélène in *Les Vêpres siciliennes* (Verdi), Tatiana in *Eugene Onegin* (Tchaikovsky), Marina in *Boris Godunov* (Musorgsky), Minnie in *La fanciulla del West* (Puccini), the Marschallin in *Der Rosenkavalier* (Strauss) or the title-roles of *Louise* (Charpentier) and *Jenůfa* (Janáček). None of these women fulfil in absolute terms the demands of the 'feminine ideal' – and yet all triumph over, or at least survive, the playing out of their rebellious moments and negotiate a life more in accordance with their own desires.[35]

But even if we accept that death or domestication forms the destiny of most nineteenth-century operatic heroines, the impact of such narratives was surely affected by the presence of their on-stage interpreters. The characters assumed by world-famous singers such as Giuditta Pasta or Pauline Viardot or Emma Calvé were temporary manifestations, assumed for two or three hours at most, and abandoned on the final applause. What the audience saw in an artform that made little pretence of verisimilitude (however much it might seek 'truth') was less the role and far more the singer. There is much to suggest that an understanding of woman's place in opera and the operatic marketplace depends on the analysis of this broader and richer canvas of the conjunction between singer and role. Rupert Christiansen makes a bold claim:

> Opera provides the strongest image of woman in any Romantic form. Neither the novel nor painting gave women such an open field of action, such a number of revolutionary possibilities. Nowhere else was a woman put so firmly at the structural centre. The great prima donnas of the period both seized and forged these possibilities, performing with an intensity and individuality unknown in the eighteenth century.[36]

We might dispute the broad sweep of this statement – French grand opera, for example, rarely placed women 'firmly at the structural centre'.[37] Nevertheless, throughout the period opera articulated women's experience in a manner that undeniably privileged the display of female vocal and histrionic talents, and that secured for the prima donna (even after the arrival of the *tenore di forza*) the most consistently powerful position at the box-office. Her commercial viability was reflected in her salary: singers such as Angelica Catalani (1780–1849), Maria Malibran (1808–1836), Adelina Patti (1843–1919) and Nellie Melba (1861–1931) were the highest paid theatrical performers of their day. And if the prima donna was a striking, even iconoclastic figure in terms of her public life, professional career and financial independence, so too was often the manner of her performance. A review of Giulia Grisi in Marliani's *Ildegonda* at Her Majesty's Theatre, London, in 1837 emphasises the distance some singers exhibited from bourgeois notions of female decorum:

> The whole of Grisi's performance . . . was marked by extraordinary boldness, energy, and power. Her ability in sustaining herself against that immense body of voices and instruments in the finale already mentioned, was quite tremendous. What she wants is tenderness of expression: her very mode of taking her notes is in keeping with her general character of performance – it is abrupt and defying: 'You may take it if you like; if not you may let it alone.'[38]

If there is doubt about the effect of opera's fictional characters on their female audience, there is ample evidence (as later chapters will show) that the singers themselves had perceptible influence in inspiring social change. I have written elsewhere of film historians' findings that twentieth-century female spectators were adept at subverting codes of representation and, in Sue Rickard's words, of 'actively identifying with feminine power in whatever form it appears'.[39] In the nineteenth-century opera house too, the singer's demonstration of ideas of womanhood not as a fixed entity but as a performative construct opened up access to other readings and other possible dimensions for female experience and engagement. From the 1850s, more and more middle- and upper-class women sought to make a career on the operatic stage: not in order to *be* Lucia, but in order to be the woman who *played* Lucia one night, Lucrezia the next, and Susanna the next – in other words, to be a woman who might adopt and relinquish a number of different personas. For example, in 1852 Giulia Grisi sang Anna Bolena (Donizetti), Donna Anna (Mozart), Fidès (Meyerbeer), Lucrezia Borgia (Donizetti), Norma (Bellini), Desdemona (Rossini), Valentine (Meyerbeer), and Elvira (Bellini) – in other words, an abandoned queen, an outraged young woman, a devoted mother, a murderess, a vengeful lover, a wronged spouse, a disobedient daughter and a wayward hysteric. Grisi, in displaying her abilities to assume and then discard all these different roles, simultaneously proved herself to be perhaps the most important factor in the making of this multifaceted onstage image of womanhood.

Opera's combination of an emphasis on fictionalised female experience with the most acclaimed and yet contentious manifestation of the woman artist in this era has inevitably invited claims about the wider pertinence of opera to women. Placing female involvement as both performer and protagonist in late eighteenth-century opera in a broader political context, Brigid Brophy declares that women singers 'could not fail to procure a further degree of emancipation for women in general'.[40] Tom Sutcliffe similarly sees opera as 'actively working for sexual equality', alluding to the manner in which harmonic structure and acoustics favour the female voice: 'The diva can dominate the stage in her redemptive sacrificing vein, her voice riding the orchestra far more tellingly than the female speaking voice dominates debate.'[41] Other arguments extend beyond aspects of visibility and audibility in analysing the possible meanings of opera for women. Hélène Cixous's essentialist definition of a 'feminine practice of writing'[42] as a 'privilege of voice' emanating from the instinctual realm of the Imaginary rather than from the phallocentric order of the Symbolic finds confirmation in opera:

> An endless choir swollen by sobs and silence, breathless gasps, hysterics' coughs.
>   That is the origin of opera. And I say that only men capable of that emission, those tormented ones who give in to their femininity, can love opera.
>   The others, builders, deny themselves this passion.[43]

The most recent influential theorist on this topic, however, is Carolyn Abbate, who writes eloquently of 'opera's capacity to disrupt male authority', referring to 'how opera, with *music* that subverts the borders we fix between the sexes, speaks for the envoicing of women'.[44] Her illuminating analyses dissect the multiple meanings inherent in opera: taking Clément to task for concentrating solely on the narrative plot, she argues that the 'locus of women's operatic triumph' is 'in the overwhelming sound of female operatic voices and the musical gestures that enfold those voices into a whole'.[45]

If such perspectives suggest a more positive framework for the exploration of ideas of gender in the Ottocento opera house, a problem nevertheless lies in the legacy of Clément's insistence on questions of 'power': were women disenfranchised by opera or emboldened by it? Did opera collude in the repression of women, or counter it? The difficulty here occurs at the point of generality. Certainly, as the following pages will reveal, there are instances that confirm Clément's thesis – and as many others that counter it. A more contemporary, subtle and, I think, accurate view is that throughout its history opera, like other forms of theatre, provided a forum for traversing gender confines, in a complex interplay of both corroborative and transgressive acts. The underlying question of this book therefore concerns the nature of this negotiation within the nineteenth- and early twentieth-century context: the encounters between societal constraints and artistic licence; the exchanges and accommodations made between traditional hegemonies such as the 'feminine ideal' and more subversive practices and discourses of representation. In short, for the artist of the period – and also arguably for the female audience – opera was much more than simply a barometer of female political power. It was a métier for female labour, a focus for female spectatorship, a sphere for female aspiration: it was not merely an artform, in the sense of a closed cultural manifestation; it was, on the contrary, also a lived experience – chaotic, shifting, irreducible.

THE OPERA HOUSE AND ITS AUDIENCE

Such questions disturb the view that the opera house's élite position within cultural hierarchies would preclude any hint of subversive activity. In her discussion of the reception of *La traviata* in London in 1856, Lynda Nead describes the nineteenth-century opera house as a place where the 'wealthy and respectable classes barricaded [themselves] in the theatre from the dangerous hordes outside on the streets'.[46] Even in Britain, this image of the opera house purely as the stolid, stuffy protector of bourgeois morality is misleading. Whilst the ruling establishments of Europe and the Americas undeniably made efforts to manipulate opera for their own ends (whether through censorship of libretti and theatrical presentation, or through financial and social strategies surrounding the production of opera), we also know that opera often evinced a more acute consciousness of contemporaneous political and social questions and also reached a much broader audience than its elitist image might suggest. For example, Jane Fulcher's analysis of French grand opera 'as politics and politicised art' challenges the assumption that this genre was 'engineered' specifically for consumption by the French bourgeoisie, and instead demonstrates how 'at its most powerful grand opera was integrally engaged in a direct provocative dialogue with the real or actual political world'.[47] Part of her investigation deals with the political unrest exacerbated by works that dealt overtly with issues of revolution and freedom, such as Auber's *La Muette de Portici* (1828): a work associated both with the Brussels uprising in 1830 and again with the short-lived Italian rebellion against Austrian rule in 1848.[48] Although in occupied Italy opera was regarded by the Austrians as a useful device to distract the populace from thoughts of revolution,[49] the sentiments expressed within certain works (such as Mayr's *Atar, ossia Il seraglio d'Ormus*, Rossini's *Guillaume Tell*, Bellini's *Norma*, or Verdi's *I Lombardi alla prima crociata* and *La battaglia di Legnano*) were on occasion read by patriotic elements in the audience as encoded exhortations to sustain the struggle for liberty.[50] According to Wagner, the opposition to Austrian rule in Prague in 1848 took similar advantage of a 'revolutionary chorus' from Kittl's opera *Bianca und Giuseppe, oder Die Franzosen vor Nizza* (set to Wagner's own libretto);[51] whilst in Russia in 1874, the 'potentially subversive effects' of Musorgsky's *Boris Godunov* were manifested by students 'singing an anti-czarist chorus' from the opera in the streets.[52]

As for the opera audience, 'wealthy' did not necessarily mean 'respectable', even in prudish Britain. The Regency courtesan Harriette Wilson 'learned to be a complete flirt' during her frequent attendance at the opera;[53] Chorley's review of London opera-goers between 1834 and 1838 included the 'most notorious and beautiful' Marguerite Blessington, who sat provocatively opposite the Royal box;[54] some decades later, the soprano Emma Eames was dismayed by the dubious morals of the *fin-de-siècle* doyenne of Covent Garden, Lady de Grey, and her aristocratic cronies.[55] And throughout the era, the opera house was open to spectators who were neither wealthy nor respectable, as the *Musical World* complained writing about Her Majesty's Theatre in 1839: 'Women of more than doubtful character are now to be commonly seen in the boxes; and the pit is half-filled by foreign ruffians, shopmen from Regent and Oxford

Streets, and *Bonnets* from the adjoining hells.'[56] In France in 1847 workers were actively encouraged to attend Adolphe Adam's new Opéra-National (doomed to a short existence by the 1848 revolution),[57] although Anselm Gerhard makes the point that the low wages of the proletariat meant that an excursion to the opera for a labourer would have been 'wholly atypical'.[58] So too in Italy, although this country, having invented opera, took a special interest in its progress. The opera house was at the heart of bourgeois culture,[59] and the operatic audience extended to artisans and tradesmen. 'Popular' prices in some theatres deliberately encouraged this broader spectatorship; a further democratization of the opera-going experience may be glimpsed later in the century with the construction of the *politeami* (large arenas offering a mixture of opera and other entertainments) such as the Teatro Costanzi in Rome, and the refashioning of the upper areas of certain theatres including the Teatro della Pergola in Florence (1867) and the Teatro Regio in Turin (1906) in order to accommodate a larger, more socially diverse audience.[60] Similar reform was also evident in Germany. Wagner's theatre at Bayreuth was deliberately designed without side-boxes on egalitarian principles, in order to attract operatic 'pilgrims' rather than rich aristocrats[61] (although Wagner's initially intended dress code of 'morning coats and grandes toilettes' suggests operatic democracy was tenable only within certain limits).[62] In tsarist Russia in the early twentieth century, Sergei Levik noted that the opera audience of the Narodnïy Dom in St Petersburg consisted of 'the lower ranks of the civil service, the middle intelligentsia, the students and shopworkers', in contrast to the aristocratic patrons frequenting the Imperial theatres such as the Mariinsky.[63] In the USA, opera found a socially mixed audience at venues such as Niblo's Garden and Palmo's Opera House in New York; in New Orleans in 1845 the *Spirit* declared that 'nothing is so popular as opera with all classes';[64] in San Francisco in the 1880s, Emily Soldene recalled the music-hall atmosphere of the 'comfortable and cosmopolitan' Tivoli, a theatre 'open all the year round, admission and seat fifty cents' where 'Offenbach and Sullivan, Wagner and Adam, Donizetti and

Boito, Meyerbeer and Bizet, Gounod and Weber, Auber and Mill-öcker, interpreted by artistes of respectable capacity, a good band and an excellent chorus, are successfully run in one continuous procession' throughout the year, whilst the audience smoked and drank 'amid soft murmurs of "Good", and "Bene", and "Bravo", and "Bis"'.[65]

As such instances demonstrate, opera spread far beyond the élite houses of the European and American capitals. Many smaller towns (in Germany and Italy especially) had opera houses that played on a regular basis, and touring companies of all nationalities traversed the world's continents. The operatic impresario Max Maretzek produced opera in Cuba and Mexico, dealing equally with bandits and violently aggressive audiences;[66] Colonel Mapleson shepherded his troupe through the provinces of Great Britain and Ireland, and across the United States as far as San Francisco;[67] Emily Soldene staged some of Britain's earliest performances of Bizet's *Carmen* in Leicester, and then in Liverpool, Glasgow and Dublin;[68] Giulia Tess spent a year with Giuseppe Gonsalez, who led his Italian company of two hundred personnel across Russia, China, South-east Asia and Australia in a mammoth tour (one of many) that began in 1914 and ended four years later;[69] Frances Alda gained her first professional operatic experience by travelling the Australian provinces with Williamson and Musgrove's Light Opera Company.[70] And if the working classes entered the opera house not at all or only very rarely, then opera in various forms reached beyond its conventional theatrical confines into other more accessible environs, via the marionette theatres of Italy;[71] the magic-lantern shows of Germany such as the one based on Wagner's *Ring* cycle designed by Paul Hoffmann in 1887;[72] the innumerable instrumental transcriptions of operas, performed across the whole spectrum of musical activity from amateur pianists to brass bands;[73] the inclusion of operatic arias in the music-halls and other popular venues;[74] and even the countless burlesque works such as W. H. Oxenberry's *Norma Travestie* (1841) or C. H. Hazlewood's version of *La sonnambula* (c. 1859) that played in the cheaper theatres. In 1839 the *Musical World* acknowledged the accuracy of the maxim that the 'true test of the merit of an Opera is the hand-organ'.[75] This is not to deny the massed ranks of privilege that occupied the major opera houses and who sought (with varying success) to establish opera's exclusivity, but to indicate that we cannot glibly dismiss the operatic experience during this era as belonging only to the élite few.

Indeed, even within those élite circles, opera sometimes occasioned suspicion. As 'high art', it often had closer links with the avant-garde than might be supposed – it was to some extent working within the boundaries of what constituted 'artistic' rather than what was considered morally or politically acceptable. Various outcries against opera throughout the period indicate distrust of this artform as morally reprehensible and subversive (if Queen Victoria, a model of respectability, often thoroughly enjoyed the opera, her comments on *Faust* to her daughter suggest she thought she was seeing something rather risqué);[76] and, as in the eighteenth century, it continued to be regarded by some detractors as oppositional to the prevailing ideas and cult of masculinity.

In short, the female singers of the era thus inhabited an operatic marketplace that was not only a remarkably diverse and extensive arena, encompassing a wide range of venues, audiences, aesthetic and performative experiences, but one in which the boundaries for challenge to received opinion were fluid and mutable.

METHODOLOGY AND STRUCTURE

The shape of this book is determined by the arc spanning the most ephemeral relationship between women and opera, as revealed in the ideas and images of the female singer, and the most concrete point of female interaction with the operatic stage, as demonstrated by the singing actress. The journey between these two positions, exemplified by the female singer's efforts to gain access to the operatic stage via vocal training and career development, the kinds of roles and conventions that she found awaiting her in the opera house, and the performance modes and interpretative effects she employed in enacting such roles, absorbs the greater part of this book. The first two chapters therefore examine the alarm generated by the professional female singer in nineteenth-century society, the kinds of strategies employed (consciously or unconsciously) to contain or at least lessen her influence, and the responses of some women to the figure of the prima donna and the development of their own professional ambitions. Chapter 2 draws on the image of the singer in nineteenth-century fiction, a topic I addressed in an earlier essay and that has since been pursued by a number of scholars:[77] its juxtaposition here with other dimensions of the prima donna's experience will, I hope, provide a useful contextualisation. In Chapters 3 and 4, I turn from image to actuality, and assess the 'real' experience of the young female singer in attempting a career on the operatic stage, especially with regard to the stage mother, patronage or sponsorship and tuition. The emphasis of the last three chapters is on the professional life of the prima donna: the degree to which she was supported or hindered in her career by notions of gender and the reality of women's lives within the operatic marketplace; the relationship between career, voice and role; and the development of the singing actress.

As will be already apparent, representation and fact are closely intertwined throughout this topic. Prima donnas were engaged in the business of the representation of fictional characters but they were also represented (and indeed represented themselves) in the media. Information presented as historical 'fact' (such as biographical details, events in a career, or aspects of stage practice) has itself often been subject to a process of representation: its absolute veracity clouded by misinterpretation or false recall or simple inaccuracy over the course of a hundred years or more. A critic's review of a performance must necessarily be suspect in an era when corruption amongst reviewers was rife;[78] the 'history' of an opera company as penned by an impresario such as Mapleson or Maretzek is far less likely to be an objective record than a colourful, exaggerated account produced with the aim of earning cash for its penurious author (many impresarios incurred considerable debts from their operatic adventures). Material from the archives of opera houses often relates primarily to the economics of the opera business. Personal experience, spectators' responses, performance conventions or peculiarities, cultural images and suchlike exist only on the margins of historical evidence, and yet are of enormous value in our attempt to decipher custom and practice, ideologies and theories. Some of the following chapters therefore deal with the representation of facts; others with the facts of representation; almost all at some time make use of both elements. Importantly, both fact and representation together constitute a discourse (in Foucault's sense of a conduit of 'power-knowledge') that reveals to us a much fuller understanding of the female operatic experience of this era.[79]

Much of my approach accords with the aims for a feminist methodology in theatre history laid out by Tracy C. Davis, the three thematic areas of the book roughly corresponding to the three questions she regards as essential components in a feminist inquiry: 'How does the ideology of the dominant culture affect women's status?'; 'How do social, class, and economic factors affect privilege?'; and 'How is the status quo maintained or challenged in artistic media?'[80] Feminist methodology in the performing arts, however, has relied heavily in the past three decades on Laura Mulvey's notion of the 'male gaze' and the supposed passivity of the female performer. This concept, defined by Mulvey in 1975 using Lacan's theories of psychoanalysis, has been challenged by recent feminist writers in a number of disciplines – by film scholars such as Jackie Stacey and Sue Rickard, by dance historian Sally Banes, and (perhaps more obliquely) by musicologist Carolyn Abbate.[81] My own view is that whilst Mulvey's notion of the 'male gaze' was an invaluable stimulus to the early debate of female representation and audience reception, it should not be applied indiscriminately to every male spectator, nor should it be allowed to overshadow the exploration of what might be termed the 'female gaze'. I suggest that we should seek to acknowledge and uncover the multiplicity of spectators' readings of theatrical image, instead of excluding such diversity by amassing these responses under a single label.

The notion of multiplicity is pertinent also with regard to other methodological features of this study. There is, in my view, no single, over-arching theoretical position that encapsulates convincingly every aspect of every female singer's life within this particular historical and geographical framework. Real women singers' experiences were necessarily varied and disparate, according to individual circumstance. Certainly, there are specific arguments to be made within thematic areas; each chapter attempts to do so. But in general I have sought to demonstrate the richness and variety of experience across the era, and to illustrate that whilst theoretical interpretations might be made of certain changes and developments both within and without the profession, the microcosm of individual experience does not always neatly reflect the broader sweep of historical movement. Theatre and music history inevitably entails dealing with the complexity of real-life subjects who elude neat categorisation or reduction to a single narrative. In methodological terms, I share with Le Goff the notion that 'it is possible to write *histories*, but not *history*'.[82]

In the course of my investigations, I have examined archival sources relating to opera production; public documents such as memoirs, autobiographies, newspapers and periodicals; private material such as letters and diaries; fictional accounts of the singer and the opera-goer; critical assessments of the operatic stage; and a wide range of operas composed between 1815 and 1930. And because of the nature of my topic, I have deliberately attempted to give sufficient space to the voices of the women who sang or witnessed the singing of others during this period. A considerable part of the evidence presented here is therefore anecdotal, because individual feelings and experiences are rarely recorded in any other fashion. Such sources are fragile, burdened with the dangers of inaccuracies, omissions and self-censorship. Clearly, we should approach this evidence with great care; yet to dismiss it entirely would be equally unproductive: in many instances it constitutes the only available accounts of the individual lives and careers of these women. And within these accounts are voices, it seems to me, that deserve to be heard again, albeit in a different and far-removed context from their own. If Giorgi Righetti's phrase 'I write for the truth' claims too much in our modern understanding of historiography, I too would nevertheless willingly share her other aim: 'I want to verify some facts that have been too bizarrely expounded, or believed with excessive ease.'[83]

A woman who wants her own way is a prima donna. A woman who makes complaints is a prima donna. A woman who changes her mind is a prima donna . . . A woman who refuses compromises is a prima donna. A woman dedicated to her talent is a prima donna.[1]

In 1844, the *Strenna teatrale europea* published an article by Benedetto Bermani entitled 'The life, death and transmigration of the *Prima Donna assoluta*'. It depicted in ironic fashion the fictitious career of 'Clelia', and began by dismissing the qualities usually expected of a singer: 'Voice! talent! feeling! education! But what does all this have to do with moulding a *prima donna assoluta* of our times?' Instead, Bermani listed the true requirements of a putative prima donna:

> Flirtatiousness, beauty, ability in intrigues, a sufficient dose of charlatanism, some of the great airs worthy of a rather misplaced celebrity, much impertinence, a scrupulous and (when necessary) convulsive attachment to one's *convenienze*, costumes that hide little and display much, affectation, limitless demands, honourable and insolent eloquence when speaking of one's triumphs, arrogance towards the *seconde* singers, malicious gossip against one's rivals, a look that promises, a hand that presses, a . . . etc., etc., here are just a few of the principal constitutive ingredients of three-quarters, four, five, nine-tenths of the *prime donne assolute*.[2]

The subsequent recounting of Clelia's career is designed precisely to illustrate this image of a vain, affected and temperamental creature. At the age of sixteen, she is the 'modest, quiet daughter of a cobbler'. But when her vocal talents are discovered by a rich *dilettante*, she enters upon the operatic stage – and so her moral downfall begins. Within two years, she has become 'one of those sublime caricatures', of which only the stage offers the 'complete model'.[3] The smoothest silk is too harsh for her skin, her satin-shod feet disdain to tread the cobbled streets, whilst her bejewelled hands attest to 'a soft, voluptuous and inert life'. Even so, she is still only a *seconda donna*, whose place at the opera house has been obtained by a hefty bribe from the *dilettante*, now also her 'protettore' (with all the implications of a sexual relationship this term often carried). Yet by the mere device of proclaiming herself as a 'prima donna' in the musical and theatrical journals, Clelia miraculously becomes one, and soon she is travelling from one major city to another. Unfortunately, her artistic prowess does not increase with her material development; her voice deteriorates, and she begins to sing out of tune. Despite this – or rather, Bermani claimed, because of it – her 'right to be a *prima donna assoluta*' becomes ever more assured:

> Moreover, the qualities that in our times must form a *prima donna assoluta* acquired in Clelia a prodigious development, since the caprices, the pretensions, the impertinences towards the impresario, the insolent manners towards the poor maestro and the orchestra players, the envies and jealousies of the stage, the art of securing for herself many admirers by having many lovers, and the thousand other qualities of a similar nature necessary, as it seems, in order to form an incomparable Norma, an unequalled Lucrezia, an unrivalled Lucia, attained in Clelia an enviable apogee. She sang horribly out of tune, but on the other hand was almost always absent from the rehearsals; she did not know the divisions of time in the musical phrases, but she knew how to share out her time in appointments; she had neither accent nor expression, but she smiled like an angel at every declaration of love; she acted deplorably on the stage, but was full of life and seduction at other moments. Clelia neglected the accessories, but assiduously cultivated the fundamental qualities necessary to her position – she was in short a *prima donna assoluta* to the letter.

And as this list of calumnies suggests, there is a further defect: sexual licentiousness. Her first 'protettore' is replaced by a second and then a third, and then 'Clelia began to have one for every city in which she found herself.'[4]

It is hardly necessary to relate the rest of this sorry tale – Clelia's desperate attempts to cling to the power she possessed despite the onslaught of age, or her eventual enforced retirement in genteel poverty. Bermani has made his point about the perils of the operatic stage for the young nineteenth-century woman. However, the context in which this article was published is also deserving of note. In the rest of this Italian year-book of operatic events, there are other descriptions of singers, which proffer quite different impressions and images. For example, there is a biographical item on the soprano Felicita Forconi (1819–?), which directly contrasts with the portrait of the hapless Clelia. Here, Bermani's much derided attributes of 'Voice! talent! feeling! education!' are all clearly delineated: Forconi is presented as a fully trained musician, who studied dramatic performance with one of the foremost Italian actors of the day (Antonio Morocchesi); her stage presence and dramatic gifts are applauded; her vocal technique is judged excellent; her face and figure are commended as interesting and expressive rather than beautiful; and even her moral gifts ('Virtue has in her a rival') are admired. Like Clelia, Forconi's travels from *piazza* to *piazza* are recorded: her career began in her native town of Florence, and then included Pisa, Milan, Lugo, Brescia, Bologna, Perugia, Mantua, Rome, Cremona, Piacenza, Udine, Turin, Berlin, and the scene of her latest triumphs, Copenhagen. But unlike Clelia in her dubious amatory adventures, Forconi (we are told) is about to contract a most favourable marriage 'to one of our Lombardian gentlemen of excellent family' – the ultimate reward, perhaps, of the female stage artist's good behaviour and propriety.

There are also a number of sonnets and odes – to both female and male singers – that exalt the singers on a quasi-religious or mythological plane. The author of an ode addressed to the young contralto Marietta Alboni (1826–1894) claims she has been sent to assuage his griefs: praising her 'portentosa voce celeste' ('portentous heavenly voice'), he implores her to reveal her name 'Se non pur vieni dal paradiso' ('If you do not come from paradise').[5] Another ode, this time to Erminia Frezzolini (1818–84), similarly locates the singer's effects on her listener within a supranatural context:

> Salve, Erminia gentil; ben ti ravviso
>> Alle vaghe sembianze,
>> All'or soave ed or fulmineo sguardo,
>> Figlia d'Italia sei; d'alte speranze
>> Animator sorriso!
>> Se irata tuona la tua voce, è un dardo
>> Al cor del più gagliardo;
>> Se in dolce suon la moduli, nell'alma
>> Come prece d'un angiolo discende.
>> Per te l'Arte si rende
>> Ognor secura di sua nobil palma.
>> Che se, a turbar tua calma,
>> Invido alcun t'arride,
>> Deh nol curar; te dagli oltraggi suoi
>> Il merto tuo divide;
>> T'ammira un mondo, che bramar più vuoi?[6]

> [Hail, gentle Erminia; well I perceive
>> From your beautiful features,
>> From your now soft, now threatening glance,
>> You are the daughter of Italy; the smiling inspiration
>> Of high hopes!
>> If your voice thunders in anger, it is a passionate blow
>> To the most robust heart;
>> If modulated in sweet sounds, your voice
>> Descends into the soul like the prayer of an angel.
>> Through you Art renders itself
>> Always sure of its noble victory.
>> And if, to disturb your calm,
>> Some envious one assails you,
>> Oh have no care; your merit divides you
>> From its injuries;
>> A world admires you, what more would you desire?]

We might usefully ask: what was the effect of these differing portraits of the prima donna? After Bermani's article, are we meant to read Forconi's biography with a wry smile, as if at a carefully contrived fiction of a different sort? Should we now perceive the odes and sonnets as the irresistible flattery that brought Clelia to her fate? (Some of these poetic ecstasies were of course commissioned by the singers themselves, as a form of advertisement.) Or is the opposite true – are we to regard Bermani's tale as an irreverent and exaggerated sneer at the honest artistry of the female singer, whose real identity is portrayed more accurately in the other articles and descriptions?

In short, this single edition of the *Strenna teatrale europea* offers a multiplicity of conflicting images of the prima donna, typical of those visible in Europe and America throughout much of the period and disseminated through a wide range of conduits: journalism, musical and theatrical criticism, published diaries and memoirs, teaching manuals, private letters and conversations, publicity material, sonnets and odes, court cases, fiction, portraits, illustrations, sculpture and cartoons. Throughout this mass of material, the female singer appears variously and broadly in three main forms: *demi-mondaine*, professional artist and exalted diva. These categories were rarely discrete entities, but often overlapped and merged. In the *Strenna teatrale*, for example, we have seen that these various images – although presented in separate units (the satirical tale of Clelia, the biographical description of Forconi, the odes to Erminia Frezzolini and Marietta Alboni) – nevertheless lay alongside each other, and that the impact of any one image was affected or mediated by the parallel images and the imprint of the whole, as the reader was invited to sample and mix the differing impressions together.

The discourses around individual singers often demonstrate a similar blurring of image. What are we to make of Elizabeth Billington (1765–1818), for example, portrayed as St Cecilia (the patron saint of music) by Sir Joshua Reynolds but also the subject of scurrilous pornographic 'memoirs'?[7] Or of Giulia Grisi (1811–69), described contemptuously by the London *Standard* as a foreign 'singing woman' when it reported the duel fought over her by Lord Castlereagh and her husband Vicomte Gérard de Melcy,[8] but of whom Princess Victoria (a particular admirer) wrote in her journal: 'She is very quiet, ladylike and unaffected in her manners'?[9] Or of Maria Malibran (1808–36), snubbed by society for her origins, profession and extra-marital pregnancies,[10] but who upon her early death was mourned as 'an inexhaustible genius' whose every sound 'fell with a holy influence upon the heart'?[11] Numerous other singers similarly straddled uneasily the fault lines between 'diva' and 'whore'.

Opera itself provided a telling illustration of the manner in which the 'idea' of the singer was constructed from a number of components, in the shape of Offenbach's *Les Contes d'Hoffmann* (1881). The poet Hoffmann, drinking in a tavern with his male friends, relates his 'folles amours' with three women: Olympia, the epitome of dutiful femininity who entrances her audience with her roulades and trills, but who is then revealed as merely a mechanical doll; Antonia, the 'artist', whose beautiful voice kills her by overstraining her constitution; and Giulietta, the courtesan, who persuades Hoffmann to surrender his reflection to the devil and to kill his rival. However, these female characters prove to be but different facets of Hoffmann's mistress, Stella. An Italian prima donna, Stella is 'trois femmes dans la même femme / Trois âmes dans la seule âme! / Artiste, jeune fille et courtisane':[12] she encompasses Antonia's voice and artistry, Olympia's technically proficient but empty display, and Giulietta's fatal eroticism. Similar analogies were already common currency in descriptions of real singers, as in this account of Jenny Lind (1820–87) written in 1855 by the opera impresario Max Maretzek:

> Under the protecting tutelage of Meyerbeer, she was as the unconscious nightingale who sings for the mere sake of singing. When in the guardianship of Lumley, she became the mere peacock of vocalism, airing her many-colored notes in the mid-day sun, for the purpose of deafening us to the song of others. And at last, with Barnum, she displayed herself as the Syren whose delicate tones warbled the American gold-finches into her outstretched fingers.[13]

In Offenbach's opera, the prima donna Stella equally fails the test of true 'womanliness'. When she finally appears in person, the drunk and disillusioned poet condemns her: 'Vous êtes Olympia? Brisée. . . Antonia? Morte! . . . Giulietta? Damnée.'[14] Her subsequent exit on the arm of Hoffmann's triumphant rival, Lindorf (the devil-figure who has plagued all Hoffmann's attempts to woo Olympia/Antonia/Giulietta), emphasises that she is sponsored by satanic elements. Hoffmann remains to be comforted by his own Muse, an angelic female figure who promises to appease his sufferings by enabling him to transform his grief into art. The opera's final images of Stella and Hoffmann thus explicitly uphold the association of female art with the disruptive forces of evil, and male art with the forces of goodness and morality.[15]

This fractured perspective of female vocal artistry was by no means new: it had been in evidence since (and arguably long before) the birth of opera in the early seventeenth century. Bermani's description of Clelia, for example, rehearses all the central points made by Benedetto Marcello in 1720.[16] Yet the prima donna was perhaps a particularly puzzling phenomenon for nineteenth-century society. In the midst of an era that was attempting through various kinds of indoctrination (social, cultural, political and educational) to restrict woman's access to the public domain, the prima donna stood indomitably on the operatic stage demonstrating musical prowess, financial independence, sexual freedom – and eliciting in return praise and monetary reward. Already in place before the notion of the 'feminine ideal' reached its corseted apogee in the mid-Victorian period, and still prominent in the later age of the New Woman at the *fin-de-siècle* when various singers lent their support to the women's suffrage movements, the prima donna provided a powerful – and disturbing – example of women's capabilities beyond the domestic confines.

The reverberations of this disturbance ripple through the era's images of the female singer, with differing degrees of intensity. In terms of the critical reception by the musical and theatrical press, much daily reviewing was unremarkable, comprising accounts of working professional women, their approach to their craft, their success or otherwise. This is not to suggest that such reviews did not also contain reflections of the contemporaneous ideology – only that for the most part, illusions to particular notions and expectations of gender were often implicit rather than explicit. But the greater agitations collected around the question of power: that is, discussions of the prima donna at a philosophical or moralistic or conceptual level centred on the perception of the *cantante* as an agent of female potency. No other woman (except in the generic sense of Woman) in this era encompassed such a range of interpretative possibilities, was both so idolised and so despised; she was, in short, a living metaphor for her sex.

Inevitably, different responses to and interpretations of the possibilities of such potency – particularly within the era's context of discussions about the political position of women – are apparent. One perception of the prima donna (promulgated predominantly by women authors and singers) was as a *proto-feminist*, a role model of female endeavour and achievement. Another contrasting and more negative view regarded her at best with uneasy admiration, and at worst open hostility. It would be false to assume, however, that approaches to the prima donna can be divided neatly into opposing camps. Rather, the discourse surrounding the female singer fulfils Foucault's thesis on the broader functions of discourse 'as a multiplicity of discursive elements that can come into play in various strategies':

> There is not, on the one side, a discourse of power, and opposite it, another discourse that runs counter to it. Discourses are tactical elements or blocks operating in the field of force relations; there can exist different and even contradictory discourses within the same strategy; they can, on the contrary, circulate without changing their form from one strategy to another, opposing strategy.[17]

As we shall see, attempts by various bodies to 'fix' the image of the singer within a particular construct or discourse were rarely, if ever, successful.

The contradictions evident in discourses relating to the prima donna moreover cannot be glibly assigned to gender issues alone, but also reflect the wider context of opera itself during this era, and its separate dimensions as a pleasure palace, an artform and an industry – categories that clearly connect with and influence the different images of the singer as *demi-mondaine,* diva and professional stage artist. Such images were also partly determined by specific modes of writing. In fiction, an author might fantasise about the singer and attempt to fashion her according to his prejudices and or desires; in formal criticism or biography, the author might judge the professional skills, merits and demerits of the singer with regard to established codes of performance; in poetic adulation, the author might be a rapt spectator paying homage to the singer – even, perhaps, attempting to recapture in words what Walter Benjamin describes as the 'aura of the work of art'.[18] At times, the boundaries between these modes of writing became indistinct: sonnets could encompass a form of review (the ode to Frezzolini draws detailed pictures of her performances in different roles); fiction often drew heavily on the biographies of real singers (as, for example, in the novels by George Sand and Willa Cather discussed in the next chapter); formal criticism sometimes strayed into purple prose (as in one reviewer's lyrical welcome of Carolina Ungher's return after illness in *Figaro* in 1837, or the ornate language of *fin-de-siècle* critics like James Huneker).[19] How the singer was portrayed therefore depended as much on the mode of writing as on the author's ideas and perceptions. And this discourse – both factual and fictional – did not simply reflect the practices of the operatic market place; it was itself an active participant in developing certain aspects of the profession. As an advertisement of the merits of particular singers, it constructed celebrity, which in turn increased audiences. As a conduit of ideas about the operatic world, it encouraged other women to consider the kinds of rewards – and penalties – offered by a life on the stage. And as a means of information about methods of singing and dramatic performance, it educated both artists and spectators.

THE DEVIL'S CHOIR, OR SIREN VOICES

Underlying the nineteenth-century representation of the singer were the sinews of a much older idea: *la longue durée* of the figure of the siren. From her appearance in ancient Greek religion and mythology, the siren has symbolised the powers of voice, music, knowledge, sex and pleasure:

> You will come to the Sirens first of all: they bewitch any mortal man who approaches them. If a man in ignorance draws too close and catches their music, he will never return to find wife and little children near him and to see their joy at his homecoming; the high clear tones of the Sirens will bewitch him. They sit in a meadow; men's corpses lie heaped up all around them, mouldering upon the bones as the skin decays.[20]

The siren's original manifestation was as a mourner, and carrier of the dead to Elysium; the chief lure of her singing was its promise of hidden knowledge of the past, present and future. But these more positive aspects of the siren's nature disappeared after the arrival of Christianity. The early church employed her first as a warning against heresy;[21] then against female public performance[22] (Jerome writes to a widow in AD 394: 'Repel a singer as you would some bane. Hurry from your house women who live by playing and singing, the devil's choir whose songs are the fatal ones of sirens');[23] and finally as an example of the perils of eroticism and worldly pleasure – she was listed in mediaeval bestiaries and amongst the monsters in Gothic decoration;[24] Dante met her in purgatory;[25] Spenser portrayed her in the 'halfe Theatre' of a secluded bay.[26] And she had other manifestations in other fables, as the Celtic Birds of Rhiannon, or the *rusalki* of Slavonic mythology, or the German water-sprites or *undines*. The precise details of these creatures vary, but the enticing, emasculating and fatal power of the female voice remains as a constant.[27]

No era, however, saw a greater proliferation of images of the siren and her sisters than the nineteenth century – or, perhaps, a greater variety in her use as a metaphor. The Lorelei stalks her victims through the pages of German romantic poetry (such as Heine's *Die*

Lorelei, 1823, or Eichendorff's *Waldesgespräch*, 1837) like a vengeful *Doppelgänger* of the drowned 'fallen woman' that was a similarly prevalent character in art and literature. In Britain, the siren appears in the context of imperial colonialism, as the naive (but so erotic) 'wild girl' of the primitive world in works such as Byron's poem *The Island* (1823) or Kingsley's novel *Westward Ho!* (1855). Théophile Gautier's poem *Cærulei oculi* describes an unsettling encounter at the water's edge with the 'sirène' who awakes 'la violence / D'un irrésistible désir' in her victim.[28] Later in the century, Ibsen viewed the siren through the glass of Darwin's theories of evolution in *The Lady from the Sea* (1888);[29] in Gabriele d'Annunzio's play *La Gioconda* (1899), the self-mutilated Silvia seeks consolation with the mysterious La Sirenetta;[30] Chekhov centred *Uncle Vanya* around the title-role's obsession with Helen, a 'mermaid'.[31] The extraordinary frequency of visual representations by *fin-de-siècle* European artists is documented by Bram Dijkstra ('it must have seemed to the visitors to the yearly painting exhibitions that these creatures were virtually everywhere');[32] and he explains this fascination by aligning the sirens with the emergence of the New Woman, offering as evidence the free, naked sirens – the very embodiment of passion and strength – that rejoice on the rocks at the sight of Ulysses' ship in John William Whiteley's picture 'A Sail!' (1898).[33]

Various influences account in part for the popularity of the sirens during this period: the increasing predilection for all things belonging to ancient Greece, which manifested itself throughout Europe in intellectual and cultural discourse;[34] the dominant society's coded fear and distrust of women, exemplified in the numerous depictions of female hostility;[35] the absorption with the domain of the supranatural; the conflict between public approbation of morality and private vice. But a vital factor was surely also the era's interest in music and music-making – particularly the prominence of the prima donna and opera itself within the musical landscape.

Here, the songs of the siren had undoubted resonance. Modern theorists such as Michel Poizat have developed Lacanian-based explanations of the innate eroticism of the human voice, and its quality of utterance or 'cry';[36] or, like Roland Barthes, explored semiological ideas to account for the ineluctable attraction of the 'grain of the voice'.[37] In an era predating psychoanalysis and deconstruction, the nineteenth century leaned instead towards the myth of the siren to explicate the listener's response to the singer. But the myth was also extended to embrace opera itself and the opera house. Nineteenth-century debates concerning the meaning and purpose of music had been stimulated in part by Rousseau's *Essai sur l'origine des langues* (1764), which argued that music had a moral function and should be regulated accordingly. The era's ensuing definitions of what thus might constitute musical decadence often included opera, and owed much to siren analogies.[38] This was hardly an innovative perspective – opera in France, Germany, Britain and even Italy had long been regarded by some critics as symbolizing precisely a kind of feminised musical seduction[39] – but it gained greater credence in the newly moralistic climate. In 1796, Jean Baptiste Leclerc wrote of the 'licentiousness' with which music 'prostitutes itself in the theatre' like a 'votary of Bacchus' who 'lards herself with ornaments and seduces instead of using her natural charms'.[40] Britain, failing to develop its own operatic traditions as successfully as its European neighbours, displayed a particular fondness for this line of criticism. In 1814 the critic and essayist William Hazlitt described the 'Opera Muse' as 'a tawdry courtesan, who when her paint and patches, her rings and jewels are stripped off, can excite only disgust and ridicule'.[41] Four years later, despite (or perhaps because of) occasionally reviewing opera for the *Examiner*, he returned even more vehemently to the attack, labelling opera as 'a species of intellectual prostitution' virulently opposed to nature:

> The Opera is the most artificial of all things. It is not only art, but ostentatious, unambiguous, exclusive art. It does not subsist as an imitation of nature, but in contempt of it; and instead of seconding, its object is to pervert and sophisticate all our natural impressions of things . . . Not only is all communication with nature cut off, but every appeal to the imagination is sheathed and softened in the melting medium of Siren sounds. The ear is cloyed and glutted with warbled

ecstasies or agonies; while every avenue to terror or pity is carefully
stopped up and guarded by song and recitative . . . and there is hardly a
vice for which the mind is not thus gradually prepared, no virtue of
which it is not rendered incapable!'[42]

He concludes with a grimly xenophobic warning that recalls
precisely the sirens' reputed powers of emasculation: 'It may serve
to assist the *euthanasia* of the British character, of British liberty, and
British morals, – by hardening the heart, while it softens the senses,
and dissolving every manly and generous feeling in an atmosphere of
voluptuous effeminacy.'[43]

'Effeminacy' was only one product of opera's pernicious effects. In
1809 Leigh Hunt wrote about the 'Private Boxes' which were part of
the recently rebuilt and refurbished Covent Garden: 'Could there
possibly be easier opportunities for the whole progress of seduction
and sensuality – for vanquishing the weak, and rioting with the
abandoned?'[44] Liszt's criticisms of La Scala in 1838 for a Parisian
music journal included implications that the boxes were used precisely for such seductive purposes – a charge angrily denied by the
Italian press.[45] (Were such claims justified? Ugo Foscolo's letters to
his lover in 1801 certainly allude to their romantic encounters at La
Scala;[46] Stendhal's memoirs of the theatre a few years later make
similar suggestions.[47]) Fiction added its own contribution to this
debate. The doomed elopement of Natasha Rostov and Anatole
Kuragin in Tolstoy's *War and Peace* (1869) begins with their first
meeting in an opera house. Initially, Natasha is repelled by the falsity
of what she sees on stage but by the end of the opera she regards it as
'perfectly natural', having fallen 'completely under the spell of the
world in which she found herself'. So too has her moral judgement
weakened – her earlier sober thoughts about her fiancé Prince
Andrey have been replaced by the erotic charge of her encounter
with Kuragin in his sister's box.[48] The young heroine of H. G. Wells's
Ann Veronica (1909) finds herself similarly imperilled when the opera
house itself colludes in Ramage's seductive advances as they watch
Wagner's *Tristan and Isolde*: the 'great hazy warm brown cavity of
the house' draws her eyes into its depths, the comfort of the box in

which she sits allows her to be fully absorbed into the 'glory of sound and colours' emanating from the stage, whilst the music 'confused and distracted her, and made her struggle against a feeling of intoxication. Her head swam.' Only the return of the houselights in the auditorium restores her 'self-command' and allows her to fight off both her own sexual desires and the importuning Ramage.[49]

But it was of course the female singer who provided the fullest embodiment of the siren myth – as she had done from the beginning of operatic history.[50] It is difficult to find a singer who was not awarded the epithet of 'siren', in a review, or an ode, or a portrait: Isabella Colbran was a 'gran Sirena';[51] Maddalena Grassi had only 'le dolci note' of the siren (see fig. 1); Giuditta Pasta was a 'sweet Syren';[52] Lucia Vestris, a 'modern Siren';[53] Angiolina Tiberini, 'quella incantatrice sirena';[54] Fanny Salvini-Donatelli, a 'nuova ed ardente sirena';[55] Angelica Catalani, 'la meravigliosa sirena';[56] Anna Bishop, 'la sirena de Albion';[57] Adelina Patti, 'la sirena per eccellenza'[58] – to cite but a few. The sheer ubiquity of the term causes one to question its meaning: did it signify nothing more than a lack of imagination on the part of the nineteenth-century writer? Perhaps. But in the siren, nineteenth-century society found an image of the singer that encapsulated a number of different and sometimes contradictory dimensions. If opera was the 'power' art-form in the 'power century',[59] an era fascinated by all forms of supremacy, the siren was undoubtedly the 'power' singer: the epitome of irresistible success. As a template of charismatic performance and vocal achievement, the siren offered an idealised model to which the professional singer might aspire – and against which she might be judged. Opera enthusiasts used the idea of the siren to explain their championship of a particular singer: Stendhal, for example, wrote that 'many notes' of Giuditta Pasta's 'remarkably rich voice' were 'not only extremely fine in themselves, but have the ability to produce a kind of resonant and magnetic vibration, which, through some still unexplained combination of physical phenomena, exercises an instantaneous and hypnotic effect on the soul of the spectator'.[60] This element of mystique undoubtedly served its place in defining celebrity; particularly in

MADDALENA GRASSI

Sirena ell'è: tremar virtù non puote,
Delle Sirene ha sol le dolci note.

Figure 1.1. Maddalena Grassi, portrait

the earlier years of the century, when a significant social divide still existed between performer and spectator, it might also have had its uses in sanctioning the sometimes fanatical adulation aroused by women of a lower social class, or by those singers like Benedetta Rosmunda Pisaroni, disfigured by smallpox, who did not fulfil conventional ideas of beauty. And in an artform that with its conventions and artifices always risked ridicule, the enlisting of mythological creatures conferred a certain – sometimes much-needed – sense of dignity on its protagonists.

But if the image of the siren might have empowered the female singer in some ways, in others it enhanced long-standing ideas about her sexual availability and motives[61] – a product in part of her links with the courtesan during the previous two centuries and the un-conventional approach to sexual mores of some singers.[62] The no-menclature 'prima donna' was used as a synonym for 'prostitute' by Victorian writers such as Henry Mayhew;[63] in Italy the terms 'vir-tuosa' and 'prostituta' were similarly interchangeable;[64] and the sense of female singers as erotic objects is further underlined by anonymous pornography purporting to be the memoirs of singers – including not only Elizabeth Billington, but also Lucia Vestris (1787–1856) and Wilhelmine Schröder-Devrient (1804–60).[65] The use-fulness of the term 'siren' was that it retained these associations with an unfettered eroticism, but unlike 'prostitute' or 'whore' it could be used in polite (that is, public) discourse. A letter written by Bellini in 1835, when the composer was trying (unsuccessfully) to arrange a marriage with a rich heiress, reveals a common prejudice: the girl's uncle was withholding his consent because of his 'fears that I, a theatrical man, would bring into his house all the singers in the world, or else would fall in love with all the prima donnas, whom he describes as the most seductive women of the Inferno'.[66] Maretzek claimed that while Erminia Frezzolini (1818–1884) 'sang like a syren on the stage, and enchanted the public at large, she acted also the part of a syren in private life, and drowned her adorers in a whirlpool of excitement'.[67] When Luisa Tetrazzini justifiably sued her former financial agent for embezzlement in 1905, his attorney attempted to discredit her by describing her as 'the siren who lured this young man from his home'.[68]

But it is in fictional literature where the influence of the siren in defining the image of the prima donna is particularly apparent. Writers of both sexes found the professional female singer a most useful heroine: her varied life, her precarious balancing act between success and failure, her forays into both the *demi-monde* and the glittering society, all provided rich material. The iconoclastic actions of the prima donna and her relationship to the feminine ideal, however, were often perceived in markedly different ways. As will be demonstrated later, some women writers were concerned with challenging the notion of the siren. For many others (predominantly male), the siren myth provided a kind of classical explication of the singer's unusual position in society, her submission to the lure of the stage rather to the guidance of husband and domesticity, and her attraction of numerous admirers.

The common concern of most male-authored novels dealing with the prima donna was to subdue the rebellious and subversive siren within her – and thus render her accessible to male domination. Even violence was acceptable in order to attain this goal: in E. T. A. Hoffmann's witty and grotesque novella *Councillor Krespel* (1818), the hero resorts to defenestration as a means of controlling his prima donna wife (a desperate act, but one that had an operatic precedent given that it was legendarily threatened by Handel during a contentious rehearsal with Francesca Cuzzoni in 1722).[69] Marriage sometimes (although not always) provided a more peaceful solution, as in Gaston Leroux's *The Phantom of the Opera* (1910); motherhood was employed to similar purpose by George Meredith in *Vittoria* (1866); whilst George Moore elected to confine the singing heroine of *Evelyn Innes* (1898) and its sequel *Sister Theresa* (1901) within the walls of the convent (in a later edition, he permitted her return to the world as a social worker). Only the heroine of James Huneker's *Painted Veils* (1920) is allowed a long and lustrous career – although it is clear that damnation awaits her at its end. The need for such control was imperative because prima donnas are invariably drawn as being possessed of extraordinary will power and determination. Inevitably in this era, these elements of female ambition and achievement were perceived as having damaging consequences on male prestige and self-image, and are often depicted as intentional acts of aggression that signify integral character traits of the singer herself. Thus Hoffmann's Angela proceeds to make life a 'torment' for her husband Krespel through the tempestuous irrationality that is an endemic attribute of her voice: 'All the self-will and capriciousness of every *prima donna* who ever sang was, according to Krespel, united in Angela's tiny frame.'[70] The title-role of *Evelyn Innes* similarly 'lived in defiance of rules, governed by individual caprice';[71] whilst the Wagnerian soprano Istar in *Painted Veils* is described as a 'heartless, ungrateful creature' who was 'composed of harps, anvils and granite'.[72]

The eroticism of the prima donna is manipulated to the full by these authors. In novels such as *Vittoria* and George Gissing's *Thyrza* (1887), the singer's innate sensuality is indicated merely by her capacity to attract admirers and her propensity to give precedence to her emotions rather than to what duty prescribes. Elsewhere, the prima donna's supposedly exaggerated appetite for sex is demonstrated by her engagement in activities deemed outside the 'norm' of sexual relationships. Before her reformation, the heroine of George Du Maurier's *Trilby* (1894) is promiscuous, sharing her body 'capriciously, desultorily, more in a frolicsome spirit of *camaraderie* than anything else'.[73] Far more shocking for the *fin-de-siècle* reader than such extra-marital interludes, however, was the episode of masturbation that occurs after Evelyn Innes (whose very voice is 'full of sex')[74] has severed her relationship with both her lovers because of an increasing religious vocation, but is nevertheless unable to control her lust:

> She loved Owen no longer, and if she yielded, an hour's delight would be followed by a miserable terror and despair so abject that she might kill herself. But God seemed far away, and as she lay staring into the darkness images of fierce sensuality crowded upon her, the fever that consumed her was unendurable, her will was being stolen from her, and with the rape of her will her flesh hardened and was thrust forward in burning pulsations. She held her breasts in both hands, and bit her pillow like a neck, and her reason seemed to drift and sicken, and her body was her whole reality.[75]

Huneker's *Painted Veils*, where Istar is depicted as 'the Great Singing Whore of Babylon', attempts even more exotic adventures. Istar's disregard for the era's sexual conventions is stressed by both her bisexuality – she humiliates her chief male admirer by seducing his mistress – and her willing sexual submission to an African-American man in the midst of a quasi-religious drunken orgy in the Deep South. Moreover, the erotic content of both Moore and Huneker's novels was a deliberate commercial strategy, signalling the emergence of the earlier depictions of the prima donna found in pornography into the literary mainstream. Moore described *Evelyn Innes* as 'one of the most powerful literary aphrodisiacs ever written', whilst Huneker referred to *Painted Veils* as 'frankly erotic'.[76]

Another interesting feature in these novels is the construction of a counter-image to the siren – an idealised, passive version of the female singer. In some, this is merely implied by the use of a male teacher who instructs the aspiring but ignorant young singer in the making of her voice. (It is noticeable that apart from in Huneker, female vocal tutors are ignored, although teachers such as Mathilde Marchesi and Pauline Viardot had an international reputation.[77]) The triumphant operatic success of Christine Daaé in *Phantom of the Opera* is due solely to the mysterious tuition she receives in rapt frenzy from her unseen Angel of Music (later revealed to be the phantom himself); he transforms her insignificant instrument into a 'seraphic' voice possessing 'superhuman notes'.[78] Daaé's willingness to accept male guidance and her adherence to the strictures of the 'feminine ideal' contrast with the behaviour of the novel's other prima donna, the 'heartless and soulless diva' Carlotta.[79] *Councillor Krespel* and *Trilby* offer more extreme fantasies of the 'idealised' prima donna. In *Krespel*, this image appears in the form of Antonia (the daughter of Krespel and Angela), who inherits her mother's vocal talent but not her temperament. Her femininity, defined by her passive nature and frail physique, is both imperilled by her singing and yet itself a direct source of her particular vocal timbre. Her extraordinary voice stems from an 'organic defect' in her chest that 'gives her voice its wonderful power and the strange tone which . . . resounds beyond the sphere of human song',[80] but which so weakens her that the act of singing endangers her life. Forbidden to sing by

Krespel, Antonia transmutes her voice into her father's violin. But the siren within her will not be silenced: erotic love finally releases Antonia's repressed voice, and she dies as a result of one last glorious bout of song.

The character of Trilby is based wholly on the quality of unknowing. At the outset of the novel she is tone-deaf, just as she is blind to conventional moral codes: both vocally and morally she wanders through the keys of her life without regard to system or tradition. This wayward femaleness must be organised by male control, and so her lover Little Billee becomes responsible for her moral education whilst Svengali undertakes her musical tuition. Through her hypnotic assimilation of Svengali's knowledge, Trilby's singing is finally a 'revelation of what the human voice could achieve':[81]

> her voice was so immense in its softness, richness, freshness, that it seemed to be pouring itself out from all round; its intonation absolutely, mathematically pure; one felt it to be not only faultless, but infallible; and the seduction, the novelty of it, the strangely sympathetic quality!
> . . . The like of that voice has never been heard, nor ever will be again. A woman archangel might sing like that, or some enchanted princess out of a fairy tale.[82]

But this voice is entirely hidden from Trilby herself – she is unaware that it even exists. The self-will, vanity and determination required for a performing career belong entirely to Svengali, and he is only able to imbue her with qualities so antipathetic to her nature when her conscious mind is asleep. Thus Trilby's innocence and naivety are untouched by the consequences of fame and fortune; she is preserved from affectation, adopts no hauteur towards old or new friends, and retains her sweetness of character. Du Maurier created the 'ideal' prima donna by subtracting the key element of the singer, will-power, from his heroine and reducing her to the status of a passive instrument. Antonia at least herself sang through the medium of her father's violin; Trilby is even less fortunate:

> That Trilby was just a singing-machine – an organ to play upon – an instrument of music – a Stradivarius – a flexible flageolet of flesh and

blood – a voice, and nothing more – just the unconscious voice that Svengali sang with . . .[83]

SONGBIRDS AND MUSIC GIRLS: VOCALISING FEMININITY

Refashioning the siren's voice into a more harmless instrument was not merely a fictional device. The early Christian church, by pro-scribing women's voices from men's hearing, had aped the advice of Circe to stop the ears of Ulysses' crew with unmelted wax. Nine-teenth-century society – or at least some elements within it – favoured the approach of another Greek hero, Jason, who conquered the sirens by means of Orpheus and his lyre:[84] the sirens, out-sung and out-charmed, reportedly committed suicide in despair. Such became the new strategy. The much-vaunted 'moral' qualities of man-made music were pitted against the sirens' elemental, wilful vocalising through the teaching of specific kinds of singing. This battle to convert the siren into a songbird became a standard item in the education of women, fought within the wider context of the era's absorption with music.

The extraordinary growth of domestic music-making within the middle and upper classes during the nineteenth century (reflected in increased sales of instruments, printed music and tuition)[85] was fuelled in part by the perceptions of its role in building the new bourgeois society. In 1838, a correspondent to the British periodical *The Musical World* elaborated a much-debated theory:

> Music acts upon the moral feeling. Simple and beautiful melodies refine it; pure and majestic harmonies connected with them, correct, ennoble, and confirm it; the significant and characteristic movement, order and feeling of relation throughout, work powerfully on the mind, and the connexion of the parts, when properly displayed by a sufficient performer, awakens high and heavenly thoughts and elevates devotion.[86]

Such abundant benefits were thought to result also from performing music. The practice of music offered an important source of controlled entertainment, instilling the lesson in children that effort reaps achievement, drawing the family around the piano to participate in a mutual experience, and facilitating vital social links via musical parties and soirées.[87] In wealthy families, music-making was often shared with or provided by professional performers, the event thus becoming an exclusive concert enabling the organisers to display taste and cultural knowledge in their selection of musicians, and to patronise the talents of rising new stars.[88] But a further factor for this upsurge in amateur music-making lay in the definitions of gender that accorded middle- and upper-class women a specific role as a private performer on the domestic stage.[89] In 1800 the *Allgemeine musikalische Zeitung* articulated what was to become a standard dictum in female education:

> every well-bred girl, whether she has talent or not, must learn to play the piano or to sing; first of all, it's fashionable; secondly (here the spirit of speculation comes in), it's the most convenient way to put herself forward in society and thereby, if she is lucky, to make an advantageous and matrimonial alliance, particularly a moneyed one.[90]

Musical expertise was in effect a visible sign of gentility – the middle-class appropriation of perceived aristocratic values deriving from the long European tradition of domestic music-making amongst upper-class women since the Middle Ages.[91] It also demonstrated the family's financial status in affording expensive lessons and instruments (although as the century progressed teachers became increasingly plentiful and the cost of instruments diminished considerably).[92] And musical performances were not simply exhibitions of innate talent; they were also evidence of 'feminine' labour, of industrious hours spent on scales and arpeggios, as the *Strenna teatrale europea* assured its readers in 1838:

> Knowing how to sing or play has now become the principal talent of a young girl: the father takes pleasure in it, the mother rejoices in it, the grandmother is delighted by it, the relatives, acquaintances and neighbours all welcome it: in a word it is a treasure, a miracle, an inexhaustible source of delight that one has in the family: and woe to her

if she does not already know by memory the best items from *Giuramento*, woe if she does not know how to perform instantly the *cracovienne* of Saint Romain, the overture of *Zampa* or that of *Guglielmo Tell!*[93]

Women's choice of instrument was nonetheless commonly restricted by the codes of femininity.[94] The adolescent George Sand owned those generally approved: 'I had in my room a piano, a harp and a guitar.'[95] Singing and piano playing were the only 'fit subjects for girls and women'[96] according to the Berne conservatoire in 1858, in a stance typical of almost all the emerging European music institutions until the 1870s.[97] Camilla Urso (1842–1902), a French violinist whose career began in the 1850s, recalled the objections against women playing the violin because 'it lacked grace in the appearance and movements of the performer';[98] instruments such as the cello or the French horn, which required even more pronounced unwomanly posture and muscular development, were played by only the most daring of women until the latter part of the century;[99] professional orchestras denied access to all female instrumentalists with the exception of the harpist.[100]

In contrast, the pianoforte was considered particularly appropriate for female study, not only as a vehicle for individual prowess but also for its social functions.[101] A pianist could provide simple background music to a family evening, dazzle visitors with technical and musical accomplishment, supply the music necessary for dances or recitations, and accompany other instrumentalists and singers. The harp was similarly favoured (its angelic connotations fitted well with the 'feminine ideal', as well as requiring much exposure of graceful bare arms), as were other smaller stringed instruments like the mandolin and the guitar.[102] But all these instruments – piano, harp and guitar – had more in common than their capacity to be played in accordance with feminine gestic codes. They all had a function of self-accompaniment, thus enabling the nineteenth-century woman to fulfil possibly her most idealised musical occupation – that of a singer.

Singing was regarded as the source of all music: in singing, the singer *became* music. The Austrian doctor and music historian Peter

Lichtenthal described it in his treatise on music in 1807: 'The human voice is the first, the most pure, the most exceptional instrument in the world, and a natural human voice, glad and melodious, certainly prevails over the best instruments.'[103] Such ideas surface again and again in the literature of the period, as in this later extract from the Italian journal *Boccherini* in 1874:

> the throat of a singer is the instrument that nature herself has created; therefore, it is the most beautiful instrument that is known, because it is the most effective at moving our affections, the most fitting for the language of the passions, the most admirable for sweetness, for vigour of expression and sentiment: in short, the prototype of all the musical instruments created by man, and of which the most appreciated is exactly that which best approaches the human voice; but this vocal organism is likewise the most delicate instrument in its structure, the most difficult to know and manage.[104]

Vocal dominance in the hierarchy of musical instruments extended to notions of music's power. If music in general was believed to exert a positive moral influence on its listeners and practitioners, then the act of singing in particular was regarded as the most effective regulator of human behaviour – providing, of course, that it accorded with specific standards regarding text and musical style. An article in *The Musical World* in 1837 claimed that the teaching of singing is 'almost the only branch of education, aside from divine truth, whose direct tendency is to *cultivate the feelings* . . . The chief object of the cultivation of vocal music is to train the feelings.'[105] The manner in which singing could be so manipulated is illustrated by the theories of the German composer, journalist and singing teacher Joseph Mainzer (1801–51). A former priest, Mainzer specialised in teaching children and adults from the poorer sections of the community, and his efforts to make the art of singing available to all were widely applauded. (Berlioz was one exception – impressed with Mainzer's early concerts with a choir of working-class men in Paris, he was later dismissive of the lack of technical progress and Mainzer's choice of repertoire.[106]) Mainzer began his career initially in Germany, until his political activism awoke the interest of the authorities and he was forced to leave the country in 1831.[107] Resuming his teaching briefly in Brussels, he then found a more settled existence in Paris from 1833 until his classes were banned in 1839. He spent his final decade in Britain, where he introduced his teaching methods first in London in 1841, then Edinburgh and finally Manchester. His ideas were disseminated through the press in various countries. In Germany he published his theories in *Singschule* (1831), and later wrote predominantly for European music periodicals: in Belgium for *L'Artiste*; in France for the *Revue et gazette musicale* and also for several left-wing journals including *Le National* and *Le Réformateur*; in Germany for the *Neue Zeitschrift für Musik*; and in Britain for *Mainzer's Musical Times and Singing Circular* (which he founded and which survives even today as the *Musical Times*).[108]

Mainzer argued that the teaching of singing was 'preferable to any other mode of attaining a more general influence upon all classes of people',[109] because of the way in which words, moral precepts and expressive melody combined to affect the performer in a particularly direct fashion.[110] His book *Singing for the Million* (1841), essentially a translation of his earlier *Singschule*, made sweeping claims for the efficacy of vocal training on children. Singing was not simply a 'luxury', he declared:

> it perfections [*sic*] the sense of hearing, purifies the voice, strengthens the lungs and ameliorates the heart. Singing in taking from school its stiffness renders it more gay and attractive, the paternal home more sacred, and adds to the sublimity of public worship; it softens the rigours of poverty, makes the rich benevolent, consoles those who suffer, makes the happy happier; as it diminishes sorrow, so it doubles pleasure.[111]

Although he himself was regarded in some quarters as a revolutionary (partly because of his political views and the fact that his classes enabled large numbers of the working class to congregate), Mainzer's use of singing nevertheless thus supported fundamental bourgeois values: as an aid to health, educational prowess, filial devotion, religious worship and moral indoctrination.[112] His ideas recurred throughout the nineteenth century in the European musical press, as part of various campaigns to extend the teaching of singing in schools and the wider community.[113]

Some commentators, however, applied aspects of Mainzer's theories – specifically, that forms of singing and music could assist in the ordering of society – directly to the education of women, as two British writers demonstrate. John Ruskin's *Sesame and Lilies* (1865) provides the first example. Distrustful of the professional environs frequented by the prima donna and regarding woman's proper role to be a noble but passive servant of man,[114] Ruskin unsurprisingly decreed that female music-making should be at the service of others rather than a reflection of internal passions:

> In music especially you will soon find what personal benefit there is in being serviceable: it is probable that however limited your powers, you have voice and ear enough to sustain a note of moderate compass in a concerted piece; that then, is the first thing to make sure you can do. Get your voice disciplined and clear, and think only of accuracy; never of effect or expression: if you have any soul worth expressing, it will show itself in your singing; but most likely there are very few feelings in you at present, needing particular expression; and the one thing you have to is to make a clear-voiced little instrument of yourself, which other people can entirely depend on you for the note wanted.[115]

There is no suggestion here that woman herself might gain pleasure from her singing; only that she must cleanse her voice of its troublesome egotistical desires, and subject its purified tone to the demands of others.[116] Ruskin's dictums drew a derisory retort some years later from the music critic and feminist sympathiser George Bernard Shaw: 'I earnestly advise the young ladies of England, whether enrolled in the Guild of St George or not, to cultivate music solely for the love and need of it, and to do it in all humility of spirit, never forgetting that they are most likely inflicting all-but-unbearable annoyance on every musician within earshot, instead of rendering "assistance to others".'[117]

Another Victorian commentator, the Rev. H. Reginald Haweis, echoed some of Mainzer's theories in his widely translated and reprinted *Music and Morals* (1873), and offered female domestic music-making as a consolation for women's narrow lives. Despite his largely conventional views, Haweis was sympathetic to the female plight, believing that woman, 'though capable of so much', was 'frequently called upon in the best years of her life to do but little, but at all times society imposes upon her a strict reticence as to her real feelings'.[118] This paucity of fulfilling occupations combined with the severe repression of emotions had dangerous consequences: women became either 'dissatisfied or listless' or 'frivolous, wicked, exaggerated caricatures of what God intended them to be'. Even more threatening was the possibility of open revolt:

> To set women to do the things which some people suppose are the only fit things for them to do, is often like setting the steam-hammer to knock pins into a board . . . The steam-hammer, as it contemplates the everlasting pin's head, cannot help feeling that if some day, when the steam was on, it might give one good smashing blow, it would feel all the better for it.

Music, having the 'power of relief and a gentle grace of ministration little short of the supernatural', was Haweis' solution to such problems, providing – he thought – a much-needed outlet for women's emotions. He pictures the female singer or pianist as a solitary music-maker with half-closed eyes confiding her 'heavy burden' to her art:

> That girl who sings to herself her favourite songs of Schubert, Mendelssohn, or Schumann, sings more than a song; it is her own plaint of suffering floating away on the wings of melody . . . Let no one say that the moral effects of music are small or insignificant. That domestic and long-suffering instrument, the cottage piano, has probably done more to sweeten existence and bring peace and happiness to families in general, and to young women in particular, than all the homilies on the domestic virtues ever yet penned.[119]

Haweis' depiction implies that women's self-will could be successfully focussed into an artistic rather than a political voice. The use of music as a safety-valve for mental, emotional and sexual frustration would preserve the status quo of the middle-class home, and encourage women to accept their domestic imprisonment with renewed obedience and compliance.[120]

The notion that singing could actively affect the character was complemented by the idea that the voice also *revealed* the character. Women were warned that any secret harbouring of inappropriate feelings would be immediately apparent to the listener, as *The Young Lady's Book* (1832) demonstrated: 'Habits of querulousness, or ill-nature, will communicate a cat-like quality to the singing, as infallibly as they give a peculiar character to the speaking voice.'[121] Even serious musicians subscribed to this theory. One periodical in 1838 reprinted the claims of German music critic and composer Johann Friedrich Reichardt that 'There is no token more characteristic of the mind and temper, none on which we can place a fuller reliance, than the human voice.' As evidence, he cited the physiognomist Johann Lavater: 'The voice is very frequently an involuntary expression of the individual . . . The voice, like the face, becomes better or worse as the character improves or deteriorates.'[122]

The most powerful disseminator of this notion that women's singing was an almost infallible guide to their internal selves was fiction. Nineteenth-century novelists constructed numerous fictional representations of the private performer. As with attributes of physical beauty, a character's beautiful voice signified elevation to heroic status. In *The Bride of Lammermoor* (1819), Walter Scott first depicts Lucy Ashton playing the lute and singing, her 'silver tones' matched by her 'exquisitely beautiful, yet somewhat girlish features';[123] Esmeralda in Victor Hugo's *Notre Dame* (1831) displays a 'fantastically warbling voice' that has 'an indefinable charm – something clear, sonorous, aërial – winged, as it were'.[124] The type of voice, manner of singing, and content of song were all used in defining female sexuality. In the northern European countries, a 'sweet' tone was the preferred timbre for the genteel young woman (and one *The Musical World* duly applied to the youthful Queen Victoria in 1837: 'Her Majesty, besides being a good performer on the pianoforte, sings remarkably well; her voice is a mezzo soprano of very sweet quality').[125] The heroine of Hermann Hesse's *Gertrude* (1910), by singing only 'for one or two friends and for my own pleasure', fulfils all the requirements for maidenly modesty: 'She sang in a high, pure voice, and it was the sweetest thing I ever heard in my life'.[126] Other fictional accounts use descriptions of female singing to reveal a character's internal distance from the absolutes of the 'feminine ideal'. In Austen's *Emma* (1816) the innate romanticism of the otherwise cool and reserved Jane Fairfax is betrayed by her singing of Italian songs,[127] when the staple diet of most British drawing-room music was English translations, ballads or arrangements of folk songs. The impassioned and irresistible singing of Natasha Rostov in *War and Peace* presages her moral downfall; listening to her, her mother is suddenly aware that 'there was too much of something in Natasha, and that it would prevent her from being happy'.[128]

One of the most explicit delineations of desirable and undesirable manifestations of the domestic singer can be found in Marguerite Blessington's *The Two Friends* (1835). Here, the deviously flirtatious Urquhart sisters perform 'many of the most difficult duets and trios of the Italian school' with such skill that 'even those accustomed to the voice of a Pasta or Malibran might have listened with pleasure to them'. But their virtuosity is allied to an unwomanly lack of sensitivity: their listeners would have preferred 'less science, and a little more *sentiment*, in their singing'.[129] The dangers of the Urquharts' dazzling yet soulless technique are made plainer a few pages later, when one of them admits disconsolately the reason for their trills and roulades: 'We have sung ourselves into hoarseness and sore throats, to witch with music some *brutes*, over whom our harmonies produced less effect than did the sounds of Orpheus over his . . . Let us then abandon all active exertions to gain husbands, and leave it to chance.'[130] These unsuccessful sirens had much to learn from Blessington's heroine, Cecile Bethune, who unconsciously attracts her future lover, Desbrow, by merely *listening* to the Urquhart sisters sing. Cecile's passivity marks her out as a perfect specimen of genteel womanhood and an ideal object for the male gaze; indeed, it is her very immobility as a spectator at the impromptu concert that enables Desbrow stealthily to stand behind her, feasting his eyes on 'her graceful form and ivory shoulders' and even (with the aid of a mirror) her 'lovely face and bust'. His admiration is made complete by her 'reiterated declaration' not to sing herself as she was 'so little of a proficient in music that she never played or sang in society': 'Desbrow thought that the voice and accents in which her refusal was uttered, was the most harmonious he had ever heard.'[131]

Of course, Cecile finally does sing, if only to provide the reader with an example of true songbird delicacy. Instead of the Urquharts' ambitious operatic repertoire, Cecile sings 'simple airs, that charmed away many an evening hour', and her manner of singing is suitably devoid of the sisters' meretricious technique, for 'if her voice wanted science, it amply compensated for it, in sweetness and pathos'.[132] The consequence of her limited musical learning acts as another restraint against any unseemly desire to display: as Lady Ayrshire says, 'my Cecile can sing and play well enough to please the few friends before whom she would not object to perform'.[133]

The perceived danger of the professional siren therefore lay not so much in the act of performance, but in the fact that her singing was consciously and publicly used for her own purposes, as a means of procuring financial and sexual independence. Fears about the prima donna's challenge to the feminine ideal, and ideas on how to counter her corrupting influence in the education of young women were still expressed in the early years of the twentieth century, as is illustrated by this extract from *The Music Student* in 1911:

> We have only to think of the lives of certain famous singers in the past to see what conceited, demoralised, despicable creatures the false study of music made of them. Take Catalani, for example, with her wonderful gifts, her natural purity of heart, and generosity and compare them with her insufferable conceit as a singer, her intolerance of a rival, her exorbitant demands for fees, her reckless treatment of operas by having them cut to pieces that she might introduce airs with variations by Rode to show off her voice, and then you will realise to the full how utterly demoralising the study of music can become if improperly pursued.[134]

The categories of siren and songbird thus remained integral to the discourses concerning the female singer throughout the period. One might even argue that nineteenth- and early twentieth-century society's most desired and unattainable 'ideal' of the singer was in fact an embodiment of both these extremes: the charisma, irresistibility and vocal genius of the siren, mixed with the sweetly docile temperament of the songbird. But we should not underestimate the oppositional tensions between this binary pairing in the operatic marketplace: bad girls, as modern celebrity demonstrates, make good copy – and opera as an industry had an insatiable need for publicity. As we saw in the *Strenna teatrale europea*, the contrasting images of the singer created a dynamic of interest and variety for the public. But by the end of the period, sirens and songbirds were no longer sufficient epithets to describe singers. In *Bedouins* (1920), a collection of essays on music and aesthetics, James Huneker employs a whole host of images to convey his impression of the soprano Mary Garden (1874–1967):

> A condor, an eagle, a peacock, a nightingale, a panther, a society dame, a gallery of moving-pictures, a siren, an indomitable fighter, a human woman with a heart as big as a house, a lover of sport, an electric personality, and a canny Scotch lassie who can force wails of anguish because of her close bargaining over a contract: in a word, a Superwoman.[135]

Superwoman? That Garden was regarded in such terms owed much to the era's changing views of womanhood in the wake of the 'New Woman' and the suffrage movement, as well as to her own ingenuity in constructing her public image.

Oh, I am happy! The great
masters write
For women's voices, and great
Music wants me!
I need not crush myself within
a mould
Of theory called Nature: I have
room
To breathe and grow
unstunted.[1]

So proclaims the prima donna protagonist of George Eliot's dramatic poem 'Armgart' (1871), flushed with the triumph of her operatic debut, savouring the ecstasy of the moment when the cage-door of Victorian domesticity was at last flung wide and a seemingly limitless horizon of possibilities lay before her. A very different concept of female experience was thus evident in the debates surrounding the prima donna. Visible not only in female-authored fiction but also in journals, letters, memoirs and biographical material, this counter-image to the siren and the songbird was the product both of women's response to the singer as a spectator, and of their own engagement in music-making. In her manifestation as a symbol of achievement and independence – a voice of freedom – the prima donna was, indeed, a kind of 'superwoman'.

This more positive depiction of the prima donna was an important element in the shaping of late nineteenth-century ideas of womanhood. But it also had a particular impact on the singers themselves. The gentrification of the stage and the eventual social acceptance of the stage artist did not happen solely because public theatres became more respectable, policed environments. It happened in part because the boundaries between the private and public world were re-drawn, as more and more women engaged in forms of domestic performance. Their participation in the act of singing and their acquaintance with professional singers helped to readdress some longstanding prejudices.

Fiction again provided a powerful arena for articulating different concepts of the prima donna. Three authors in particular – George Sand, George Eliot and Willa Cather – returned more than once to the theme of 'performing heroinism', first manifested in Mme de Staël's *Corinne* (1807).[2] All three regularly attended and enjoyed operatic performances; their fictional responses to the theatrical world addressed not only the nature of the opera singer's craft, but what it meant to be a female artist in a time when women were regarded as incapable (in Schopenhauer's words) of producing a genuine artwork of lasting value.[3] Their imaginary singers were portrayed as proto-feminists evincing indomitable self-confidence, dedication to their art, intelligent creativity and unconventionality of manner, ideas and behaviour. But another important thread runs through their writing: the appearance in various guises of a real singer, Pauline Viardot (1821–1910).

Younger sister of the equally famous soprano Maria Malibran, Viardot was a prima donna of prodigious talent. A highly intelligent musician, a gifted composer and a compelling actress, she triumphed over a somewhat flawed instrument to achieve a reputation as a truly remarkable performer. Charles De Boigne wrote that she was not 'a *chanteuse*, a *cantatrice*', but rather 'an *artiste*': 'Whoever asks himself if Madame Viardot is pretty, if she even has a voice? In her singing there is so much expression, so much drama, passion, *furia*, that one listens to her without seeing her; one is ravished, transported, with no thought of discussing the quality or extension of her voice.'[4] Indeed, she made her greatest impact when the maturity of her interpretative powers more than compensated for her vocal difficulties, as in her final role as Orfeo in Berlioz's revival of Gluck's *Orfeo ed Euridice* at the Théâtre Lyrique, Paris in 1859. Viardot (the first female interpreter of this work, originally composed in 1762 for the castrato Gaetano Guadagni) sang this part more than one hundred and fifty times, in a rendition renowned for its emotional commitment and musical intelligence[5] – Flaubert described it as 'one of the greatest things I know'.[6] But in her life beyond the opera house she also acquired a social standing and respect – a dignity, perhaps – that had been denied to her sister Maria.[7] This was a result not only of her own personality, but of the discourses surrounding her.

Viardot's closest female friend in the early years of her career was George Sand. In a remarkable letter written in June 1842, Sand delineates the kind of task she believed lay ahead of the young singer. Describing her as 'the first, the only, the great, the true singer' as well as 'chaste and modest', possessing an 'incredible goodness of heart' and 'inexhaustible kindness', Sand urged the singer to devote herself to her art with missionary zeal:

> you are the priestess of the ideal in music and your mission is to spread it, to make it understood, and to bring the recalcitrant and the ignorant towards an instinct for and a revelation of truth and beauty.[8]

Sand's passionate admiration was given fictional shape in her two-volume romantic novel *Consuelo* (1842), celebrating Viardot's character and profession in its depiction of an eighteenth-century opera singer. In keeping with her theories of 'idéalisation', Sand combined her knowledge of Viardot's personality with her own vision of the ideal artist to create her novel's protagonist:[9] challenging the notion of the prima donna as erotic siren,[10] she instead presented the female singer's profession 'as sacred . . . the loftiest that a woman can embrace'. She used a man, Consuelo's lover Albert, to argue that originally the arts and religion were one: 'Music and poetry were the highest expressions of faith, and a woman endowed with genius and beauty was at once a sibyl and a priestess.' But 'absurd and culpable distinctions' destroyed women's liturgical participation in religious ceremony:

> Religion proscribed beauty from its festivals, and woman from its solemnities. Instead of ennobling and directing love, it banished and condemned it. Beauty, woman, love, cannot lose their empire. Men have raised for themselves other temples which they call theaters, and where no other god presides.

Admittedly, these new temples had become 'dens of corruption', but Albert believed that Consuelo 'would be as pure in the theater as in the cloister', and that nature had specifically formed her to 'shed over the world' her 'power and genius'. In reassessing the source and motive of female creativity, Consuelo recognised 'sentiments which she herself had frequently experienced in all their force':

> Devout, and an actress, she every day heard the canoness and the chaplain unceasingly condemn the brethren of the stage. In seeing herself restored to her proper sphere by a serious and reflecting man, she felt her heart throb and her bosom swell with exultation, as if she had been carried up into a more elevated and more congenial life.[11]

Consuelo, dedicated to her art and faith, is 'Consolation personified';[12] her innate goodness and 'tender and sensitive heart' disseminate compassion, hope and renewal to all those around her. Sand (as author and in the guise of Albert) thus lifts the prima donna from the mire of male degradation, and accords her a moral status of unimpeachable virtue. But because of her artist's nature, Consuelo the woman is also provided with freedom: she has a 'love of liberty, and a proud and lofty independence';[13] she relishes danger and 'deeds of courage and address';[14] she willingly assumes male attire, is physically strong and agile, and invariably frank and outspoken in her opinions. Sand showers gifts on her heroine like a fairy godmother: she invents a husband who supports and cherishes her professional life, grants her motherhood of five children, organises a satisfying career (which ends only when Consuelo's voice finally fades), and involves her in political intrigue and adventure. Importantly, she also finds Consuelo an operatic role (Predieri's *Zenobia*)[15] in which she could be 'herself', and 'manifest, in their full force, all her purity, strength, and tenderness, without, by an artificial effort, identifying herself with an uncongenial character'.[16] In marrying Consuelo's 'otherness', signified by her assumed gipsy identity and artist's calling, with her virtuous and generous character, Sand confirmed and illustrated Consuelo's own statement: 'I would make art loved and understood, without making the artist . . . feared or hated.'[17]

Sand, in idealising Viardot as Consuelo, immersed herself and the reader in an enjoyable (if wordy) wish-fulfilled fantasy of the prima donna's life, motives and attributes. George Eliot's depiction of a professional singer in her dramatic poem 'Armgart' is more problematic, but again Viardot is a visible if oblique influence on the text. Eliot and her partner G. H. Lewes were personally acquainted with Viardot: Lewes recorded an occasion on which Viardot attended one of their social gatherings and 'sang divinely and entranced every one, some of them to positive tears'.[18] Like Viardot, Eliot's heroine Armgart is a 'plain brown girl', who makes her debut as Gluck's Orfeo,[19] the role that marked the culmination of Viardot's stage career. Viardot's fictional representation as Consuelo (Eliot is known to have read Sand's novel) is also evoked: Armgart's teacher Leo is surely named after Leonardo Leo, an eighteenth-century composer whose music Consuelo uses to teach singing to the young Joseph Haydn. The truncation of Armgart's career and her final decision to teach is further reminiscent of Viardot's own situation at the time Eliot wrote the poem. Finally, Viardot is possibly reflected as the 'Paulina' who sings Leonore in Beethoven's *Fidelio* (another of Viardot's most successful roles) on the night when Armgart had hoped to return to the stage.

Throughout the poem the shadow of Viardot/Consuelo therefore appears variously as Armgart's alter ego, foremother and rival, symbolising female artistic prowess, whilst Eliot, in the shape of her own rebellious and strong-willed heroine, explicitly defines the significance of the prima donna as free woman. Armgart's voice liberates her from the conventional constraints of her sex: it supplies her life with 'meaning';[20] it is the instrument which gives her soul 'freedom',[21] releasing the 'rage' that would otherwise have made her a 'Maenad' setting fire to forests in her wrath:

> 'Poor wretch!' she says, of any murderess –
> 'The world was cruel, and she could not sing:
> I carry my revenges in my throat;
> I love in singing, and am loved again.'[22]

Moreover, her singing has wider implications: it is a refutation of the argument that 'Nature has willed' woman's role as one of 'pure subservience', for it is nature herself who has given her both ambition and voice, 'such as she only gives a woman child'.[23] This use of maternal imagery to describe the prima donna's creativity recurs throughout the poem, subverting the Victorian equation of mother-hood with domesticity, and aligning it instead with a powerful depiction of female autonomy. In return for her maternal guardianship, her voice repays Armgart with the unique privileges of the prima donna. Because 'the great masters write / For women's voices', not only is she afforded access to the otherwise male world of music-making but her talents also cannot be usurped by male expertise:

> Men did not say, when I had sung last night,
> ''Twas good, nay, wonderful, considering
> She is a woman' – and then turn to add,
> 'Tenor or baritone had sung her songs
> Better, of course: she's but a woman spoiled.'[24]

Rather, the reverse is true: Armgart's Orfeo suggests an appropriation not only of a role designed for a male singer, but perhaps also of the very nature of Orpheus himself and his supposedly 'moral' music. The suggestion that Armgart should relinquish this active music-making on the public stage to 'Sing in the chimney corner to inspire / My husband reading news'[25] is met with scorn. Claiming that she can 'live unmated, but not live / Without the bliss of singing to the world',[26] she refuses marriage to the wealthy, aristocratic Graf who believes ambition has 'unwomaned' her:[27]

> I will not take for husband one who deems
> The thing my soul acknowledges as good –
> The thing I hold worth striving, suffering for,
> To be a thing dispensed with easily,
> Or else the idol of a mind infirm.[28]

If Eliot heightened the feminist connotations of the prima donna as career woman, she also countered Sand's exuberant romanticism by delineating the transient nature of the singer's art. In an earlier essay of 1855, Eliot had written sympathetically of the temporality of the performer's career: 'the memory of the *prima donna* scarcely outlives the flowers that are flung at her feet on her farewell night'.[29] In 'Armgart', Eliot elucidated the double tragedy of the prima donna who loses not only her creativity and public recognition but also her emancipated status. Armgart's voice is 'murdered' through illness, leaving her 'meaningless', a 'power turned to pain',[30] the mere 'torso of a soul'[31] forced to contemplate a future she bitterly names as '"The Woman's Lot: a Tale of Everyday"'.[32] Some claim that this loss of voice is a punishment for Armgart's denial of femininity;[33] I think Eliot (who was herself at the time of writing the poem in a state of 'almost total despair' about the continuation of her own creative gifts) makes it plain that the 'burthen' of the artist's rank is indeed this 'peril' of failure that Armgart had proudly accepted: 'I choose to walk higher with sublimer dread / Rather than crawl in safety.'[34] Moreover, it is the understanding of a male artist in a similar predicament, the composer Leo, that finally reconciles her to a future without her voice. Although she believes she will henceforth be a 'broken thing',[35] Armgart's decision to 'bury her dead joy', to disseminate her gifts to other women in a new career as a teacher, and to acknowledge, in the final image of the poem, that her rival Paulina 'sings Fidelio, / And they will welcome her tonight'[36] implies a continuation of and support for women's artistry.

Eliot returned to the complex figure of the prima donna in her last novel, *Daniel Deronda* (1876), developing a number of themes raised in 'Armgart'. Armgart's evocation of the 'murderess' who 'could not sing' is here realised in the person of Gwendolen Harleth, a drawing-room singer who vainly seeks the operatic stage in order to avoid marriage and to 'achieve substantiality for herself and know gratified ambition without bondage'.[37] But Gwendolen lacks the requisite talent and vocation: she must instead marry the odious Grandcourt, and although she does not precisely murder him, she makes no attempt to save him from his death by drowning. The absence of 'voice', of an instrument of woman's self-determination, imperils not only Gwendolen herself, but also the man who denies her freedom.

Armgart's destiny as a teacher is elaborated in another figure who emerges later in the novel: Mirah Lapidoth, whose 'exquisite'[38] voice was not 'strong enough'[39] for the stage, who failed as an actress because she had 'no notion of being anybody but herself', who found theatrical life 'repugnant' and rebelled against it,[40] and who instead built a new existence for herself by teaching singing and performing at modest concerts. Mirah has no desire to make 'great claims' for herself;[41] and the smallness and fragility of her voice, 'like a thread of gold dust',[42] is echoed in her acceptance of the feminine role in its entirety: in her purity of character, her dutiful devotion to family, and her eventual marriage to Deronda.

In contrast, the singing of the former prima donna Alcharisi provided a 'chance of escaping from bondage', from eluding the oppressive domesticity her orthodox Jewish father imposed upon her. Alcharisi wanted to 'live a large life, with freedom to do what everyone else did, and to be carried along in a great current, not obliged to care'. She castigates her son, Daniel Deronda, when he assumes an understanding of her:

> You are not a woman. You may try – but you can never imagine what it is to have a man's force of genius in you, and yet to suffer the slavery of being a girl. To have a pattern cut out – 'this is the Jewish woman; this is what you must be; this is what you are wanted for; a woman's heart must be of such a size and no larger; else it must be pressed small, like Chinese feet; her happiness is to be made as cakes are, by a fixed receipt.' That was what my father wanted . . .[43]

Alcharisi is the most vehemently feminist of Eliot's singing heroines, and the most separated from notions of womanliness. She lacks the 'talent to love':[44] wholly absorbed in her career, she gives away the care of her baby son because she 'did not want a child'[45] and because she wished to defy her dead father by denying him a Jewish grandson. Yet she defends herself from the unspoken accusation that she must therefore be perverted:

> Every woman is supposed to have the same set of motives, or else to be a monster. I am not a monster, but I have not felt exactly what

other women feel – or say they feel, for fear of being thought unlike others.[46]

Daniel Deronda was the child of her father's dictates: the product of a forced marriage and a patriarchal concept of woman's place. Implicitly, Alcharisi's real child is her art: a wholly female art she alone gave birth to and nourished, and which brought her a precious nine years of liberation and achievement before, as if in a 'fit of forgetfulness', she began to 'sing out of tune'.[47] Despite her subsequent marriage to a Russian prince and the five children that second relationship produced (the traditional rewards of a 'womanly' woman), life without art remains eternally impoverished for Alcharisi, it is 'little more than a sense of what was'.[48] As in 'Armgart', the penalty paid by the prima donna is the pain of this continual yearning when her capacity to create has ceased. Nevertheless, the overriding image of Alcharisi is of a woman who, though now ill and dying, found absolute freedom and fulfilment in her career: a woman who 'was never willingly subject to any man'.[49]

Towards the end of her novel *The Song of the Lark* (1915), Willa Cather (an experienced reviewer of opera and music) wrote that 'Artistic growth is, more than anything else, a refining of the sense of truthfulness. The stupid believe that to be truthful is easy; only the artist, the great artist, knows how difficult it is.'[50] This, then, is the heart of Cather's portrayal of the prima donna, for her heroine Thea Kronborg is just such a 'great artist' engaged in the long, hard struggle to fulfil ambition and achieve artistic maturity. An amalgamation of the real singer Olive Fremstad (1871–1951) and Cather herself, Thea is born and raised from plain 'rough people'[51] in a small town in Nebraska: her earliest inspiration is Wunsch, her alcoholic German music teacher who, via a score of Gluck's *Orfeo ed Euridice*, and his memories of the Spanish prima donna who sang the title-role, enthuses Thea with the idea of an operatic career. The Spanish singer is, of course, Viardot, although she is never named as such; but she is clearly recognisable in Wunsch's description of a woman who is '"ugly; big mouth, big teeth, no figure . . . A pole, a post! But

for the voice – *ach!* She have something in there, behind the eyes",
tapping his temples.'[52] It is again this potent appropriation of the
male music-god Orpheus by the female voice of the prima donna
which, encapsulated in the recurring lines of Gluck's famous lament
('Che farò senza Euridice?'), accompanies, inspires and comforts
Thea in the years ahead.

Cather drew an unglamorous picture of the prima donna's profession. Thea is a 'strange, crude girl'[53] to whom nothing comes easily;
her learning is painful and tedious, and even as a mature singer she
grimly comments: 'I have to work hard to do my worst, let alone my
best.'[54] Her career contains 'many disappointments' and 'bitter, bitter
contempts',[55] yet she is eventually rewarded, not by monetary success or worldly approbation (though she achieves both), but by 'full
possession of things she had been refining and perfecting for so
long':[56] by the rare sense of creative fulfilment and freedom that is
the direct result of her hard work, her determination and her 'fierce,
stubborn self-assertion'.[57] Throughout this account of the making of
an artist, Thea's gender is virtually incidental. There is no suggestion
that her female sex excludes her from following such a path, nor any
overt alignment of the prima donna with women's emancipation:
simply the figure of a strong-minded, independent woman energetic-
ally forging a life for herself. However, Thea's conception of art
perhaps reflects Eliot-type notions of a womb of creativity:

> what was any art but an effort to make a sheath, a mould in which to
> imprison for a moment the shining, elusive element which is life itself –
> life hurrying past us and running away, too strong to stop, too sweet to
> lose . . . In singing, one made a vessel of one's throat and nostrils and
> held it on one's breath, caught the stream in a scale of natural intervals.[58]

And onstage there is a distinctly feminist perspective in Thea's
interpretations of Wagner's heroines: she transforms the limpid Elsa
in *Lohengrin* (who collapses into death on the departure of her lover)
into an abbess, a woman 'made to live with ideas and enthusiasms,
not a husband', a woman who, rather than dying, is 'just beginning'.[59] Effectively combining elements of both Sand's optimism and

Eliot's realism, Cather constructs a warmly human prima donna: a woman who dreams and achieves, whose abrupt and resolute character inspires love and respect in those around her, and who embodies the prosaic, earthy qualities of dedication and honesty that Cather believed were so essential to the creation of genuine art.

In entering the discourses surrounding the prima donna, these women writers challenged the dominant myths about women's voice, illuminated aspects of the singer's profession and its rewards and penalties, and argued for woman's right to creativity. The singers themselves largely welcomed their efforts. Viardot was highly flattered by her portrait in *Consuelo*, even demonstrating its influence in both her correspondence and her later actions.[60] Eliot's *Daniel Deronda* also met with approval; the soprano Clara Louise Kellogg (1842–1916) cited the pragmatic advice given to Gwendolen Harleth as essential reading for those young women singers 'who think of trying to make a career'.[61] And although Fremstad was less convinced by the accuracy of her counterpart in *The Song of the Lark* (reportedly saying to Cather with characteristic frankness, 'My poor Willa . . . it wasn't really much like that. But after all, what can you know about me? Nothing!'),[62] she also felt the novel was the only account of operatic life where 'there was something doing' in the singer.[63]

DRAWING-ROOM PRIMA DONNAS

It is impossible to estimate the degree of influence exerted by these novels (and others like them) on the wider female readership. There are occasional clues that they might have aided the legitimisation of the singer's profession: in her 1877 address on 'Woman as a Musician' to an American feminist organisation,[64] Fanny Raymond Ritter (1840–90) described Consuelo as 'the ideal character of a pure and noble artist woman, too deeply imbued by lofty enthusiasm for her fine vocation to barter its true principles for transitory success, social flattery, or pecuniary advantage'; and employed her in support of her representation of real prima donnas as exemplars of woman's musical achievements.[65] Much of Ritter's quasi-feminist essay (the first such survey of female musical endeavour) concerns the woman singer, who following her banishment from the early church re-emerged in the middle ages as the composer of her own songs, contributing significantly to the folk music tradition[66] – an argument that contrasted sharply with Haweis' depiction of the female singer as mere consumer of male product.[67] Ritter's emphasis about the usefulness of singing to modern women also differed from that of Mainzer, Ruskin and Haweis. Whilst supporting the common asso-ciation between music and morals (to her, music was 'the art of order, unity and harmony'), her vision of the female singer is not a dispossessed songbird whose warbling signifies her passivity, but rather a beneficent activist:

> [The singer] also exercises a positive moral force upon her hearers. The voice is an instrument which the singer carries with her; and as goodness, beauty and happiness are almost the sole objects of unperverted artistic expression, and as even grief and terror are themselves ennobled when illustrated by art, the singer, merely by the action of communicating elevated emotion to her hearers by means of her voice, becomes, for the time, a moral agent.[68]

Ritter's discussion also assumed that a professional career might be considered, thereby offering singing as an activity connected to female development and financial independence, rather than a sop for domestic boredom or a device to contain women's will. Even for those not endowed with sufficient talent to become one of the 'great songstresses', Ritter believed that singing was a valuable occupation:

> every woman possessed of a tolerable voice and ear, and unhindered by actual physical infirmity, should devote some portion of her time to the practice of singing, if only for health's sake. Singing, which is regulated by respiration, is the most important element of the gymnastic science; it is an aid to circulation; it heightens the spirits, adds grace and activity to the movements, and animation to the face.[69]

This argument about the health benefits of singing was used by many teachers and singers of the day, and had a particular import for middle- and upper-class women who often led sedentary lives constrained in corsets and heavy, tight-fitting dresses. Some even claimed that singing was a defence against consumption: in 1855 the *Gazzetta musicale di Milano* declared that singers were less liable to this affliction because the larynx was fortified with daily exercise.[70] The deep breathing necessary for singing was another oft-cited factor. Lillian Nordica declared that 'Singers are usually healthy, for that is one of the first requirements; the great amount of oxygen of which they make use tends to expand and develop the body';[71] an article in *The Music Student* in 1913 went further by claiming that the increased oxygen not only revitalised the singer but also increased brain power.[72] Obviously, if deep breathing was required, so was the physical capacity to accomplish this. Did the popularity of singing, which required the free, unfettered movement of the torso, contribute in some way to women's growing awareness of the harm done to their bodies by corsets? At the renewed outset of this fashion in the 1820s, the Italian opera critic Carlo Ritorni had warned his female readers in *L'Eco* (and reprinted his article in *Annali del teatro della città di Reggio*) of this 'predilection for an ugly, unnatural and pernicious fashion',[73] and listed in great detail the maladies that ensued from the use of corsets.[74] Some singers do not seem to have heeded such warnings: Patti's short breath has been attributed to her wasp-waist – although we should not assume that her posed photographs were necessarily an accurate depiction of her on-stage costumes.[75] Enterprising corset-makers fashioned garments specifically designed for singers, such as 'Marion's Resilient Bodice and Corsaletto di Medici', advertised in the *Musical World* in 1853: 'Vocalists and others cultivating sustentation of the voice and the power and fulness of its tone will find these an invaluable acquisition.'[76] But by the end of the century, any such practices were increasingly challenged. The need to avoid dangerous 'tight lacing' for the singer is mentioned in an interview in the *Musical Herald* in 1900 with Madame Bessie Cox, a prominent teacher in London;[77] Luisa Tetrazzini, renowned for her magnificent breath control, declared outright that 'singers cannot wear tight corsets and should not wear corsets of any kind which come up higher than the lowest rib. In other words, the corset must be nothing but a belt';[78] whilst Nordica stressed the need for 'comfortable' clothes: 'an inch in the waist does not matter to the public, but if your gown is even that degree too tight, the lower ribs and the lungs are cramped, and you need perfect freedom both of lungs and shoulders'.[79] In the *Music Student* in 1913, Ernest Hunt launched a direct assault on women's dress, declaring that 'Men breathe better, as a rule, than women; for the clothing of women (and especially the corset which most of them wear) is against all free expansion of the lungs.' Advising the need to allow for a four-inch expansion of the chest for good breathing, his solution was to dispense absolutely with corsetry. Given the role of corsets in reinforcing modes of femininity, such advice again hints at the freedoms obtainable by the female singer.

But many women had another and more direct source of information about the female singer than books, pamphlets or newspapers: that of their own experience of music-making as drawing-room prima donnas.[80] Echoes of women singing resonate through the journals, letters and memoirs of the period. Rich or poor, they sing alone, or with family and friends, or in an infinite variety of larger social gatherings. Four instances from Britain provide a useful example. In 1838, Elizabeth Gaskell recalled the music-making of her cousins in her childhood home:

> The last time I was there . . . one or two of Shakespeare's ballads: 'Blow, blow thou winter wind', and 'Hark, hark the lark at Heaven's gate sings', &c, were sung by the musical sisters in the gallery above, and by two other musical sisters . . . standing in the hall below.[81]

The diary of Lady Monkswell similarly abounds in references to various vocal enterprises: for example, in 1873 she herself took part in a choral concert for Princess Louise;[82] whilst in 1892 she spent the day at Abinger Hall, where the guests were entertained by Lady Farrer, who 'sings well enough to earn her bread by it'.[83] The duets between Ethel Smyth and her sister Mary, whose family were of typical upper-middle-class Victorian stock, became 'a feature at home dinner-parties' in the 1870s.[84] In 1901, the working-class diarist Ruth Slate recorded the dissatisfaction of her consumptive younger sister, Daisy, 'because she can not play or sing. So I am to commence and teach her.'[85] Even the youthful Queen Victoria studied the art of singing, as her letter to her uncle, King Leopold of Belgium, reveals:

> I have resumed my singing lessons with Lablache twice a week, which form an agreeable recreation in the midst of all the business I have to do. He is such a good old soul, and greatly pleased that I go on with him. I admire the music of the Huguenots [Meyerbeer's opera] very much, but do not sing it, as I prefer Italian to French for singing greatly. I have been learning in the beginning of the season many of your old favourites, which I hope to sing with you when we meet.[86]

Their reasons for singing varied according to individual character and circumstance. For the newly enthroned young Queen Victoria, singing lessons plainly provided an antidote to her more tedious royal duties. This perception of music-making as purely an enjoyable, sociable pastime also occurs in the diary of Lady Monkswell, and in the letters between the working women Eva Slawson and Ruth Slate. For other women, the act of singing had greater significance. In an echo of Haweis' ideas, the poet Anna Wickham (1884–1947) found consolation in her singing for an impoverished childhood in which she was constantly beset by 'feelings of inferiority': 'Singing was a retreat from loneliness and isolation. I used to sit in the hammock on the verandah swinging to and fro in an ecstasy of pleasure at singing.'[87] Bernard Shaw's mother Bessie (who possessed a 'mezzo-soprano voice of remarkable purity of tone')[88] used her energetic forays into the Dublin world of amateur singing as compensation for a disillusioning marriage in which she was forced to cope with 'a hopelessly disappointing husband and three uninteresting children'.[89] Elizabeth Gaskell and her husband encouraged the 'really fine'[90] singing of their eldest daughter Marianne 'because her only talent seems to be for music and we want her to view this gift rightly and use it well'.[91]

Amongst this latter group of serious performers, connections between domestic singing and the prima donna's image as 'free' woman might be most readily made. Anna Wickham, Bessie Shaw and Marianne Gaskell all used their singing to gain access to a professional environment (either as performers or teachers) and thereby a measure of financial independence. The increasing presence of middle- and upper-class women on the professional stage from the 1850s onwards was often a direct result of their participation in the amateur circuit. To some, a career was a means of escape from the domesticity otherwise awaiting them. The American novelist Gertrude Atherton recalled sharing her 'dreams of a future when I should be free to live my own life' in the late 1880s with Sibyl Sanderson (1865–1903), the daughter of a wealthy San Francisco judge:

> we used to take long despairing walks over the steep hills of the city, wondering if we should ever get out of it. She wanted to be an opera singer, and her father wouldn't hear of it. A few years later she was the rage of Paris and Massenet had written *Esclarmonde* for her debut. At that time, however, life seemed a dreary waste.[92]

One of the most detailed descriptions of the manner in which domestic singing fed this dream of a professional career is provided by the journal of Marie Bashkirtseff (1859–84). Born into Russian aristocracy, Bashkirtseff spent most of her life in France and was afforded a degree of freedom uncommon at that time, eventually studying art in Paris until her promising career was curtailed by her early death from tuberculosis. Her journal was published in France in 1887, and in Britain and North America in 1890. Despite stringent editing by her mother (who excised passages containing slang expressions, sensual descriptions of male lovers and even Bashkirtseff's 'violently critical attitude to women's conditions'),[93] the diary created an uproar. Far from adhering to the profile of a polite nineteenth-century *demoiselle*, Bashkirtseff sweeps through these intense and private entries as an energetic woman of independent spirit. Commentators such as Marion Davies applauded the 'courage' this 'real woman' displayed in revealing herself so honestly;[94] other (largely male) critics castigated Bashkirtseff for her lack of womanly values.[95] Perhaps one of the most alarming aspects of her rebellion was her subversion of the image of the archetypal accomplished young woman into a pursuit of the unfeminine goal of fame and achievement. Nowhere is this more apparent than in her use of music.

Although proficient in a number of instruments (typically, piano, harp and mandolin), Bashkirtseff was primarily a singer; in her perceptions of the purpose of her singing, she diverged noticeably from the idealized path of the domestic performer. Her triumphant declaration 'I am my own heroine' was particularly resonant here: for Bashkirtseff, the act of singing was a potent exercise of her will, a voicing of ambition and desire, and a route to fame and fortune. The first entry in the published diary (written at the age of fourteen)[96] reveals that her choice of career was inspired by both her own experiences of singing and her naive perception of the prima donna; in a word, she luxuriated in the future she imagined awaited her:

> Life will be perfect thus. I dream of nothing but fame, of being known all the world over. Fancy appearing on the boards, of seeing thousands of spectators waiting with beating hearts for the moment you will begin to sing! To know as you look at them that they'll be at your feet at a note from your voice! To survey them haughtily! (I am fit for most things.) This is my dream; this, this is life, happiness, everything.[97]

Bashkirtseff's adolescent attitude to her singing was far removed from the required modesty and genteel usefulness of a young lady's vocalising as stipulated by Ruskin or Blessington. Bashkirtseff sought activity, not passivity: in her own words, she wished to 'do' rather than simply 'be'. Her aim was not the steady holding of a note in choral singing, but the display of individual prowess and the reaping of just rewards. With the example of the adulation and attention heaped on female opera stars, singing appeared to offer the young Bashkirtseff a status comparable to that of a 'princess',[98] as well as the physical pleasures of the act of singing itself:

What happiness, what delight to sing well! One fancies oneself all
powerful, one imagines oneself a queen! One rejoices at one's gift. It isn't
the pride of gold or of a title. One is more than a woman, one feels
immortal. One is freed from the earth and soars to heaven! And then all
those people who hang on to your lips, who listen to your song as if it
were divine, who are electrified and enchanted . . . You sway them all . . .
Next to actual royalty this is the best thing to strive after.[99]

Above all, perhaps, she regarded singing as the ultimate expression of
female sexuality: 'Singing is to a woman what eloquence is to a man:
a power without limits.'[100] But Bashkirtseff's own professional ambitions came to naught. Plagued by the consumption that would finally
overwhelm her, her singing voice first faded and then vanished.

Bashkirtseff's responses to the act of singing, both as performer and spectator, provide a valuable insight into the manner in
which some women regarded the display of musical talent. Domestic
prima donnas of similar ambition to Bashkirtseff were assisted by
the structure of the amateur circuit, which often brought them into
direct contact with their professional counterparts. Such opportunities were to some extent governed by social position and wealth.
Giovanni Pacini recalled his visit to Vienna in the 1820s, where 'the
young Baroness Laickham sang like a little angel';[101] and again the
aristocratic music-making in Paris in 1830 at the salon of the Russian
Princess Bagration.[102] In 1842, Felix Mendelssohn admired Queen
Victoria's phrasing and intonation, her long breath, and 'beautiful
feeling and expression' when she sang two songs to his accompani-
ment.[103] At a soirée at the Prussian embassy in Paris in 1861, Wagner
had 'the strange experience of hearing the Neapolitan Princess
Campo-Reale sing Isolde's closing scene . . . with lovely German
enunciation and a surprising accuracy of intonation' – accompanied
by no less a pianist than Camille Saint-Saëns.[104] Charles Villiers
Stanford applauded the amateur singers of a Dublin choral society,
including a Mrs Hercules MacDonnell, 'a dramatic soprano with a
voice which would have rivaled even the greatest *prima donna* of
her day' and who was 'in every sense an artist both technically and
musically'.[105]

Even given that many musicians were dependent on the support and interest of rich dilettantes and perhaps therefore inclined to exaggerate instances of musical ability, the sheer quantity of such comments suggests that there was a considerable degree of skill amongst some female amateur singers. An important factor in the development of vocal abilities to such a high degree was that middle- and upper-class women had both the time for extensive study and the financial means to procure good tuition. This did not necessarily preclude the emergence of singers from other sections of society, particularly in mainland Europe where there was greater access to free tuition in certain training institutions. Pacini recalled one of his former pupils at the Liceo musicale in Viareggio, the 'impoverished daughter of a street vendor' whose career had been made possible only with the aid of 'charitable persons'.[106] In Britain, the working-class soprano Susan Sunderland (known as the 'Yorkshire Queen of Song') built a substantial professional career from her amateur beginnings on the oratorio circuit in the mid-nineteenth century. Nevertheless, whilst exceptional talent occasionally triumphed over barriers of class and financial hardship, few singers from poor backgrounds had equivalent opportunities of education and vocal tuition to those of their wealthier counterparts.

Links between amateur music-making and the professional sphere were various, according to the combination of ability, social position and financial means on the part of the dilettante singers. As we have seen, salons and private concerts were one important strand of such encounters. Visible from the beginning of the period in élite households, these events found their first popular flourishing in Paris in the 1830s, and quickly spread throughout Europe.[107] Their prominence in the spectrum of musical activity during the era is reflected in the press and periodicals, where they were increasingly reviewed with almost the same level of seriousness as wholly professional concerts. In these select, private gatherings, amateurs and professionals not only shared the same platform but also often sang together. At one such soirée at Buckingham Palace on 12 June 1840, Queen Victoria and her ladies-in-waiting (Ladies Sandwich, Norreys,

Williamson and Normanby) performed various operatic duets, quartets and choruses with the famous tenor Giovanni Battista Rubini and the equally famous bass Luigi Lablache: Victoria herself sang a trio from *Die Zauberflöte* (in Italian translation) with the two professionals, as well as a duet from Ricci's *Il disertore per amore* with Prince Albert.[108] But much more public fusions between professional and high-class amateur talent became common as the century progressed. In Palermo in 1891, Tina Whitaker Scalia crowned her significant career as a dilettante singer by performing before a royal audience with Francesco Tamagno at a public concert to inaugurate the Grande Esposizione at Palermo: she sang 'Casta diva', Gounod's cantata 'Gallia o Jerusalem', and a duet from *Il Guarany* (Gomes) with Tamagno. This was by no means her first such occasion: she had previously sung duets with other professional singers, such as Maria Alighieri Spezia.[109] Some dilettante singers particularly courted professional artists: two socialites in New York, May Callender and Carol de Forest, figure in several singers' autobiographies. The American soprano Emma Eames (1865–1952) recalled the 'most delightful musical parties' they gave in their shared Fifth Avenue apartment, adorned with photographs inscribed by singers such as Lilli Lehmann, 'bearing dedications in praise of [May Callender's] talent'.[110]

Middle-class amateurs found access to other encounters with professional performers under the aegis of high-ranking amateur music societies that sprang up throughout Europe. Berlioz described 'L'Académie de chant' in Berlin (one of many throughout Germany) in 1843, composed almost entirely of amateurs singing alongside professionals: 'society ladies do not think it all demeaning to sing in a Bach oratorio alongside Mantius, Boeticher or Mademoiselle Hähnel.'[111] Stanford records a similar occasion in Dublin in the 1860s when the 'cleverest and most gifted' amateur singer of 'The Society of Antient Concerts', Mrs Josephine Geale,[112] sang operatic excerpts with Jenny Lind before an audience that included Queen Victoria. Geale defied at least one convention about the domestic female singer, because she had 'by some extraordinary art, manufactured for herself a tenor voice of rare Italian quality which she controlled with the best Italian skill'. (Despite Lind's initial 'amazement' at being asked to perform with a female tenor, Stanford claims that at the end of the first rehearsal, 'no one was more appreciative of [Geale's] powers than that most critical of artists'.[113]) Sometimes amateur singers were used when – for various reasons – professional artists were simply unavailable. For example, in 1862 Wagner staged three concerts in Vienna of segments of *Der Ring* in order to show his 'hidden enemies' that there were other means of acquainting the public with his work 'besides the theatrical performances which it was so easy for them to impede': the majority of the singers for this pioneering venture came from the resident company at the Court Opera, but the three Rhine Maidens were played by amateurs.[114]

There was even a whiff of superiority in the notion of amateur music-making; its freedom from the taint of money was, according to some perspectives, a sign of its status as a more thoroughly 'artistic' enterprise than professional activity.[115] And if the popularity of singing meant that the audiences of opera houses often comprised unusually knowledgeable spectators (at least in contemporary terms), this did not necessarily lead to a better understanding of professional practice, as the scathing comments of Frances Alda (1879–1952) testify:

> In New York I know half a dozen society women, amateur singers, who will tell you how much better they are than the artists engaged at the Metropolitan. Once I sat through an opera in a box with one of these women, and heard her criticism of the singing of a great and finished artist who was the star of that performance. All the lady's remarks revealed to me, a professional singer, was how very much she did *not* know about the art of singing. But I don't doubt that several other persons in the box were impressed.[116]

Clearly, engagement in domestic music-making was here used to score points over both social peers and the luckless prima donna who was the target of such criticism.

Nevertheless, the musical and social association between amateur singers and their professional counterparts must surely have increased the ambition of some drawing-room prima donnas. The history of one private singer, Lillie de Hegermann-Lindencrone (1844–1928), both supports and questions this assumption. Born into a respectable upper-middle-class American family, de Hegermann-Lindencrone's talents as a singer suggested that a professional career was a distinct possibility. She was brought by her mother to London in 1859 (aged only fifteen) to study with Manuel Garcia II, and was later taken to Paris for further tuition with Garcia's sister, Pauline Viardot. However, within two years of her arrival in Europe she married a wealthy Parisian, Charles Moulton. Her marriage brought her into the most elevated spheres of European society, including the court of Napoleon III, and her reputation as a singer in this élite environment appears to have blossomed yearly. Intelligent, witty and attractive, she combined evident musical gifts with social acceptability and as such must have been perceived as an ideal addition to the court circle – indeed, she might almost be regarded as a superior kind of court musician. Although she sang for pleasure, she obviously invested considerable effort in the development of her voice, studying with the Italian baritone Enrico Delle Sedie (1822–1907), the influential singing teacher and violinist Heinrich Panofka (1807–87), and also with the famous theorist of dramatic and vocal performance François Delsarte (1811–1871).[117] She received coaching by Auber,[118] and was applauded by other notable musicians of the era such as Rossini, Gounod and Massenet.[119] Her repertoire ranged from operatic arias to songs composed by herself and her husband, and her amateur engagements encompassed a wide variety of events. Amongst appearances at social occasions, she performed in a 'naïf and banal' operetta composed by the Marquis d'Aoust before the Emperor and his family,[120] sang for an audience of convicts in an American prison,[121] warbled folk-songs for Abraham Lincoln,[122] performed a *Benedictus* especially composed for her by Auber in the chapel of the Tuileries (accompanied by the orchestra of the Conservatoire),[123] was given instruction by Jenny Lind on how to execute the perfect trill,[124] and in 1867 sang a duet with this same prima donna at a private dinner given by Auber.[125] Her exploits were recorded with discreet anonymity in the French press: in 1863, *L'Art musical* describes that 'An American woman of remarkable beauty, Mme. M., is the object of a lively admiration in our Parisian salons. She possesses a magnificent voice, and she sings, although an amateur, as a great artist.'[126]

Her success on the select amateur circuit in Paris would seem to bear out her claims that Garcia had regarded her as having the talent to make a professional career if she had so wished. In a letter to Viardot he supposedly wrote, 'I send you my pupil. Do all you can to persuade her to go on the stage. She has it in her.'[127] De Hegermann-Lindencrone never relates her reasons for refusing such an opportunity, but her account of a performance of *La traviata* given by Christine Nilsson at the Théâtre Lyrique, Paris, in 1865 perhaps offers some clues. She was provided with seats in a box that allowed her to see the manoeuvrings backstage, and whilst she found it 'intensely amusing to see how things were done, and how prosaic and matter-of-fact everything was', she also was dismayed that 'Everything looked so tawdry and claptrap: the dirty boards, the grossly painted scenery, the dingy workmen shuffling about grumbling and gruff, ordered and scolded by a vulgar superior.' If she had secretly yearned to be part of theatrical life, this experience proved that her decision not to sing publicly had been the right one: 'If ever I thanked my stars that I was not a star myself it was then.'[128] Watching Nilsson after the performance only confirmed this feeling; the singer's smiles as she collected her bouquets 'faded like mist before the sun the minute the curtain was lowered, and she looked tired and worn out'; the darkened stage that had been 'so brilliant a moment before was now only a confused mass of disillusions': 'I went home, glad that my life lay in other paths.'[129]

For a singer such as de Hegermann-Lindencrone, amateur circles obviously supplied freedom and fulfilment enough for her musical talents – the life of a working prima donna seemed shabby and constrained in comparison. Why, then, did she contemplate a professional career in 1871? The impresario Maurice Strakosch prevailed upon her to undertake a series of concerts in New York, and with the support of her family de Hegermann-Lindencrone accepted. She was billed as the 'Diva du Monde', and the audiences flocked to see her decked out in the Worth costumes which she had ordered so that 'if the public don't like me they can console themselves with the thought that a look at my clothes is worth a ticket'. The most probable reason for her change of heart was that the court society she had previously known had vanished as a result of the revolution of 1870, and with it disappeared the extravagant, elegant atmosphere that she had used as a backcloth to her performances. Public approbation was perhaps now sought as an alternative to her former captive but élite audience. However, her initial response to this changed situation suggests she found it an intensely satisfying experience:

> To feel that I can hold a great audience, like the one that greeted me the first night, in my hand, and to know that I can make them laugh or cry whenever I please – to see the mass of upturned faces – is an inspiring sensation. The applause bewildered me at first, and I was fearfully excited; but one gets used to all things in the end. My songs, 'Bel raggio' (Rossini), and 'Voi che sapete' (Mozart), and 'La Valse de Pardon de Ploërmel' (Meyerbeer), were all encored and re-encored.[130]

But after this and several similar concerts, de Hegermann-Lindencrone's foray into the professional world abruptly ceased. Why this was so remains unclear. Perhaps it was due to an oratorio performance where she was 'dreadfully nervous and unstrung' and made a number of minor errors – suggesting that the drawing-room prima donna's experience was not wholly sufficient for professional purposes.[131] A more likely possibility is that her retirement was the result of her husband's sudden death from a brief illness. Although she eventually resumed her amateur singing, her dalliance with the professional stage was at an end.

Nevertheless, the engagement of de Hegermann-Lindencrone and other dilettante singers such as Georgina Weldon (1837–1914) in professional music-making demonstrates both the refusal of the amateur singer to be constrained to the private sphere and the gradual erosion of the previously antipathetical attitudes of 'society' (on the part of some women at least) towards the prima donna. If at the beginning of the nineteenth century, the vast majority of singers had emerged from families of working musicians or actors (*figlie d'arte*, as the Italians termed them), by the middle of the period there were clear signs of an important shift in the profession. Marietta Piccolomini, the niece of a cardinal, was the first high-profile female upper-class entrant: she made her debut in the early 1850s, following the steps of another Italian aristocrat, the tenor Mario some twenty years earlier.[132] A determined stream of middle-class novices was also now apparent, led by singers such as Camilla Sodese and (more successfully) Clara Louise Kellogg. By the *fin-de-siècle*, Victor Herbert's satirical ballad about a stage-struck princess captured the mood of the eager acolyte of the operatic stage:

> I long to be a prima donna – donna – donna
> I long to shine upon the stage.
>   With my avoirdupois
>   And my tra la la la la,
> I'd be the chief sensation of the age.
> I long to hear them shouting 'Viva' to the diva.
> Oh, how lovely all that must be
>   That's what I'm dying for,
>   That's what I'm sighing for.
> ART is calling for me.[133]

In 1830, Maria Malibran had lamented that the term 'actress' was only 'understood in the most unfavourable and revolting sense of the world'.[134] Now it seemed that 'Art' was indeed calling loudly to many women, regardless of social station, as a brief survey of some of the most prominent late nineteenth- and early twentieth-century singers demonstrates. Louise Edvina was the Honourable Mrs Cecil Edwardes, sister-in-law of Lord Kensington;[135] the father of Elisabeth Höngen was a builder; Sybil Sanderson's father was a judge; Olive Fremstad was the daughter of a Swedish physician and lay preacher; Maggie Teyte's father was a hotel-owner; Cicely Gleeson-White was the daughter of a literary editor; the father of Iva Pacetti was the head operator in a textile factory; Eva Turner was the daughter of an engineer; Lotte Lehmann's father was a civil servant; Nellie Melba's father made bricks; Geraldine Farrar, Emma Eames, Kathleen Howard, Amelita Galli-Curci, and Lucrezia Bori were all from respectable middle-class families. The presence of these women, engaging consciously in an operatic career, was a sign that the old divide between stage and society was finally becoming a thing of the past.

SUFFRAGE

The idea of the professional female singer as a 'voice of freedom' also found a new political framework in the question of women's suffrage that became increasingly pressing during the latter part of the nineteenth century. Singers' responses to progressive images of womanhood such as the New Woman remained mixed, however. Some did not involve themselves at all in any political matters. Emma Eames, for example, might have remained in complete ignorance of the women's suffrage movement, as she 'never dared read a newspaper. Having an emotional nature that was ready to respond to and dramatize any suggestion, I became horribly agitated upon reading of murders, suicides, robberies and sordid political juggling, and had to abandon my daily paper altogether.'[136] (One wonders how she dealt with the violent fictional world of the operatic stage.) Other singers declared their negative attitude towards women's emancipation in unequivocal terms. In her memoirs in 1928, Ernestine Schumann-Heink fulminated against the pace of modern living, which she blamed on the fact that women nowadays 'are interested in everything and anything except home-making':

> Women in their proper place – the home, that is the final solution. Woman has nothing to do with politics, in my opinion, except through her husband and children. Let the husband have a happy home, find his home fire burning as it used to be, good food on his table, relaxation after his work, let the wife attend to all these things, and she then is the greatest influence in politics that she could wish, through her men folk.[137]

Yet could her views have carried more weight with her readers than the actuality of her life as described in those very same pages, by the proud possessor of a career that had lasted fifty years? Rescuing first her parents from poverty, then paying off the debts of her first husband who had abandoned her, raising the four children from this relationship as a single working parent, nursing her second husband through long years of ill-health and unemployment whilst also giving birth to three more children, and all the while singing in some of the most prestigious opera houses in the world – can Schumann-Heink really have been unaware that nothing in her own life accorded with the cosy domestic picture she envisaged for others? Or was it simply that, like many working women torn between the demands of family and career, she saw the domestic life she had *not* had with rose-tinted spectacles?

The renowned German singing teacher Mathilde Marchesi (1821–1913) demonstrated a more ambiguous approach to the 'Woman Question'. She condemned the physical labour of women in Vienna she witnessed in 1878, describing them as 'poor white slaves' in whose cause 'no one has yet risen',[138] and also declared that 'woman's emancipation would remain a chimera' as long as women indulged themselves in 'frivolities' such as the 'revolting' fashion for hennaed hair.[139] However, like Schumann-Heink, Marchesi regarded being separated from her children as 'the greatest sacrifice to my art', and considered that the best place for most women was indeed the home – although she interestingly blamed men for no longer making that possible:

> We women, as in olden times, should concentrate our interest on our households, and devote all our energies to our families. Only in rare instances and exceptional cases, where a young girl shows particular talent and strongly developed tastes, should she be allowed to choose a career. This, however, is hardly possible nowadays, the forced emancipation of woman having struck a severe blow at home-life. I say *forced*, because many less gifted girls and women are compelled from sheer necessity to take to teaching music, painting, sculpture, literature, languages, etc. In these times of constant excitement and continually

increasing wants, when men no longer show the same energy and spirit of self-sacrifice as heretofore, it follows naturally that women should try to emancipate themselves so as not to be dependent on the will and unscrupulousness of men, who often ill-treat them physically and morally.[140]

Clearly, Marchesi perceived herself and others like her to be in the mould of Eliot's Armgart – set aside from the usual roles of women because of exceptional talent. This was perhaps the most common interpretation of their position amongst the prima donnas. Frances Alda tried to find an explanation for her own lifestyle by dividing women into categories:

After all, there are three kinds of women. There is the woman who is all mother. There is the woman whose sole *métier* is love. And there is the worker. I am a worker. That doesn't mean that I don't care about young people; because I do. Nor does it mean that men have not meant a great deal in my life; because they have. But it means that I have in me the capacity for concentrated work, and that I actually derive a pleasure from this. That is, when I know it is getting me somewhere that I want to go.[141]

This categorising of herself as a 'worker' nevertheless was regarded by Alda as something different from political activity. When she married in 1910 and her husband (the impresario Giulio Gatti-Casazza) suggested that she should adopt his name in future, her response was ambivalent in political terms:

I was a long way from being a feminist or taking a keen interest in suffrage. Mrs Pankhurst and Rosalie Jones and the other vigorous exponents of women's rights who were then making the front page for picketing government offices from soap boxes or leading parades down Fifth Avenue, seemed to me rather pitiful and ridiculous.

But I was a worker, and I loved my work. I was honestly proud of the career I had made for myself and which belonged to the name of ALDA which Madame Marchesi had given me.

For Alda and many other singers, the crucial distinction therefore seems to have been one between 'woman' and 'artist'. After her wedding, the Swedish soprano Olive Fremstad sent Alda a telegram: 'Remember you married as a woman. Don't give up the position you have attained.'[142] Such women essentially regarded themselves as having two separate identities – and of the two, the 'artist' was by far the most important. Like Alda, the singers would protect their 'artistic' self with steely determination if inappropriate demands were made on it by notions of womanly behaviour. Nevertheless, this attitude did not necessarily translate into an automatic understanding of the demands of other women for similar rights.

Such appears to have been the position of many female singers. But others involved themselves actively in the growing campaign for women's suffrage. In America, for example, opera singers appeared in the five-day 'suffrage bazaar' held at the Hotel LaSalle in Chicago during the winter of 1911–12;[143] and similarly in the 'Night of the Interurban Council Fires' during the New York City Campaign of 1915.[144] One of the most active workers was Nordica, who participated enthusiastically in a variety of suffrage events, including giving a paper at the Women's Musical Congress in Chicago in 1893 and performing in a feminist pageant at the Metropolitan Opera House in 1911.[145] Perhaps her political ideas were further radicalised during the summer of 1908, which she spent in London on a concert tour,[146] and where she must have been at least aware of the important suffrage marches on 13 and 21 June. Certainly, her interviews to the press in 1909 demonstrate the influence of the Pankhursts; unlike the more timid American movement, Nordica fully supported the notion of militant action:

> 'Smash windows?' said Mme. Nordica to a group of reporters. 'Yes!
> When men take the view that to gain an end warlike methods are
> excusable, they are heroes. Many a man has fought and gone to
> prison for his principles, and I think no great reform has been brought
> about without there being those willing to cast themselves into the
> breach and fight. It is all very well for those in power to keep on their
> way, ignoring us. We have to draw attention to ourselves. If we are to
> be heard, why, we have to make ourselves obnoxious, perhaps, at
> times.'[147]

There is some limited evidence to suggest that Nordica was part of a network of singers who similarly became involved in the suffrage movement. We know she publicly declared at least one attempt to convert another prima donna to the cause: Mary Garden, with whom she shared an Atlantic crossing aboard the *Savoie* in May, 1912. Garden reputedly began the journey sure that Nordica 'will not succeed in converting me', although her reasons have a tongue-in-cheek ring: 'My love for the home is intense! probably because I have neither husband nor home.'[148] (There is no indication as to whether Garden's opinions were intact when they reached London. Certainly five years later she declared that 'suffrage will do women no good'.[149]) It seems more than probable therefore, given this incident and the evangelistic nature of the suffrage movement in general, that Nordica also sought the conversion of other singers. Did she in fact persuade others to the cause? And who might have converted Nordica herself?

One answer perhaps lies in the membership list of the Actresses' Franchise League: a British organisation established in 1908 by professional actresses committed to securing women's suffrage.[150] The first objective of the League was: 'To convince members of the Theatrical profession of the necessity of extending the franchise to women'.[151] The membership list included several opera and concert singers: Marie Brema, Maggie Davies, Hilda De Angelis, Alice Esty, Vera Holmes, Aida Jenoure, Agnes Larkcom, Liza Lehmann, Rosa Leo, Jean Sterling McKinlay, Bertha Moore, Decima Moore, Mary Palgrave Turner, Esther Palliser, Madeline Lucette Ryley, Lucy Carr Shaw and Amy Sherwin. Other women on the AFL list (Mrs Oscar Beringer, Mrs Thos. Meux, Mrs George Giddens and Mrs Sydney Valentine) were married to musicians. And there are many other names on the membership list about whom little or nothing is currently known.

The most prominent – both professionally and politically – of these women was the British mezzo-soprano Marie Brema (1856–1925), who became a Vice-President of the AFL. Having made her stage debut unusually late, at the age of thirty-five, Brema swiftly established an international operatic career including appearances at Bayreuth, the Metropolitan Opera House and Covent Garden. Like Nordica, she was made of a character that would have found politics almost child's-play after the trials of public singing. A correspondent to *The Musical World* in 1908 witnessed her handling of a fractious member of the audience in Paris, where she dealt firmly with a heckler who didn't like her repertoire: 'Brema fastened her eyes on him, where he sat in the gallery, went ahead with the song, and fairly bit the words out at him. And the audience cheered her.'[152]

It might have been Brema who converted Nordica, for the two women had often been part of the same company, and had sung together on various occasions: at Covent Garden in 1892, 1893, 1898 and 1902; and at Bayreuth in *Lohengrin* in 1894. And it is interesting to note that several of the singers who sang with either or both of these women were also known to be public supporters of the women's suffrage movement: for example, the American soprano and AFL member Esther Palliser (1872–?) also sang at Covent Garden with both Brema and Nordica in 1892 and 1893, and with Brema alone in 1894; the soprano and composer Liza Lehmann had been closely acquainted with Nordica since at least 1894.[153] The American contralto Eleanora De Cisneros (1878–1934), another 'determined campaigner for women's suffrage',[154] had also performed with Nordica in 1907 as part of Hammerstein's Manhattan Opera Company. Other known activists include the Russian soprano Lydia Lipkowska (1882–1955), who delivered speeches on behalf of women's suffrage on the streets of New York,[155] and the Wagnerian singer Anna Bahr-Mildenburg (1872–1947), who with her husband Hermann Bahr recruited the composer Ethel Smyth to the movement.[156] Whilst such tentative links are hardly proof of a flourishing network of pro-suffrage singers, they nevertheless seem too noticeable to dismiss as mere coincidence. Such a network would certainly accord with policies in the wider international suffrage movement, which thrived on a web of personal contacts.[157]

Perhaps these women would always have been part of the suffrage campaign, even if they had led domestic rather than professional lives. But it was women's engagement in the world of work that gave many the confidence to challenge the patriarchal hegemony and demand equality of political rights, opportunity and pay. Those singers allied to the suffrage movement were women who made a tough living on the stage, who knew that great determination and strength of character were required to 'make oneself heard' by those in power, and who weren't afraid to 'draw attention' to themselves. Their readiness to demonstrate publicly their political commitment was a small but telling indication that the prima donna's 'voice of freedom' could be deployed not only to secure personal liberty but also in pursuit of a wider cause.

As the sirens' death by suicide after their defeat by Orpheus turned out to be mere rumour (at least two were alive when Ulysses sailed past their island a year later),[158] so the strategy of containing women by a specific ordering of the female voice thus proved unsustainable. Whether as a result of her personal appraisal of the prima donna, or of her response to the fictional representations of singers cited earlier, or of her experience of her own music-making, the drawing-room singer either subverted the moral intent of music tuition by claiming her right as 'agent' rather than 'object', or (like Piccolomini, Bashkirtseff and de Hegermann-Lindencrone) she interpreted her singing in terms of potency and freedom and moved inevitably towards a professional career.

Rosa Ponselle, perhaps the most extraordinary voice of her generation, stated that the best advice she could offer to 'ambitious girl students' was *Be sure of proper guidance in the initial stages when you study singing!*[1] Solid technical grounding was a fundamental requirement for the aspiring prima donna – and yet surprisingly hard to obtain. This was an era in which ideas of singing changed considerably, and determining precisely what constituted 'proper guidance' became increasingly difficult.

No previous century had witnessed such extensive and rapid changes in vocal technique. The whole approach to the upper third of the tenor voice from the late 1830s onwards, for example, was entirely new; the repercussions of this technical development were felt by all voices.[2] Such modifications arose mainly in response to compositional demands and shifts within the operatic marketplace, including the construction of larger auditoriums. The florid, delicate ornamentation of the *bel canto* operas of the early decades gave way to the declamatory, dramatic vocal lines and the bigger, louder orchestras of the mid- and late nineteenth century, finding perhaps their most extreme manifestation in operas such as Richard Strauss's *Elektra* (1909).[3] New, 'heroic' styles of singing were demanded by these operas: in consequence, singers grew ever more obsessed with volume and power, whilst many teachers abandoned the former, empirical methods of imitation and basic exercises in favour of newer – sometimes outlandish – theories to supply additional strength and stamina.[4] One such example appeared in the *Gazzetta musicale di Milano* in 1846, which reported a new 'system' invented by Francesco d'Eyrel. He claimed his technique doubled the vocal range of the singer 'without any fatigue or effort', thereby enabling singers to 'accommodate their voices to modern musical compositions'. The

Gazzetta enjoyed a moment of heavy irony: 'Imagine what an advantage! In such a manner we would have sopranos with four octaves! basses and baritones with more than three octaves!'[5] Real science nevertheless made itself felt in determining change in vocal tuition, led by Manuel Garcia II's invention of the laryngoscope (an instrument for visually examining the vocal chords) in 1855, and the subsequent development of his controversial theories of *coup de glotte*.[6] Soon, 'science' became the supposed guarantor of the effectiveness of a particular approach to vocal technique, as is apparent in the tediously obscure jargon employed by numerous later singing manuals and handbooks, with their emphasis on pseudo-scientific solutions to vocal problems.[7]

Change was also facilitated by the more open discussion and dissent about vocal technique than had occurred previously, courtesy not only of genuinely diverse ideas but also of an expanding musical press that encouraged the dissemination of such debate. By the middle of the century, as developments in compositional practices and vocal technique made significant impact, increasing numbers of articles in the musical press referred to the 'decadence' of modern singing.[8] By the latter part of the century, these articles had been supplemented by a host of books on the topic, of which Enrico Delle Sedie's *Riflessioni sulle cause della decadenza della scuola di canto in Italia* (1881) is perhaps the earliest and best-known example.[9] But accusations or anxieties about decadence were evident long before the beginning of the period. In 1791, Saverio Mattei's report on the state of the Conservatorio della Pietà dei Turchini in Naples complained that a change in teaching methods from the former strict schooling in *solfeggi* to a more lax approach that permitted students to indulge in the '*rondoncini* and the *canonetti* of French guitar' (which 'tire neither the chest nor the lungs') had corrupted the ears of the pupils, and had led to the 'decadence of the art of singing'.[10] And yet Mattei's views had surely been influenced by an even earlier letter from Pietro Metastasio in 1770, who claimed that the previous 'laborious type of training' that had made voices 'firm, robust, and sonorous' (instead of weakened by newer practices of 'arpeggios, runs and trills') had already been abandoned.[11] These cyclical laments about the quality of singing demonstrate that the latter nineteenth-century concerns were in part a response to the ephemeral nature of singing – a sign, even, of the falseness of memory. The idealisation of older techniques is also interestingly visible only with regard to singing, which received distinctly different treatment in this era from the discussions on the playing of other instruments; there, in general, extensions to technical ability and range of expression were welcomed. This debate around vocal techniques was made even more telling because of the great expansion in the educational market-place, evident, as we shall see, in the considerable increase in both numbers of private teachers and the founding of music colleges and conservatoires. Such growth of competition exacerbated the splintering of the old ways of teaching. As early as 1861, Oscar Commettant declared: 'There exist sixty-six different methods of singing published in France! It is assuredly too many.'[12]

In this climate of rising doubt about the correct way of singing, finding a suitable tutor was a complex and confusing process. The new influx of singers from middle-class, non-professional backgrounds from the 1850s moreover ensured that pupils were both wealthier and more gullible than ever before, facilitating the emergence of inadequately qualified teachers. Most such recorded examples stem from the latter part of the period: perhaps a sign of a rise in bad practice, but also perhaps indicative of a new mindset in the consumer – a desire not only for 'value for money', but for assured results. Nonetheless, the sheer quantity of complaints about the quality of teaching is telling. Frances Alda demanded that vocal tutors should be licensed (in the same manner as 'physicians and dentists') in order to get rid of the 'bad and dangerous singing teachers' she claimed were ruining the 'perfectly exquisite natural voices' of their unlucky pupils.[13] Lotte Lehmann described how poor teaching nearly ruined her early chances: 'Had I followed the advice of one teacher I would have given up singing entirely, had I followed another I would have sung, but never in opera.'[14] Some of these dubious teachers had never themselves sung or even been taught how to sing, but attracted pupils on the basis of their connections with an opera house or a notable singer – such as a New York tutor who had simply been the secretary-valet of the tenor Jean de Reszke,[15] or another who (according to Emma Calvé) had originally been 'the lady's maid of a famous opera star'.[16]

Almost every singer, teacher or critic knew of anecdotes concerning one or more of these 'quacks', as Bernard Shaw termed them, each of whom firmly believed that they alone held the key to the perfect art of singing.[17] Reputable singers publicised the worst excesses of the charlatans, both in a genuine effort to deter naive pupils from falling into their clutches and also to demonstrate the usefulness of their own practices by comparison. In a series of lectures given in Paris in 1913–14, the French singer and composer Reynaldo Hahn criticised the 'ridiculous, even criminal' means employed by some tutors, such as the insertion of a spatula to 'enlarge the mouth and pharyngeal cavities', along with a flat ruler 'to dilate and elongate the four pillars of the uvula and those of the larynx by constantly pushing them back towards the soft palate when they resist the restraints of the spatula'.[18] Other methods approached physical assault:

> But what can I say of the teacher – now deceased; I knew him well, he was the soul of a gentleman – who would have his students lie on the floor, then place several volumes of the *Larousse Encyclopaedia* on their stomachs and sit forcefully upon them, causing the victims to shriek with pain. Following this exercise, he would stand up and announce triumphantly: 'You see, you *do* have a B-flat! The only question is how to get it out.'[19]

The Musical Times assembled a catalogue of some of the most ludicrous and dangerous practices cited by Blanche Marchesi in her memoirs *A Singer's Pilgrimage* (1923):

> The large piece of lead used by a Dresden teacher to keep a pupil's tongue down (and which slipped into the interior of one victim, and had to be X-rayed and fished out); the wire cage, to ensure the open mouth (price one guinea, and made in one size only, with Procrustean results);

the use of prunes or chestnuts in the cheeks to double the sound by keeping the cheeks from touching the teeth; breathing exercises, prone, with bricks on the chest for the fortifying of the muscles (one of Marchesi's male pupils told her he had reached the total of thirty bricks); the tumbler of water balanced on the chest of a woman pupil, also prone: her breathing was right if the water remained unspilled (unfortunately it never did); tightening a leather belt, running up and down stairs, and panting like a dog – three methods of improving breath control; Italian water at five shillings a bottle ('In Italy the voice is good because the water is good: if you drink Italian water . . .'); and, leaving the water for the air, there was 'amoniaphone', sold in tubes (another five shillings), alleged to be compressed Italian air ('Italian air gives voice; if you breathe Italian air . . .') – these and other practices described by Marchesi suggest the dark ages rather than the 20th century.[20]

Despite such condemnation, some of the 'quacks' nevertheless made a good living – at least for a while. One colourful example was George J. Vandeleur Lee (1830–?), the Irish singing teacher of Shaw's mother and his sister Lucy, and (according to Michael Holroyd) a model for Du Maurier's fantasy figure, Svengali: a notion supported by Shaw's description of him as a 'mesmeric conductor and a daringly original teacher of singing'[21] and by Lee's extraordinary manner of insinuating himself as a resident into the Shaw household. This Svengali-prototype, who had had no formal music education himself, claimed to have developed the 'Method': a theory of singing that mixed certain *bel canto* principles with the pseudo-scientific language favoured by so many teachers of the day, and which for a while apparently had some success. His real notoriety began when he left his home town of Dublin in 1873, in order to establish himself in practice in London. There, according to Shaw, Lee discovered that 'good teaching did not pay, because the only people who could afford to pay ten guineas for twelve lessons could not be induced to take more than the twelve'. His only solution in the face of such philistinism was to discard the long-term vocal objectives of his cherished 'Method' and adopt a more brazen approach:

So he told [his pupils] that he would in six weeks shew them how to sing like Patti; and he took care that at the end of their dozen lessons they should be able to make a much louder noise than at the beginning, which caused their friends to declare that their voices were immensely improved.[22]

For a while, it seems, this ruse succeeded, and Lee became the darling of the town. But after a few seasons his popularity faded, presumably because his pupils failed to develop successes comparable to those of Patti. Having sacrificed the principles of good singing in order to avoid starvation, he nevertheless died in poverty.

What was regarded, then, as good teaching of singing? The emphasis on an essentially straightforward approach of 'simple scales and exercises' appears to have borne continual fruit across the centuries, despite changes in musical style and theories of voice production.[23] Yet a methodology of great simplicity requires a teacher of corresponding subtlety and experience. Clara Kathleen Rogers (1844–1931), an opera singer who eventually (like so many of her colleagues) turned to teaching, offered a list of the ideal vocal tutor's qualifications in her treatise *The Philosophy of Singing* (1893):

The teacher must possess – 1st, an absolute and unerring feeling for the perfect vocal sound; 2d, he must recognize immediately the smallest deviation from that perfection; 3d, he must be able to analyze in what that deviation consists, and in what particular perversion of process it has its immediate cause; 4th, his knowledge of the vocal mechanism must enable him to adapt the proper exercises to the actual needs of the pupil; 5th, he must be able to constantly furnish the pupil with examples of the perfect sound, either in his own voice or the voice of another, and also to point out immediately the sporadic occurrences of the correct sound in the voice of the pupil himself; 6th, he must be endowed with infinite patience, discretion, hopefulness, and last, not least, with an intense interest and love for his work. These are not common qualities, but neither is an intelligent and perfectly equipped teacher a common product.[24]

As Rogers implies, few teachers met the requirements of this list. Her fourth point had particular relevance, because throughout the period a principal source of antagonism between tutors and their pupils was methodology. In 1833, Nicola Tacchinardi described the problems that arose when the individual needs of the pupil were ignored in pursuit of a rigid idea of singing:

> There are very few tutors who teach singing that do so according to the nature and the inclination of the student: they have only one method, and that must be applied to all, like a saddle for every horse. Fortunate is he who encounters his own natural disposition in the method of the tutor; otherwise, he will be forced to swim against the current. There are those here (and in every country) who teach singing because they know music and how to accompany singers, but they know as much about singing as I do of chemistry . . . The singing teacher should not have any fixed method, but rather the knowledge and the communication skills of how to establish one for each scholar, according to his natural inclination and the quality of the voice.[25]

This emphasis on a personal tailoring of approach is also apparent in accounts of another highly prominent tutor of the early nineteenth century: Manuel García I, father of both Maria Malibran and Pauline Viardot. A former pupil, the Countess de Merlin, left this intriguing description of his teaching:

> In proportion as the voice of the pupil improved, it was García's custom to prescribe exercises more and more difficult until every obstacle was surmounted; but he rarely noted down a set passage for his pupils. His method was to strike a chord on the piano, and to say to them, 'Now sing any passage you please'; and he would make them execute a passage in this way ten or twenty times in succession. The result was, that the pupil sang precisely that which was suited to his voice, and suggested by his taste. Solfeggi exercises, performed in this way, presented a character of individuality, being suggested by the feeling of the moment. Another advantage of this mode of practice was, that the pupil gained a perfect mastery over his voice by dint of exercising his own inspirations, and that he was at liberty to follow the dictates of his own taste without fear or hesitation.[26]

The freedom suggested here and its implications for the empowerment of the singer are remarkable. But concern with developing the

student's individuality became less noticeable as the century progressed. Increasing competition within the marketplace of musical
education was one factor that led teachers to claim that it was their
own particular 'method' which developed pupils' voices; the industrial era's emphasis on greater productivity might equally have
encouraged a 'one size fits all' attitude. Methods became weapons
in the war to attract students. Manuel Garcia II's controversial theory
of *coup de glotte* was attacked fiercely by other singers and vocal
teachers. The teaching of Jean de Reszke (whose formidable reputation as a master technician arose because he began his career as a
baritone but then rebuilt his voice into that of a tenor) was similarly
criticised: one singer declared that de Reszke 'was sent for over a
quarter of a century the cream of Europe and America and turned
out nothing but skimmed milk – with *one* exception: Maggie
Teyte'.[27] Mathilde Marchesi, another of the most notable tutors of
the era (counting Nellie Melba among her pupils), was condemned
for producing nothing but 'neat *voci bianche*'.[28]

One of the most contested aspects of methodology from the
middle of the period onwards concerned differing approaches to
respiration: a key element in the search for increased vocal power
and stamina occasioned by the new compositional techniques.[29] In
the past, respiration had been hardly mentioned in previous
manuals;[30] now, however, the issue of 'clavicular' versus 'abdominal'
versus 'thoracic' breathing surfaced again and again in periodicals,
articles and books of the period.[31] The Italian baritone Leone Giraldoni (1824–97) 'criticized the rib-cage breathing that was the official
method taught at the Paris Conservatory' (he himself was an advocate of 'diaphragmatic breathing');[32] Lilli Lehmann argued that the
common German terms for vocal respiration ' "Atemstauen" (breath
restraint), and "Stauprinzip" (law or principle of restraint)' induced a
rigidity and stiffness in the breathing mechanism, instead of making
the singer realise that 'only from an eternally alive form with elastic
muscular action can the breath flow, the tone resonate'.[33] In Britain a
letter by Josiah Richardson in *The Musical World* in 1890 declared that
'Abdominal breathing is best; I know it; I practise it myself, and teach

it myself with excellent results', and took to task a previous letter-writer (Mr Garry) who had claimed with equal vehemence that 'inspiration *must* be through the nose *alone*'.[34] Far more preferable to the student caught between such extremes, surely, must have been the eminently reasonable approaches of singers such as Reynaldo Hahn, who stated that abdominal, thoracic and clavicular methods of breathing all had their merits, and that singers 'need to know how to breathe in every way, using each of these methods according to circumstances.'[35] In this frenzy of methodological claims and counter-claims, only Verdi – envisaging a future in which the singer was freed from the restrictive hegemony of vocal teachers, and instead guided only by the principles of good musicianship and his or her own inspiration – seemed to recall the past trust in the singer as an autonomous artist:

> For singing, I should like the students to have a wide knowledge of music; exercises in voice production; very long courses in solfeggi, as in the past; exercises for singing and speaking with clear and perfect enunciation. Then, without having any teacher perfect him in vocal style, I should like the young student, who by now should have a strong knowledge of music and a well-trained voice, to sing, guided only by his own feelings. This will be singing, not of such-and-such a school, but of inspiration. The artist will be an individual. He will be himself, or better still, he will be the character he has to represent in the opera.[36]

Such a range of theories about vocal production must have made finding the right teacher a bewildering experience for the novice singer. The anonymous female author (possibly Blanche Roosevelt) of an article entitled 'Singing Lessons in Paris', published in *The Musical World* in 1890, relates her sampling of the available tutors in her search to learn the 'French method' of singing in the early 1880s: first she visits 'Madame Della Grange'[37] but finds that she only teaches the 'Italian method'; then she begins lessons with Christine Nilsson's teacher, Pierre Wartel,[38] but unfortunately he dies shortly afterwards; next, she accompanies a friend to Mathilde Marchesi's studio and is impressed by Marchesi's 'faculty of penetration'; and finally she settles down to study with Pauline Viardot, only to learn at last that in Viardot's opinion there was no 'French school' of singing as such but merely *good* schools' based on sound Italian principles.[39]

Mary Garden also seems to have experienced difficulties in finding the right teacher when she arrived in Paris in 1896; her letters to her sponsor Florence Mayer provide us with a detailed account of her search. She and her American teacher Sarah Robinson Duff (who had accompanied her to Paris) toured a number of studios before settling on the Italian tenor Giovanni Sbriglia (1829–1916). Initially, Garden is enthusiastic about Sbriglia's emphasis on building a 'new box' (the chest), and even about the fact that she had not sung a note for two lessons but merely practised humming exercises in order to bring her tone further into the mask. But there are indications that something is not quite right. Being in Paris is like a 'beautiful dream', she writes, 'but when I went down to Sbriglias & had him pull my breast and stomach almost off why I knew it to be real He uses you like a ball – takes a hold of you where ever he sees a place that is not held high enough –'.[40] Perhaps Sbriglia's lack of inhibitions about physical contact were entirely innocent. But in Garden's memoirs this re-told incident sounds close to sexual harassment, as Sbriglia supposedly also told her 'to unbutton the front of my dress': Garden claims that she left his studio at that point, 'roaring with laughter'.[41] However, the reasons she offered to Mayer for leaving Sbriglia were vocal ones:

> I began with Sbriglia as you know – and tried hard to make myself believe that his method was what I wanted, but just couldn't – I didn't like the way he used the voice, he took me up too high, always to 'F' and 'G' and it was a struggle – I never came out of that studio that I did not have a sore feeling in my throat – So Mrs Duff and I heard some of his women pupils & they sang wretchedly and Mme Sbriglia plays the piano for him and has about as much expression in her work as a piece of wood, and Sbriglia is known not to understand what *style* means – So I just made up my mind that was not where I wanted to go –

Garden's search for the right teacher began anew. Her description of this investigation reveals the questionable manipulations some tutors employed to secure good-quality pupils:

So we tried other schools, and the one that had the most favourable impression was Boughy[42] – He is considered a fine master and I really rather liked him, but after going through them all & trying them all, and to my great pride to see [*sic*] they all wanted me – I ended up with the only teacher for the human female voice Marchesi[43] – The dearest woman, the most interesting teacher, and it just suits my every wish – Music? Well, if you wish to hear music just go to her opera class – She has invited Mrs Duff and I there any day we can go[44] – It is considered a great honor to go I know – Mrs Duff asked to bring a friend of hers there one morning and Madam Marchesi distinctly said 'No' – You know she is really jealous of Mrs Duff – She cannot quite understand how Mrs Duff has been able to teach & place the voice – and the old lady does not mind showing it – Well we told her I would take three lessons a week, and what do you think, she gives me a lesson every day – and a private one at that.[45] Why Mrs Duff and I are so surprised we don't say a word for fear it might be a dream. She said my voice & quality was beautiful & spoke of my intelligence (*intelligence* please to understand –) and yesterday she said I reminded her very much of Eames,[46] and she also said my voice was a much better voice than hers – Now that coming from that woman who never gives praise to anyone meant a great deal to me – We are to do wonders this winter – She told me what to eat & what not to eat & not to talk in the air, and is so dear in everything – She said to me – 'Do you think you will learn to love me very much' – I told her I had done so already – and I do[47] – She won't let me hum one note, she says it is ridiculous such a thing – She gives one all the exercises we have in our studio oh very very slowly, stand perfectly quiet looking straight ahead[48] – not to any side, & stand on both your feet – She says to Mrs Duff in fun – "My how that girl wants to show her foot" – When I stand on one & [put] the other to one side – I have had nothing but exercises – and am perfectly happy over the thought I am with Marchesi and I feel I can accomplish wonders – Sbriglia is good with men – not with women – Every one in Paris who knows anything about voice placing will tell you that, still we found it out for ourselves –[49]

Once again Garden finds that her first impressions prove errone-
ous, and her relationship with Marchesi is soon sundered. In her
memoirs, Garden claimed that she chose not to return to Marchesi
because of her emphasis on *coloratura* singing, and also because
Marchesi failed to remember her after Garden returned from a
holiday in Carlsbad.[50] However, Frances Alda (another pupil of
Marchesi's and a close friend of Garden) stated that Marchesi had
'refused' to teach Garden 'because she did not think the young
American girl was sufficiently respectful of her ideas and criticism'.[51]
Unfortunately, Garden's letters to Mayer only fleetingly refer to her
reasons for leaving Marchesi, although she quotes another singer as
saying that 'Marchesi is altogether too old now & does not pay
enough attention to her pupils.'[52] Instead, Garden finally found the
teacher she was to remain with for the next two years, Ange-Pierre
de Trabadelo.[53] She later stated that it was Trabadelo's first remark
that put her at her ease: ' "Sing for me in a normal, natural way", he
said, "as if you were singing by yourself at home." I wasn't being
asked to sound like a freak. I turned to Mrs Duff and said: "This is
my teacher." '[54]

Whilst finding the right teacher was of crucial importance, experienced singers nevertheless warned against moving frequently from
one tutor to the next in the hope that vocal problems would be
remedied merely by a change in approach. A lack of progress was not
necessarily due to faulty tuition, as Luisa Tetrazzini made plain:
'There are bad teachers, of course, but often the pupils are worse
and will not listen to advice.'[55] Caruso was equally insistent that the
responsibility for effective learning lay as much with the student as
with the tutor: 'Many too ambitious students are their own worst
enemies in the culture of their voices . . . Their teachers should give
up trying to make them listen to reason and devote their attention
to those who merit it and want to study seriously.'[56] Some pupils
realised too late the dangers of following their own enthusiasms
rather than their tutor's cautious counsels, as the anonymous pupil
of Viardot mentioned earlier demonstrates: Viardot, she wrote, 'did
all she could for me; gave me reasonable music to sing, and made

me understand what I was doing. If only I had been a more sensible pupil I should have profited immeasurably.'[57] Frequently, novice singers were either unaware of the degree of time and effort that needed to be invested in their voices, or they had an inflated idea of their vocal talents. Lillie de Hegermann-Lindencrone found herself in this situation when she arrived in London in 1859 to study with Manuel Garcia II thinking that she 'only needed a *few* finishing touches to make me perfect'. Instead, she was told that she had 'not the remotest idea of how to sing' and was sent off for six months' complete vocal rest before he would consent to give her lessons.[58]

The expectations of the effects of teaching were substantial, promulgated largely by the teachers themselves. Maria Malibran was perhaps the most publicised example of a faulty voice that was improved by her father's tuition. But the novice might have been discouraged by the fact that many other singers claimed to have succeeded with comparatively little vocal education. The German mezzo-soprano Elisabeth Höngen (1906–77) was rare in admitting that before her long years of training her voice was 'small and ugly'.[59] More common were those singers who declared that tuition merely polished already present abilities: for example, Zinka Milanov (who made her debut at the age of twenty in 1927) acknowledged the excellent tuition she received from Milka Ternina, but claimed that her voice was 'all there from the very beginning' and merely 'needed to be fortified and disciplined'.[60] Maretzek mocked the propensity of certain prima donnas to assert that their vocal skills were evident in the cradle:

> The biographies of most divas are nearly alike, the only slight differences being that some, when small babies, could hum and repeat the gems of an opera at a single hearing, whilst others could do the same without ever having heard them, and still others could sing them before they were composed.[61]

But we should not assume all singers exaggerated the extent of their innate talent. Milanov, an extraordinarily accomplished technician and one much admired by her fellow singers,[62] probably assessed her early potential accurately. For such artists, technical difficulties were few, and needed only minor correction.[63] The soprano Amelita Galli-Curci was largely self-taught before her first stage appearance as Gilda at Trani in 1912: she was one of a host of singers (including Giulia Tess, Sara Scuderi, Gemma Bosini Stabile and Ines Alfani Tellini) who arrived on the professional stage with little prior vocal training. The most notable example of abundant natural gifts was Rosa Ponselle. Exactly how much training Ponselle had, and from whom, remains unclear, but there is little doubt that it was relatively minimal even by the standards of the day. She gained most of her experience as a vaudeville singer before being heard by Caruso; and then only a few months later made her astonishing debut at the age of twenty-two as Leonora in *La forza del destino* at the Metropolitan in 1918.[64]

CONSERVATOIRES

An alternative to private tuition was enrolment in one of the various music colleges established in Europe and America through the century. The model for such institutions was the Paris Conservatoire, founded in 1795 and which admitted female singers and certain instrumentalists;[65] Milan did likewise in 1807. Soon women could study in Vienna, London, Brussels, Parma, Leipzig, Venice, Berlin, Bologna, Prague and Berne, or in a host of other cities. Something of the scale of development can be seen in France: in 1850, there were only around twenty *écoles de musique* – by 1862, there were sixty-five.[66] Access to such tuition was less easy in southern Mediterranean countries: for example, a 'Scuola di Canto per le Donzelle' (later the 'Collegio di Musica delle Donzelle') was established in Naples in 1806 but was closed again in 1832 by Ferdinand II, on the grounds that it threatened public morality.[67]

Even where women were permitted to enter the conservatori elsewhere in Italy, problems remained. Access, for example, was not equal for both genders: certainly in the early decades of the nineteenth century, the number of *posti gratuiti* available to female students were generally fewer than those for male students. Once within the institution, inequalities persisted. Florimo made the point that during the brief existence of the Collegio per le Donzelle in Naples, the girls were taught not as future members of the profession, but almost exclusively in order to become 'good mothers of families'.[68] This approach is also evident during the early years of the conservatorio in Milan. The articles and regulations of 1807 state that both boys and girls will be instructed in 'reading and arithmetic' until the age of thirteen, but then: 'for the boys, reading of some history book or literary treatise; for the girls, needlework'.[69] Further information on the nature of such tasks is given a few paragraphs later: 'In the hours of reading aloud for the boys, the girls will employ themselves in the work for the linen of the Conservatorio, or their own according to the need.'[70] It is one of the many contradictions of the era's approach to female singers that they were criticised for being uneducated and ignorant, and yet appropriate education was so often denied to them. Under such circumstances, it is not surprising that the first appointment of a woman at a more senior level within the conservatorio at Milan was not made until the 1870s.[71]

Efforts to establish access for women to the conservatori met with resistance by some elements in society. At Parma in the 1830s, it seems it was only the desire of the governing duchess, Maria Luigia (a committed *dilettante* musician herself), that eventually overrode various objections about suitable accommodation. Even so, the first site for the girls' school in the Ospizio delle Mendicanti facing the Borgo Reale had to be abandoned: 'the lessons being continually disturbed by curious passers-by who were lingering in the public street', and the school was moved in 1835 to the Ospizio delle Esposte instead.[72] At Naples, following the first edition (1869) of Florimo's history of musical education in the city and his argument that it was 'shameful' that 'one of the greatest cities of Europe and the seat of so many celebrated conservatori' should be deprived of a 'music college for women',[73] the legal framework for such an institution was finally established in 1872. However, owing to a lack of suitable accommodation this plan was abandoned, and instead only a *Scuola esterna* for female students was opened in 1874.[74]

In all the Italian *conservatori*, whether for *posti gratuiti* boarders or external pupils, the girls were kept strictly separate from the boys. The regulations of the Liceo Comunale Musicale di Bologna in 1833 stated that the lessons attended by both genders must be arranged 'in a manner that avoids the boys and girls finding themselves together'.[75] Nor were girls to be left alone. Article 70 of the regulations at Parma declares that 'The female pupils will always be accompanied by relatives or by persons entrusted by the same'; article 71 continues, 'A female pupil will never be allowed to stay alone in the School, but will have to wait until another girl finishes the lesson and withdraws at the same time, or until someone arrives to collect her.'[76] In Paris, girls were similarly chaperoned to lessons, a practice still apparent (or at least protected by the regulations) later in the period according to *L'Art musical* in 1861,[77] and equally enshrined in the policies of provincial conservatoires such as Rennes in the 1880s.[78]

Who were these young women, and what happened to them? Parma offers us a particularly vivid insight, as Dacci's history records not only the names of the students (as Melzi does), but also notes their success or failure and eventual career. In 1833 five female pupils (Lucia Giglioli, Luigia Giovannini, Drusilla Bernini, Carolina Gabbi, and Carolina Lusignani) were admitted: all apparently made professional careers.[79] But the second year's intake was less successful. Of the five admitted in the winter of 1834, only one (Teresa Tessoni, a contralto) was contracted by an opera company; the remaining four withdrew from the school for reasons of health. A further eleven girls were then enrolled in the spring and summer. Seven left within a year, again apparently either for health reasons or for 'inaptitude'; two became chorus singers, and one was contracted in opera houses as a mezzo-soprano. Only one girl remained at the school for more than two years: Carolina Filippini left in 1843 at the remarkably late age of twenty-five, having passed a total of nine years at the conservatorio – her efforts resulted in a career not as a diva but as a 'corista distinta'.[80] Nor did fortunes seem to improve much in later years. In 1866, thirty-six students were admitted to the conservatorio, of whom seven were women. Two were harpists (the first such instrumentalists in the history of the institution) and sisters: they withdrew after only a month, but later emerged as successful professional musicians.[81] Another of the seven was a pianist (only the second in the conservatorio's history), who eventually became a teacher. The remaining four students were singers: all left within a year because of 'lack of aptitude' or because they chose to abandon their study of music.

The evidence from Parma and Milan suggests that the output of successful female students from the Italian conservatori during the first three-quarters of the century might have been surprisingly small. It is equally apparent, however, that some of those students who found their experience of the conservatorio unsatisfactory continued to study privately. Fosca Fava (b. 1855) spent three years at the conservatorio between 1871 and 1874; she withdrew 'spontaneously' (the expression used when the conservatorio regarded a student as promising and his or her departure therefore inexplicable), studied privately, and was then 'acclaimed in various national theatres as *primo soprano*', before later abandoning her career.[82] Adalgisa Gabbi withdrew in similar fashion after two years' study in 1874 in order to perfect her studies with the 'celebrated baritone' Felice Varesi in Milan;[83] she too enjoyed a considerable professional career.

There is a perceptible difference in the attendance of northern European and American women from that of their southern European counterparts in the conservatoires. Numbers of women students increased significantly in Germany during the era: the Leipzig conservatory began in 1843 with 33 male and 11 female students – in contrast, Dr Hoch's Konservatorium opened in Frankfurt in 1878 with 97 female and 42 male students.[84] In Britain, there was a similarly clear increase, demonstrated by the initial intakes of three important institutions. In 1823 the Academy of Music (later to become the Royal Academy of Music) enrolled 21 students in its first year, 10 of whom were women; in 1883 at the newly established Royal College of Music in London, out of a total intake of 335 students, 124 students were female singers (as compared with only 13 male singers);[85] in 1897, its founding year, the Royal Manchester College of Music enrolled 151 students, of whom 112 were women.[86] Some men found this inrush of female musicians disturbing: in 1908, the composer Charles Villiers Stanford complained that the music colleges were being overrun by women.[87]

In contrast, no such large increase is visible in the Italian institutions during the same period. This may be attributable to the fact that there were many more smaller conservatori and *licei* in Italy, whilst in Britain at least, students tended to be concentrated in a few larger colleges. Numbers of students also seem to have been more tightly controlled by the Italian authorities, especially where the conservatori were still largely dedicated to the principles of *posti gratuiti*; Pasquale Amato, himself the product of the conservatorio in Naples, made a pertinent argument against the practice of privately funded training:

> In America a pupil suddenly determines that he is destined to become a great opera singer and forthwith he hires a teacher to make him one. He might have been destined to become a plumber, or a lawyer, or a comedian, but that has little to do with the matter if he has money and can employ a teacher. In Italy such a direction of talents would be considered a waste to the individual and to the state . . . I consider the Italian system seems a very wise one for it does not fool away any time with incompetence.[88]

The discipline in many Italian institutions was also severe, restricting students' engagement in external concerts and other activities unless sanctioned by the conservatorio.[89]

Nonetheless, there were significant advantages in participating in an established college, including a broader-based musical education, association with other students, and (in contrast with private study) the facilitation of access into the profession. Appearances in college performances might be rewarded with press coverage: a production of *Ildegonda* at the Conservatorio di Milano in 1845 is prominently reviewed on the first page of the *Gazzetta musicale di Milano*, with the young principal Carlotta Sannazzaro acclaimed in laudatory terms: 'Rarely on the musical horizon appears a star that barely at the dawn of her career already assures a splendid zenith like la Sannazaro. . . Her musical education honours more than ever the establishment to which she belongs.'[90] Towards the end of the century in Paris, winners of the 'prix' of the conservatoire were almost automatically awarded contracts by the Opéra: indeed, the regulations of the Opéra in 1879 enabled it to have prior claim on the students at the end of their studies 'in preference to any other lyric theatre', thus creating considerable conflict with the rival establishment of the Opéra-Comique.[91]

Conservatoire education also theoretically protected students against the worst excesses of the private tutors. In practice, however, this last point was a matter of debate throughout Europe. In a letter from Paris in 1871, Bizet wrote that 'The teaching at the Conservatoire is pitiful':

> There is one such professor of singing who indulges in the most dissolute extortion. A monsieur Z. . . obliges his pupils to take some particular lessons at his home, at ridiculous prices, and, when the pupils can no longer pay, he accepts their linen, their effects, their jewellery, which madame Z. . . resells to a second-hand clothes trader [*une marchande à la toilette*].[92]

Shaw too railed against the standard of the singers who emerged from the London music colleges in the 1880s and 1890s: the 'ordinary Academy pupil' was a young woman who 'after a brief trial of her thin and colourless perfections on the public, takes to helping herself out by brute force, and presently grinds away her voice and takes to teaching the art in which she has failed'.[93] Lilli Lehmann (who had acquired her own vocal training from her mother) related the new institutional way of learning to the industrialisation of the era, and castigated a system that rewarded unsuccessful performers with a licence to teach:

In former times eight years were devoted to the study of singing – at the Prague Conservatory, for instance. . . But art today must be pursued, like everything else, by steam. Artists are turned out in factories, that is, in so-called conservatories, or by teachers who give lessons ten or twelve hours a day. In two years they receive a certificate of competence, or at least the teacher's diploma of the factory. The latter, especially, I consider a crime that the state should prohibit.[94]

Moreover, as Lotte Lehmann discovered at the Berlin Imperial Opera School, conservatoires also denied the students the freedom of choice available to the private pupil when difficulties occurred between pupil and teacher. Charlatanism or simply bad practice was therefore often as much in evidence within the formal educational institutions as within the private tuition marketplace.

STUDENT LIFE

What, then, do we know of student life for the female singer at that time, whether as a private pupil or as a student at a conservatoire? The evidence on this question is slight, and in the early part of the century almost non-existent – at least, from the perspective of the singers themselves. But we certainly know what successful singers and teachers thought student life *ought* to be in the latter years of the period. Articles, interviews with singers, and singers' autobiographies invariably stress the 'work, hard work, endless work' (in the words of the soprano Frieda Hempel) necessary for the novice.[95] Geraldine Farrar said that the 'very first requisite' of the would-be prima donna is an 'iron will' in order to 'work like a galley slave';[96] Frances Alda wrote that success as a singer depends on the pupil's 'capacity for study, for learning . . . for work';[97] Lilli Lehmann declared that the study required by the singer 'occupies an entire lifetime'.[98] Presumably, this emphasis on effort was a genuine response to the vast numbers of young women who regarded singing as an 'easy' career to fame and fortune and did not realise it also involved lengthy disciplined study. But was it not also an attempt to validate women's work, to demonstrate that behind the diva's glamorous image lay a serious artist engaged in laborious tasks? If so, some commentators thought the protesting was overdone. An article in *The Musical Standard* in 1914 quotes the opinions of the soprano Emmy Destinn, who warned young women who considered singing an easy alternative to the confines of the home: 'Domestic work may often be drudgery . . . but it is a picnic compared with the drudgery those have to undergo who want to become opera singers.' Unfortunately, Destinn claims, 'barely one in a hundred girls' who attempt this path 'have the courage or the brains to make such sacrifices and do such work'.[99] The reporter is unimpressed:

> We know that the life of the singer is not all honey, but what calling is? . . . Nevertheless, we know musical artists who have a very good time of it, and if by chance if they happen to captivate the fancy of the public as Miss Destinn most surely has, then the returns for a youth spent in unremitting labour are great indeed. Many an opera singer has retired on a fortune long before most men – and no women – have begun to 'make their pile'.

So what was the reality of student life? As I mentioned earlier, published accounts of singers were invariably self-censored and concerned with constructing a particular image for public consumption, and can only offer us a limited understanding. Nevertheless, it might be fair to assume that experiences differed, according to temperament and circumstances. Kathleen Howard, eminently sensible, financially very well supported by her patrons and chaperoned by her sister, provided us with this measured account of student life in Paris during 1905–06:

> But I should not recommend Paris as the best school for the ordinary American student of singing, who has no real opportunity to penetrate into French life. There is no lack of sincerity in the real French institutions, the Conservatoire, the schools of art, the Sorbonne – there are found concentration, competition, and keenness enough. But the foreign student does not ordinarily come into contact with those institutions. In the Paris vocal studios, as I know them, there is a dissipation instead of a conservation of energy. The students expect to

win the crown without running the race, and money and influence play too great a rôle. They (vocal students, I mean) tend to exaggerate their little emotions into *grandes passions*, and hold the most disproportionate view of their own importance. I do not mean to say that I agree with a certain singer who brought back harrowing tales of immorality among American singers in Europe. Amongst all the hundreds of vocal students I have known, I never met one case of flagrant misbehaviour. In general the girls live quietly and strive according to their lights, though there is not one in twenty with resolution enough to concentrate on the hard work necessary for a great career. The temptation is to fritter away both time and money on the things that don't matter.[100]

Given that there was still a considerable body of opinion that deemed study abroad and alone an unsuitable occupation for a young woman, Howard's emphasis on the propriety of student life was perhaps judicious; yet equally it may have been a totally honest description of her own particular experiences. In contrast, the English mezzo-soprano Marguerite d'Alvarez (1886–1953) studied at the Brussels conservatoire between 1904 and 1907, and certainly engaged in incidents of 'flagrant misbehaviour' – that is, sexual exploits and adventures. Her memoirs, however, were published posthumously in 1954, and thus respond to a different perception of sexual morality.[101] Would she have been as frank about her experiences if she had been writing, like Howard, in the early 1920s?

Singing was not the only recommended area of study for the aspiring prima donna, whether a private student or enrolled at a conservatoire. Even before the beginning of this period, some teachers advised a broad education for the development of the 'perfect singer', as in this counsel from the Bologna teacher Lorenzo Gibelli (1719–1812):

[she should] know all that concerns music and the essentials of her own language and of acting, and should also have furnished her mind with knowledge of the civil, political, and religious history of the peoples of the world, of the civilisation and customs of different social classes, if possible of all times, not to mention enough philosophy to teach her the course of human passions.[102]

As Rosselli points out, it is unlikely that many students achieved such a formidable range of knowledge. However, professional singers often argued that far more was demanded of them than simply a good voice. Emma Calvé deplored the 'ignorance' of some students, and declared that 'a high intelligence, a well-informed mind, a sensitive and generous heart' were required of the singer: 'History, literature and languages – all these are essential to the development of an interesting artistic career.'[103] But success probably depended above all on the factor described by Blanche Marchesi: she claimed that Garcia rightly converted Rossini's dictum that the essential ingredients for a good singer were 'Primo voce, secondo voce, terzo voce' into 'Primo character, secondo character, terzo character'.[104] It was character that enabled all the different elements of voice, personality, intelligence, creativity, and knowledge to be knitted together into the fabric of a serious artist.

For those singers who were exceptionally gifted and who later enjoyed commensurately exceptional careers, the period of training often seemed relatively tranquil and uneventful – or at least, was made so in the retelling. The Russian soprano Félia Litvinne, studying privately in Paris in the 1880s with Anna Barthe-Banderali and Pauline Viardot, apparently had a thoroughly enjoyable time despite the poverty she endured. To all intents and purposes, she sailed through whatever small obstacles impeded her vocal development until her debut with Victor Maurel in *Simon Boccanegra*. Her older sister Céline, however, clearly suffered at the hands of the elderly Gilbert-Louis Duprez, who, although enthused by her 'incomparable' voice, made her repeat difficult passages too often; she also damaged her voice by smoking.[105] It was Félia who had the brilliant career; that of Céline – even though it was her talent and ambition that had originally brought the family from St Petersburg via Milan and Naples to Paris – never even started.

We must not assume that women's growing interest in a career on the operatic or concert stage emancipated all those who attempted it. Various voices were raised in warning against the aspiring prima donna's ambitions – especially when they entailed expensive periods of study abroad. Clara Louise Kellogg wrote soberly of the 'lighthouse of success' that lured many young women to 'break their wings' against its implacably enclosed beam,[106] and described the 'shoals' of young women who came to her in Paris and Milan 'begging for just enough money to get home with. I have shipped many a failure back to America, and my soul has been sick for their disappointment and disillusionment. But they will not be guided by advice or warning. They have got to learn actually and bitterly.'[107] Far more women than those fortunate few who made a name for themselves were compelled to accept that they had neither the physical nor the mental nor the emotional equipment to fulfil their ambitions. The American mezzo-soprano Eleanora de Cisneros believed European training should only be undertaken once a singer had 'completed her studies in America under a good teacher', and described some of the disasters that occurred when singers lacked the necessary attributes and schooling:

> I know of many American girls, however, who have gone to Italy, and not had such good fortune. They should never have gone at all, for they had neither the voice, nor the temperament, the knowledge of tradition, nor command of the language. Of three such girls who were in a party being taken over by a teacher who promised them an immediate debut, two had spent all their singing lives in church choirs, and while good enough in oratorio, had no operatic style and didn't know what Italian opera is. Another poor girl I remember, whose brother had mortgaged heaven knows how much property to give her a chance at opera. She had neither voice, figure, nor temperament. She should have been kept at home, where she might have done something in small concerts.[108]

What happened to these women? One example is the poet Anna Wickham (1884–1947). A friend of the cellist and feminist May Mukle, Wickham arrived in London in 1904 from her parents' home in Sydney, Australia, to study singing. Her first teacher was George Dukes, a 'good voice producer' but a man she found 'rough', who 'bullied' her. Moreover, her aunts (with whom she was living) 'talked so much about the necessity of hard work that I sang more than ever out of tune'. She was then taught by Madame Randaeggar (the wife of a well-known teacher at the Royal College of Music), who claimed that Wickham would 'set the Thames on fire in eight months'. Still Wickham does not seem to have been able to settle to her work: she was lonely, unable to find friends, and saddled herself instead with a fiancé (the journalist William Ray) who declared in an angry scene that she should give up her ambitions and marry him instead.[109] Finding herself caught between Ray and another admirer, Patrick Hepburn, she left for Paris, believing that if her voice was any good she should get the best instruction possible. She unsuccessfully applied for entrance to the Conservatoire, and was then taught privately by Jean de Reszke, who supposedly told her that she 'had the best voice he had ever had from England'.[110] But within a few short months she abandoned Paris for marriage to Hepburn; a career that had once looked promising leaked insidiously away.

What went wrong? Although it is impossible to judge in retrospect, she seems to have had some kind of potential as a singer – at least, her son remembers her possessing 'a truly remarkable voice with a range of three octaves and a very full tone in the upper register'.[111] Wickham herself largely blamed her husband for both interrupting her studies and for his lack of support thereafter, whilst he argued that she never would have had a career anyway. Perhaps what her brief autobiography reveals is that although singing was important to her, it was less so than her need for companionship and her desire to experience life. (Marchesi would no doubt have hissed 'character, character, character' at her.) And crucially, Wickham also seems to have been on her own – without the support system of stage mother or patrons or even good friends enjoyed by many (if not all) the successful singers. She in part blamed her isolation as a result of class, claiming that had she been part of Sydney's fashionable society, she would have been sent to study in Europe through a subscription of patrons.[112]

Another casualty of the era was Susy Clemens (1872–96), the daughter of Mark Twain. Susy had a 'fine soprano voice' and ambitions for the operatic stage.[113] In the early 1890s she was taken to Europe by her parents to study with Blanche Marchesi, but her vocal abilities were increasingly marred by a physical weakness that nowadays probably would be diagnosed as a form of anorexia.[114] Marchesi sent her away to recuperate, as Susy recorded in a letter to her closest female friend (and possibly her lover): 'Marchesi said some pleasant and unexpected things about my voice but insisted she could do nothing with me in my present state of health.'[115] However, Susy never sufficiently regained her physical strength, and eventually returned to America. There she died in 1896 of spinal meningitis. In the hours shortly before her death, she wrote approximately a thousand words of what appear to be delirious ravings centred on the opera singer Maria Malibran. It began as follows:

> [You?] will be held by and obey me in order that you can hold & command the world. Say I will try not to doubt and I *will* obey my benefactress Mme. Malibran Now I can better hold you. You must not deliberately question me & my wisdom while I am only making the destiny which you feel in your heart possible. I do not allow such treatment Say 'I will obey Mme Malibran' 'I freely decide to obey Mme. Malibran.' Now go on and *hold* this song. Nothing but indecision Go on Go on . . .'[116]

These feverish scribblings have caused some puzzlement.[117] Was Susy engaged in an imaginary conversation with Malibran? And if so, why? However, Susy (on her father's advice) was a recent convert to a kind of 'mental science' that mixed elements of hypnotism and spiritualism,[118] and it is clear that this form of 'treatment' was being actively employed in her efforts to become a singer[119] – an approach all too reminiscent of the Svengali style described in *Trilby* (1894). Surely, these last writings of Susy owe something to the sessions she spent with the 'mind-curists':[120] the building of belief in her talents, the adjurations to 'obey' so that she can 'hold and command the world', the use of a famous but long deceased prima donna as a kind of guardian angel empowered to remove the doubts and anxieties about her capabilities. If so, Susy Clemens perhaps stands as an example of the desperation experienced by those young women whose dream of operatic success slipped into nightmare.

But the fullest account of a singer who 'almost made it' is that of Viola Tree (1885–1938). Her experiences at the end of this period illustrate the vast social changes that had occurred in the profession. She too was a *figlia dell'arte*; but this was no social outcast fettered by the red silken rope, like Maria Malibran in the 1820s. Tree was the daughter of Sir Herbert Beerbohm Tree, one of the first knights of the British stage. Her circle of close friends included aristocracy and the Oxbridge set of Edwardian England: even the prime minister, Herbert Asquith, was a fond correspondent. Her career began as an actress, in her father's company: her favourite role was Trilby. Perhaps it was in her playing of this character that her dreams of a singing career began; certainly it was at this time she decided that she would never have a 'great career' as an actress, but might do so as a singer. Two years of study at the Royal College of Music went well, including opera performances and concerts where she made 'quite good money'. Then, in 1910, she decided to spend a year in Italy, in order to acquire a 'more powerful voice'.[121] Accompanied by her singing teacher, Visetti, she travelled to Milan, and there began two years of study.

Personally acquainted with a range of musicians – including Tosti, Grainger, Quilter, Tovey, Fauré and Debussy – as well as many actors, Tree can hardly be considered a novice in the theatrical world. And yet in many respects she showed as much naivety as the most cloistered middle-class entrant. In particular, her expectations far exceeded her talents, if not her future potential. Tosti's letters of introduction opened all kinds of doors for her, including that of the leading publisher and impresario of the day, Tito Ricordi. He advised her on a suitable teacher – Madame Arkel – and identified with blunt honesty the source of her current difficulties: 'these high notes are worth fifteen cents'.[122] Perhaps, with slow and patient study, this problem would have been resolved. But Tree's ambitions, and also her temperament, did not permit such a methodical approach: she sought stardom, and as quickly as possible. She clearly still saw herself in some way as Trilby; when her teacher says that she has three separate voices, or that she can't decide if Tree is a soprano or a contralto, Tree recalls only the comments made about Trilby's miraculous extended voice.[123] But progress is slow – sometimes non-existent. Within six weeks her voice is making a 'strained, cracked sound'.[124] Over the next two years there is some sporadic improvement, but Tree obviously never builds a solid technique, or really understands what her voice should be. She never sings at all, except at her daily lessons; whether this is at the bidding of her teacher or from her own inclination is uncertain. She goes continually to other teachers and other impresarios, looking for answers and advice – looking, perhaps, for Svengali – and finding only conflicting opinions that leave her ever more confused. In effect she loses ownership of her voice.

Unlike Wickham and Clemens, Viola Tree did finally perform on the operatic stage – briefly, in two performances of *La traviata* at Cormons. It was here that perhaps the real damage to her voice began, courtesy of attempting a role beyond her natural vocal tessitura and singing with a bad cold. A temporary hoarseness became chronic. Trying to get well again for her debut as Salome almost six months later at Genoa, the middle of her voice by now non-existent, she makes a final disastrous rehearsal for the impresario and conductor:

> The first passage of *Salome* wants delicate and petulant singing, right in the middle of one's voice. I started on the right bar, but it was simply a blank – the voice was not there.
>
> I must have gone on singing in a rather doped way, for they stopped me, and put me on the big aria – 'Sono in-amorato [sic] del tuo corpo', with its silvery nightingale passion. It is on very high notes, with large drops into the bass, and I suppose I made something of it; but I knew it had taken all my strength, and that in the morning I should have no voice left. I was very glad that it removed the last doubt. We all said very little, our group just melted away.
>
> I think, knowing the truth suddenly, and however bitterly, always gives you a thrill of exultation, for the moment at all events. I had the feeling of certainty, of courage, which all the castles in the air had never given me.

In response to the subsequent telegram to her waiting husband in England ('Useless, darling . . . Tell Mother gently'), he writes only: 'Most dear Viola, come home quickly.'[125]

Amongst the correspondence Viola Tree reprints in her autobiography is a letter from another close family friend, Bernard Shaw. His advice about the whole notion of tuition illustrates how far the profession had moved from eighteenth-century practices. Responding to Tree's anxieties about her voice and the effect of nerves, he argued that she should abandon her studies:

> Don't you know that there are no perfect voices, and never will be? Don't you know that the teachers who profess to manufacture those voices (just one year more, whilst the guineas last) can't sing themselves, and can't show a single pupil with such a voice? Don't you know that when — appeared as a pupil of —, and — as a pupil of —, they simply paid for six lessons, and the right to make the announcement, with perhaps a cadenza or two, and a little correction of their Australian and Liverpudlian pronunciation of French and Italian?[126] Don't you know that the people who know how to sing may be divided into those who taught themselves, and those who were taught – like De Reszke and myself – by their mothers? . . . I know what can be taught and what cannot; and I know the tricks of the trade; and I can most positively assure you that every night you spend off the stage, every note you sing without paying audiences listening (bar your scales in the morning), is a night further from success, and a thousand-pound-note-worth of youth and beauty thrown away. You'd better by far sing 'Annie Laurie' on Margate Sands, and take a collection in your hat afterwards, than sing 'Una voce', or 'Bel raggio' for the fiftieth time at a professor's piano, and dream of paralysing the Scala with it next year. *Next year never comes*: remember that. 'Credit given tomorrow' is an instructive Italian trattoria sign.[127]

Shaw's argument that singing can only really be learnt through actual engagement in public performance, however modest, was echoed also by Ricordi: these two men, wrote Tree, gave her the only consistently good advice of her career. Had the industry of training – the development of the musical institutions, the expansion of private teaching – really served to develop talent and prepare it better for the profession? Or had it, with its codifications and muddled methodologies, its plethora of conflicting claims, its abandonment of the ideas of artistic individuality in favour of a processed product, simply confused and disenfranchised the novice singer? If at the end of the period, the myth of Svengali had become an appropriate metaphor for the aims and claims of the teaching industry, too often the student singer – like Viola Tree – was merely reduced to a Trilby *before* his guidance, to a wandering, uncertain voice.

The development of a career – especially in an era that regarded working women and even more, *theatrical* working women with deep distrust – was rarely the result of the singer's solitary labour. The creation of stardom required concerted efforts by at least one or more members of the family. Clara Schumann, herself the daughter of professional musicians, described in her diary in 1840 the travails of Elise List (1822–93), a singer from an ordinary German middle-class family with a 'heavenly, beautiful voice'. List's attempts to begin a professional career were marred by nerves, which Schumann attributed to a lack of family support:

> Elise suffers and complains of stage-fright; she wants to please everyone, and that won't work. Everyone gives her different advice, and thus she will end up completely confused, unless she makes her appearance resolutely and decisively and sings what *she* wants [to sing]. I pity her: she has neither a musical father nor a musical mother who could advise her. But it is astonishing how broadly this girl has educated herself without any guidance and despite resistance on the part of her parents (earlier that is).

List never sufficiently overcame this problem, and her putative career subsided into marriage. Her younger sister Lina might have suffered as a consequence; although Lina had a 'great talent for music', Schumann remarked that 'it will be suppressed in her; the mother wants to make a housewife of her because [a career in music] did not work out with the two oldest [daughters]. How pitiful is such a thing!'[1]

The engagement of mother, father or husband in the daily business of career building was often seen askance, however. Both stage mothers and husbands attracted particular scorn, because both disrupted the conventional gender models: stage mothers by inter-vening in the male-dominated environment of the operatic market-place; husbands by being financially dependent on their wives' success. Only the father of the prima donna could behave in a manner more appropriate to the century's ethos, by ensuring his daughter's protection and – at the same time – selling her as a commodity.

In the earlier decades of the period, it is the stage father who seems more obviously in evidence. Isabella Colbran is accompanied by her father to Paris (and later is apparently so bereft of his guidance on his death that she marries Rossini);[2] Nicola Tacchinardi exhibits his barely adolescent daughters in concerts;[3] Garcia schools the young Malibran so severely that she learns to sing perfectly even whilst sobbing.[4] Both Tacchinardi and Garcia were singers themselves, and their tutelage of their daughters into the family profession was a normal part of artistic life. But by the mid-century, two fictional accounts in music periodicals depict another type of father – the bourgeois man who, having lost all his wealth, exploits his daughter's talents to rebuild the family fortunes.[5]

Fathers continued to be important figures in their daughters' ca-reers as the century progressed; but stage mothers also became more prominent, despite the opprobrium that met their efforts. In his remi-niscences in 1890, Willert Beale presented them as an indispensable but troublesome item in the prima donna's entourage:

> If unmarried, [the prima donna] is guarded by her mother, or a duenna representing her maternal parent, to whom all must bow down to be sure of a favourable reception by the songstress. The impresario, if a prudent man, will conciliate mamma before attempting to discuss a new costume, or any topic not specified in the agreement, with her daughter. The agreement apart, he will not prosper in his business relations with his leading lady without mamma's approval.[6]

Such mockery was a well-established tradition: Benedetto Marcello devoted an entire chapter to the stage mother in his satirical exam-ination of Italian opera in 1720.[7] She also found her way on-stage in various operatic farces. In Haydn's *La canterina* (1766), the stage mother colludes with her daughter's amorous intrigues, advises her on the kind of make-up she should use in order to outshine her rival artists, and interrupts her singing lesson with dictates on vocal technique.[8] In Donizetti's *Le convenienze ed inconvenienze teatrali* (1827/1831), Mamm'Agata attempts to increase the importance of the role of her daughter, the seconda donna – but instead ends up by ousting the Musico and taking the role herself.[9] In both operas the stage mother is played by a baritone, which increases the comic possibilities of the role but also betrays the fact that many of these protective and resolute mothers were seen as positively masculine in the manner in which they defended their daughters' interests. Beale supplied further credence to this notion:

> The mother of a prima donna is equal to any emergency. She is at once a clever foil, a ready-made excuse, a permanent apology, an efficient representative, and as excellent a means of evading an unpleasant proposition as any sleeping partner ever referred to. She has been described as a man of business in long clothes, and often represents the self-constituted mother of a complete Italian Opera Company. To fill such a position with *éclat*, the authority in question should be of uncertain age, of a tall dragoon-like figure, bold and energetic in speech, penetrating in voice, and conciliatory in manner, when boldness has effectually subdued any rebellious thoughts in minds of her large family.[10]

The influence of Donizetti's representation of the stage mother (based on Antonio Sografi's earlier plays) is also evident in other respects. In the 1830s, *Il pirata* published an article entitled 'Le madri dell'attrici';[11] in the 1850s, the *Corriere delle dame* did a similar item under the heading of 'La Mamma Agata'.[12] In both, the stage mother is demonstrated as a fiction: these are not 'real' mothers, but fakes – 'madams' who prey off the greedy ambitions of young women, and who whore their supposed 'daughters' to the richest, most influential persons on the operatic circuit. The legacy of these derisive and unflattering portraits exists still; one much respected scholar describes events surrounding the casting of Donizetti's *Maria Stuarda* in 1835: 'The *comprimaria* role of Anna was coveted by Rafaella

Vernier, a contralto without appreciable talent, whose mother actively campaigned for her daughter's engagement (shades of *Le convenienze!*), but eventually that part went to Teresa Moja.'[13] The implication here is clearly that Vernier's mother had no business interceding on her daughter's behalf. Other stage mothers are simply excised from their daughters' history: a dictionary entry for Gemma Bellincioni states that she was taught by her father, when her autobiography makes it clear that it was her mother who was responsible for her tuition.[14]

That stage mothers should be dismissed in such terms even now testifies to the enduring power of their image as meddlers and sycophants. As we shall see, some mothers undoubtedly invited justifiable ridicule. And yet, many were indeed 'indispensable', and deserving of more serious consideration. Their involvement and support were important factors that made a career possible for a number of singers, and ensured that their daughters gained wider horizons of opportunity than had been previously open to themselves.

Who then was this 'man of business in long clothes'? Investigating her identity and contribution is by no means straightforward. In Bermani's tale of Clelia, her father is transformed from a cobbler into 'a venerable captain': 'These transmutations are extremely common in the family trees of the *prime donne assolute*.'[15] Maretzek made similar claims about the stage mother:

> The next important step in the life of many divas when arrived at the age of discretion, is to give to their mothers a suitable and becoming education, so as to make them fit for the high position they are destined to occupy as mothers of divas behind the scenes, and to make them presentable to the future worshipers at the shrine of the coming operatic divinity.[16]

The tendency to represent the maternal parent in the best possible light is indeed evident in many descriptions of the singers' families, as Mathilde Marchesi demonstrated: 'My beloved mother was to me the incarnation of everything that is good, noble and beautiful. She was, in fact, not only an exemplary wife and mother, but was also the beau-ideal of a German woman.'[17] Frieda Hempel similarly praised her mother's physical beauty and 'perfect disposition': 'we all idolised her', she wrote – even though two pages later clear tensions are apparent over her mother's preferential treatment of Hempel's brother.[18] Exaggeration and sentimentality thus obscure many singers' accounts of their families. But this was not always due simply to a singer's vanity, or even a desire to protect the parent in the eyes of the public by drawing a veil over personal shortcomings: rather, it also indicates anxiety about conforming to the new morality of the stage. A singer's family background, and particularly possession of a 'good' mother, was evidence of a certain level of social standing and respectability. These deliberately effusive portraits were perhaps also attempts to distance real mothers from the satirical images in the press and other literature.

Some stage mothers limited their involvement in their daughter's careers to encouragement, support and practical assistance. The German contralto Ernestine Schumann-Heink (1861–1936) recalled the efforts of her invariably pregnant and poverty-stricken mother to secure her a career by finding her singing teachers,[19] persuading her husband that choosing a life as an opera singer did not mean that their daughter would become a 'bad woman',[20] colluding in the lies that enabled Schumann-Heink to attend the audition that began her professional career (against the wish of her father), and then caring for her daughter's babies when the young singer was abandoned by her first husband and forced to pay off his debts. Without such aid, Schumann-Heink might never have achieved success.

Other mothers engaged in the building of their daughter's career, accompanied them into the workplace, and acted as their agents – with mixed results. Their attempts at negotiation are often recorded negatively by impresarios, suggesting both a certain prejudice against these women and also, at times, their own lack of knowledge and expertise. In July 1836, Spontini wrote to Friedrich Wilhelm III of his triumph in securing a contract with Clara Heinefetter despite 'so many difficulties and obstinacies on the part of this singer and her mother': the correspondence as a whole, however, reveals that

Spontini was exaggerating in order to convince the king (the real source of the contractual 'difficulties', owing to his wish not to engage Heinefetter) that a hard bargain had been struck.[21] Benjamin Lumley deplored the efforts of Marietta Piccolomini's mother to protect her daughter in the 1850s:

> The spirit and ardour of the 'pet' never for one moment flagged. Yet she must have had much with which to contend, both within and without the walls of the theatre. The Countess Piccolomini, her mother, although born in a higher sphere, was, in all her connexion with the stage, the veritable type of the '*mere* [sic] *d'artiste.*' Now she discouraged her sprightly and buoyant daughter by constant grumblings, predicting that every new part she undertook would be a '*fiasco*'. Now she harassed the management with complaints that her daughter was being worn to death by exertions and over-fatigue . . . But Marietta was never happy except when she found herself upon the stage, 'I have a hard task between you', I said to her, good-humouredly; 'your mother complains that I make you sing too much, and you that I make you sing too little.'[22]

Marchesi claimed that a pupil of hers was forbidden to accept a 'good engagement' because her mother determined that she should only sing leading roles: 'As no theatrical manager would accept such an insane proposition, and as the obstinate mamma would not give in, the poor girl had to relinquish her artistic aspiration.'[23] Attempts to intervene directly in the artistic process were especially unwelcome, as we can see from Henry Wood's description of a rehearsal in Manchester in 1912:

> An American soprano,[24] I remember, introduced to this country by Oscar Hammerstein, appeared at one of the concerts, and I know I went to a good deal of trouble over a rehearsal with her in Queen's Hall. The frequent stoppages, unfortunately, were misinterpreted by her mother who was sitting just within the little curtains at the side of the platform. She seemed to think I was interfering with her daughter's interpretation; at all events, she came on to the platform. She then made a little speech in which she expressed her opinions rather definitely. I explained that I was doing everything I could for her daughter. Then she began to argue which was more than I could endure. To the intense amusement of the

orchestra I dismissed the lady by saying: 'In any case, Madam, *I don't conduct mothers!*' It was a few minutes before they quietened down and we could proceed with the rehearsal.[25]

It is clear that stage mothers and fathers were not always motivated by selfless concern for their daughters' interests. Some singers, groomed by these energetic parents for operatic stardom from their earliest years, found their professional life had been designed not to afford them personal fulfilment but as a means of providing fame and fortune for the whole family. In the mid-1820s, Eugène Malibran recognised that a proposal of marriage for the young Maria Garcia, newly emergent as one of the most exciting operatic artists of the decade, would disturb the aspirations of her 'severe' father (who had so relentlessly drilled her in her singing) for financial security;[26] Maria, all too eager to escape the attentions of her paternal taskmaster, married him nonetheless twenty-two days later. A similar tension is visible in the history of British soprano Clara Novello (1818–1908), daughter of Mary Sabilla Novello and the composer and music publisher Vincent Novello. Clara's interest in performance was provoked by her father's music-making, but it was her mother's ambition of making her into a 'famous prima donna' that was the driving force behind her career.[27] Dubbed the 'Wilful Woman' by Leigh Hunt,[28] Mary Novello arranged for Clara to study in Paris and Italy, took her to visit Rossini, and chaperoned her at numerous professional engagements. Despite the success that resulted from such careful organisation, Clara herself harboured secret desires for domesticity. A collision course with her mother was inevitable; when in 1843 Clara decided to marry an Italian aristocrat (Count Giovanni Battista Gigliucci), Mary Novello was incensed. Her biographer claims she regarded 'Clara, the prima donna, as partly of her own creation and to her pride in her daughter she added pride in her own achievement and her hopes, as she had told Sir John, of financial gains'. In Mary Novello's eyes, Gigliucci was not an eligible suitor, but 'the destroyer of her handiwork', whom she bitterly resented.[29] Clara proceeded with her plans, and following the wishes of her husband gave up singing altogether. Mother and daughter were finally reconciled after several years' estrangement, perhaps because the marriage was genuinely successful, perhaps also because Clara eventually resumed her professional life when Gigliucci's financial and political position suffered during the turmoil preceding Italian unification. Given her willing return to the stage, was Clara's earlier preference for marriage rather than career primarily a desire to escape parental control? Were many of the freedoms associated with the life of a prima donna largely non-existent in cases such as this, where the singer was kept in a permanently childlike state by a well-meaning but overbearing parent?

Problems about marriage and financial control resurface in the experiences of the American soprano Emma Eames. When Eames, having only recently achieved public success, wanted to marry, her mother insisted that she wait for a period of two years or until Emma had paid off the debts Mrs Eames had incurred during the funding of her daughter's vocal training.[30] Eames disobeyed and married secretly in 1891 in London, creating a split with Mrs Eames that lasted for nine months.[31] But marriage finally gave her proper knowledge of the financial side of her career for the first time:

> Incidentally, this same winter also saw me have a bank account that was entirely my own, and draw my first check. Hitherto my mother had never allowed me to have a separate account or to know how much I had. In fact, I had never been given any but the haziest idea of my financial affairs until that winter. When my uncle, General Thomas Hyde, of Civil War fame, decided that I must have my chance in Boston, he and my mother made all the arrangements without taking me into their confidence. And then, after we left Boston and went to Paris, my mother assumed the management and control of all moneys; and it was not until my marriage on August 1, 1891, that I had the handling of the money which I had earned.[32]

Unlike that of Clara Novello, Eames's marriage ended in divorce. In both these instances, we see that certain prima donnas differed little from many women during that era in needing to use marriage as a device to escape parental domination. A career was by no means an immediate route to autonomy.

Given the difficulties many singers encountered in marriage,[33] however, it is hardly surprising that stage mothers attempted to protect their daughters' prospects so vehemently. If Novello and Eames risked confrontation on this issue, other singers accepted parental rulings with sometimes unfortunate consequences. Amanda Norton, the mother of Lillian Nordica, found herself in a quandary when her daughter decided to marry the rich but unpleasantly boorish Fred Gower, and was reminded of an earlier conversation with the soprano Clara Louise Kellogg:

> We met Miss Kellogg in St Petersburg, and found her very unhappy to think she had made her musical career, but in her advancing age was *alone*. She blamed her mother very much – for she had several opportunities to marry well, but her mother persuaded her from her own judgment, and now she is sorry, too late. Lillian said then, she would never wish to find herself old, and without sympathy. So I can only say, 'Do not be in a hurry.' But of course I can say nothing against Mr Gower.[34]

Chaperonage was a primary aspect of the stage mother's responsibilities, as a means of protecting the singer herself from unwanted sexual advances and also her reputation from scurrilous gossips. Kellogg was subject to the close scrutiny of her mother throughout her career – a consequence of her middle-class family's claims to respectability and their ignorance of her professional milieu. Mrs Kellogg's anxiety about her daughter's safety and reputation was such that she continued to accompany Clara's long tours even when she herself became old and ailing.[35] Although her mother's presence undoubtedly gave the genteel Kellogg access to the morally suspect environs of the theatre, the singer found such chaperonage more of a hindrance than a help in the development of her career. She described her mother as a 'very strait-laced and puritanical' woman who 'hated the atmosphere of the theatre' even though she 'gloried' in Kellogg's successes:

To her rigid and delicate mind there was something dreadful in the free and easy artistic attitude, and she always stood between me and any possible intimacy with my fellow-singers. I believe this to have been a mistake. Many traditions of the stage come to one naturally and easily through others; but I had to wait and learn them all by experience. I was always working as an outsider, and, naturally, this attitude of ours antagonised singers with whom we appeared.

Not only that. My brain would have developed much more rapidly if I had been allowed – no, if I had been *obliged* to be more self-reliant. To profit by one's own mistakes; – all the world's history goes to show that is the only way to learn. By protecting me, my mother really robbed me of much precious experience. For how many years after I had made my début would she wait for me in the *coulisses*, ready to whisk me off to my dressing-room before any horrible opera singer had a chance to talk with me![36]

Such assiduity was not merely a product of the Victorian age, nor of prudish American mothers. As late as the 1920s, Iva Pacetti recalls annoying Toscanini at La Scala by arriving at rehearsals 'chaperoned by my mother'.[37] Her contemporary Sara Scuderi, another Italian soprano, was accompanied around the opera-house circuit by her 'very strict' mother for twenty-eight years, and was clearly discouraged from giving reign to her 'private emotions' by establishing relationships with men. When her mother became a 'total invalid', Scuderi retired in order to look after her because she felt she 'owed a great debt to her' and did not wish to leave her in the care of others. Leaving the stage was a 'hard decision'.[38]

If the prima donna's own mother was unavailable, other women could perform this dual role of protector and companion. Lillie de Hegermann-Lindencrone remarked on the cleverness of Christine Nilsson in providing herself with just such a figure in Paris in 1865, who had 'surrounded herself by a wall of propriety, in the shape of an English *dame de compagnie*, and never moves unless followed by her. This lady (Miss Richardson) is correctness and primness personified, and so *comme il faut* that it is actually oppressive to be in the same room with her.'[39] Singers themselves might also function as quasi-stage mothers or chaperones for their colleagues. The opera impresario Henry Mapleson recorded the intervention of Therese Tietjens (1831–77) on behalf of a young singer, Mlle. Guarducci, who had been the object of the 'rather conspicuous' attentions of the Duke of Cirillo in 1859. Tietjens suggested that Mapleson ask the Duke what his intentions were towards the singer; when 'no satisfactory answer could be obtained, Mlle. Tietjens took Guarducci entirely under her charge, and all communication with the Italian nobleman was put an end to'. Tietjens then refused to allow the thwarted lover to see Guarducci again unless he proposed marriage. This he did, and a wedding (attended by the opera company) duly took place. This guardianship of Guarducci by her knowledgeable colleagues also protected her subsequent professional and financial interests: Mapleson states that he supervised the drawing up of a marriage settlement in which it was stipulated that Guarducci should retain the 'liberty to resume the exercise of her profession, and take the whole of the benefits she might derive therefrom for her own use'.[40] (The marriage was apparently successful.)

An intriguing portrait of one particular mother–daughter relationship emerges through the autobiographies of two singers: Gemma Bellincioni and her daughter Bianca Stagno-Bellincioni. The mother in question here is Carlotta Soroldoni, mother of Gemma – and herself a professional singer. Bellincioni was a *figlia dell'arte*; yet for much of her childhood she had very little access to the stage. Rather, she was sent away to school, in part so that Carlotta could accompany her husband on tour (and thus limit his infidelities). In Bellincioni's autobiography, her mother receives relatively orthodox treatment, mentioned dutifully in the second sentence of the book: 'a good musician and prize-winner from the Conservatorio di Milano, she gave me singing lessons, thus initiating me in my future career'.[41] As both tutor and chaperone to her daughter, Carlotta schooled Bellincioni in vocal technique during her adolescence, and then accompanied her during her early years of professional engagements. Moral supervision was uppermost in her mind. When they met the ageing but still roguish tenor Tamberlick, he looked at Bellincioni appreciatively and said 'Bella ragazza. . .' ; 'Ma buona', retorted her mother promptly and pointedly.[42] Carlotta defended Bellincioni vigorously during various disputes in the company, endured miseries of indigestion at her daughter's treatment by gossipy rivals, and even threw herself on to the stage in the middle of a performance to protect Bellincioni from the consequences of a violent argument between another singer and a critic.[43] It was Bellincioni's father, however, who undertook the business management of his daughter's career, and the negotiations with impresari and agents.[44]

Although Bellincioni was obviously closer to her father, she nevertheless wrote about her mother with reserved affection. Her own daughter Bianca's portrait of her grandmother, however, was much sterner. Where Bellincioni only hinted at differences with her mother (was the latter still alive at this point?), Bianca was more forthright. Her grandmother was 'rigid of body and character', a strict conformist to the moral codes of the day, and a dictator in appearance, attitudes and ideas.[45] Only reluctantly and for economic reasons did she permit her two daughters a theatrical career, and her tutelage of Gemma's training was severe:

> Everything was forbidden that was not study – preparation for the career that had to be considered seriously; for hours and hours she kept her daughter at the piano to sing vocalises and scales that had to be, as she said, like pearls. No recreation, no dreams, no possibility of growing close to anyone.[46]

But despite Carlotta's watchful chaperonage, Bellincioni fell in love with a married tenor some twenty-six years her senior, Roberto Stagno, during a South American tour. Even here, Bellincioni remains circumspect:

> Then began the battle with my family, who did not intend to lose the authority they had until then maintained over me . . . but Stagno was not a man to draw back before an obstacle. He sustained me by showing me a wholly new horizon to pursue in order to reach the artistic destination that he was dreaming of for me, emancipating me from all those little bourgeois ideas in which I had lived until then.[47]

Again, Bianca is more open, describing her grandmother's reaction to the relationship as 'severe and inflexible'. Fighting with all the weapons she possessed, this 'exasperated, exasperating woman' tried to restrict Stagno's access to her daughter, locking her in her room at night, and keeping up a barrage of veiled allusions to his 'conscience as a mature man, to his responsibilities'. All was in vain. We might assume that Bellincioni's emancipation from the 'little bourgeois ideas' included sexual activity: certainly she fell pregnant. She no longer saw her family: she herself was 'disgusted' by their lack of understanding and made no step towards them; her 'good and affectionate' sister was too timid to take the initiative and in any case was kept in the dark about the coming event; her father sometimes muttered a word in her defence, but 'all were directed and dominated by the inflexible baton of Carlotta Bellincioni, wounded to the deepest sensibility of her principles and perhaps . . . to her maternal heart that wrongly she never spoke of'.[48] Bellincioni therefore gave birth alone in Budapest, where she was singing, aided only by the elder sister of her father, who defied the family disapproval to be with her. Her relationship with Stagno seems to have irrevocably broken the ties with her mother – at least, both Bellincioni and Bianca are silent on the matter of whether the rift was ever resolved.

Bellincioni's history illustrates the degree to which breaking social conventions of sexual behaviour could create as much friction within the family of the late nineteenth-century artist as it might amongst the most bourgeois of households. And it is again apparent how the family saw the prima donna daughter as making all their fortunes: Bellincioni describes how, immediately after signing the contract for her South American tour, her father rented first an apartment 'in order to give himself some airs fitting the position' of the father of a rising star, and then before she had even embarked on the voyage, had bought a small villa as the 'nest destined to accommodate the Diva' on her return.[49] Bellincioni's liaison with an unsuitable man thus jeopardised the well-being of all. But it is possible also to see Carlotta's behaviour not simply as the manoeuvrings of a domestic dictator, but as awkward attempts to protect her daughter from disappointments she had herself endured. A former prima donna herself, who had found it difficult to combine career, children and marriage, she was initially reluctant to encourage Gemma's ambitions; once decided, however, she implemented a rigorous regime of training in order to provide her with the best chance at success. Similarly understandable is Carlotta's extreme anxiety about Bellincioni's affair with Stagno: clearly unhappy with her own inconstant husband (they later separated permanently) and well aware of Stagno's reputation, Carlotta obviously wished to protect her daughter from a similar fate.

A rather more positive image of the relationship between stage mother and prima donna is illustrated by Amanda Norton and her daughter Lillian Nordica: two women perhaps more temperamentally compatible than Bellincioni and her mother. Unlike Carlotta Soroldoni, Mrs Norton belonged to that group of women for whom the musical and artistic circles of the prima donna were far removed. The Nortons eked out a precarious living, settling finally in Boston where Edwin Norton set up as a photographer with little success. Lillian was the last of six daughters. An older sister, Wilhelmina, had already shown considerable promise as a singer, but died of typhoid fever before her ambitions could be realised.[50] When two years later the Nortons discovered that their youngest child displayed similar talent, Lillian's latent possibilities as a prima donna were carefully cherished. In 1875, Lillian moved down to New York for further training, accompanied by her mother. Amanda Norton's life would now be spent almost permanently with Lillian, returning home only for brief periods, until her death in 1891. Her husband died in 1881.

Amanda Norton provides a rare example of a nineteenth-century stage mother whose own voice has survived, via the correspondence she wrote to her family of her daughter's travails and triumphs. During Lillian's long period of study in America and then Europe, mother and daughter survived only by pouring everything beyond what was required for the most frugal existence into lessons and tuition designed to build the young singer into a prima donna. At times, Amanda Norton blanched at the risks they were taking: 'The distance between us and home! The work ahead!!! The critical world!!! The expense!!!! The danger of losing health!!!!!'[51] In another letter home in 1880, two years after their arrival in Europe, she revealed that she was 'horrid homesick, but I do not say it to Lilly, for she has enough to do, and think of, without worrying about me, so I have only to bear it and say nothing'.[52] But success on a grand scale was not far away. Lillian's elder sister Onie was bowled over by the life-style she found on a visit to Paris in 1882: 'The half can never be written nor told . . . Lillie lives in Paris with magnificent apartments such as I never was in before, with servants and horse and carriage and coachman, can entertain any of her friends or relatives who will take the pains to come and see her, and she has done it all by the *sweat of her brow.*'[53]

There is little evidence that Amanda Norton involved herself directly in negotiations with opera house managements, although she was more than capable of springing to her daughter's defence if she considered it necessary. In 1882, she wrote a stinging rebuttal to newspaper accusations that Nordica had procured the applause of the audience by means of 'an unusually powerful claque' during her successful debut at the Paris Opéra.[54] Her exposure of corruption and bribery amongst opera reviewers was published in the Boston *Home Journal*, and the 'detractors and commentators, the mockers, advisers, and critics retired in confusion'.[55] Here at least a stage mother's intervention secured an honourable outcome for her daughter.

Determined, sensible, courageous, loyal, inordinately proud of her daughter ('I wonder, every time I hear Lilly, how she can have such strength and nerve'),[56] and above all consummately devoted to Lillian's welfare, Amanda Norton fleshes out a different truth behind the two-dimensional satirical portraits of the stage mother. She was indeed a 'mother', with all the partiality and vehemence that might imply. She even survived the crucial marriage problem with her relationship with Lillian intact, despite her own (later justified) reservations about the suitability of her son-in-law. What Nordica herself felt she owed to her mother's support and companionship was perhaps expressed in her book *Hints to Singers* (1923):

> It is *Very Difficult, Almost Impossible, for a Girl to Start Out Alone Upon a Career;* she needs the helpful protection of an older person. I can never tell all that I owe to my mother, so just, so discerning, so thoughtful of my welfare, and of my every interest; and to my father, who made it possible for her to be with me in those earlier years of my musical life . . . Both proved untiringly and fully their deep sympathy for my undertaking.
>
> My Mother spurred me on by her criticism, for she was a severe critic; she shielded me from everything unpleasant that might distract me from my work. Her devotion to me and to my career meant the sacrifice of home ties, and the very giving of her life that we might enjoy the privilege of study and travel together . . .
>
> That is the love and the devotion that goes to make a career, and which receives no public recognition. In such a life of unselfish, of absolute affection, there is no thought of self, no faintest wish for self-aggrandizement. It was enough that she lived in the success of her child.[57]

For these two women, at least, a prima donna's career was made through a genuine and affectionate partnership between mother and daughter.

PROTETTORI AND PATRONS

If the family was an important element in the aspiring prima donna's life, so too were protettori and patrons. There was a subtle distinction between these two types. The role of a protettore might encompass any or all of a number of activities, ranging from sexual partnership, management of business and financial affairs, and social and professional patronage. Fundamentally, it was a person who knew more than the singer about the operatic world, and able thus to guide them appropriately.

Alessandro Micheroux,[58] formerly the singing teacher of Giuditta Pasta, later also functioned as a kind of protettore for her in the

1820s: his correspondence to her is full of advice about her voice, her roles, her negotiations with opera houses, and her dealings with wealthy society patrons. In 1826, for example, he advises her on a point of etiquette towards the Duchess of Berry and the Queen of Naples:

> I enclose the letter of the Duchess of Berry for Her Majesty the Queen. Paër, who received the news of your day of departure, has given it to me with the note of her travelling companion, transcribed here: 'Sottom greets his friend Paër and sends him the letter Her Grace brought yesterday to the Opéra in order to deliver it to Madame Pasta as had been *agreed*; she not having arrived, [the Duchess] sends it to you in charge for her.' There has therefore been a misunderstanding. Now you must write two lines in Italian to Her Grace soon in order to ask her pardon for the misunderstanding, and tell her that you had waited for the Order to go up to her box up until the end of the performance; and then you must thank her for the honour she has done you and the goodwill she has for you. My brother will be able to direct you as to the formalities of the letter and all else. Do not lose time.[59]

In the same letter, he urges her not to make her forthcoming debut in Naples with *Medea*, citing the historical context of earlier performances of this opera at the San Carlo, and the factors peculiar to Pasta's own voice:

> The middle notes of your voice are almost always veiled. This defect is not only precious but indispensable in order to obtain the magical effect in the inflections of an expression I would call 'mysterious': as, for example, in the 'Mi chiami a seguirti fra l'ombre'. In order to obtain this effect, however, the orchestra must not play too loud, since it is necessary you do not force your voice; otherwise that veil, that darkness of timbre clouds the tone and stops it from ringing. Unfortunately, this clamour of the orchestra is a constant accompaniment when Medea sings. And this disadvantage is exacerbated because your singing is always strong [*di forza*] and of a wrathful expression. Therefore your voice loses all its sweetness, and remains inferior to the effect it must produce. The vastness of the auditorium of the San Carlo doubles this disadvantage.[60]

Whether or not Pasta agreed with Micheroux's perceptive analysis is unclear: nevertheless, she did in fact make her debut as Medea a month later, and scored a great success despite her adviser's reservations.[61] (From Micheroux's following letter, it appears she suggested that she had had no alternative.[62])

Micheroux's relationship with Pasta was affectionate, but seemingly purely platonic: he makes frequent references to her husband and family, and writes to her using the formal 'voi' instead of 'tu'. Other rapports between protettore and protégée included a sexual element, such as that between Isabella Colbran and the powerful impresario Domenico Barbaja, or a few years later between the agent Camillo Cirelli and the soprano Giuseppina Strepponi. Their relationship began in 1834; in 1837, Strepponi gave birth to Cirelli's child.[63]

The fact that the role of protettore implied specific knowledge of the operatic marketplace was one reason why such figures were commonly male. But women were also involved in such supportive activities, although the term 'patron' more aptly describes their often more distant relationship from the daily business of operatic production. Female patrons in the earlier part of the era tended to be the aristocratic hostesses of grand salons, like Giulia Samoyloff in Milan in the 1820s and 1830s, or the Princess Cristina Belgiojoso in Paris during the 1840s. The involvement of this stratum of female society continued throughout the period. The Russian soprano Félia Litvinne (1860–1936), motherless, impoverished, and trying to make her debut in Paris during the 1880s, recalled 'a great Russian lady, the comtesse de Galve', who took an interest in her: 'she was goodness itself, and offered me some small subsidies'. The countess gave her two concert dresses (one in white satin, the other in black) and when to this gift was added a pair of diamond earrings, Litvinne declared: 'my joy knew no limits'.[64] She also introduced her to another society hostess, through whom Litvinne met Victor Maurel and subsequently made her debut as Amelia in *Simon Boccanegra* at the Théâtre Italien. In Germany, Ernestine Schumann-Heink met similar kindness in Nina Kienzl, a 'remarkable woman' who had the 'deepest interest' in the young singer and arranged useful introductions to established singers and influential people,[65] including the Princess of Teck and the Queen of Saxony.[66] Lady de Grey provided a comparable service for selected singers in London: after Nellie Melba's unhappy debut at Covent Garden, Lady de Grey invited her to return to sing Juliette (Gounod), citing the interest of the Princess of Wales as an extra fillip and promising her that things would be 'very different': 'You will be under my care and I shall see that you do not lack either friends or hospitality.'[67] She was right: from then on, Melba's London career was assured.

But as bourgeois society developed, many wealthy middle-class women also became involved in musical circles, either via the women's clubs, musical associations, or simply through their own domestic music-making.[68] Urged by commentators such as Fanny Raymond Ritter to support the development of music, many such women gave not only their time but their money.[69] The financial aid provided by such patrons was an invaluable prop for many singers. If women from all social backgrounds increasingly sought a career on the operatic stage, not all had an equal chance. Money, as Clara Louise Kellogg warned, played an important part in securing the first rungs of a singer's career:

> There is something else which is very necessary for every girl to consider in going on the operatic stage. Has she the means of experimenting, or does she have to earn her living in some way meanwhile? If the former is the case, it will do her no harm for her to play about with her voice, burn her fingers if need be, and come home to her mother and father not much worse for the experience. I sympathise somewhat with the teachers for not speaking altogether freely in cases like these. There is no reason why anyone should take from a girl even one remote chance if *she* can afford to take it. But poor girls should be told the truth. So I said to my young Connecticut friend: 'My dear, you are trying to support yourself and your mother, aren't you? Very well. Now suppose you go on and find that you can't – what will you have acquired? Look how few singers ever arrive and, if you are not one of the few, will you not merely have entirely unfitted yourself for the life struggle along other lines?'

Herewith I say the same to four-fifths of all the girl singers who, in villages, in shops, in schools, everywhere, are all yearning to be great.[70]

In Kellogg's analysis, by the *fin-de-siècle* the operatic profession had become an enclave for the few who could afford expensive training – that is, middle- and upper-class women. Good vocal tuition alone could cost a considerable amount,[71] but for singers outside Europe an additional factor was necessary: foreign travel, in order to study with French, German and Italian tutors in the musically sophisticated atmosphere of the continent. This trend had begun in the middle of the century. An article in the *Gazzetta musicale di Firenze* in 1853 commented on the presence of 'more than a half dozen' American students assiduously practising their solfeggi in the city 'with the intention of becoming singers of Italian opera', whilst elsewhere in Italy were 'English and French students – tenors, sopranos and basses – who adopt Italian surnames, and try to sing *di petto*, instead of singing from the throat and the nose as they do in England and France'.[72]

By the latter part of the period, the thirst to study abroad had been further fuelled by articles and books such as the pianist Amy Fay's immensely popular diary of her own sojourn, *Music Study in Germany*. First published in America in 1880, in Britain in 1886, and later in French and German translations, it was estimated to have inspired over two thousand students to study abroad – even, much to Fay's satisfaction, becoming a standard text for girls on leaving school.[73] The book's introduction, however, contained a more cautious rider that she hoped 'no American girl who reads this book will be influenced by it rashly to attempt what she herself undertook, viz.: to be trained in Europe from an amateur into an artist', because 'the trials and difficulties with which a girl may meet when studying art alone in a foreign land' should not 'be underrated'.[74] Yet the lively account of her experiences – her associations with foremost musicians of the age such as Clara Schumann, Liszt and Hans von Bülow (to name but a few), her attendance at concerts given by Wagner, her witnessing of the unusual spectacle of a woman, Alicia Hund, conducting a male orchestra in a performance of Hund's own symphony,[75] and perhaps above all her obvious delight that in Germany 'ladies can go anywhere alone',[76] thus enabling her to attend concerts and other 'public amusements' as an independent spirit – all combined to present a irresistible picture of the enjoyment and fulfilment a woman could find in the pursuit of a career.

For British, American and Australasian singers especially, a training period in Europe was essential. Europe offered important benefits: the study of French, German and Italian; the increased opportunities for a debut in one of the numerous smaller opera houses; the acquisition of European sophistication and gloss; and last but certainly not least, vocal tuition from the most famous teachers and repetiteurs of the day. Moreover, such was the fear of provincialism in Britain and America that many home-grown singers found it difficult to obtain proper acceptance for their talents, as the mezzo-soprano Eleanora de Cisneros claimed in an interview with the New York Herald Tribune in 1907:

> [Experience in opera] she cannot gain in her own country, for a substitute's position at one of our own opera houses or even a debut in an important role, does not seem to give her the chance to become a real star. She must gain her reputation abroad, and then be re-engaged for American opera through the booking agencies of Italy or some other country.[77]

Paris exerted a particularly powerful pull; by the mid-nineteenth century, the city had become 'an intellectual mecca' for American singers, who arrived to study with renowned tutors such as Anna LaGrange or Mathilde Marchesi.[78] Other favoured destinations were Milan and Berlin. But foreign study was extremely expensive. De Cisneros suggested a student would need about $120 a month for lessons, food and lodging in Italy; extra money would be required for 'clothes or doctor's bills'. For poor girls, the only solution was to find sponsorship from wealthy patrons. In 1896, Clara Butt received £300 from her patron to fund six months' study in Paris with Jacques Bouhy and a further six months in Berlin with Etelka Gerster (her family, whom she was virtually supporting, were provided with another £600 to compensate for her absence).[79] Eight years later, another British singer, Maggie Teyte, was given £1,000 for two years' study in Paris with Jean de Reszke.[80] The largest known expenditure, however, belongs to the American soprano Geraldine Farrar, who had acquired a patron, Mrs Webb, to fund her European study in 1899. It is somewhat difficult to envisage the legal terms of the contract if it was indeed as she described it:

> My father sold his store in Melrose and realized a sum sufficient to reduce materially the amount of the first loan we had from Mrs. Webb. This sum, according to the terms of a written contract drawn up by Mrs. Webb's lawyer and duly signed by my father and mother as my legal guardians, was to be an indefinite amount, advanced as required, and to be repaid at an indefinite date when my voice should be a source of steady income. The only actual security given was that my life was insured in Mrs. Webb's favor, so that in case of my death she would be fully compensated for the risk and loss she might sustain.[81]

The total sum provided by Mrs Webb apparently approximated thirty thousand dollars: a staggering sum for the early 1900s. Farrar claims to have repaid 'every dollar' within two years of her return to America.

How did these relationships between patron and protégée function? What was expected from the singers in return for the financial aid they received? And how did the singers perceive the role of their sponsors? Obviously, individual factors played a large part in determining the success or otherwise of such relationships. The American mezzo-soprano Kathleen Howard, for example, seems to have been very fortunate in her sponsors. Trying to obtain work as a singer in New York in the early 1900s, she discovered the impasse that faced many prospective prima donnas: 'No one would engage me without experience and no one would give me the opportunity to become experienced.' Europe and further training was the obvious solution, but Howard realised that although she had many of the basic attributes and qualities necessary for success as an opera singer, she lacked the one essential qualification – financial support. Enter the patron:

Friends of mine in the church, Frank Smith Jones and his wife, offered to finance me through my years of preparation and for as long afterwards as I might need their aid. These real friends were behind me for years, and I owe them more than I could repay.

The purse provided by the Smith Joneses bought not only Howard's vocal and dramatic training, but also a companion who was a kind of chaperone: 'They made it possible for me to have my sister with me, for me, a rather delicate girl, an inestimable benefit.' Certainly, the patrons are drawn as altogether amenable in Howard's autobiography. When the initial sum for the first year of her Paris education proved only 'half enough', it was duly increased the following season;[82] when Howard obtained contracts in the German opera houses which required her to supply her own stage costumes, her benefactors provided her with a 'beautiful wardrobe' designed by a famous Paris costumier; when in 1912 she was offered a concert engagement in Bergen, Norway, they financed her journey (the cost of which otherwise would have consumed all her profits from the fee);[83] and when she finally made her debut at Covent Garden, they sent her 'an extra cheque to impress London with'.[84]

Some relationships between patron and protégée could be intensely close. Maggie Teyte was virtually adopted by her wealthy middle-class patrons, Mr and Mrs Victor Rubens, at the age of sixteen: she went to live with them, called Mrs Rubens 'Mama', and 'severed all connection' with her own family. The Rubenses paid for her training in Paris with de Reszke, and Mrs Rubens accompanied her on her early engagements.[85] An article in the *New York Herald Tribune* in 1907 relates another instance of sponsorship where the protégée – one Ada Chambers – was taken into the house of the patrons supposedly in order to allow them to 'study her voice under all conditions'; more probably, it was the suitability of the candidate that was the object of their scrutiny.[86]

We are given a fascinating glimpse of one such relationship between sponsor and protégée in the unpublished letters of the soprano Mary Garden to her sponsor Florence Mayer, written during Garden's years of training in Paris between 1896 and 1899. In later years, the singer was keen to declare that her success was purely the result of her own 'hard work',[87] but in truth her career benefited immeasurably from the support of a number of influential women.

Born into a lower-middle-class Scottish family who settled in Chicago in 1887, Garden was typical of many young women who sought an operatic career.[88] Her formal singing tuition began at the age of sixteen with a well-known teacher, Sarah Robinson Duff. Chicago already had something of a reputation as a city that produced female singers by the dozen. In 1890, *The Musical World* printed 'The Story of a Prima Donna', a satirical tale about a nice middle-class girl whose singing rescues her family from poverty and destitution. In desperation Olivia de Ponsonby decides to 'use the music I learned in wealthier days to obtain subsistence' for herself and her mother. On Christmas Eve she bravely ventures out on to the street, where her warbling is heard by a stranger who recalls a debt he owed her once rich but now alcoholic and penurious father. On returning home that night, Olivia discovers an unexpected present:

> Olivia rushed to her stocking. What rapture was hers when she found in it a new grand piano and a receipted bill for two years' study with the most famous voice culturist in Parkdale. Olivia, it is unnecessary to remark, was a Chicago girl.[89]

Clara Louise Kellogg, writing of her experiences of giving masterclasses throughout North America, commented drily: 'I believe there are, or were, more would-be *prime donne* in Chicago than anywhere else on earth.'[90]

Garden was certainly one such eager and fortunate novitiate, later claiming she owed much of her vocal success to Sarah Duff.[91] But undoubtedly her teacher's greatest gift to Garden's future was in arranging her period of study in Paris, a trip far beyond the financial capabilities of her family. Duff's pupils included a number of society women: amongst these was Florence Blum Mayer (1872–1934), the young wife of David Mayer (1852–1920), the wealthy owner of the largest department store in Chicago. Through Duff's mediation, the Mayers agreed to finance Garden's training in Paris in 1896. Over the next three years, Garden wrote to Florence Mayer (and occasionally to David Mayer) of her progress, her studies and her life in Paris.[92]

As protégée and patron, Garden and Florence Mayer were initially relatively intimate: they shared not only a singing teacher but also a corset-maker, and Garden was privy to various items of gossip about Mrs Mayer's extended family. As months, then years pass, the warmth of their intimacy cooled. Perhaps this was a natural result of two women separated not only by a large ocean, but by increasingly different lives. Perhaps, however, it indicates that the relationship between sponsor and protégée proved to be far more complex than either party had anticipated at the outset.

Garden was a rather awkward young woman: 'very young and very emotional' is how she later described herself.[93] Tact was obviously not one of her strongest characteristics, as she betrayed in this inept apology written in December 1896: 'I did not remember in time to send greeting to all my American friends but I hope they will forgive me, and another Xmas when I have more time to throw away I shall remember them all.'[94] There are various indications of Garden's 'many selves' in the course of these letters, most noticeably centred around the tensions between the world from which she had emerged and the one towards which she was heading. On the one hand, she strives to inhabit the social milieu presumably favoured by her sponsors. Thus we hear in 1896 that she has attended the 'fête des fleurs' rather than the Grand Prix of the salon, because this is the preferred destination of the 'nicer people';[95] and we are given notice of her encounters with well-known socialites such as Fanny Reed. Similarly, she stresses her ladylike behaviour in only visiting the Café de Paris with a suitable companion: 'a divine place, only I never could go only with someone whome [sic] I know very well – and not a Frenchman'.[96] (Should we believe such statements?) And throughout the correspondence, she attempts to assure her patrons that she is leading the modest, hard-working, quiet life of a model student.[97]

But other aspects of Garden seem at war with notions of genteel behaviour, although arguably rather more fitting for the development of her artistic potential. In later years Garden stated that her 'motto' had always been 'liberty':[98]

> I believed in myself, and I never permitted anything or anybody to destroy that belief. My eye never wavered from the goal, and my whole life went into the operas I sang. I wanted liberty and I went my own way.[99]

This desire for independence is frequently seen in her correspondence with her patron – as are also the Mayers' contrasting attempts to exert greater control over the young singer. Tensions inevitably arose as a result. For example, Leon Grehier (the Mayers' French lawyer, who regulated the flow of money from sponsor to protégée) had obviously been cautioned about the young singer's self-will prior to his first meeting with Garden. His initial letter to Mrs Mayer contains the telling comment: 'I will as you say not allow myself to be dictated to.'[100] One of their first disputes was over 'suitable' accommodation. Garden was determined to live on her own (rather than with other American women who would presumably act as chaperones),[101] a battle she finally won after spending a compromise period with a French family on the face-saving grounds that she was studying the language. A further cause of friction was Garden's failure to write as often (it would seem) as Florence Mayer wished. Occasionally she even seems to snub her patron, whose original standing as a fellow singer had now dropped to amateur status against Garden's burgeoning professionalism. There is surely more than a whiff of patronage in Garden's advice to Mrs Mayer regarding the latter's forthcoming lessons with Mrs Duff: 'Don't fail to get all you can, for really everything she brings home will mean a great deal to those who accept it & work with it intelligently.'[102] Other factors may have disturbed the Mayers. Although Garden was constantly hinting that she was about to achieve great things, actual success eluded her. In this context of non-achievement, her busy social life and her enjoyment of the pleasures of Paris perhaps rang hollow in the ears of her patrons.

Eventually, the relationship between Garden and the Mayers snapped under the strain of clashing expectations and supposed duties. The story of how this break occurred is confused. In her autobiography, Garden claimed that the Mayers had offered to assist her with her studies in Paris 'for three years',[103] but then cut off her income after only eighteen months and without prior warning. Desperate and unable to pay the rent, Garden was then supposedly visited by a woman at the behest of her sponsors, who told her that the Mayers had received anonymous letters suggesting that she had 'lovers', and had even given birth to a child. Garden, incensed by such accusations, showed the woman the door.[104] Shortly afterwards, the soprano Sibyl Sanderson assumed the role of her protector, and a few months later in April 1900, Garden made her successful debut at the Paris Opéra-Comique in Charpentier's *Louise*.

What actually happened between Garden and her former patrons? Garden's complaints that she was abandoned by the Mayers are contradicted by the letters. It is clear that the Mayers did indeed support her for the full three years that Garden claims she was promised, and it is equally clear that the money then ceased with apparent abruptness, causing Garden considerable distress. Precisely why remains confused. It might be thought that three years of financial aid, with all the hints of grand debuts coming to nothing, was enough for any one family to cope with, and that the Mayers simply ran out of patience and interest. However, in what was possibly her final desperate plea for money, Garden implies that there was a specific charge against her, emanating from mutual acquaintances in Paris: 'I cannot understand the affair – I only know that some one is my bitter enemy and is doing me so much harm.' She was much puzzled by those who were 'busy to say anything against me – whether the truth or not': 'why they are so I am sure I can't tell, for I never do any one harm, nor wish them harm, and live my life very quietly paying attention to no one'.[105] Certainly, it is clear that the Mayers kept a watchful eye on their protégée, both through Leon Grehier and through friends in Paris. Whether such reports were the source of their suspicions is unclear.[106]

But again, Garden herself may have fuelled doubts about her conduct in Paris. A mysterious Spanish holiday in 1898 might well have been the sort of incident to encourage rumours of a secret confinement, or even an abortion.[107] No evidence of a child has emerged. Another cause of dissent might have been Garden's ecstatic meanderings on the fun she enjoyed when a young and single relative of the Mayer family came into town ('I have had with him the happiest days that I have had since coming here – because I felt so free to do what I liked').[108] Was Garden, whose career still showed no real signs of blossoming at this stage, setting her sights on marrying into the family instead? There was also some kind of financial dispute between Grehier and Garden in 1899 over missing receipts for tuition.[109] Were accusations made against Garden? Or was 'that brute Grehier' (who remained oddly vindictive on the subject of Garden in his later letters) even one of the 'disgusting men' Garden implies were prepared to trade favours for her sexual acquiescence?[110]

There was a further postscript to the affair. In 1909 the American newspapers were full of a story that the Mayers had demanded payment of their 'loan', because Florence Mayer had been slighted by Garden at the Manhattan Opera House.[111] Garden paid up, and the Mayers pledged to use this money to fund the study of further novice singers. There is no evidence they ever did so.

This correspondence undoubtedly raises more questions than answers, and it is unlikely the full story of the sponsorship will ever be known. What is apparent is that neither party fully understood the circumstances of the other. Garden makes it plain that there were other, dark factors with which she was having to contend in the battle to establish a career, such as sexual harassment;[112] and although the most explicit of these accusations was made when her financial allowance had been stopped and might therefore have been an attempt to shame the Mayers into continuing their patronage, her despair is convincing. On their part, the Mayers may have been too naive to realise that Garden was in a highly vulnerable position; or alternatively, they might have felt she herself was to blame if she was indeed in a difficult situation. And what did such patrons expect from their sponsorship? Various other singers regarded their patron's financial support as a loan, and repaid it accordingly.[113] In 1909, Florence Mayer claimed that 'it was clearly understood that Garden was to return to us the money advanced for her musical education, if successful'.[114] Garden, somewhat unreasonably, stated that the Mayers should have accepted her emergence as an artist of the first rank as the proper reward for their financial investment, and that this was the arrangement she had originally established with them.[115] A letter she wrote as she crossed the Atlantic to begin her training might support this claim:

> When I sit here and think I am almost in Paris to realize my only hope & love on Earth – why I am too over come for words or thoughts – That's all – and then I think – all this due to a little woman in Chicago and her kindheartedness – I have said Thank you so many times & now the only way of showing my appreciation is to see what I can do to make her proud of me in the future.[116]

If they had remained on friendly terms, would Garden's subsequent success really have been regarded as sufficient payment? And if so, would there also have been social obligations that Garden would have been expected to fulfil – perhaps providing a box for the Mayers when she sang, introducing them to other 'stars' of the operatic world, being prepared to attend their parties or dinners as an attraction for other guests?

But the public row between Garden and the Mayers perhaps found another shape in a short story by Willa Cather entitled 'Scandal', published in 1920.[117] There are a number of similarities to the Garden/Mayer scenario: the heroine, Kitty Ayrshire (hints of Garden's Scottish background?) is a dynamic, defiantly 'new' singer who is the target of vicious gossip reporting that she has given birth to a child abroad. Rumour also links her with Siegmund Stein, a New York Jewish 'patron of the arts' and department store owner (exchange New York for Chicago, and this description then bears a marked resemblance to David Mayer), who has long since unsuc-cessfully sought to add the beautiful Kitty to his list of sexual conquests. However, if he can't actually have her, he wants to make the rest of the world believe that he has. He hires a look-alike model of Kitty, and makes sure that they are glimpsed together in sup-posedly furtive companionship in various restaurants and other night-spots. Cather's sympathies lie clearly with Kitty Ayrshire, and she displays unpleasantly anti-semitic responses in her construction of the character of Stein. However, we also know that Cather, as a music critic, was well informed about the operatic world, and that at least two of her other fictional opera singers were based on real prima donnas.[118] Does 'Scandal' constitute another telling of the relationship between Garden and the Mayers? Or was it simply a fantasy on the theme of rich patron and famous prima donna?

MARRIAGE

Unlike the vast majority of women in this era, the financially inde-pendent prima donnas could regard marriage as an option rather than a necessity. Most did marry, nonetheless. For some singers, loneliness and the insecurity of life on the stage were influential factors: in a letter in 1845, Jenny Lind wrote 'how difficult it is to stand all this racing about – alone! – alone! with the certainty of having to rely on my own judgement in everything, and yet so absorbed at the same time in my rôles'.[119] Other singers feared the isolation of a single life when their operatic career had ended, as Amanda Norton revealed in her comments about both her daughter Lillian Nordica (who did not wish to be 'old and without sympathy') and Clara Louise Kellogg.[120] Public life as a single woman also had its dangers. La Moda reported in 1836 that a man named Olivierio Dupeget, armed with two pistols, had been arrested for attacking the uncle of Giulia Grisi whilst trying to force his way into the singer's box at the Théâtre-Italien in Paris. Grisi complained that Dupeget had been stalking her for over three years, and that on three occasions he had approached her at home. (Dupeget's lawyer argued that his client's reason had been disturbed 'by the beauty of Madamigella Grisi' and that he believed she loved him – the court eventually accepted his plea of madness and his original sentence of a month's imprisonment was quashed.[121]) It is perhaps significant that it was less than three months after this incident that Grisi made her ill-fated and short-lived marriage to Vicomte Gérard de Melcy.[122]

Certain marriages, like that of Adelaide Comelli and Rubini, or Grisi's later union with Mario, or (half a century on) Toti Dal Monte's second marriage with the tenor Enzo de Muro Lomanto, were happy and fulfilling. But finding a suitable husband, as the high divorce rate amongst prima donnas makes plain, was by no means easy – especially for those singers who wished to continue their careers. The shadow of the siren emerges again in the notion that marriage to a working prima donna constituted a form of emasculation, as is evinced by Maretzek's caustic comments about the 'prima donna's husband'[123] and also by a letter from Tchaikovsky to his father in 1868 concerning his proposed nuptials with the Belgian singer Désirée Artôt (1835–1907). Tchaikovsky's closet homosexuality precludes us from reading this letter as a true depiction of his reluctance to marry Artôt, but he presumably offered reasons here that would be generally understood and accepted by others:

First of all her mother, who is always with her, has a great influence over her daughter and is against our marriage; she finds me too young and probably fears that I shall force Artôt to live in Russia. Secondly, my friends, and especially Rubinstein, are doing all they possibly can to prevent me from realising this plan. They say that becoming the husband of a famous singer I shall have to play the miserable part of my wife's husband – i.e. will have to travel with her to all corners of Europe, live on her money, lose the habit of work and stop doing so; in one word, that when my love for her cools there will only be left hurt pride, despair and ruin. This could be prevented if she agreed to leave the stage and live with me in Russia but she says that in spite of her love to me, she could not think of dropping the career which gives her fame and money and to which she is accustomed . . . so I in my turn am not sure of being able to sacrifice all my future for her sake; as it is obvious that I shall then lose the opportunity of going forward along my own road.[124]

Artôt (with the strong support of her mother) is depicted as resisting the suggestion that she sacrifice her career for domesticity. Other singers did not. Clara Novello not only relinquished her professional life for marriage to Count Gigliucci in 1843, but even humbly accepted the absence of a piano in their Italian *palazzo* during the first years of their marriage, as proof to her jealous husband that she loved him more than music itself.[125] Marietta Piccolomini embraced once again the social sphere she had temporarily left for the stage on her marriage to the Marchese Francesco Caetani della Fargna in 1860: her singing was henceforth mostly restricted to private salons (with the one exception of a later visit to London to assist Lumley). The Italian dramatic soprano Esther Mazzoleni (1882–1982) retired from the stage in 1926 after a successful career of twenty years because she fell in love with a 'pearl of a man', a notary who refused to become a 'diva's husband and follow her around' – Mazzoleni 'never regretted' her decision, and settled down to raising their two children and developing a new profession as a teacher.[126]

Other singers were similarly only too happy to exchange their precarious careers for the comforts of domesticity – especially upper-class domesticity, given that their public visibility and financial success often secured the prima donnas advantageous marriages to men of wealth or title.[127] Such alliances were even possible early in the era when the prima donnas were still regarded as social inferiors and rather dubious figures. Henrietta Sontag (Countess Rossi), Maria Alboni (Countess Pepoli), Sophie Cruvelli (Baroness Vigier), Rosina Mazzarelli (Countess Tolomej di Siena), Adelaide Tosi (Countess Poli), Stefania Favelli (Marchesa Visconti Ajimi), Caroline Naldi (Countess de Sparre) and Giuditta Grisi (Countess Barni di Lodi) all made titled marriages before the middle of the nineteenth century. In 1843, the *Musical World* heralded Novello's nuptials with a degree of cynicism:

> This lady is the fourth Warbler who has married a titled spouse within these few years. The other three are Miss Stevens (Countess of

Essex), Miss Foote (Countess of Harrington), and Miss Bolton (Lady Thurlow) . . . We should recommend every lady vocalist to set her cap at a duke or a *plum* (nothing less); never mind age or *imbecility* – a carriage, a title and a dish of turtle-soup, make up for *all other* deficiencies.[128]

Or did they? Whilst some singers adjusted successfully to a different way of life, there are clues that others experienced difficulties akin to those of Eliot's Alcharisi. Chorley suggested that the social elevation of Henrietta Sontag (a 'daughter of the people')[129] through marriage to Count Rossi did not compensate fully for the loss of her professional life, because of the 'keen and vivid' pleasure she showed whenever she could discuss 'some question of Music' instead of the 'regulation nothings' dictated by polite society. When dwindling family finances forced Sontag (1806–54) to resume her career twenty years after her retirement, Chorley concluded: 'I cannot but think that she rejoiced in her return to the stage.'[130] Lilli Lehmann (1848–1929) seems to have been aware of her priorities from the beginning of her career when, in 1869, she refused an offer of marriage to a count: 'The title of Countess held no attraction for me, my vocation was everything. I desired to advance, to attain, to become and continue independent.'[131] Her antipathy towards marriage was perhaps a result of the experiences of her mother, the soprano Marie Loew, who had abandoned her successful career at the age of forty on her marriage to Carl Lehmann: a tenor who drank, gambled and displayed a violent temper. Loew eventually left him, was unable to return to the stage and instead supported her two small daughters by playing the harp in an opera house orchestra for a wage that was little more than a pittance.

Numerous singers throughout the period and in various countries similarly found their actual or prospective husbands demanded the cessation of their careers. The engagement of Jenny Lind to Captain Harris in 1849 in Britain foundered when her fiancé, not content with insisting she leave the operatic stage, wanted to include a clause in the marriage settlement that precluded her from ever working again.[132] We might think such an attitude peculiarly Victorian; yet over seventy years later in Croatia, Viorica Ursuleac (1894–1985) ran away from her first husband in the early 1920s when she discovered that he 'would not hear of my continuing' a career.[133]

Even (or perhaps especially) when marriage permitted the prima donna's continuation of her profession, another danger loomed. As Nordica wrote wryly: 'I have found that women who earn money in large sums are looked upon as legitimate prey by adventurers.'[134] Legislation preventing married women from owning property or signing legal documents without their husband's consent until the latter decades of the nineteenth century (precise restrictions varied from country to country) meant that prima donnas were often unable to exert sole control over their salaries.[135] Giulia Grisi, for instance, was forced to pay a substantial part of her fees to her estranged husband de Melcy even after the couple were legally separated.[136] Pre-marital contracts (such as that proposed by Lind's adviser)[137] could avoid this problem to some extent. But even after the passing of protective legislation later in the era, singers such as Luisa Tetrazzini (1871–1940) frequently found their hard-earned fortunes dissipated in the hands of plausible rogues.[138]

If in much of Europe for the greater part of the period, married women could not sign contracts without their husband's authorisation, certain Italian states prior to 1860 demonstrated a more progressive attitude on this issue. The *Codice civile universale austriaco*, introduced in the Lombardo-Veneto regions under direct control of Austria in 1816, abolished marital authorisation. Elsewhere in Italy, older customs persisted. The new *Codice civile* (1865) of unified Italy drew a middle course between these extremes. Recalling the reasoning behind the new laws, Rosmini stated that the 'liberal principles of the age . . . no longer tolerated the absolute incapacity of a woman when deprived of the consent of her husband'. But this apparent freedom was ring-fenced by an important clause, on the grounds that 'it seemed prudent and cautious to prevent the dangers and very grave difficulties that might derive from her absolute independence to both the family and herself'. In consequence, a married woman only had the right to sign contracts solely on her own authorisation *provided that* her contractual obligations did not conflict with 'the fulfilment of her duties towards her husband and her family'. This effectively meant that a contract with an impresario or a theatrical company would be regarded as void if 'in order to fulfil its obligations the married woman would have to abandon the marital home'. The decision as to whether a contested contract was legal or not was therefore dependent on circumstances of the most 'delicate order', including both economic factors and also those of a more personal nature:

> If the husband is infirm, if the children are very young, or if there are daughters to take care of, who would argue that to leave the marital home in order to work outside does not infringe her duties as wife and mother?[139]

Moreover, Rosmini makes it plain that this particular clause was inserted in order to protect masculine pride:

> Neither was it so much the fragility of the sex, the *infirmitas consilii* ['weakness of knowledge'] described by Cicero, that induced our legislators to preserve in many cases the husband's authorisation, since the full capacity to undertake obligations has been given to single women and widows; rather, it resulted from reflecting on the need to attribute to the husband an authority, a power, that served to ensure the smooth running and protect the interests of the conjugal union, of that family of which he is the head and guardian and legitimate representative.[140]

It is difficult to know what tensions this might have provoked amongst married singers: domestic differences were most commonly held in private. But one dispute between a working prima donna and her husband earlier in Britain extraordinarily found its way into the public domain in 1839. Anna Bishop (1810–84) was the second wife of the composer and conductor Henry Bishop (1786–1855), her one-time singing teacher at the Royal Academy of Music. Over the eight years following their marriage (including the birth of three children), her career developed as his waned, and culminated in a series of concerts with the acclaimed French harpist and composer Nicholas Bochsa

(1789–1856). But Bochsa was also a man with a shady past, wanted in France for fraud. In 1839 Anna Bishop secretly left her husband, ostensibly to go on tour with Bochsa. Her husband, unusually, turned to the press, as *The Times* reported on 15 July 1839:

> For several days paragraphs have appeared in some of the daily journals in which reference has been made to the conduct of a lady who has justly attained a prominent rank in the list of our native vocalists, and on Saturday it was formally intimated that Mrs Bishop, the wife of the celebrated composer, had abandoned her home leaving her husband, as may be readily imagined, in a state bordering on distraction, and the three young children without the care and protection of a maternal hand. It was further stated that Mrs Bishop had proceeded to the continent in the company of Bochsa, the harp-player . . . The state of mind in which Mr Bishop has been since the receipt of his wife's communication will readily be imagined. We lament at the same time to say that [Anna Bishop's mother] Mrs Riviere's senses appear to have left her forever . . .[141]

Anna Bishop's brother, Robert Riviere, wrote to the newspaper in defence of his sister, demanding his brother-in-law refute the suggestions made against Anna. When Henry Bishop failed to comply, Riviere sent to the *Times* a copy of the letter Anna had had delivered to her husband shortly after her departure:

> Your late extraordinary and unjust conduct, so little deserved by me, your cold and unfeeling manner, your mind so strangely different to mine, the uncertainty of our future means, and above all the future welfare of my children have at last roused my spirits and decided me to think and act for myself, and I have accepted an engagement for a few months, which, in enabling me to make further progress in my profession, will also allow me to provide for my children from time to time, as I have always done. I would gladly have informed you of my intention, but your manner and injustice have repulsed me; in fact no true confidence ever existed between us, and we do less than ever understand each other. You have only two courses to pursue – the one to ruin us all (and you and the children more than me), by making a *fracas* in the world; the other to view my absence as it really is – viz., the

fulfilment of an engagement. This will not, in the eyes of the public, look differently to any other of my tours, unless you choose to give some other colour to the thing. Think well before you act: you can make the children miserable forever. Don't leave them to the mercy of strangers and circumstances, as [you did] your former family. You know me well enough, that in promising to provide for the children to the utmost I can, I do not deceive you. Do not think I act from the impulse of the moment. I declare most firmly, that I am determined to pursue my plans, and that nothing on earth can make me change. I have worked for all since you married me, and I will do so still if I find you act as a friend to them. The voice is precarious, I am near 30, and we have not saved a penny; we have three children; you do not gain much, and (do not be offended at my saying so) most of the bulk of our expenses have fallen on me. Fagging and fagging merely to live, is a dreadful idea. We cannot expect so good a year as last; I gained upwards of 1,100*l.*, you about 400*l.*; of all this very little remains. And all you can reckon on as a certainty during the next three years is 200*l.* from D'Almaines and 36*l.* from the Academy. You know you will not be engaged at any theatre; something decisive must be done. You say the house cannot be kept under 1,000*l.* a-year. This must not be. No professor of respectability spends so much, and I must say, that in providing an entire change must take place. The professional gentleman who will give you this letter will consult with you on this subject and he will let me know the result, as any communication for the present will be painful to both. The engagement I have contracted with Mr Bochsa (to whom I owe already so much, as you know, and who has been so cruelly treated by you, although you cannot with any real foundation find fault with his conduct towards me) is more than I could have expected. I am to have half the profits of each concert, or dramatic entertainment; one clear benefit once a-month; if I have a permanent engagement as *prima donna* I am to receive the two-thirds of such engagement, and to provide any master necessary for me at his own expense. I have a proper document from him for the fulfilment of the above. You said I should have masters that money could procure; but where is the money to come from? We have none. You know well that on the continent you can do nothing for me, as some time must elapse before I should be known; but with Mr Bochsa, he will, of course, give concerts immediately, and push the speculation with his usual energy. When I know how you act you shall know where I am.

I leave you money enough to go on with. I have received the money for the concert here, but of course with the deductions of the carriage, &c., which I had agreed to pay for the month's use of. This money I regard, indeed, as my own, as you called forth every exertion to prevent my succeeding, and it has been with the greatest effort and pain that I did succeed. My father and his family have been my only supporters in my last struggle.[142] I kiss my dear children tenderly, and God bless them; and hope my exertions will prove, as I intend them, for their benefit.

ANN BISHOP.

P. S.– I should have said that in the engagement I am not to sustain any loss. I returned to Mr Bochsa 90l. for the three weeks' illness I had in Edinburgh. I take Miss Younge with me as a companion.

July, 1839.[143]

Her husband's response to the publication of this letter a day later included this paragraph:

I would willingly have spared the pain of a public answer to any part of Mrs Bishop's letter, but justice to myself demands my most solemn denial of our ever having lived otherwise than on terms of perfect unanimity and the utmost confidence, until a few weeks since, when, in consequence of what had passed, I considered it my duty, in the presence of her father, on the authority of a husband, and with the feelings of a husband, and the father of her children, strictly to forbid any further intimacy with Mr Bochsa.

In defiance of this injunction, and without any professional engagement for her being proposed to me by Mr Bochsa (as on former occasions), or any reason existing to prevent my accompanying her, she, wholly without my consent and clandestinely, left her home to proceed to the Continent under the circumstances which have been stated . . .[144]

We cannot know which of the two parties in this marriage were telling the truth – perhaps neither; perhaps (in their own way) both. Anna Bishop's later relationship with Bochsa suggests that her husband's suspicions might have been well founded; his claims that the couple had never previously exchanged a cross word seem highly unlikely from Anna's almost clinical analysis of their recent history. But this public exchange of letters is a remarkable testament to the way in which the prima donna disrupted the social conventions of the day. In effect, Bishop was able to challenge the private domestic order because of her public position in the wider society, and the economic freedom this afforded her. Her determination to 'pursue my own plans', her insistence on her right to 'succeed' (and moreover that her success had been achieved entirely through her own efforts), her clarification of her position as the family breadwinner illustrate how far the lives of real women differed from the much-peddled image of the 'angel in the house'. This was Nora slamming the door long before Ibsen's *A Doll's House* dared depict a similarly violent end to a marriage – and it was a door slammed conspicuously in public. Strangely, perhaps, the ensuing clamorous scandal was played out to a more peaceful conclusion. Anna spent the next seven years abroad with Bochsa, undertaking a long series of concerts and operatic performances;[145] meanwhile the terms of a formal separation were drawn up with her husband, finally granting her legal custody of the children.[146] When she returned to Britain with Bochsa in 1846, her triumphant successes in English opera and concert tours demonstrated public acceptance. Perhaps even more interesting is that despite this extraordinary scandal, Henry Bishop was knighted in 1842, the first British musician to be honoured in this way.[147] Clearly, his reputation had survived relatively intact. Nevertheless, there were long-lasting repercussions for other members of the family. Bishop's biographer claims that her parents never really recovered from the shame of their daughter's departure from the marital home: her mother especially withdrew into 'deep melancholia' and became virtually bedridden.[148] Bishop's relationship with her eldest daughter was broken entirely; that with her younger twins re-established only in their adult lives. But her professional and personal partnership – a seemingly happy union on both counts – with Bochsa continued until his death in 1856.

We should remember that the role of the 'husband of the prima donna' was a less than enviable position in the eyes of many. Like the stage mother, the husband was seen as an anomaly within the usual gender roles. Impresarios complained of their interference in the smooth running of the company;[149] journalists mocked their presence.[150] If some men preferred their wives to relinquish their performing career, it seems possible that this owed as much to their own reluctance to undertake a particularly despised role as it did to any wish to curtail their partner's freedoms. Some husbands attempted escape by developing their own interests. Giuditta Pasta's husband, a former lawyer and then minor tenor, apparently coped surprisingly well for most of their marriage, accompanying his wife on her endless tours. But a series of letters between the couple between 1825 and 1826 chart his only recorded effort to establish a career of his own. He signed up for an ill-fated tour with García in North America: the money never materialised, he was ill and lonely, and his letters home became increasingly plaintive. Why didn't Giuditta write more often? How could she have allowed three months to pass without even taking up the pen to write to him? When would she send the money? He laboriously listed the cost of his ticket home and the amount he needed to pay his debts in New York; far from wishing to reprove his wife for her mysterious delay, he nervously added, 'I attribute that which has the appearance of neglect to a sentiment of confidence that, deriving from our own heart, one presumes in others.' Once home again, he remained close to Pasta for the remainder of their lives together; the temporary rift seems to have been healed.[151]

Other husbands appear to have failed completely to adjust. Nordica's first husband, Frederick Gower, 'flew into a frenzy' every time she sang at home (he had already put an end to her public career), and burnt her music and her operatic costumes.[152] Nordica eventually left him; shortly after, Gower disappeared whilst attempting to cross the English Channel in a hot-air balloon. Perhaps believing that marriage to a fellow artist would provide a more supportive relationship, Nordica then wed Zoltan Döme: an unsuccessful tenor for whom she generously arranged a Bayreuth debut, but who sent her death threats after their marriage collapsed.[153] Her third husband, George Washington Young, was a businessman who effectively bled Nordica's wealth dry. 'I have been duped, betrayed, deceived and abused', she wrote.[154]

Nordica was especially unlucky in her choice of male partners, but many prima donnas found marriage unsatisfactory. The unconventional attitude of some singers to marriage has been interpreted on occasion as evidence of lesbianism. Certainly, we must assume that a number of prima donnas preferred same-sex relationships, even though documented evidence is rather thin. In 1836, Louis Gentil claimed that Marie Flécheux, following an abortion and through her 'hate for the authors of the pains she suffered, has abandoned herself to the sapphic song and the *mode lesbien*'; and now insisted on taking a lover from the *coryphées*. And yet even this rare acknowledgement of homosexuality seems to have been a deliberate rumour spread about by a predatory male, one Schneitzhoeffer, who attributed the ballet girls' 'resistance to his ignoble desires' to 'some ugly practices between women'.[155] In other cases, there is perhaps too great an assumption that women portrayed as erotic objects must necessarily themselves be sexually active, whether in heterosexual or homosexual terms. But for some, the pleasure of singing was simply much greater than sex. Germaine Lubin claimed that she was 'never a sexual woman' and that 'sex never interested me'; it took her a long time 'to realize that the men I really loved were Tristan, Siegfried, Lohengrin, Tannhäuser, and heroes of that sort'.[156] Perhaps it is not surprising that Emma Eames should compare her 'artistic passion' so favourably with a love affair, that Lucrezia Bori thought herself wise to have remained 'wed' to her profession because her heroines 'never let me down, nor did my public',[157] or that Mary Garden refused to marry, finding men were poor substitutes for the endless fascination of her working life: 'My career never gave me any pain. It never gave me anything but joy, and what man could give that?'[158] Far from feeling deprived of affection, Garden gloried in her liberty and solitude:

> When I sit and think that I can be alone in this world, that I can go into my bedroom and sleep alone, it gives me a shiver of freedom. That is my ecstasy, that knowledge of freedom.[159]

'Vissi d'arte, vissi d'amore'   In her autobiography, Emma
                    Tosca, Act II   Eames wrote: 'A career is a won-
                                        derful and a terrible thing'. There
were of course as many experiences of professional life as there were
female singers; each sampled her career differently according to vocal
and dramatic ability, personal circumstances and geographical location. Above all, the developments in the operatic marketplace and
the mechanisms for operatic production meant that the nature of
professional life was signally different for singers at the beginning
of the period from those at the end.

Attempting to reconstruct something of these individual experiences is a frustrating, fitful process: a letter, an archival document, a
portrait, a newspaper review all provide fragments of lost lives, but
frequently find little substantiation or clarification. One fact seems
evident, nonetheless: that the discourses around the singer were as
powerful and influential (if not more so) in shaping experience as the
actual behaviour of the singers themselves.

CONVENIENZE

In *Europe: A History* (1997), Norman Davies lists the component
processes of the modernisation that occurred in the nineteenth
century. The history of opera similarly demonstrates the influence
or even the direct impact of these processes: for example, the
category of 'mobility of labour' is visible in the development of the
operatic circuit and the numerous touring companies; the emergence of the money economy affected the transition of singers' pay
from costly presents to hard cash; the 'standardization of weights and
measures' is reflected in the international agreement of a fixed pitch;

the advancements of science and technology find diverse manifestations in the shape of Garcia's laryngoscope, the fashioning of new stage machinery and the introduction of first gas and then electricity into the opera house, the development of recording technologies; and so on. But there is one category that at first glance sits rather oddly with the history of the operatic stage and in particular with the history of the operatic singer: 'women: dependency and subordination'.[1]

Given that the stage performer enjoyed unusual freedoms and independence in contrast to the domestic 'feminine ideal', it is tempting to mount an argument that demonstrates opera's singularity to the processes of modernisation in this particular respect. We can point to the high wages earned by female singers, the cult of celebrity that fêted their successes, or the increasing numbers of middle- and upper-class women who sought to embrace a career on the stage from the 1850s onward as exemplars of the way in which the prima donna was perceived as precisely the opposite of a dependent and subjugated woman. And yet this category of subordination has greater import than a superficial glimpse allows.

Women's greatest freedom on the operatic stage occurred between approximately 1800 and 1840. At this juncture, the prima donnas enjoyed their most powerful moment in operatic history: they influenced compositional practices; they determined musical and dramatic interpretation; and they affected management decisions about the running of the opera house, the content of the season, the employment and use of other artists, and so forth. Indeed, one might even argue that the opera (as composition, performance practice, and system of production) of these decades was the artform in its most 'feminised' state: at least, in the sense of its fluidity,[2] the lack of fixed boundaries,[3] its responsiveness to individual circumstances and conditions[4] – and certainly as the dominant society would have understood the term as meaning irrational, emotional, wayward. The complaints of many late eighteenth- and early nineteenth-century critics about opera are often couched in language that reflects the era's wider debate about women: they speak of the emasculating tendency of opera, its excess, its madness.[5] But this epoch is also perceived as opera's most decadent period: David Kimbell describes the 'easy contempt' with which many historians regard the early nineteenth-century Italian stage and its 'innumerable tasteless and trivial abuses';[6] 'sad and squalid' is another scholar's appraisal.[7] More often than not, it is the singers who bear the brunt of criticisms for the parlous state of the operatic stage. Berlioz attributed to these 'charming monsters' every conceivable blame: 'the number of bastard works, the gradual degradation of style, the destruction of all sense of expression, the neglect of dramatic proprieties, the contempt for the true, the grand and the beautiful, and the cynicism and decrepitude of art in certain countries'.[8]

At the heart of such comments lay an essential debate not only about the integrity of the artwork, but about the very *identity* of the artwork: was the artwork the composition, or was it the performance? This was the question that would absorb and affect the development of the operatic marketplace throughout the period. As the era began, however, few would have doubted the answer: the artwork was the performance. And the performance was essentially of a singer's individual characteristics and talents, and the way his or her particular qualities – both vocal and theatrical – were given greater accent or shape within the compositional frame.[9]

The privileging of performance brought a commensurate privileging of performers – at least, the most important ones – within the theatrical hierarchy. Much of the criticism levelled against singers was provoked by the *convenienze* that marked out their status: a series of professional codes concerning billing, roles, fees, privileges and so forth. Variations on these codes had been in existence from the beginning of opera, and had long been the butt of satirical humour. Benedetto Marcello's *Il teatro alla moda* (1720), Carlo Goldoni's *L'Impresario delle Smirne* (1755) and Antonio Sografi's *Le convenienze teatrali* (1794) and *Le inconvenienze teatrali* (1804) were amongst the most influential and biting attacks.[10] But the clearest delineation of the *convenienze* in the early nineteenth century was provided by the tenor and impresario Nicola Tacchinardi in an essay, *Dell'opera in musica sul teatro italiano e de' suoi difetti* (1833). In line with Marcello, he attributed the source of such practices to the vanity of the singers: their principal ingredients were 'envy for the *primo*, presumption, intrigue and ignorance'. If you asked the singers what 'convenienze' meant, he argued, they would reply that it means not to be oppressed; but since they define as 'oppression' everything that doesn't agree with their own 'caprices and various ideas', then the *convenienze* merely give birth to an eternal discord of dissent and argument.[11]

But what exactly were the *convenienze*? First of all, they concerned billing: the layout of names on the posters erected outside the theatres. As Tacchinardi explained, the method most prevalent at the beginning of the era was as in this bill from the Teatro Regio in 1816 (see fig. 2), with the singers labelled in order of status.

In the early years of the nineteenth century when the 'primo soprano' changed from being a castrato to a female singer, this meant that the women invariably had top billing. Gradually, however, this convention changed: in order to 'avoid the continual tittle-tattle' and to remove 'the absurdity of all these *assoluzioni* and these *primati*', the singers were listed in terms of the character they played.[12] The order of the characters nevertheless caused some further difficulties. Should these be laid out according to the status of the role within the opera, or in order of appearance? If the latter approach was followed, this effectively denied the prima donna the top billing she might legitimately expect, because her entrance on stage was often situated after the opening numbers. But billing was only the start of the frictions:

> *Convenienze* or continual arguments over the choice of the operas; *convenienze* for the distribution of the numbers in the operas; *convenienze* about the roles if they have not been balanced correctly; *convenienze* for the carriage that must accompany them to the rehearsals and to the theatre; *convenienze* for the dressing-rooms or changing rooms and for the lighting of the same; *convenienze* about the obsequious visits of the impresario, of the theatre owners and managers, of the composer, of

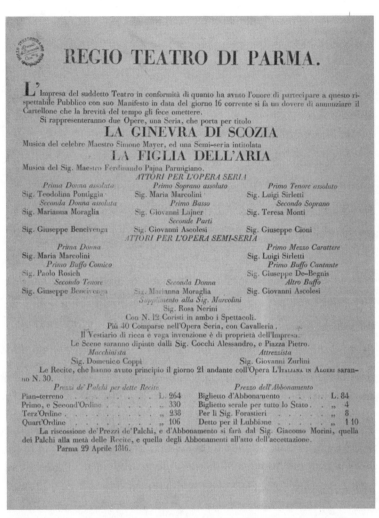

Figure 2. Poster dated 29 April 1816 from the Archivio storico del Teatro Regio, Parma

the first violin and others. In short, all is *convenienze*, or leads continually to disorder and argument, and everyone tends to outdo each other, not by way of emulation but because of envy and intrigue.[13]

It can hardly be denied that these codes could be and were manipulated by unscrupulous artists. But the wholesale condemnation sometimes seems a little stretched, and has led to certain misreadings of professional behaviours. The notion of the *convenienze* as driven solely by 'caprice' and 'envy' continues in the perspective of some modern historians, with eighteenth- and nineteenth-century disputes between singers and opera house managements being labelled as egotistical in origin. In the words of one scholar, 'Artistic and professional issues, as they would be understood today, entered into [the singers'] views of the world only marginally, if at all.'[14] The difficulty here is that 'artistic and professional issues' were indeed an important part of a singer's considerations, but were framed within an entirely different context from contemporary practices.

We should thus resist the myth-making of the satirists and view the *convenienze* a little differently, within the context of a growing marketplace in which the singers were a form of commodity. A concern with one's status was not simply artistic or personal vanity: it was a real recognition of the way the market operated. And we cannot ascribe certain personal characteristics (self-interest, for example) to only one party in the various disputes that occurred within the opera house. Tacchinardi made the point that when the *convenienze* were broken or ignored, it was the impresario who suffered: 'Then follows an open war during the whole season, and trouble for whom? for the impresario.'[15] As it is often the impresarios who relate with most relish their difficulties with singers in this respect, it is hard to resist the notion that often the discourse surrounding the business of the *convenienze* was essentially depicting a dispute between management and workers.

The characterisation of singers as grasping and difficult is also sometimes overdone on other accounts: was it ever possible, for example, for a star to become a 'star' without being concerned at all about status? And even when the artist might have been relatively relaxed about such things, the people around the artist – the agent, or the family-as-agent – interposed to demonstrate their contribution to the building of stardom; there was thus additional negotiation in order for these extra personnel to underline their own value. If the prima donna attracted the most severe criticisms for this kind of behaviour, Tacchinardi argued that this was largely due to the family entourage that surrounded her – husbands, fathers and mothers – who all contributed to the demands made on the management and the composers. In contrast, male singers often travelled alone: 'The men attacked by this contagion are fretful and exacting, but as they do not form a family business [*ditta sociale*], as the women do with their husbands, fathers and mothers, their obstinacies are in consequence more pliant and less clamorous.'[16]

The contract was the primary vehicle for enshrining the singer's status. Perhaps the most powerful contract awarded to a female singer was that drawn up in April 1826 between Giuditta Pasta and John Ebers of the King's Theatre, London – a city described as the 'milch cow' of musicians and singers, paying vastly more than mainland European houses.[17] Pasta's contract covered a season of three and a half months, for a total number of thirty performances; she was contracted to sing as both '*Prima Donna assoluta*' and '*Musico assoluto*' (reflecting the nature of the roles she sang, both soprano and contralto, female and male). The contract stated that she would be paid £2,300 (the highest fee of Ebers' regime between 1820 and 1827);[18] she would receive the whole fee in advance – £500 in Paris where she was living, £500 on her arrival in London, and the remaining £1,300 before her debut; in all the operas, she would have the right to choose which roles she would sing; she was not obliged to sing more than six times a month, or to sing in any other concerts at the theatre apart from Ebers' benefit evening; she would sing no operas beyond those named (*Tancredi*, *Giulietta e Romeo*, *Otello*, *Semiramide*, *La rosa bianca e la rosa rossa*, *Nina* and *Medea*), with the exception of a new opera expressly composed for the King's Theatre – on condition she was entirely happy with her role; she would be afforded a benefit evening, presenting a new opera chosen by herself, the costs of which would be borne entirely by the management; she would be permitted leave of eight days; she would be able to sing in any private or public concerts, providing this did not interfere with her operatic performances; a box would be at her disposal during the length of her engagement, plus twelve tickets for the pit and twelve for the gallery on every night she played; she would choose the costumes necessary for her roles, all paid for by the management; finally, if the management failed to adhere to any of the contractual clauses, she would have the right to suspend all performances – the theatre remaining dark until the dispute was resolved. One of the clauses bears repeating in full:

> In all the operas in which Madame Pasta will perform, she alone will choose the actors, the distribution of the roles, the absolute direction of all that which regards the rehearsals, and all else for the *mise en scène* of the said operas. No-one will have the right to intervene in the rehearsals nor interfere with anything concerning the performance of those operas; it is of course understood that Madame Pasta will respect the ranking of the actors.[19]

Even for the period, this was an unusual contract, affording Pasta an extraordinary degree of authority over every aspect of the production process and allowing her to mould the performances precisely to her artistic vision. Moreover, Ebers published the contract in his memoirs of 1828, thereby making public the image it presents of the all-powerful prima donna. But it marked a high point for the female singer. This level of control over operatic production would increasingly pass from the artist to the management as the century progressed: the history of the singer during that era is traced through the often troublesome journey from one point to the other. In future, only by combining both performance and management were singers able to wield similar power later in the period.

But before the downward path began, one singer attempted to go even further. Ebers published another contract from 1826, this time proposed by Angelica Catalani. It includes – albeit phrased differently – many of the same clauses concerning roles and staging. Its major difference was that Catalani did not ask for a fee; instead, she sought half the 'general receipts of the Theatre for the season', although expecting Ebers to withstand 'every possible expense', including rent of the theatre, performers' salaries, tradesmen's bills and so forth. This was in essence a proposal of shared management but without equal costs – and it is not surprising that Ebers rejected it.[20] It is worth noting, however, that this time the contract was between the impresario and Catalani's husband ('Conditions between Mr Ebers and M. P. de Valabrèque'),[21] rather than with Catalani herself.

These London contracts differed substantially from the norm on mainland Europe, where singers rarely had the same degree of control over every aspect of the production. In general, contracts (whether with impresarios or with opera house managements) established the fee, the length of employment, numbers of agreed days for illness and leave, and the rights to benefit performances. Nor were there substantial differences between those issued to female and those to male singers. Adelaide Comelli's three-year contract with the impresario Domenico Barbaja in 1821, for example, is almost exactly the same as that of her new husband Giovanni Battista Rubini, beyond the fact that when she sang in the 'Ridotti Imperiali' the management undertook to furnish the costumes, and provide her with a maid when travelling.[22]

The legal formality of contracts did not preclude dissent. An immediate source of conflict concerned the operas. Certain contracts specified the roles to be played by the singers (as between Pasta and Ebers); other, less precise arrangements (often when the impresario was unsure of the programme of the coming season, or, as with Comelli and Barbaja, where the contract extended over several years) could cause considerable difficulties. One such example occurred in 1832 at the Teatro Regio, Parma, concerning – appropriately enough – a production of Donizetti's *Le convenienze ed inconvenienze teatrali*. The Hungarian soprano Lina Roser Balfe (wife of the composer Michael Balfe), had been contracted to sing three operas.[23] On arriving, she discovered that the impresario, Claudio Musi, also wanted her to sing the role of the Prima Donna in *Le convenienze*. She refused, arguing that this exceeded the agreed number of roles, that the part lay too low in her voice, and finally (clearly the most important factor) that the character was 'a woman of extreme impudence, or rather, a shameless character, who is impossible for me to perform'.[24] She claimed that Musi had initially acquiesced to her refusal, assigning the role to Margherita Rubini; but she had then discovered he had contracted another soprano, Letizia Cortesi, for the role at Roser's own expense. The ensuing row involved the court management of the theatre, as both Roser and Musi appealed for justice.

The eddies and cross-currents in this dispute illustrate some of the conflicting tensions within an opera house. There is little doubt that Roser was distressed far more by the character of the role than by its tessitura or the fact that it exceeded the agreed number. We might accuse her of a lack of sense of humour (when did it ever really harm a theatrical career to indulge in a spoof?); plenty of other prima donnas were happy enough to play the role – Pasta even used it for a benefit evening. Roser was obviously less secure in her reputation, or less confident in her ability for comedic playing. She was also pregnant, and, at the time of her formal complaints to the management, extremely tired – even fainting onstage at one point.[25] In total, from 26 December to 11 March, she sang forty-six full operatic performances, and participated in nine other benefit evenings – remarkably, she seems to have missed only one performance through ill health. By any standards, this was an exhausting schedule. Perhaps her reluctance to play the Prima Donna meant that she simply wasn't in the mood for games – particularly ones that publicly mocked (even if indirectly) her own commitment and hard-working existence. Finally, she played her strongest card: she offered to sing the role, and leave it to the audience to judge its effectiveness.[26] Such a suggestion undoubtedly sent a chill down the back of the impresario and the court administrators, with its implication of a studiedly disengaged performance. Musi backed down, the season ended, and before leaving, Roser wrote a thank-you note to Conte Stefano Sanvitale, expressing her gratitude for his help in seeing off Musi.[27]

We must assume that to sing a role that did not display a singer's talents to the full was considered a greater professional risk than that of displeasing the management. Certainly, some singers resisted with stubborn determination. At Berlin, a heated and protracted debate grew between Gasparo Spontini and Caroline Grünbaum (1814–68), who in 1834 refused to sing the title role in Spontini's *Olimpie*. Her father argued that the role was too strenuous for her age and did not suit her voice;[28] Spontini claimed that it was less difficult than Alice in *Robert le diable* (a role she had recently performed) and that she could have sung it easily.[29] The dispute, increasingly acrimonious, was never resolved, and someone else finally sang the part.

Convenienze also extended to compositional practices within the operas. But here again, there are signs that modern historians have sometimes exaggerated the extent to which prima donnas made nuisances of themselves. Kimbell, for example, makes a telling edit in his presentation of Carlo Ritorni's remarks about the singing of the final cabaletta. Ritorni's original wording of 'But then the prima donna, *or whoever was the principal singer*, turned their mind to appropriating the final applause, by closing the opera with their own rondo'[30] [my emphasis] is reduced neatly to 'the prima donna . . . turned her mind to the task of appropriating the final applause for herself', as if only women were so disposed to argue this point.[31] Suspicion might also be cast on another instance: Tacchinardi's daughter Fanny Persiani purportedly complaining about the conclusion of *Lucia di Lammermoor* in 1833. William Ashbrook remarks that 'In *Lucia* there is a double set of aria-finales, with Lucia's (the mad scene) preceding Edgardo's. One of Donizetti's letters reveals that this arrangement irked Persiani considerably while *Lucia* was in rehearsal.'[32] But this impression is due to a misreading of one of Donizetti's letters to the impresario Lanari in 1836, regarding the composition of *Pia de' Tolomei* for the Teatro della Pergola in Florence. Ashbrook translates Donizetti's letter thus: 'In *Lucia* I was the victim, because she was certainly not the brightest star, and I myself heard her many times say:"The curtain will fall after the aria of la Persiani!"'[33] The unabridged passage provides a different story:

The contract with Sig.ra Tacchinardi remains today an embarrassment, although not through her fault: when this capable singer does not do her duty, everyone says that it is in order to favour the operas of her husband; and you yourself have seen proof of this in Florence. In *Lucia* I was the victim, since she was certainly not the brightest star, even though she had a scene that at the rehearsals made Duprez tremble with fear and I myself was told many times, *the curtain will fall after the aria of Persiani*. The outcome was entirely the opposite. . . I do not know the reason for it, but however it is certain that in order to avoid any rumour it is advisable that the good *Fanny* expends her breath, if not more, at least as much as she does in her husband's operas. From all this comes that before signing your contracts I wish to know definitely which operas will be given both before and after mine, so that I might not have the displeasure of hearing myself told, *she does not sing yours like that of her husband*, or even *she has not taken the trouble*.[34]

Rather than being determined to outdo Duprez, Fanny Tacchinardi Persiani emerges as being concerned to shine only in her husband's operas, and therefore deliberately withholding her full abilities in the works of other composers (in Donizetti's opinion, at least). We might surmise, therefore, that this apparent example of a prima donna's demands for the fulfilment of her *convenienze* never existed – although it raises intriguing questions about the tensions within Persiani's marriage.

To quibble on these particular instances is not to deny that other singers were indeed capable of bad behaviour. But singers' demands about their roles in terms of arias, transpositions or additional items were born quite naturally out of an older perception of the relationship between singer and composer. In the eighteenth century, operatic composition was more nearly a collaborative process. Some composers actively enjoyed this partnership in creativity, particularly when a strong mutual respect existed between the two artists: Mozart wrote warmly of his working relationship with the tenor Anton Raaf, for example, and his delight in tailoring an aria 'to fit a singer as perfectly as a well-made suit of clothes'.[35] In the early part of the nineteenth century, this practice was still commonplace: Rossini's contract for *Il barbiere di Siviglia* with the Teatro di Torre Argentina, Rome, in 1815, stated that he was required to 'adapt' his music to the particular vocal talents of the singers, and also to make further alterations arising from the 'advantages and demands of the singers'.[36] As late as 1854, Meyerbeer told Rosine Stoltz to make whatever changes were necessary for her to sing Fidès' aria in Act 5 of *Le Prophète*, even if this meant cutting the middle section because it lay too high for her: 'I always believe that a role must lie well within the singer's vocal range for it to be effective. Therefore, should you find that some notes are not within your good range, it would be advisable to change them though it is important that you do this in such a way that the character of *cantilena* is not changed in the process.'[37]

At its most fruitful, where creative genius found correspondence between composer and singer, this practice of adjustment was highly rewarding, ensuring that both opera and performance appeared to the best advantage. If Pasta made her early reputation with works written for other singers (*Tancredi*, *Otello*, *Medea*), her essence as an artist left an indelible imprint in the works composed for her: Donizetti's *Anna Bolena*, and Bellini's *La sonnambula*, *Norma*, and *Beatrice di Tenda* offer a superb tracing of her performance abilities. But the need to write specifically for certain voices also arguably extended composers' artistic vision. Meyerbeer lavished particular care on writing for his singers, assiduously researching the peculiar qualities of each voice for which he composed. Verdi's *I Lombardi alla prima crociata* was penned for Erminia Frezzolini: her presence 'encouraged Verdi to develop his own, highly original vocal style, and eventually influenced the entire creative process'.[38] I have argued elsewhere that echoes of Wilhelmine Schröder-Devrient can be found in many of Wagner's operas:[39] he himself was effusive in his acknowledgement of her influence, stating that 'she had the gift of teaching a composer how to compose, to be worth the pains of such a woman's "singing"'.[40] Only three roles were written specifically for her, Adriano in *Rienzi*, Senta in *Der fliegende Holländer*, and Venus in *Tannhäuser*, but the effects of her artistry surface in other, sometimes unexpected places in Wagner's compositions. One hint may be found in the comments he made to Cosima in 1878 on *Tristan und Isolde* (1865): 'How did I ever achieve the rapture of the 2nd act? I know, it was through seeing Schröder-D. as Romeo, and it isn't so silly to have a woman in that role, for those little runts of men, and particularly tenors, can never do those lovely wild embraces.'[41] This indication that Schöder-Devrient's ardent performing style found musical manifestation in *Tristan und Isolde* is interesting not simply in itself, but also for the notion that operatic representation of impassioned masculinity in the mid-nineteenth century might have been influenced by female performance of *travesti* roles.

If instances of mutual creative attraction led to a real flowering of innovation on the operatic stage, however, shotgun weddings between composer and singer were often less successful. Rehearsing *Bianca e Fernando* in Genoa in 1828, Bellini was insistent that Adelaide Tosi perform his music exactly as written, despite her laments that it was 'music made for children'; Tosi's reluctance vanished when the cabaletta was a public success, and Bellini made a point of the fact that this momentary dispute between them was resolved in 'extreme cheerfulness'.[42] Verdi was more irritated by Sofia Loewe's dislike of the *terzetto finale* of *Ernani* in 1844; perhaps she had wanted a 'Rondò' instead, he wrote drily, and meanwhile 'poor Ernani was treated horrendously on the first evening'.[43] But whilst such disagreements might have been aggravating, one wonders whether there was nevertheless sometimes a positive aspect to these debates: whether being forced to address the nature and quality of composition in performance terms wasn't as productive a process for the composer as the discussions with librettists – and certainly better than isolation from the realities of the operatic stage.[44] The singers were after all concerned as much with the success of the finished product as the composer and librettist; Sofia Loewe's ideas about the finale of *Ernani* were seconded by Piave, the librettist, which might suggest that she had valid doubts about the structure of the opera, not merely the lack of opportunity for an *aria di bravura*.[45]

In short, early nineteenth-century singers saw opera as primarily a vehicle for the display of their talents, and the composer's task as shaping his musical conception to suit their artistic profiles. As late as 1853, Felice Varesi blamed the supposed 'fiasco' of the premiere of *La traviata* (in which he sang Germont) on Verdi's failure to write sufficiently well for the particular vocal abilities of his cast.[46] This was not merely misplaced ego. From the singers' perspective, the demands of the operatic marketplace in the pre-repertory period were on the expression of their performative individuality: a score's popularity might last only one or two seasons; a singer's career could last twenty years. In the 1820s, Micheroux advised Pasta to continually look for new operas, because the principal thing in London as elsewhere was 'new musical scores': it would be 'ridiculous' if she enclosed herself in the 'old circle' of her then standard roles of Tancredi, Medea, Desdemona, Romeo and so forth.[47] But when new scores were unavailable, the trick was to find novelty through different means. One such device was the *aria di baule* ('baggage aria'): an interpolated aria, sometimes especially written for the singer, sometimes an addition from an entirely different opera.[48] The purpose of the *aria di baule* was to demonstrate the singer's most appealing qualities – vocally and dramatically – to the full. In 1847 Jenny Lind added the aria from Meyerbeer's *Vielka* (a role composed especially for her, and which showed off her voice extremely well) to the Lesson Scene in Rossini's *Il barbiere di Siviglia*, to add a touch of novelty to an opera which by then was familiar territory.[49] But even these personalised additions could create conflict, as the contralto Clorinda Corradi recorded during a season at the Teatro Comunale in Bologna in 1829:

> In Tancredi the prima donna will not be Kinterland, [*sc. Maria Cascelli Kyntherland*] but instead a certain Orlandi contracted by Bandini, and who has never yet sung in the theatre. Kinterland rejected the role because in Tancredi Pasta sings an aria by Nicolini that Kinterland herself sang in the Voto di Jefte, for which she is so piqued that she did not want to sing any more. . .[50]

If the aim of the interpolated aria was to demonstrate something of absolute individuality in performance, then the singing of the same piece by two different singers invited unfair comparisons – Kyntherland clearly did not relish standing on stage as Pasta essayed an aria already performed by herself earlier in the season. (Later in the era, when the *arie di baule* had long disappeared, similar frictions still arose over the use of cadenze: Bellincioni relates the row that erupted in the 1880s when she appropriated the carefully guarded cadenze of the senior prima donna in the same touring company, and then sang them in performances of the same role – thus stealing the other woman's thunder.[51])

Arguments about maintaining the integrity of the composition, however, became increasingly more pressing. The moral of Sografi's late eighteenth-century play rested entirely on this point: that the performers do not have the right 'to disfigure the poetic productions of the best talents that Italy has had, or to exasperate the most excellent composers of music who distinguish themselves in our times'.[52] It is debatable, nevertheless, whether these arguments for transferring the notion of the artwork to the composition rather than the performance were viable in a situation where the theatre was a social meeting-place as much as a performance venue, or indeed where twenty or more performances of the same work were given in close proximity. Demands that the audience listen with silent, rapt attention to the same opera over and over again, in the manner that modern audiences attend contemporary productions, were probably unsustainable. Early Ottocento spectators watched opera as we watch television, with a mixture of casual interest and concentration, interspersed with conversation, food, and visits from friends and acquaintances.

But to regard this period as therefore devoid of good performance is misleading. In terms of an 'event', it is questionable whether homogeneity of production values necessarily lead to a greater effectiveness. The old ways were ridiculed for their lack of overall dramatic and more especially musical logic; and yet such coherence at the end of the century did not in itself save later operas from all charges of absurdity (see, for example, Joseph Kerman's stinging dismissal of *Tosca*).[53] Certainly, the attention of the early nineteenth-century audience towards the stage was *segmented*: each individual element was examined within its own sphere, so to speak, without being necessarily considered as part of a whole. This does not mean that there was a lack of informed criticism (the journals and periodicals demonstrate otherwise); or, as will be apparent in the following chapter, a lack of performance values. And where an audience was already very familiar with a particular opera, the change in the order of the acts, the addition of a new or different aria, all added something fresh and new to the experience. In 1840 Countess de Merlin maintained that although the custom of performing different acts of operas was 'at variance with common sense' and an 'absurd' practice, it was 'not revolting to the ear of the amateur'. Her argument was based on the notion that the 'sense of hearing' had three stages: 'its first developement [*sic*], its perfection, and decay'. She claimed that the unexpected repositioning and sampling of certain acts in different contexts enabled her to appreciate these works with new insight:

> This custom of performing separate acts of operas confers the charm of novelty on many old productions. I have often listened to musical compositions which appeared to be invested with additional freshness and beauty, merely by the modifications produced on my feelings by time and place! – How many confused and fugitive recollections – how many sensations of the mind may be conjured up by the electric strains of songs which we have once listened to carelessly, and perhaps unconsciously![54]

But by the end of the decade, all had begun to change. The world outside the theatre was also changing; a new era of reform pursued the revolutions (sometimes abortive) and uprisings that sputtered through Europe from 1848 onwards, and it left its trail across the operatic stage. The greater part of the efforts of composers, librettists, impresarios, and publishers (urged on by the critics in the flourishing musical press) was to impose a kind of order on the seeming chaos of the early nineteenth-century opera house. Thus the practice of introducing *arie di baule* was increasingly banished,[55] and demands for new arias that better fitted the singers' voices were refused;[56]

gradually, the composer gained ascendance and operas were no longer adjusted to display individual talents but became *in themselves* the dominant or fundamental component of the performance process; the composer was no longer a commercial purveyor of melodies (Rossini), but refashioned as an Artist (Wagner).

Similarly, the introduction of the conductor imposed order within the pit: where once singers regarded the *primo violino* or *violino principale* as the aid to their performance,[57] the conductor as tyrant (Toscanini is perhaps the best known example) held increasing sway by the end of the era. The control of time, perhaps the musician's and especially the singer's most prized commodity in the shaping of performance, was handed to the conductor. The search for a unified production concept[58] brought an equal discipline to the area of dramatic interpretation: first in terms of authenticity of costume (no-one must wear anything other than the prescribed garments, thunder the prompt-books);[59] and then in terms of actual staging, marked by the arrival of a director who stipulated what kinds of gestures and movements would be used, and when. The individuality of the singer's performance is undoubtedly still – just – apparent at the end of the period (see Garden or Shalyapin), but the Svengali-like notion of the director as the only person who can unlock the genius within the perfomer would gain in currency as the years pass. The libretti equally betray increasing unease with the practices of the past. The kind of narrative incongruency which marked earlier operas would give way to the insistence on dramatic unity, on 'realism', which was often simply another word for 'logic'. Those additional elements external to the libretto that interfered with the dramatic unity of an operatic performance – the positioning of an unrelated ballet between two different acts of an opera, for example – were also abandoned.

Even the earlier practices of managing a career were brought under newer controls. The family was still in evidence (Viola Tree recorded that Lucrezia Bori was much approved by her Italian audience in 1911 because she travelled accompanied by her father and brother);[60] but in general the arrival of the theatrical agent established a new, more formal system. If at the beginning of the period, many opera houses still had close links with governments or courts (the Berlin Hoftheater, the Teatro Regio at Turin), by the end of the century opera had become (with some exceptions) an almost entirely commercial enterprise. The demands of the marketplace effected certain changes: the irrationality of the court opera house, where a prince or monarch could decree the performance begin with the latter half of the opera followed by the *first* half of the opera (Parma) or request unscheduled extra performances of the opera (Paris, 1820s) or intervene actively in the hiring or firing of singers (Berlin, 1830s), gave way to the logic of commerce.

We might regard this entire construction of a series of controls and brakes on previous operatic practice as a kind of 'masculinisa-tion' of the system of production, in which the development of 'order' and 'rationalisation' is equated with progress and the needs of a modern marketplace. The prima donna still nominally retained the appearance of status, but the prima donna-*as*-opera, in the manner in which Pasta-*was*-Norma, had all but vanished. When we see Emma Eames, a prim, middle-class girl, achieve pre-eminence on the operatic stage of the 1890s, therefore, it is only partly accurate to consider this a victory for a widening definition of what was or was not appropriate behaviour for a woman of her class. Her liberty in developing a career was offset by the tightening controls that limited and regulated operatic practice: her individual freedom as a woman was countered by a loss of freedom as a professional artist.[61] By the end of the period, in 1930, one hundred years after Giuditta Pasta was performing *Tancredi* at the Teatro Comunale in Bologna, the profes-sion bore only a superficial resemblance to the site of artistic licence she and her colleagues had enjoyed.

MANAGEMENT AND MONEY

Professional life throughout the period was governed to a large extent by the relationships between singer and management: a term that loosely encompassed impresario, theatre owner, court administrator, publisher, composer, librettist, conductor and stage director. Some – indeed, probably most – of the relationships singers enjoyed in their working lives were cordial and productive. Bellini wrote that Pasta made even him weep in the early performances of *Norma*;[62] Meyerbeer told his wife about the herculean task of staging *Robert le diable* in Berlin in 1832: it would have been impossible without the 'goodwill, enthusiasm and hard work of the singers', and he could not praise them enough for their commitment.[63]

But problems could nevertheless arise. Singers answered to at least three separate but interrelated authorities: the audience, the impresario or artistic management, and the owners of the theatre (a notably influential element in the European court theatres). Some singers became adept at manipulating the possible tensions between these parties: the power acquired as a result of public approbation could easily be used as leverage against unacceptable (or what were considered unacceptable) demands on the part of the management; appeals to the theatre owners or court or government authorities could bring pressure to bear against the impresario.[64]

Many disputes between singers and impresarios were due primarily to ineffective managerial strategies rather than so-called artistic temperament. Lack of parity in the treatment of the singers, as was evident in the 1820s and 1830s in Berlin, clearly fuelled dissent. Lack of money was another factor: during the production of *Lucia di Lammermoor* in Naples in 1835, Donizetti wrote that 'As Persiani has not been paid, she does not want to rehearse'[65] – an all too frequent lament made by singers. Lack of integrity when making offers of employment or honouring contractual arrangements was perhaps the most common fault of all. An extraordinary row surfaced in Paris in 1825: both Fodor and Pasta had been promised performances of *Semiramide* – Fodor as her debut opera, Pasta for her benefit. The dispute made its way into the press, and became public debate as supporters of both singers argued their different merits and justifications. It only subsided when Castil-Blaze published a long tract: in it, he said with measured fairness that both singers would perform the role equally well, and both were equally right in their claims – it was the management's error, and should be openly acknowledged as such.[66]

Female singers were often drawn as difficult, awkward to deal with, and intemperate in such disputes. Following a troubled rehearsal between Spontini and Josefine Schulz[67] in Berlin, Karl von Brühl referred to her as 'a woman whose lively and quick-tempered character impedes every kind of moderation'.[68] One wonders how many of these impressions were owing not to genuine character traits of the singers, but rather to the tensions that arose from the unusual position of women negotiating on equal – sometimes superior – terms with men, in an era that presumed a quite different relationship between the genders. This did not necessarily lead to worse treatment of the female singers at the hands of male impresarios; but it did seem to create more noise and antipathy in the various disputes. Schulz's outburst against Spontini (as described by Brühl to the composer) offers an example of the kind of complaint interpreted as excessive; she had apparently complained of 'the lack of consideration for her and the hardness with which you treat her, forcing her often to sing even when she feels ill; that she had always fulfilled your desires with the greatest exactness; she had consented, to please you, to perform successively the most tiring roles in your operas; but she sees now that all her compliance was useless, from now on she does not want to do any more than her strict duty.' A letter two months later refers to her pregnancy: it is possible that she was already pregnant at the time of her outburst against Spontini. But Spontini had the knack of upsetting almost all his singers, even those he favoured and tried to support, such as Schulz.

Certain disputes with the prima donnas seem unfathomable to the modern eye. What exactly, for example, upset Giulio Ricordi so much in 1871 about Teresa Stolz's contractual demands regarding the forthcoming production of *Aida* that he writes to Verdi with his hands 'trembling with rage'?[69] Her letter seems perfectly courteous: her conditions well within then current practices – with the possible exception of the first one, regarding the guarantee of her fee either by the municipal authorities or by a bank.[70] Despite Ricordi's severe reply (in which he tells her that 'never in my life have I felt a displeasure so lively and a disillusion so strong' as on receiving her letter),[71] shortly afterwards Stolz had accepted the contract – apparently on the terms she had first suggested.[72] Given that all was finally accepted, and that the size of fee did not appear to be an issue, perhaps this dispute arose as much as a result of vocabulary and phraseology as from any real unreasonableness on her part.

Opera house managements frequently sought advice from other theatres on the reliability and value of singers before contracts were finalised. An extraordinary letter from the composer Giuseppe Rastrelli in Dresden in 1833 to Spontini about Schröder-Devrient illustrates (if true) how difficult a singer could be:

> This singer, having arrived here on 3rd September last, sang, after some days of rest, *Fidelio* and a week later Desdemona in *Otello* in Italian with the greatest commitment; the Royal Direction [*Real Direzione*] therefore believed this singer would continue with the same zeal in performing her roles twice a week. But she immediately declared that she had not come to Dresden in order to lose her voice, but in order to rest (it is an agreeable 'rest' to enjoy a salary of 5,000 thalers). After which, the principal part in Wolfram's opera, *Schloss Candra*, was entrusted to her, for which she showed extreme reluctance, not coming to the first five rehearsals with piano – first with the excuse of indisposition, then with tiredness. In order to remove every impediment, these rehearsals were next held at her house, as she wished, in the hope that things would improve. I assure you, signor Cavaliere, that it takes a great deal of patience to study an opera with this *cara signora*, because at rehearsals she only sings *sottissima voce*; whatever seems a little high to her, she sings an octave lower; in the somewhat difficult passages, she does not pronounce any words, vocalizing always on *a a a* – the mistakes she makes in the first piano rehearsals are made again in the orchestral rehearsals, and later in all the performances, as she did in Wolfram's opera, and almost always in the same situations: clear proof that she studies nothing for herself, falling again always into the same defects. Poor Wolfram suffered much for this signora, who had the rudeness, in a moment of impatience, to throw her part at the feet of the composer and stamp on it. The opera had to be postponed for some days, because

the orchestral rehearsals, and particularly the dress rehearsal, went so badly, on account of this singer! One hoped things might go better, but in vain; all happened as I said above. The composer conducted his opera once, and I three times: all went very well, beyond that which Devrient was singing.

After this she studied Bellini's *La straniera*, for which she demonstrated excellent care, and almost one hoped that things would change for the better. But the keyboard rehearsals began again in her house – something that displeased me very much because of the thousand distractions that are there (now pictures, now books) which take away from the singers the attention necessary for study. At the end of every rehearsal there was an importuning visit from some Polish nuisance that disturbed us very much. I complained to the Signori Maestri of this disorder, but it seems everyone trembles before this Armida enchantress. The orchestral rehearsals of *Straniera* went *almost* like those of *Schloss Candra*, because of the aforementioned defects: lack of study, of attention etc. She did not arouse in this opera the enthusiasm that she was hoping; on the contrary, I assure you that the great furore of before is almost extinct, and only the Polish still listen to her. As for her moral conduct, I cannot tell you anything new, dealing with her as little as I can, and not trusting too much in others' assertions on this point; however, I believe she is what she was, since until now she has not given any sign of conversion. Among her admirers is Count Potocki, whom I've seen every time at her house at the end of rehearsals. Before long, the in-laws of this unattractive and married young man will come to lead him away and put an end to every disorder.

Here, my dear Sig. Cavaliere, is as much as I can tell you in all conscience regarding signora Schröder-Devrient, begging you wholeheartedly to put into execution as soon as you have read this letter that which you promised me to do, as I glean from your last [*the burning of the letter*].

The Royal Direction has gained nothing in contracting this singer, who sings what she wants and as she wants, dealing with too much confidence – on the contrary, impertinence – with the aforesaid administration.

I believe that if she ever knew how I write to you, she would kill me for certain. I therefore implore you to make sure this does not happen.[73]

This fascinating letter documents every aspect of Schröder-Devrient's professional and moral conduct: the use of the epithet 'Armida enchantress' to describe her effect on the senior administration of the theatre; the financial value of her work (supposedly nil); her impertinence towards the management; the desire of Rastrelli that the letter should be destroyed (was she really too powerful to cross?); the way her chief admirer, Count Potocki, needed to be rescued by his family from her clutches. Jumping on the score of a struggling composer would hardly endear her to her colleagues, of course; but it is significant that she appears to have shown greater respect for other, more established works (*Otello*, *Fidelio*, and *La straniera*) that have better stood the test of time. In contrast, Wolfram's compositions do not even merit an entry in *Grove Opera*. Perhaps Schröder-Devrient's antipathy to the score was simply a sign of (albeit exasperated) good taste. Interestingly, even this description of her attitude and behaviour did not derail the contractual negotiations at Berlin: the management might have been forewarned, but her reputation at the box office nevertheless overrode every other component.

Perhaps the greatest disputes, however, regarded fees. The common perception of singers was clearly as shallow, meretricious figures obsessed with money. The 'Old Price' riots at Covent Garden, when the audience erroneously believed that the change in the seat prices was entirely the responsibility of exaggerated demands by Angelica Catalani, set the tone for the era.[74] I cited earlier the remarks of de Boigne on Pauline Viardot, and his eulogising of her as an 'artist'; but these remarks also concluded with a sting in the tail: 'But there is no light without shade – every medal has its reverse. This exceptional talent is rather a talent for study, for the workroom, for book-learning. These great inspirations, these demonstrators of vast erudition worship the golden calf as do common singers, rushing from north to south, from south to north in order to make money, and too often sacrificing themselves to an overwhelming desire to produce showy effects.'[75] Almost every impresario highlighted the supposed greed of the singers, as if their own intervention in the operatic marketplace was entirely selfless and philanthropic. Articles in the press (both musical and otherwise) emphasised the artists' earnings with a disapproving tone: the *Harmonicon* in 1830 wrote about the 'exorbitant recompenses paid to singers';[76] in 1838, the *Corriere dei teatri* argued that the fees obtained by opera singers were outrageously high in comparison to the meagre earnings of actors;[77] in 1851 the *Gazzetta musicale di Milano* contrasted the poverty of former singers with the riches acquired by contemporary artists;[78] in 1886 a San Francisco newspaper declared that 'Lyric artists are, as a rule, the most grossly ignorant people on all subjects, except their own special art, and money. They are intensely conceited and abominably selfish, and regard an impresario as their natural prey.'[79]

Certainly, vast sums could be made as an opera singer. The Italian tenor Giovanni Battista Rubini, careful and organised with his money, accrued a considerable fortune, and built a lavish mansion for himself and his family. Later in the century, Adelina Patti's country house in Wales, with its own private theatre and thirty-four bedrooms, was an equally well-known testament to one prima donna's earning capacity. But most singers were less fortunate. Forced to earn a lifetime's salary within a finite but alarmingly indeterminate period, with no real notion of when their voice might suddenly give out or their popularity fade, their anxiety over fees was understandable. And there were numerous expenses – travel, lodgings, costume, coaching, music, let alone the care of sometimes an entire retinue of family and supporters – that ate into their initial riches.

To the theatre managements, the singers were understandably a commodity. Status within the opera house depended on the singer's prowess at the box office. Spontini's dispute with Schulz at the Royal Opera House in Berlin was all the more unfortunate in that in 1821 he had earlier argued that she should receive a 500 scudi increase in her annual salary of 2,000 scudi: the manager, Brühl, had rejected this request because she did not 'attract people to the theatre', unlike the other house sopranos, Anna Milder and Carolina Seidler: 'The same roles sung by each singer have produced very different results at the box-office.'[80] Box-office receipts appear to have been Brühl's

only criteria on deciding salaries: Spontini's pleas that Schulz deserved to be treated at the same level as her colleagues for reasons
of parity and her usefulness were entirely ignored. The debate was
still continuing two years later. In such environments, where singers
were themselves valued not according to artistic worth or loyal
service but strictly according to financial criteria, it would be strange
indeed if they also did not view their relationship with managers in
similar terms. For their part, singers were well aware of their own
impact on the box office. In 1833, Pasta wrote to her mother from
her season in London: 'since I've been here [Laporte] makes lots of
money, the theatre is always full or crowded and yet he still com-
plains [*fa il piangino*]'.[81] In this equation of money and status,
accepting a reduced fee meant – effectively – the beginning of the
end of a career. In 1874, close to retirement, Teresa Stolz explained to
Verdi that Cremona could not pay her requested fee of 1,000 francs,
and that she did not want to go for less, 'so that they may not have
the opportunity to speak badly of me and my perhaps deteriorated
means! I want to leave the theatre with all the dignity imaginable!'[82]

Maurice Strakosch argued with justification that although it was
perfectly acceptable for the great divas – a mere half-dozen in the
whole world – to request astronomical fees, the problem was that
lesser singers expected the same level of financial recompense, in
theatres that could not possibly sustain it.[83] Greed was an undeniable
factor in such miscalculations. But so too was ignorance: the public,
often inaccurate discussion of salaries and earnings must have surely
increased some singers' ambitions about the size of their fee. Ebers
commented that during Pasta's London season in 1826, the press
reported 'with the usual correctness of statements relative to Opera
affairs' that she was earning two to three hundred pounds a night; in
fact, Ebers said, her nightly average was around £76.[84] In 1838, *Figaro*
reported that 'In a single evening, Giulietta Grisi earned at London
sixty thousand fiorini!!'[85] The *Cosmorama pittorico* marvelled in 1857
that various French and Italian papers had claimed that the consul of
Brazil had offered Angiolina Bosio 'the sum of 30,000 francs for ten
months; more, a guaranteed benefit of not less than 50,000 francs;

more, a carriage, servants, travel for four persons; more, *all those conditions she wished to establish*': in fact, the *Cosmorama* had established that such reports were wholly false, and that the impresario responsible for signing European artists had declared that he would not dream of making such a proposition.[86]

The conviction that singers were continually overpricing their abilities undoubtedly influenced management decisions. Opera singers were some of the first artists to have access to a wide international marketplace; this gave them manoeuvrability of an unprecedented order.[87] It is difficult to know in this context whether singers' demands were genuinely unreasonable, or whether it was the sheer measure of the fees they were able to command that provoked such continual comment – much as the fees of modern celebrities from footballers to soap-stars do so today. Then as now, however, more could not be paid than the market would bear. Most singers attempted to determine the level of their fees in the context of what they had been offered by other impresarios and opera houses. But hard bargaining could lead to offence. The negotiations between Malibran and Edouard Robert of the Théâtre-Italien in Paris in 1829 illustrate how manipulative employers could become when they felt under undue pressure. Robert's letter to Vicomte de Laferté was full of flattery for Malibran's 'immense talent', of which he declared himself 'the most ardent and sincere admirer', plus a ludicrously exaggerated portrait of the conditions in Italian theatres which awaited her if she refused the contract;[88] to his colleague Severini the next day, however, he described her as 'that rapacious leech', and claimed it would teach her a lesson if they were able to hire Pasta instead.[89] Not for nothing did Alessandro Micheroux advise Pasta: 'Do not delude yourself about the caresses of the Impresario.'[90]

The impresarios also affected the way the singer's relationship to money was portrayed in the press, both through their complaints and the doctoring of their own image. They presented themselves to the public with all the largesse of beneficent providers, concerned only with throwing a good party for the guests. *I teatri* reported the impresarial efforts of Andrea Bandini at the Teatro Comunale in Bologna in 1829 in the flattering terms often repeated elsewhere: 'not heeding the grave cares or the enormous expense, but nurturing only the desire to be worthy of the people of Bologna, surpassing the promises made, he knew how to give us four scores of the highest quality'.[91] In absorbing the financial risk of the undertaking, the impresarios could thus effectively appear as gallant champions of the operatic enterprise. In contrast, the singers found themselves cast as the ones who spoiled the fun by introducing the coldly mercenary element of money. Both male and female singers were implicated in this prejudice; but women suffered more from the distance between conventional gender images and reality. If their bourgeois sisters stayed at home and made music in the comfort of their drawing rooms, ran the contemporary logic, why weren't these women doing the same? The notion of women actually *wanting* a career seems to have been alien to much of society. Although an admirer of Violante Camporese's amiability and ladylike behaviour, Ebers nevertheless claimed that like every singer 'she was griping in her demands on the treasury'. But, he argued, this financial obsession was inevitable: 'For the only object which can induce a woman of character and education to come on to the stage being the hope of emolument, the organ of acquisitiveness may naturally be expected universally to develop its power with proportionate strength.'[92] Such views were commonplace. Many biographical items and fictional portrayals in the earlier part of the period emphasise that it was only the need of money, following a family's financial disaster, that had persuaded an otherwise respectable girl to enter the profession. Even singers themselves used such reasoning in their self-descriptions: in a letter by Johanna Eunicke (1800–56) to Spontini in 1825, the singer wrote about her family's 'irreprehensible reputation' in Berlin and that it was the 'wretched circumstances of the years from 1812–18' that had forced her as a girl of thirteen to undertake leading roles.[93]

But the shaping of the prima donna's motives in such purely economic terms also conversely evoked connotations of prostitution:

the singers' willingness to provide pleasure for money – and pleasure of a particularly sensual kind, often requiring physical display – trod a path only a step away from that of the courtesan. This circle could only be squared much later when the stage had been gentrified, and when women were finally permitted to regard a life of work outside the home as a valid alternative to domestic duties.

In the meantime, the discourse framing women's desire to be an opera singer only within the context of financial 'emolument' and unfeminine ambition denied the serious interest and enjoyment many opera singers had in their own careers. Even in 1840, in the final years of her professional life, Pasta wrote a proud little post-script at end of a long letter to her son-in-law: 'Between ourselves, I will confide to you (as someone very knowledgeable about singing) that yesterday evening in the duet from [*Arabi nelle Gallie*] I made a new cunning embellishment [*sghirigogolo*]: that is, I took and held a high D natural and then I skated down merrily to the low A, which made a beautiful effect.'[94]

MAKING A CAREER

One goal remained constant but elusive throughout the period: success. For some singers, success arrived remarkably easily. Isabella Colbran's career began with little difficulty;[95] Pauline Viardot Garcia met with a similarly enthusiastic response from her very first appearances.[96] Other prima donnas had a slower start, but then matured into extraordinary artists, such as Giuditta Pasta, Sophie Cruvelli and Emma Calvé. Félia Litvinne commented how the latter's initial performances were unremarkable; on seeing Calvé some years later, she was astonished at the transformation in both vocal and dramatic terms.[97]

Yet other singers appeared to have hovered on the edge of success without ever actually attaining it. The accusations that a career could be purchased through a network of the right connections seem to have little substance: or at least, it was difficult to create a solid, successful career out of the occasional opportunities such 'protection' offered.[98] Carolina Biagioli, perhaps an early example of the dilettante singer who turned to a professional career in the 1820s when her husband's earning capability was jeopardised, clearly enjoyed the full support of Rossini: he wrote letters on her behalf, he organised a concert at which she sang in London alongside famous artists like Pasta and Colbran, she even appeared at La Scala. Despite all this, her career never really took root; she wrote in desperation for financial aid in 1830, on the verge of being homeless.[99]

Sexual harassment and intrigue undoubtedly existed – particularly targeted towards the younger and more vulnerable singers. Garden's letters to Florence Mayer suggested that operatic debuts were often associated with morally dubious behaviour:

> What a life I have chosen Mrs Mayer, you have *no idea* of it, but I can't give it up now, or have no intention of doing it, only it is the lowest, hardest most disgusting life for anyone who wishes to get there on her talent alone – just to the present, I am succeeding that way, but if I am not accepted at the Opera it will be someone against me, or a clause in the contract I wont sign . . . is it to pay in the end?[100] I hope to God, yes, or I don't know what I'll do . . .[101]

Another letter suggests that the 'flawlessly armoured personality' Christiansen accuses Garden of possessing in later life[102] had been deliberately fashioned as a protection against the manoeuvrings of the operatic impresarios and agents:

> Oh! Mr Mayer the world is *so cruel* for a woman all alone! If they can put her down they do it – and one has to have a character of iron to stand up against it all and come out in the end as honest and pure as when I went into it – I'll do it, I know I will, and then when I am at last *there*, perhaps I can have my peace. . .[103]

It is possible to read Garden's comments (including further statements that unlike other singers any debut she receives will have been obtained 'honourably'), as another way of excusing herself to the Mayers for her lack of success. But there are plenty of allusions to the pressures for sexual favours in the histories of other singers.

Oscar Hammerstein's harassment of Marguerite D'Alvarez was publicly known.[104] Maggie Teyte found herself expected to service Raoul Gunsberg, impresario of the Monte Carlo Opera House where she made her first professional appearances;[105] Félia Litvinne was offered a repeat of her contract at Barcelona if she agreed to do likewise for the director.[106] Blanche Arral claimed that there were 'two distinct businesses' operating in the theatres, run by the managers: one concerned with the production of operas; the other arranging introductions between the female artists and the rich men who eyed them across the footlights, for a 'handsome stipend'. She was forced to dine with the friends of her manager, men who were 'in every way repugnant and uncongenial'; when she was inveigled into appearing at the private theatre of an elderly millionaire and then learnt she had to stay the night, she walked eight miles home in her evening dress and satin slippers.[107] Perhaps such incidents offer us a different meaning for the professional singers' frequent references to the 'hard work' required of the apprentice prima donna.

What then were the necessary elements for success? Voice and dramatic talent, certainly, as will be explored in the next chapters. But the look of an artist – preferably 'a fascinating physical beauty', as Strakosch recommended – was also important.[108] An oft-cited story, told to illustrate the era's emphasis on physical appearance, is the anecdote of Benedetta Rosmunda Pisaroni's first performances following a bout of smallpox; her disfigurement was such that she wore a mask in order to persuade the audience to appreciate her voice before she revealed the extent of damage to her face. But male artists were equally under pressure to impress the audience by their physical beauty. Tacchinardi was often criticised for his ugliness; similar stories revolve around his attempts to be 'heard' rather than 'seen'.[109] Ideas about the importance of physical beauty also varied from country to country. Ebers explained away Velluti's championship of Emilia Bonini (a 'tolerable' performer who was disadvantaged by her 'total want of personal attractions') by saying that in Italy, 'beauty is not considered so essentially necessary as in England, and, provided a singer has talents, personal appearance is little considered'.[110] The belief that the British audience was particularly choosy with regard to 'personal appearance' surfaces again in Fétis' discussion of Catalani. When the Italian librettist Lorenzo Da Ponte looked for singers in Venice, however, he was searching for voices not faces.[111] Nevertheless, beauty allied to voice was a significant asset in any country. De Pontmartin claimed that nothing more beautiful than Giulia Grisi had been seen before in the theatre: 'Her head offered all the perfections of an antique statue.' He admired the 'incredible regularity' of her features, her 'great eyes' and black hair, her shoulders and arms which resembled 'the marble of Paros'.[112] Singers such as Grisi and Lina Cavalieri (the 'most beautiful woman in the world') undoubtedly produced an erotic frisson within the audience; others, like Lind or Persiani, were merely regarded as attractive or handsome.

But confidence was a much more significant factor than physical appearance. In Modena in 1829, a young singer, Orsola Corinaldesi, made her debut in Mayr's *Ginevra di Scozia*: finding herself badly received by the audience, 'she allowed herself to be dominated by such discouragement, which hindered all the effect of her role'.[113] An unknown singer in the middle of the century complained she had still not launched her career because she lacked 'a certain confidence in myself, without which one can do nothing good'.[114] Audiences, particularly in some Italian opera houses, could be extremely hostile. Fyodor Shalyapin recalled one performance at La Scala in 1901 when 'the final act was original in the highest degree, since the entire audience took part in it. I was sorry for the French contralto, whom they mimicked, howled at, miaowing, mooing, barking, imitating her singing.'[115] Such scenes sound horrendous, yet we should remember that a far more ominous sign of the disapproval of an Italian audience was pure silence. Nevertheless, it is hardly surprising that some singers seem to have been so cowed. The mezzo-soprano Lison Frandin (1854–1911) appeared at Parma in 1884; she had made her debut at Cairo in 1881 and earlier that year had already sung at Rome, Naples and Trieste. Despite such experience, Giulio Ferrarini (secretary to the administration of the Teatro Regio) recorded after the first performance of *Mignon* on Christmas Day: 'La Frandia [*sic*], having been seized by panic, has been much inferior to what she demonstrated in the rehearsals. However, she will end by pleasing because she is a *true artist*.'[116] Later performances certainly won her much applause. But the same pattern repeated itself six weeks later with *La Favorite*; once again on the first night she was prey to 'an unconquerable panic' – once again, everything improved on the following nights.[117] Other singers were made of sterner stuff. In Naples in 1835, Donizetti claimed that 'La Ronzi has relinquished 30 performances because the public absolutely did not want her for 100 – she has been heard too much. She has very little political sense, and only shouts "*money money the whistling doesn't matter to me*"; this aggravates the public, she is wrong: and the public is wrong to whistle her, because at the moment in Italy we hear none better than her in the silence of Madame Pasta and Malibran.'[118]

Even when success arrived, it often wasn't at the right time or in the right environment. Luck was everything. A letter from Virginia Censi in 1862 talks excitedly of her triumphs in *Macbeth* at Spoleto: finally she has triumphed, she has aroused the audience to 'fanatismo' in the sleepwalking scene, her technique, dramatic action, accent and voice have all been admired. If she had to judge from the reaction in this city, she wrote, then she might be able to say that her career was assured: 'but you will see that now they will take the excuse of saying that it was not a theatre worth consideration, and I will return to the beginning . . . but one does not think about it for now – I am content and that is enough.'[119]

Good health in this search for success was a prerequisite. Strakosch declared that an iron constitution was required, to endure the long journeys and relentless pace of work for a modern prima donna.[120] When Viola Tree auditioned for Strauss, she attempted to explain away the unsteadiness of her voice as due to her train journey – that meant that the voice was 'too tender', Strauss replied.[121] Without a voice of much tougher stamp, Anna Bishop surely would never have survived her extraordinary career in the mid-nineteenth century: in the course of thirty-eight years she travelled through every major continent – Africa, India, Australasia, Asia, Europe and the Americas. Poor health was not only disastrous for singers but also a serious financial risk for impresarios: Lanari detailed the damage that befell him and the management of the Teatro La Fenice in 1839 when Caroline Ungher, forced to perform all the operas of the season owing to Strepponi's absence through pregnancy, fell ill as a result of overwork: her fifteen-day absence (even though covered by an understudy) emptied the theatre.[122] Menstruation could also cause problems. Rosmini maintained that theatrical law should recognise that during menstruation singers' voices underwent certain modifications; and that some prima donnas were medically advised to request rest or the omission of particularly difficult or tiring arias.[123] The archives contain many such petitions. A letter from Carolina Grünbaum's father in the 1830s explained that since that morning his daughter was 'in a period in which she should not sing' and requested that she might omit her first aria that evening in consequence;[124] the following year he warns Spontini that from the next Sunday Grünbaum would not be able to sing because on the preceding Friday or Saturday the 'days of her indisposition' would begin.[125] Later in the century, an intriguing entry in Ferrarini's diary listed that Chiara Bernau refused to attend the dress rehearsal of Auteri-Manzocchi's *Stella* in 1883 because of her menstruation – 'The husband shouts and weeps!'[126]

According to Rosmini, vocal changes were even more acute during pregnancy; it was therefore obligatory under Italian law that singers informed the management of their pregnant state before signing a contract. A failure to do so exposed the singers to legal redress for the damages sustained by the management if they were unable to fulfil their obligations towards the public satisfactorily.[127] The dispute of Francesca Festa Maffei with the Teatro Argentina in Rome in 1806 illustrates some of the difficulties women faced in such situations. When she arrived at the theatre to take up her contract, it was realised that she was pregnant: 'The news of the rotondity of the enormous Festa spread immediately through Rome, and the ridicule and satires began.' The government stepped in, and insisted that the impresario dispense with the contract. 'Imagine the anger of the singer, who apparently had the courage to present herself so enlarged before the public! She went to bed and miscarried.' The singer then demanded the full observance of her contract from the impresario, or damages if he refused. Claiming that the physical appearance of Festa was even worse after the miscarriage than before, the impresario held to the legality of his position; and offered Festa a mere quarter of her fee. She insisted on half; only after interventions from the Pontificate did the impresario finally agree on damages of a third of her fee.[128]

Pregnancy had other contractual implications. If a woman was married, then motherhood was regarded as a natural consequence, and no penalty was exacted as compensation for a broken contract. Indeed, one French tribunal in Nancy in 1845 ruled that a Madame Bernard was entitled to her stipend during her month's absence for childbirth, because having employed a married woman the impresario should have foreseen the 'probable interruption of service' through the arrival of children: an attitude that might seem enlightened but perhaps also led automatically to a prejudice against employing married women. But if a singer was unmarried, then the situation was very different: she was deemed to have freely 'chosen' her pregnant state, and could be made to pay a forfeit for the damage to the impresario – a harsh response, in Rosmini's view, but one that was still enshrined in theatre contract law in Italy in the 1930s.[129]

Many singers appeared to have avoided pregnancy entirely, or at least delayed it until their retirement from the stage. Motherhood undoubtedly presented special difficulties for the working artist – particularly if she was unmarried. Perhaps the fullest description of the problems pregnancy could cause to both singer and opera management lies in Lanari's account of Giuseppina Strepponi in the late 1830s, who found herself pregnant for the third time, by an unnamed tenor. Her agent (and the father of her first child), Cirelli, came to her aid; and the subsequent correspondence between Lanari, Strepponi and Cirelli reveals a classic operatic tale of illegitimate birth. The seductive trickery of a caddish lover; the necessity of hiding the pregnancy from the theatre authorities, courtesy of falsified medical certificates; the decamping to a secret location; the news of the birth and recovery; the abandonment of the child; Strepponi's desperation – Cirelli's concern – Lanari's cynicism: all is drawn here in high relief.[130] By the time that Strepponi finally found herself in a stable relationship with Verdi, her child-bearing years were tragically past.

In an era which condemned women particularly harshly when marriages failed, many singers found that separation or divorce had severe consequences on their relationship with their children. Schröder-Devrient lost custody of her four children to her first husband. Nellie Melba's son George Armstrong merits only three brief mentions in her autobiography: his father removed him from his mother's care in the 1890s. New medical procedures offered a different but drastic solution to women reluctant to become mothers: Maggie Teyte, at the urging of her husband, consented to have her Fallopian tubes tied in 1912 – it was supposedly a temporary solution, but proved permanent.[131]

Other singers managed motherhood rather well. Pasta's relationship with her daughter Clelia illustrates that despite the difficulties of frequent long absences, it was possible to enjoy a close rapport. If her correspondence with husband and friends was sometimes sporadic, she wrote regularly and with great affection to her daughter. An undated letter, probably written when Pasta became a grandmother, expresses the depth of her sentiments:

> Blessed be the day, the month and the year, blessed without end the day in which the heavens gave me my Clelia. If you want to understand the affection that I bear you, imagine what would be my existence without you. God has conceded you the first joy on earth in rendering you a mother, now I beg him [fervently] that he may want to make you also a grandmother so that you may feel in your heart this double incomprehensible love.[132]

Bellincioni similarly seemed to have developed a good relationship with her daughter Bianca. In her autobiography, she asked forgiveness from all those to whom she had said 'Amo te sopra ogni cosa' ('I love you above all else'): the truth was that she had only ever really loved two things in her life – her career and her daughter.[133]

But there were practical difficulties in combining motherhood and a singing career, especially for a single parent. In one letter in 1854, Virginia Boccabadati writes of her need to arrange lodgings so that her son didn't wake her too early in the morning: 'For the bedrooms, I would be grateful if that of Maria and the baby is not precisely next to mine, since Gigino wakes early, and if I do not sleep, I am a ruined woman.'[134]

The correspondence of Boccabadati (1828–1922) illuminates something of the shadowy life of a middle-ranking singer who never quite achieved the success of a diva. The daughter of a famous and much respected prima donna, Luigia Boccabadati (1800–50), sister of another, Augusta, and sister-in-law of the baritone Felice Varesi, she came from impeccable artistic stock. Her status as a *figlia dell'arte* was emphasised in the fact that she used her mother's name, instead of that of her father, Antonio Gazzuoli – a minor impresario and employee of Lanari. Boccabadati's early career was relatively successful: her status in the 1850s is illustrated by the fact that she was one of three singers Verdi suggested for the role of Violetta for the premiere of *La traviata*.[135] A review in *Italia musicale* in 1852 described her abilities in a way echoed in many other notices: 'she is truly an artist who knows how to support her not overly robust voice with all the resources provided by an exquisite technique and appropriate artistic feeling'.[136] Admired for her intelligence, technical prowess and spirited performances, Boccabadati was nevertheless a rather complicated person, seeming to possess neither the iron physique nor indeed the iron nerves that life as a prima donna demanded. Nine letters survive from her correspondence and friendship with the violinist and conductor Giulio Cesare Ferrarini between 1854 and 1861; unusually frank and open about her feelings, they offer us a surprisingly intimate glimpse into the arc of a singer's life. The second of her letters anticipates a forthcoming season at Macerata, which she was hoping would be shared with Ferrarini:

> If you don't come to Macerata, I am a lost woman! Do you know the
> company? . . . For goodness' sake reassure me, because in that contract
> the only thing that really made me smile was finding myself once again
> with you, who has always shown me such kindness.[137]

In the next letter she is reassured that Ferrarini will be there. She is
also evidently fully involved with her studies, despite her relatively
secure professional status. Singing clearly still enthuses her:

> I am so happy you are coming to Macerata – even more happy if you
> come for me. I propose to make much progress in these two months,
> certain that you will not refuse me your advice, which on other
> occasions has been so useful to me. I am so well, in health and voice, and
> I have so much enthusiasm and passion for my art that it seems to me
> I could do great things in a little time, but. . . I fear fortune may not wish
> to correspond to my good will.[138]

Later letters demonstrate that this season at Macerata was one of the
highlights of her professional life – at least in terms of the support
she felt she enjoyed from her colleagues. Three and a half months
later she was at Rovigo, and the picture is rather less rosy:

> The other day I wrote you two lines that I hope you will not have
> received, because I was so agitated and tormented that I really do not
> know what I might have written. Certainly I was extremely ill, and I only
> hope you will forgive me in consequence for the disconnection of my
> ideas. I come now to give you news of Traviata, which went on stage
> yesterday evening and which has pleased immensely from beginning to
> end. You cannot imagine how much philosophy, how much delicacy
> there is in this *cara musica*. There are some phrases that move one to
> tears, some moments in which one feels oneself overwhelmed by the
> most profound sadness; in the first act one experiences a false
> cheerfulness, while in the third the contrast between the situation of an
> almost dying woman and the cheerful shouts of the revellers that pass by
> on the street is so strange, that I have really had to weep on the stage in
> truth. . . I have done all that I could, being very poorly in voice and
> extremely weak. The Public showed itself to be very content. . . but I was
> not pleased with myself and returned home profoundly saddened.
> I found myself so alone, without the dear assistance to which *my good*

friends at Macerata had accustomed me so well, that my health worsened, and today we rest on my account. Let us hope I'll be able to recover by tomorrow. However, I am glad that I salvaged some effect throughout the entire last act, even though I was ill. And that famous phrase, *oh dio morir sì giovane io che penato* [*ho*] *tanto*! – it did not pass in silence; I would have been mortified by it. I hope you will come soon to hear us in this opera and to tell us your frank opinion; as for me, I can assure you that your advice is valued beyond all other and that one word of your encouragement is worth more to me than the applause of an entire Public. Therefore come and quickly![139]

Her interest in and sensitivity to the role of Violetta are self-evident: she was clearly intensely moved by the opera. Equally apparent are her own high standards and rigorous self-criticism, which perhaps played a part in her worsening health and her obvious nerves. Another letter demonstrates her anguish at her frequent illness, and its effect on her singing: 'I still don't feel well; I have a great weakness particularly in the throat, which however does not pain me at all, but I do not have enough strength to sing, which causes me such melancholy that I do nothing but weep.'[140] In the following letter, she had recovered: but it is clear that loneliness was still plaguing her: 'I am less sad since my voice is better, but I assure you that here one dies of boredom; and there is such a difference from the life I had at Macerata, that the thought of those beautiful days renders me doubly melancholy.'[141]

Somehow she survived the season; and the next letters arrived from Viterbo in 1855 where she was playing Alice in *Robert le diable*. In this role she had 'a great success'; nevertheless, it was 'very tiring'. Her health was still a problem: she explained her long silence as due to 'some very sad moments for my health', although now she felt fully recovered. The word 'sad' is perhaps intriguing, particularly in view of the fact that she talks of not having had the 'courage' to write to her friends. She was obviously also planning a visit or engagement in Paris, asking Ferrarini to supply her with a letter of introduction to the music director at the Théâtre-Italien: 'It is a country where intrigue can do much, and I – who do not know how to intrigue – I have need of some true friend that might support me should the need arise.'[142] Did she ever make the visit? No sign of it has so far emerged.

Two other important events happened in the next years: one personal, recorded in her correspondence; the other professional, visible only in the press. In 1856 she sang Violetta at Parma, with Ferrarini conducting. This should have been a repeat of the enjoyable season they shared at Macerata. Instead, it was a disaster. *La traviata* had been first performed two years earlier at the Teatro Regio, with Adelaide Cortesi in the title-role; the opera had been warmly received. But on this occasion, the cast was felt to be lacking, a 'fiasco', as *L'armonia* claimed on 31 December 1856. Boccabadati's always fragile voice had clearly not strengthened sufficiently: 'She sings extremely well, she is an artist, but one does not hear her voice.' Above all, to reproduce an opera only two years after its initial showing, and with a far less impressive cast, was considered a great error on the part of the management – a sign that repertory opera was by no means wholly established in this city.[143] A poor review was bad enough, but worse was to come. The impresario (Domenico Marchelli) then staged his next production, Rossini's *Mosè*; the first and only performance limped as far as the second act, after which it disappeared in 'a storm of shouts and whistles'; the curtain was brought down after the ballet. Marchelli hastily brought in *Traviata* again the following night: this time, the audience waited until after the brindisi in the first act, and then openly manifested 'a bold and resolute declaration' that they did not wish to hear anything more of this opera.[144] Once again the curtain was brought down, and the audience was reimbursed. A production of *Trovatore* was then bundled swiftly together a few days later, without Boccabadati; she herself found some success in the production in March of Sanelli's *Gusmano il prode*.

This was plainly a difficult season, and one that Boccabadati referred to indirectly but with obvious tension in a later letter. But it was perhaps made even more stressful by another occurrence. She was also the mother of a small child, Gigino. Apparently unmarried, she nevertheless was in a relationship with a man she describes only as 'Peppino' or 'P'; he figures in several of the letters including that of 1855. Whether this man was Gigino's father is unclear. It is interesting that Boccabadati had kept her baby, and travelled openly with him – unlike Strepponi, who needed to hide her illegitimate children fifteen years previously. But there is another letter, dated only 28 February, written to Ferrarini, when he was in the same city. She asked him to deliver a packet of letters to 'P.', as she had ended their relationship: 'My heart has changed because I believed myself to be loved only with coldness, because it appeared to me that he did not desire any more to be close to me, and because he made me despair of the future; but I have done nothing vile for which to reproach myself and I do not deserve insults. Rather than these, I will conserve the memory of the care and affection shown towards me.'[145] She requested – in true Ottocento style – that 'P.' destroy her letters and portraits himself; and asked only to keep the portrait of Gigino that Peppino gave her during that idyllic season in Macerata.

And then all letters cease, until the last of the nine arrived in 1861. It recommended another singer (Giuditta Beltramelli) to Ferrarini's care and guidance, and it also gave Boccabadati's own news, after an obviously long silence:

As for me, dear Ferrarini, I am very happy as I had always *dreamed* of being, without hope that my dream might become a reality. United to a good-hearted man who tenderly loves me and my Gigietto, my life runs calm and serene; no more emotions – and in consequence, *no more attacks of nerves;* all the days resemble each other and it is really true what a French author says: 'happy people do not have a history!' Gigino grows up good and intelligent. Let us hope that he will do well, because he has a great love of study and much desire to emulate [success]. I almost *never* sing any more, thus avenging myself for all those times when I was forced to sing sometimes in little soirées. Without pretensions or preparations, I perform by singing salon songs, and then the soul [*Animuccia*] of the Artist returns a little to palpitate; but only a little – You know, I really regret nothing of the theatre.[146]

The letter is signed: 'Virginia Boccabadati Carignani'. There is a certain poignancy in this candid acknowledgement of the stresses of the stage life, in the warmth she clearly found in her married life and the pride in her son, in the new relationship she had built with her voice in the freedom of domestic music-making. This hardworking and conscientious prima donna, relentlessly self-critical and never satisfied with her own efforts even when her performances were warmly received, did not lose all contact with her profession; instead, she turned to teaching, producing *Osservazioni pratiche per lo studio del canto* in 1893.

RETIREMENT

If Boccabadati left the stage without regrets, many other prima donnas felt differently. To Eames, retirement was 'almost unbearable'. Some chose their moment wisely: Isabella Galletti Gianoli left quietly and at the full height of her powers.[147] Others lingered on, perhaps for love of their art or financial necessity, or more probably a mixture of both. Pasta returned to London, a wreck of a voice; Nordica died on tour, still trying to find her vanishing head tones; Melba could not let go, and said farewell so many times she became a parody. Yet others never made a conscious decision to abandon the stage; the stage simply abandoned them.

Bellincioni described the final years of her professional life. In 1905, after twenty-five years of a career and still in the fullness of her abilities, she found herself invaded by an 'indefinable tiredness': more than one evening she left the theatre 'oppressed by the weight of the performance'. The acclaim of the public no longer moved her; more importantly, she no longer felt in herself that '*infinite joy of singing. . .* that kind of *fever* that had invaded me at every performance'. Conscious that 'routine' was taking the place of inspiration, and not wishing to renege on her ideals as an artist, she decided to retire. It was at that point she saw Strauss' *Salome*; the challenge of this role reinvigorated her, and she became the first Italian interpreter, playing it 110 times in three years. Only then, when she felt she had nothing more to offer her audience, did she finally withdraw from the stage.[148]

What lay beyond the final curtain? Teaching was a prime occupation, providing the opportunity to pass on hard-won experience and knowledge. Many of these singers were extraordinarily generous to their students: Adelaide Kemble Sartoris recalled her welcome by Pasta; Toti Dal Monte remembered the kindness and selflessness of Barbara Marchisio.[149] It was also via teaching that many female singers entered the published discourses around singing. One of the earliest female-written manuals of the era was Anna Pellegrini Celoni's *Grammatica o siano regole per ben cantare* (1802; final edition 1817): published in both Italy and Germany, it was prefaced by approving male comments from figures such as Pietro Guglielmi and Nicola Zingarelli.[150] Many other singers followed suit, with publications ranging from brief pamphlets to full-length studies.

And as the era progressed, a new task presented itself: the writing of memoirs. The cult in memoirs and autobiographies (often ghosted) that was established towards the end of the nineteenth century enabled singers to relive the past.[151] Many such books often seem like an attempt to describe a party to someone who wasn't there; the descriptions of glittering triumphs, the throngs of admirers, the recollections of parades and wild processions. These purple passages are the counterpart to the sonnets and odes penned in homage to the singers: a similar attempt to recapture an ephemeral experience, but from the opposite side of the footlights. If it seems overdone at times, it is perhaps as difficult to translate the breath-held silence or the wild clamour of an audience into words as it is to fix the sound of a perfectly sung phrase in the form of a poem. Emma Eames tried to explain her own feelings about her professional life:

> If one thought of the pain, the frustration, the discontent, 'divine' though it may be, one would feel the game of such a life not worth the candle. But the joy of accomplishment more than outweighs such

drawbacks. The sense of exaltation and expansion that follows the establishment of a perfect vibration between an artist and his public, brings one nearer heaven than anything else on earth. The vibrations of a *grande passion* are the only ones that can be compared with it, but these, alas! are shared with another and dependent upon that other; the artistic passion frees one, and is therefore complete and infinitely more satisfactory.[152]

'Vissi d'arte, vissi d'amore' indeed.

I do not know if a perfect Singer can at the same time be a perfect Actor; for the Mind being at once divided by two different Operations, he will probably incline more to one than the other;

It being, however, much more difficult to sing well than to act well, the Merit of the first is beyond the second. What a Felicity would it be, to possess both in a perfect Degree!

Pier Francesco Tosi, *Observations on the Florid Song* (1743)

The central dilemma of the operatic stage – its need for performers who can sing and act in equal measure – became even more pressing in the nineteenth century. In 1833 the actor William Macready recorded his impression of a performance of Beethoven's *Fidelio* (an opera he found to be 'rather heavy') given by a visiting German company at Covent Garden: 'The general acting also disappointed me; it was opera-acting – the same unnatural gesticulation and redundant holding up of arms and beating of breasts.'[1] Théophile Gautier was similarly trenchant in his criticisms of a troupe of Italian singers appearing a few years later in 1838 at the Théâtre-Italien, Paris: 'the singer must also be an actor: a nightingale perched on a tragedian . . . The artists of the Théâtre-Italien, with the exception of Lablache and Mademoiselle Grisi, seem to forget completely that they are giving dramatic performances and playing different characters.'[2] Wagner disliked what he saw of both German *and* Italian singers: the Germans 'do not articulate properly', offer only 'general hazy outlines' of their character and think 'they have sung quite "dramatically"' if they bellow out the phrase's closing note with an emphatic bid for applause',[3] whilst for the Italians, dramatic effect 'is all done by rule; thus after a period of billing and cooing an explosion makes an incomparable effect; none of it has anything to do with real life, but then of course it is precisely that which makes it "art"'.[4]

These comments all belong or refer to the 1830s, but similar criticisms are made throughout the period. Some singers – many, perhaps – were theatrically inept, or unimaginative, or simply uninterested in the dramatic dimension of their roles. But there are also accounts of operatic performances that were histrionically thrilling and innovative. Stendhal's descriptions of Isabella Colbran provide one such example. Off-stage, Colbran had 'about as much dignity as the average milliner's assistant', but onstage she instantly 'inspired involuntary respect' and 'radiated majesty'[5] – something used to good effect in her interpretation of the title-role of Rossini's *Elisabetta, regina d'Inghilterra* in 1815:

> Signorina Colbran, as Elizabeth, used no gestures, did nothing melodramatic, never descended to what are vulgarly called *tragedy-queen poses*. The immensity of her royal authority, the vastness of events which a single word from her lips could call into being, all this lived in the Spanish beauty of her eyes, which at times could be so terrible. Her glance was that of a queen whose fury is restrained only by a last rag of pride; her whole presence was that of a woman who still has beauty, and who for years has grown accustomed to beholding her first hint of a whim followed by the swiftest obedience . . . It was the *ingrained* acceptance of the manners and mannerism of despotic power . . . which characterized the acting of this great artist; all this wealth of exquisitely-observed detail could be read into the statuesque calm of her every gesture. And when, rarely, she did move, it was as though the breaking of the stillness were forced upon her from within, by the clash of turbulent passions in her soul; not once was it merely to threaten, to impress, to constrain obedience to her will. The very greatest of our tragic actors, even the great Talma himself, are not exempt from the weakness of imperious and theatrical gestures when they play the parts of tyrants and despots . . . but for all the wild applause they may elicit, extravagant mannerisms and gestures in this tradition are none the less absurd. No man in the world uses *fewer* gestures than a despotic monarch; why *should* he rant and gesticulate? He has for so long been accustomed to implicit obedience, that emphatic movement is merely superfluous; swift as lightning, an imperceptible nod brings fulfilment to his every wish.[6]

Stendhal's appraisal of Colbran emphasises that the notion of the *attrice cantante* or 'singing actress' was an active concept from the beginning of this period – and not simply a product of the *fin-de-siècle* emerging with singers such as Gemma Bellincioni and Emma Calvé.[7] It also suggests that the dramatic standards of some singers not only compared favourably with other, less proficient singers, but were equal on occasion to the best actors of the legitimate stage, extending the bounds of acting as it was then perceived. 'Opera-acting' undoubtedly existed, but it was only part of the broader picture of the operatic stage.

This and the following chapter are concerned with those singers and commentators who regarded dramatic performance as an integral part of operatic practice. As the next chapter will reveal, theory played a crucial role in developing singers' ideas and performance modes, whether this was gleaned from tutors, periodicals or acting manuals, or in collaboration with other artists (for instance, Pasta and Pallerini, Barbieri-Nini and Verdi, Schröder-Devrient and Wagner, Calvé and Duse, Bellincioni and Mascagni). First, however, it is pertinent to consider the wider context of their performances.

THE THEATRICAL LANDSCAPE

The lyric and legitimate stages, then far more closely aligned than today, saw a tremendous shift in notions of dramatic representation throughout the period of 1815–1930.[8] The fundamental change in performance modes might be broadly summarised as a move from classical stylisation to naturalism, but this should not be understood as a linear progression from inept acting towards the 'better', more lifelike style of realism. Such an attitude devalues the work of the earlier artists who, although employing expressive techniques unfamiliar to modern eyes, surely created histrionic moments as telling as those of their later colleagues. Rather, the era's concept of theatrical performance operated on an axis between the real and the ideal; the tensions and intersections between these two positions determined varying notions of what constituted 'good' acting.

Confusingly, perhaps, both schools of thought claimed 'truthfulness' as their guide. Diderot, writing at the end of the eighteenth century, provided a valuable exposition of the classical relationship between the 'ideal' and 'truth':

> Reflect, pray, on that which one calls 'true' in the theatre: is it to show things as they are in nature? Not at all: a wretch on the street will be poor, small and paltry; truth in this case will be nothing more than that which is vulgar. What therefore is the truth? It is the conformity of the exterior signs, of the voice, of the figure, of the movement, of the action, of the discourse: in a word, of all the parts of the play, with an ideal model either given by the poet or imagined by the actor.[9]

'Truth' is here revealed as a very different concept to that of 'nature': Diderot's 'truth' is one of aesthetic harmony and aspiration – not things as they are, but things as man's ingenuity intends them to be. One example of how this principle operated in performance practice is visible in the staging of death scenes. Death in the classical tradition – at least for a hero or a heroine – was essentially an act of beauty in extremis. Johann Jacob Engel (1741–1802), whose influential writings on dramatic art (*Ideen zu einer Mimik*, 1785) were translated widely in Europe in the late eighteenth and early nineteenth centuries,[10] advised on the actor's appropriate approach to a death-scene:

> I would give one rule, which, I believe, has been frequently adduced before; – that the agonies and approaches of death ought not to be represented with all the horrors which attend these dreadful moments in nature. The judicious player will soften down these horrors. His head should have more the appearance of a man sinking to a sound sleep, than of a person convulsed with strong agonies; the voice should be broken and altered, but not so as to give the effect of a disgusting rattling: in a word, an actor ought to acquire a manner of his own in representing the last sigh of expiring mortality. He should give such an idea of death as every man would wish to feel at that crisis; though, perhaps, no one ever will have the good fortune to find that wish accomplished. Contemplate (if you can find patience for the task) the abominable grimaces and unnatural distortions in which some players indulge themselves under similar circumstances, and you will acknowledge the justice of this rule.[11]

Two versions of *Otello* at opposite ends of the century demonstrate how this principle altered under the new ideas of realism. If in 1816 the 'horrors' of Desdemona's death were hidden from the audience in Rossini's *Otello* by discreetly positioning her demise behind a screen, in Verdi's version some seventy years later her murder is enacted centre-stage with gruesome ferocity: 'OTELLO grabs DESDEMONA by the arms, and throws her violently on to the bed, at which point he grabs her by the throat with his two hands. DESDEMONA, trying once more to free herself, lets out a sharp, heart-rending cry, then remains motionless, with OTELLO still strangling her.'[12]

The depiction of death, graphic or otherwise, fitted well with the broader concerns of theatre in this era. The nineteenth-century theatre was essentially a 'theatre of feeling': one that sought through the actor's portrayal of emotion to evoke similar feelings within the spectator.[13] For much of the period, the focus of relationships onstage was primarily between actor and spectator, rather than (as in naturalism's later concept of the 'fourth wall') between actor and actor. This awakening of the audience's emotional response was sought through the actor's own display of feeling – physically in gesture and *mise en scène*, and orally through timbre and rhythm of voice. Dramatic performance was therefore a highly stylised art, more akin to narrative dance forms such as ballet; the performing artist concentrated on conveying a generally recognised 'idea' of either a character or an 'affective situation',[14] rather than the individual particularities favoured by exponents of naturalism.

Opera was peculiarly well fitted to this concept of a 'theatre of feeling' – indeed, was perhaps its most prominent manifestation – primarily because of the element of music. Susanne Langer comments on the congruency of musical form with the internal structures of human feeling, and in consequence its greater effectiveness at communicating emotion: 'music can *reveal* the nature of feelings with a detail and truth that language cannot approach'.[15] Even in the more formal, number operas of the early period, music was used to provoke strong emotional manifestations: Bellini's declared intent was to engender feeling within the spectator: 'Opera, through singing, must make one weep, shudder, die.'[16] The dramatic structure of much opera enhanced this emphasis on emotion rather than complex narrative: libretti, more sparsely written than the average play, were built around a series of 'affective situations', focusing on the experience of the character in relation to a given event rather than the event itself. Later in the period, when the conventions of operatic structure had loosened and the strict division of self-contained numbers had given way to a more fluid form, music's special properties explicated dramatic meaning in a way inaccessible to mere words, as Arrigo Boito (1842–1918) argued in a letter to Verdi in 1880 during their collaboration on *Otello*:

> An opera is not a play; our art lives by elements unknown to spoken tragedy. An atmosphere that has been destroyed can be created all over again. Eight bars are enough to restore a sentiment to life; a rhythm can re-establish a character; music is the most omnipotent of all the arts; it has a logic all its own – both freer and more rapid than the logic of spoken thought, and much more eloquent.[17]

Vocally too, singers arguably displayed a far broader spectrum of sound in terms of tonality, colour, rhythm and pitch than can be achieved by speech alone, thus facilitating a more extensive illustration of the heights and depths of passion. In the age of melodrama, the legitimate actor was encouraged to imitate certain elements of the singer's vocal prowess;[18] even the doyen of the later movement of naturalism, Stanislavski, wrote that 'Speech is music' and that actors must 'let the sounds sing for themselves'.[19]

But if opera thus fulfilled many of the expectations of what constituted effective theatre, it also presented significant difficulties for the lyric artist in terms of developing a coherent dramatic performance. Some of these arose from the musical design of opera: the pattern of recitative and aria in the early period, textual repetition and ornamentation, or ensembles as in *Lucia di Lammermoor* or *Rigoletto* where musical unity belied the separate anguish of individual characters. Other difficulties stemmed from the production processes. Rehearsal – either too little or too much – presented one problem for singing actors. In the large theatres throughout the period, new operas were often allotted substantial rehearsal time, but the arrival of repertory opera from the middle of the nineteenth century brought a different approach. Lilli Lehmann stated that at the prestigious Royal Opera House in Berlin in the 1870s, 'Most of the répertoire operas, even those in which I sang a part for the first time, were given without any rehearsal, and more time was granted one only for the preparation of entirely unknown works.'[20] If such practices were testing for experienced singers, they must have been even more difficult for newcomers, such as Iva Pacetti (1898–1981) who made her operatic debut in 1920 at the Teatro Metastasio in Prato without a 'single stage rehearsal'.[21] In some instances, lack of rehearsal was due to insufficient financial resources, or (as in Pacetti's case) to the illness of another prima donna. In others, it was because the singers themselves were concerned to save their voices and energies for the performance: Emma Calvé alluded to the reluctance of both Patti and Alboni to 'fatigue themselves with rehearsals'.[22] By modern standards, accustomed to a unified production concept, this might seem inexplicable; but within the operatic marketplace of much of the nineteenth century it made good sense for singers to avoid overtiring themselves – especially in a working environment where they might be required to give as many as thirty or forty performances of the same role. Absence from rehearsals was also a result of the long distances often travelled by singers – exacerbated by the new technologies later in the period that permitted such excursions. Howard wrote that during one week in the early 1900s she sang Die Zauberflöte on Tuesday in Darmstadt, Samson et Dalila in Prague on Wednesday, Die lustigen Weiber von Windsor on Thursday in Darmstadt again, left that night for Edinburgh, which she reached on Monday and where she gave a concert the same evening, repeated the concert in Glasgow the next day, and then returned to Germany.[23] Such schedules undoubtedly placed a strain not only on the singer, but also on the rest of the cast.

Other obstacles hampered performance practice. Acoustic practicalities and the need to keep a watchful eye on the conductor, particularly where the music was especially complex, often meant that staging had to focus around the central position of the pit. Florence Easton revealed that she thought there was 'an element of the ludicrous' in all operatic acting: 'How can you *act*, if you have to hold a sustained note for six measures in the middle of an emotional climax, with your eyes glued on the conductor?'[24] Lotte Lehmann decried those singers who, unsure of their musical knowledge, depended on the conductor with 'a desperate helplessness', thus marring the illusion. Her solution was to sacrifice musical accuracy for dramatic effectiveness: 'it is much better to make mistakes, to be slightly inexact, than to stare fixedly at the conductor's pit'.[25] And always, as Kellogg described, there was the remorseless drive of the music: 'In opera one cannot be too temperamental in one's acting. One cannot make pauses when one thinks it effective, nor alter the stage business to fit one's mood, nor work oneself up to an emotional crescendo one night and not do it the next. Everything has to be timed to a second and a fraction of a second.'[26] A further factor disturbing histrionic delivery is the voice's sensitivity to emotional stimuli. Complete abandonment to the moment can mar the singer's degree of control over tonal quality and range, as Verdi made plain in 1875:

> A singer who is moved by the dramatic action, concentrates on it with every vibrant fibre of his body, and is utterly consumed by the role he is portraying, will not find the right tone. He might for a minute, but in the next thirty seconds he will sing in the wrong way or the voice will simply fail. A single lung is rarely strong enough for acting and singing.[27]

The increased dramatic and athletic demands on the singer in operas written from the latter part of the nineteenth century onwards made vocal control a particularly acute problem. Easton complained of the emphasis of 'modern grand opera' on acting rather than singing: 'We are evidently there to be seen quite as much as to be heard. And seen how? We rush around, we fall, we roll down stairs, we do everything but stand on our heads.' But, she argued, to sing well required 'repose and deep breathing': 'you cannot rage, weep or dance violently without losing your breath – and yet you are supposed to do so'.[28]

If some singers viewed such difficulties as a motive for concentrating solely on the vocal aspect of their role and limited their histrionic efforts accordingly, others chafed under the restrictions opera imposed on their dramatic instincts – and about the musical consequences wrought by the demands of the text. As we shall see, many sought to present a performance that was both musically accomplished and theatrically effective, yet at certain points in the score and the libretto one or other of these elements had to take precedence. The individual choices the singers made in these matters were a significant part of their interpretation of a role.

THE VOCAL LANDSCAPE

What was acted? The obvious answer might seem: 'character'. But as Gabriele Baldini argued about Verdi's roles, the voices are the true characters in much nineteenth-century opera, not the literary figures as expressed through the words of the libretto.[29] Dramatic action in opera exists primarily through the music, in the sense of both musical line and vocal timbre. It is perhaps axiomatic to state that the most striking changes that occurred in opera in the era were through the musical narrative: certainly, the libretti also present important differences in story-telling, but in many respects these are often less remarkable than the development of the aural depiction of the character. One has only to compare *Norma* with *Madama Butterfly*, or *Les Huguenots* with *Pelléas et Mélisande*, or *Der Freischütz* with *Wozzeck* to appreciate how much the soundscape altered on the operatic stage across the period.

The professional and aesthetic territory inhabited by female singers was thus an aural terrain. The precise organisation of sound, the manner in which it articulated particular concepts and ideas, and how these related to broader aspects of nineteenth-century society, obviously varied enormously over such a large repertoire; and it is beyond the scope of this chapter to provide detailed analyses of individual operas. But it is worth noting that this terrain was shaped not simply by vocal ability, but by conventions regarding the significance of particular timbres within a wider cultural context of gender representation.

Definitions of gender gathered significance in a number of ways as the era progressed. Prior to the nineteenth century the dress codes adopted by men and women within the same social class were remarkably similar: the clothing of the wealthy and well-born in the eighteenth century, for example, demanded rich fabrics, corsets, ornate adornment and powdered wigs for both genders. Even in the 1820s, the 'dandy' was still a familiar figure of male interest in fashionable attire. But the visual representation of gender in dress gradually became delineated according to the new ideas of masculinity and femininity as binary oppositions: men's clothing became dark, sober and restrained; women wore full-skirted dresses, emphasising their waists and displaying (for evening wear) naked shoulders and arms. This overt differentiation of the genders was regarded with the utmost seriousness: the Code Napoléon even introduced a law forbidding women to wear men's clothing.[30]

Some aspects of this cultural development of separation in the visual performativity of gender also found expression in the conventions surrounding vocality on the operatic stage. In previous centuries, gender boundaries onstage were blurred by the presence of the castrati and by the practices of cross-dressing (both female to male and male to female); and in vocal terms too the music written for men and women shared similar characteristics. Until the nineteenth century, singers were in general loosely categorised as sopranos, contraltos (both voices being either male or female), tenors or basses:[31] a nomenclature that provided in its very openness the freedom to explore the unique qualities inherent in individual instruments. Each category was regarded as having its own characteristics. According to Lichtenthal in 1807, the castrato (soprano or contralto) impressed the ear but did not touch the heart; in contrast, the female soprano voice was 'full of feeling and produces a great effect', whilst the voice of the female contralto was 'expressive and virile, and invades perfectly the soul of the listener'. The 'most beautiful' male voice was the tenor, who was 'the true painter of all the passions: his pictures bear the stamp of truth. The tenor voice is full of strength, and its effect is very great.' The bass voice was 'grand, sublime, solemn and full of gravity'.[32] And in general, the same elements of technical virtuosity were required of all singers: *messa di voce* (the swelling of sound from *piano* to *forte* and vice versa), vocal agility (the ability to execute roulades, trills and a variety of *fioriture*), a smooth, sustained legato; resonance, clarity and equality of timbre throughout the range; excellent breath control and the capacity to sing long phrases; no perceptible break between the head (*voce di testa*) and chest (*voce di petto*) registers;[33] and clear articulation of language.

The sense of both genders inhabiting liberally the same aesthetic realm in opera was still evident during the first three decades of the nineteenth century. Prior to 1830, the heroine of an opera, although usually a soprano, might also be a contralto; the hero, although usually a tenor, might again be a contralto. It is also noticeable that most of the prominent female singers of that early period were women whose timbre was comparatively dark, some of whom were actively identified as 'mezzo-sopranos' (Isabella Colbran, Giuditta Pasta, Maria Malibran, Wilhemine Schröder-Devrient),[34] playing opposite male singers whose timbre was comparatively light (Giovanni David, Adolphe Nourrit, Giambattista Rubini).

It is tempting – and justifiedly so – to see these first decades as less rigid in gender ideas. But perhaps the real impetus behind this glorious confusion of sexual identity lay in the adherence to notions of the ideal. For much of the period, music was regarded as an entirely idealised domain: even in 1860 the *Gazzetta musicale di Milano* could still claim that 'The principal *aspect* of music is wholly ideal; its sphere of action is that of a world let us not say unknown, but which has nothing in common with that in which we live.'[35] These musicalised personages of the early period were not therefore regarded as verisimilar or as reflective of real life – and therefore not especially threatening to the social status quo. But around 1830, different ideas emerged. Bellini's use of *il canto sillabico* – the setting of one syllable per note, as opposed to the Rossinian use of many notes to one syllable – introduced declamatory singing, and brought a closer mimetic relationship between word and music. Singers also began to engage more fully in the dramatic representation of a role, with an emphasis on the depiction of emotion. Both factors led to new ideas about the use of the voice, but with rather different implications for the genders. Men's voices became more declamatory, largely abandoning the ornamented vocal line. In particular, masculinity found a new articulation through the tenor voice, which underwent an important change during the 1830s via the extension of the chest register to the upper third of the range: Duprez specifically referred to the 'virile accents' he felt his role required in *Guillaume Tell*, which led to his famous *ut de poitrine*.[36] The emergence of the baritone voice, with a greater use of the upper register, also emphasised the thrusting of the natural male voice into territory once reserved for the castrati.

Although women's voices also began to adopt a more declamatory style, they nevertheless remained positioned for some time predominantly in the realm of ornamented *canto vocalizzato* – because, it was argued, this was more appropriate to the feminine gender: 'the characters of women, more ideal, easier to colour with the gentle tints of imagination, more easy therefore to locate in the sphere of a less prosaic and positive world, must in consequence feel less the need to attain the imitation of exterior nature, reflecting instead the ineffable accents of the intimate nature of man'.[37] Such ideas led to a compositional extension of the voice into the upper spheres, rather than the lower. The depiction of heroinism with its suggestions of an idealised femininity was increasingly sought through the soprano voice at its most extreme, in the high, floating tones of the *coloratura* (a broad term including what today we would call both the soprano *leggiero* as well as the soprano *acuto sfogato*).[38] The coloratura's bird-like trills, ornaments and cadenzas, her impossibly ethereal swooping above the stave, all served (superficially at least) to support the era's perception of woman as a decorative, naive creature easily distracted from the main melody of her life by the prettiness of a cunning *roulade.* In truth, the roles written for this voice demanded a steely concentration, absolute accuracy of pitch and attack, and an extraordinary degree of vocal control. Some of these contradictions are visible in the characterisation of the *coloratura* heroines: Amina in *La sonnambula* (1831) is a village maiden whose nocturnal, somnambulatory escapades lead her tantalisingly into physical and moral danger; Lucrezia in Donizetti's *Lucrezia Borgia* (1833) is an adoring mother and aristocratic murderess; Giovanna in Verdi's *Giovanna d'Arco* (1845) is both innocent virgin and fearless warrior.

Composers continued to write for this agile type of voice throughout the later period, but tended to reserve it for certain characters of emotional excess (such as Ophelia in Thomas' *Hamlet*) or showy temperament (Zerbinetta in Strauss's *Ariadne*). From the 1850s, however, two other kinds of voices dominated the representation of the heroine. The lyric soprano, emerging initially from *opera buffa*, possessed a warmer, more plaintive sound than the brilliant timbre of the coloratura, and became the voice most used to signal femininity in the middle and later period – or at least, a certain kind of fragile, trusting nature, often abused by faithless men. French opera made particular use of this voice (*Faust* and *Carmen* providing two obvious examples in the roles of Marguerite and Micaela); in the Italian repertoire at the turn of the century, Puccini also later deployed the lyric soprano to great effect. But even in the lyric roles, the demonstration of femininity was by no means always straightforward. If within the libretto of *Madama Butterfly,* Cio-Cio-San is the image of femininity, musically the picture is more complex. Several sopranos argued that the role was extremely demanding: 'one of the leading voice-killers' according to Esther Mazzoleni, who was nevertheless comfortable in dramatic roles such as Isolde.[39] Sara Scuderi similarly regarded Cio-Cio-San as a 'dangerous part', and more exhausting than Tosca: 'Tosca is not onstage the whole time, the way Butterfly is, and there is less legato and gentleness. It's easier, you know, to be angry and jealous over a big orchestra than it is to be tender, and the orchestration of *Butterfly* is heavy.'[40] As with many of the earlier coloratura roles, there was thus sometimes a clear contradiction between the portrayal of femininity and the quite unfeminine resources of physical strength and stamina needed for its enactment.

But the middle of the nineteenth century had also brought other ideas about female vocality. It is perhaps arbitrary to single out one particular moment of change; but Verdi's *Macbeth* (1847) was an important milestone, offering a quite new concept of the female voice. With its allegiance to the notion of *il brutto* instead of the classical idealism still prevalent, this opera presented one of the first female roles written not to *please* the audience, but rather to surprise and astonish. Verdi's desire to have a 'harsh, stifled, dark' sound from a singer who 'does not sing' ran contrary to the more usual emphasis on a limpid vocal beauty.[41] In aural terms, Lady Macbeth was a more radical depiction of womanhood than another famously innovative character, Carmen, was to be almost thirty years later, and similarly influential. As the century progressed, the emphasis now was on power rather than prettiness: vocal lines became broader and more sustained, roles grew longer and heavier, and a darker tonal colour was required. Singers required immense physical and vocal stamina to perform roles such as Wagner's Isolde (1865) and Brünnhilde (1870 and 1876), or to negotiate the awkward challenges of Verdian parts such as Leonora in *La forza del destino* (1862) or Elisabeth in *Don Carlos* (1867). Two closely related kinds of female voices emerged to sing such roles: the *lirico spinto*, predominantly associated with the Italian repertoire; and the even more powerful *hochdramatischer Sopran* (described by Blanche Marchesi as 'the rarest voice produced by nature'),[42] employed almost exclusively by Wagner and Richard Strauss.

The arrival of these heavier, more imposing female voices within the opera house seems at odds with the external images of womanhood. But it was part of opera's own logic: as Enrico Panofka suggested, the modification in the soprano voice was a necessary adjunct to the transformation of the tenor into a darker, weightier instrument.[43] The new concept of masculinised vocality had redesigned the acoustic territory of opera, and in order to create a coherent

Figure 3. Lillian Nordica as Brünnhilde

soundscape required a female counterpart. The *hochdramatischer Sopran* became the essential onstage partner for the *Heldentenor*: Brünnhilde to his Siegfried. Yet even if she emerged like Eve after Adam, the dramatic soprano's overtly assertive tonal stance and energy added a new dimension to the era's ideas of gender.[44] The sheer length of the central Wagnerian role, spanning three operas, was one supporting factor; so too was the considerable physical stamina needed, as Lillian Nordica revealed:

> *Great Physical Strength Is Required*, and long stage training, to sustain those attitudes demanded in a Wagnerian performance. The poses of *Brünnhilde*, for instance, on awakening in *Siegfried*; the manipulation

Figure 4. Katharina Klafsky as Brünnhilde

throughout the *Ring des Nibelungen* of her shield, helmet, cuirass, draperies, and spear; the carrying of those up over the rocks and down again, and with a horse that is not infrequently restless and terrified; the fire and smoke in *Die Walküre*, the fumes of which are so hard to keep out of one's throat; the long time that the fire is burning and the intense accompanying heat; these are but a few of the difficulties to be coped with, and to be overcome.[45]

It was this role that soon became the marker for the prima donna's endeavours: the one that defined her as having achieved the highest reaches of her art. And it was also a role that connected most readily with the developing suffrage movement, which found in Brünnhilde's 'cry of the old, free Northern woman' (in Olive Schreiner's words) a telling illustration of fearless heroism and sacrifice for a cause.[46]

Within all the female categories there was a degree of cross-over: a *coloratura* might also sing certain lyric roles; a lyric voice might darken and extend sufficiently in order to assume some items of the dramatic repertoire. As Rosa Raisa (1893–1963), one of the most remarkable *spinto* voices of her generation, commented:

> If the so-called 'lyric soprano' can sing rapid passage-work, *fioriture* and embellishments with ease and *bravura*, then she is also a coloratura soprano. And if a dramatic soprano, in addition to dramatic style and delivery, has an instinct for the pure lyric song-line, then she is a 'lyric soprano' as well. If you have the voice, the tone quality and the range, there is no reason why you cannot combine all three styles.[47]

Some roles demanded all three voices. Violetta begins the first act of *La traviata* as a bright-edged coloratura, softens into a lyric soprano in the pastoral idyll of the second act, and ends the opera as a *spinto*. Conversely, Offenbach's *Les Contes d'Hoffmann* offered the opportunity for one highly skilled and adaptable singer to undertake three separate roles: Olympia, the doll who displays her *fioriture*; Antonia, the doomed lyric heroine whose singing is the instrument of her death; and Giulietta, the courtesan who plies her erotic wares in the dark tones of the *spinto* soprano. Few prima donnas were able to meet this challenge (Jarmila Novotna was one exception), and the opera was more commonly performed by three separate singers.

Certain singers experienced the full range of the soprano repertoire through either natural or artificial development. Lilli Lehmann began her long career of forty-five years and 170 roles as a soubrette, progressing from a Rhinemaiden and Valkyrie at Bayreuth in 1876 to Brünnhilde in 1896. Other singers deliberately cultivated their voices in the direction most favoured by the operatic marketplace. Malibran and her sister Pauline Viardot both fashioned their mezzo-soprano voices into instruments capable of tackling the coloratura repertoire then in vogue, with the aid of some judicious transpositions: an accepted practice up until the mid-nineteenth century. At the latter end of the period, Nordica consciously set about the reconstruction of her coloratura-trained voice into a dramatic soprano, in order to undertake the heavy Wagnerian roles. All these efforts had their price: Viardot claimed that her desire to sing everything resulted in the loss of her voice; Nordica's change of repertoire and vocal style, although initially highly successful (she became the first American singer to perform at Bayreuth), was later cited as responsible for her early decline in vocal control.[48] Other singers had their fingers burned more immediately. Nellie Melba's attempt to sing Brünnhilde in *Siegfried* at the New York Metropolitan (a part far beyond the powers of her agile lyric voice) was simply disastrous: 'The music was too much for me. I felt as though I were struggling with something beyond my strength. I had a sensation almost of suffocation, of battling with some immense monster – a very different feeling from the usual exaltation which I had experienced in my other rôles.'[49]

Contraltos and mezzo-sopranos

The first three decades of the nineteenth century were the swansong of the contralto voice – at least, as it had appeared in opera until that period. With certain, infrequent exceptions, never again would the contralto benefit from such a range of characterisation and prominence of roles within the operatic hierarchy. The cult of the climactic and extended high note, and the move towards greater volume and heavier orchestration within larger auditoriums as the era progressed favoured (if not demanded) the soprano register. By the middle of the century, the contralto found herself largely limited to the *seconda* roles of – in common backstage parlance – 'tarts, old women and boys'. And yet there are signs that if the contralto had lost the interest of the composers, she had not yet lost that of the audience. A surprising number of letters from opera house managements to composers in this era request that a role be included for a contralto, accompanied by glowing descriptions of this or that singer's attributes. But even when such commissions were fulfilled, the roles remained secondary. In a letter written around 1852, Rossini argued that the omission of the contralto from much composition was having a detrimental effect by encouraging the new tendencies towards exploiting vocal extremes. Comparing the contralto to the *vox humana* stop on the organ, with its innate capacity for pathos, he claimed that the voice had not 'lost its natural attractions':

> The contralto is the norm by which voices and instruments should be subordinated in a fully harmonized musical composition . . . What is best is to work on the middle strings, which always manage to be in tune. On the extreme strings, one loses as much in grace as one gains in force; and from abuse they tend towards paralysis of the throat, turning as an expedient to declaimed – that is, forced and toneless – singing.
>
> Then the need is born to give more body to the instrumentation, to cover the excess of the voices, to the detriment of the musical colouring. That is the way it is done now, and it will be worse after me. The head will conquer the heart: science will lead to the ruin of art; and under a deluge of notes, what is called *instrumental* will be the tomb of voices and of feeling. May it not come to pass!!!![50]

Rossini was not alone in his consternation: various articles in the periodicals had begun to question the disappearance of the contralto. In the *Gazzetta musicale di Firenze*, Ermanno Picchi claimed that this voice was more 'persuasive' than any other, but given that it was more limited in range than the soprano, it was forced to ever greater technical achievements in order to unite the vocal registers (*di petto* and *di testa*) – thus developing a kind of technical and artistic superiority that made it an unwelcome rival to the soprano.[51] If Picchi's arguments about competitiveness seem rather stretched, he nevertheless had a point: the majority of female voices are sopranos, just as the majority of male voices are baritones: good contraltos and tenors are less common, in part because the negotiation of the registers is more demanding. The added pressures of greater volume and strength required from the middle of the period compounded the problems of blending the registers effectively.

But other factors might have colluded with the compositional neglect of the contralto. Michel Poizat advances the thesis that voices that appear 'trans-sexual' (high male voices, low female ones) hold the 'greatest fascination' for the listener.[52] Certainly, Théophile Gautier seemed drawn precisely to this aspect of his lover's voice, the contralto Ernesta Grisi. 'Est-ce un jeune homme? est-ce une femme?'

(Is it a young man? is it a woman?), he asks in the stanzas of *Contralto*, a poem addressed to the 'Monstre charmant' whose voluptuous caress has haunted his dreams:

> Que tu me plais, ô timbre étrange,
> Son double, homme et femme à la fois,
> Contralto, bizarre mélange,
> Hermaphrodite de la voix![53]

But the potential androgyny of the contralto, with its echoes of the castrati of a lost age, was simply too confusing for those elements of the nineteenth-century audience who preferred less ambiguous representations of sexuality.[54] Some of the most frequent complaints surfaced in the *Harmonicon*'s review of Rosa Mariani in 1832: 'Madame MARIANI is the counterpart of Madame PISARONI; she has the same loud, rude, unfeminine, and, to us, most disagreeable (we were about to use a stronger epithet) contr'-alto voice'.[55] Nor were such opinions confined to the earlier decades of this era: in 1896 a French doctor cited 'a low voice' (along with 'hirsute bodies and small breasts') as an indication of female degeneracy.[56]

There might have also been class-based reasons why the contralto voice was unacceptable as a representation of femininity. Lichtenthal's description of voices in 1807 identified the female *voce di petto* or chest voice as 'strident and disgusting'.[57] Such qualities were presumably regarded as inappropriate in the idealised environment of the operatic stage (particularly in the early period); but this was a sound much more evident in popular culture. In the latter part of the nineteenth century in France, the *café-concert chanteuses* and other popular singers sang almost entirely in their chest voices (a practice Reynaldo Hahn attributed to the influence of one particular singer, Thérésa);[58] early recordings of the British music hall artiste Marie Lloyd display a substantial use likewise; Sternberg's film *The Blue Angel* made right at the end of this era in 1930 (but suggestive of earlier practices) shows the cabaret artiste Rosa Valletti delivering her number in similar fashion. Most classical contraltos would of course have sung largely in a mixed register, reserving pure chest notes for specific effect – indeed, Schumann-Heink advised that only a very judicious and unforced use of the chest register was the contralto's key to vocal longevity.[59] Nevertheless, the associations between a low voice and low-class entertainment might have had unwelcome connotations in the high art arena of the opera house – even if conversely in oratorio and on the concert platform the contralto often presented a more refined image.

By the 1850s, the contralto and mezzo-soprano's access to the role of the heroine had became increasingly limited – 'feminine' representations equivalent to those played by sopranos (such as Rossini had provided earlier for the contralto in *Il barbiere di Siviglia* and *La cenerentola*) were now almost non-existent. In 1852, Verdi was invited to consider writing Violetta in *La traviata* for the famous contralto Marietta Alboni (1823–94): according to Brenna, he refused on the grounds that 'he writes his operas in order that they circulate, and a work made for Alboni would not be hired out more than two or three times a year'.[60]

There was an alternative to female characters: the 'breeches' roles, which had been a convention of the operatic stage in the previous two centuries. The popularity of these cross-dressing roles – at least for the male audience – owed much to their inherent erotic possibilities for the display of the female body (as will be discussed in Chapter 7). In dramatic terms, however, the nature of such roles changed perceptibly within the period. From 1800 to around 1845, when the gender boundaries onstage were less rigid, contraltos were often required to continue the eighteenth-century tradition of playing heroes, such as the title-role of *Tancredi* (Rossini) or Malcolm in *La donna del lago* (Donizetti). The absence of the castrato from the operatic stage was one factor; another was the undeveloped (in the modern sense) tenor voice, which with its *tenorino* quality and use of the falsetto range from g' upwards shared many characteristics of range and timbre with the contralto, and might therefore have been regarded as tonally interchangeable. There was also a real paucity of tenors in the early period, as the periodicals made plain, thus necessitating the use of female singers in male roles.

For various reasons, therefore, the contralto was regarded in the early decades as a valid candidate for the musico. Both Rossini and Donizetti contributed a significant number of such roles between 1812 and 1843;[61] Bellini followed suit by designating Romeo for a female singer in *I Capuleti e i Montecchi* (1830) – although Berlioz fulminated against this decision for 'Juliet's hero to be shorn of his manhood'.[62] More surprisingly, given his suspicion about certain operatic conventions, even Wagner composed the heroic Adriano in *Rienzi* (1842) for female voice, that of Wilhemine Schröder-Devrient.[63]

Such heroic roles became noticeably fewer after the emergence of the new tenor voice, and had all but disappeared by the middle of the nineteenth century. Criticism of the practice of 'en travesti' had been steadily increasing. In 1841, Ritorni derided the use of female voices in male roles, describing it as an 'absurdity'.[64] Above all, the contralto lacked a champion amongst the new generation of composers. We have already seen that Verdi refused to compose the title role of *La traviata* for Marietta Alboni: even less did he entertain the alternative idea of giving her the lead male role of Alfredo, apparently 'hating' transformations of this kind.[65] (When finally he did write a male role for a woman, Oscar in *Un ballo in maschera*, he perversely used a coloratura soprano.) From then on, the contralto had to be content with her other most common male role: that of an adolescent boy.

Vocally, this made perfect sense against the new tenor voice. These boyish travesti roles were often asexual, even if romantically fixated on the prima donna – such as Pierotto in Donizetti's *Linda di Chamounix* (1842) or Siebel in Gounod's *Faust* (1859). The dramaturgical usefulness of this figure (a friend dressed as a man but often displaying the warmer, sympathetic qualities of a woman) almost suggests a theatrical need for a new kind of gender: either a more understanding male, or alternatively a woman able to live a freer life beyond the domestic confines and participate equally in male society. But in the more decadent atmosphere of the *fin-de-siècle*, composers once again began to play with the sexual frisson created by a woman playing a man making love to a woman, famously sampled by

Cherubino in *Le nozze di Figaro* (1786). Rossini had earlier exploited this to the full in the relationship between Isolier (*musico*) and Adèle (soprano) in *Le Comte Ory* (1827); now Massenet, in pantomime tradition, used a female singer for Prince Charmant in *Cendrillon* (1899), whilst Strauss composed the ultimate role of this kind, Octavian in *Der Rosenkavalier* (1911).

In 1871, Panofka attempted a rehabilitation of the contralto voice, by arguing that the perception of it as inherently masculine was a common error:

> No: this voice, notable for its sweet, tender, sometimes melancholy timbre, lends itself to the roles representing the mature, good and sensible woman; but one who is also endowed with such strength of character and energy that she is able to bear with resignation the most vivid moral pains, and is rendered susceptible also to political exaltation to the point of martyring herself from real heroism. But such heroism is not that of the warrior, but rather that of the Roman matron and of many Italian women who in these modern times have known how to defy prison and who saw their sons die for the blessed cause of the fatherland, without a murmur against Providence. They were heroines, yes, but equally noble wives and adored mothers: finally, they were women in the most sublime sense of the word.[66]

Panofka's comments plainly reflect the political context of recent Italian history and the *risorgimento* movement in this reappraisal of the contralto. The use of the contralto's darker vocal timbre to signal female maturity was of course already apparent in the writing of *seconda donna* parts as companions, duennas, or mothers. Most such roles were comparatively minor, but Fidès in Meyerbeer's *Le Prophète* (1849) had introduced (according to Chorley) a 'new type' of female character:[67] 'the pathos of maternal tenderness and devotion, pure of all passion, had been hitherto unattempted, till it was tried in this opera'.[68] Four years later, Verdi also drew on motherhood in his delineation of Azucena (*Il trovatore*), describing her as 'a woman of very special character',[69] whose 'two great passions' were '*filial love* and *maternal love*'.[70] Both Fidès and Azucena were given substantial focus within the operas, exceeding that of the soprano, and their popularity (especially when performed by Pauline Viardot) might have suggested that the mature woman was to be an enduring addition to the range of contralto characterisation. But although depictions of motherhood increased from 1870 onwards, there is no real parallel with either Fidès or Azucena for contraltos in later operas. Neither La Cieca in *La Gioconda* (1876), nor Geneviève in Debussy's *Pelléas et Mélisande* (1902) nor Carmela in Wolf-Ferrari's *I gioielli della Madonna* (1911) play as active a role as their predecessors. Where a mother is given more space within the drama – such as Alice Ford in Verdi's *Falstaff*, or the Kostelnička in Janáček's *Jenůfa* – she mysteriously becomes a soprano again.

The most common deployment of the mezzo-soprano or contralto voice for younger female characters, however, was as clear identification of sexual experience. Operatic lust belonged primarily to the lower register. In the most sexually explicit arias of opera's best known seductresses, Carmen (Bizet) and Dalila (Saint-Saëns), both heroines weave their chromatic way down towards the dark reaches of tonal sensuality. Many of these roles also encompass the higher notes, but often these are used as a taunt (Carmen's b'' at the end of her seguidilla) or as a threat (Amneris' ab'' in her duet with the heroine of Verdi's *Aida*; Ortrud's repeated vengeful $a\sharp''$ in her Act II scene in Wagner's *Lohengrin*). Only Eboli's soaring bb'' on 'lo salverò' at the end of her penitent aria 'O don fatale' in Verdi's *Don Carlos* suggests not a challenge but rather her emergence as a changed woman who is now prepared to sacrifice herself to save the man she loves. The placing of such notes only at emotional climaxes obviously reflects the mezzo-soprano's vocal difficulty in surmounting the stave, but it again serves to emphasise the auditor's perception that the lower female voice could not easily attain the higher reaches of musicalised femininity except as a form of attack.

The size and nature of the contralto roles often occasioned complaint from the singers. In the early period, when singers exerted a degree of influence on the composition of operas, there are hints of open conflict. One librettist for La Scala in 1816 is warned to take account of the contralto's preferences: 'take care, when you write for

Bassi, to give her a vibrant character and a good deal of the action, since she is extremely touchy, both on principle and by temperament'.[71] Evidently, this particular singer was accustomed to agitate with some success for suitable performance opportunities. A century later, contraltos could only bemoan the kind of roles allotted to them. Louise Homer (1871–1947) complained that the soprano was always the heroine, standing in the 'limelight of nobility'; in contrast, although the contralto might 'sing like an angel', her 'operatic impersonation is one that offends or antagonizes the public'.[72] There is little sign here of the kind of modern repositioning of such roles within a more feminist context. But not all singers agreed with this negative assessment; Sophie Braslau (*fl.* 1913–22) claimed that whilst certain contralto roles were undeniably 'unpleasant types', what the audience wanted was not so much 'sympathetic characters' as a powerful projection of 'real vocal and dramatic art': 'If a contralto has a glorious voice, and her tones ring out through a crowded house; if the emotions of hatred, revenge or despair which she expresses thrill, the audience will respond and she will make a lasting impression.'[73]

But even the contralto's small repertoire was subject to the avaricious raids of the soprano: Rosina in *Il barbiere di Siviglia*, Fidès in *Le Prophète* and the title role in *Carmen* were all plundered regularly by sopranos eager to exploit the potential offered by these characters. Carmen in particular attracted singers as diverse as Adelina Patti, Rosa Ponselle (for both of whom it was a mistake, although for different reasons), Zélie De Lussan and Emma Calvé (for both of whom it was a resounding success). Similarly, many contraltos – if they possessed sufficient range – struggled to attain a grasp on the soprano repertoire. Wagner's use of a heavier voice provided some possibilities here – Marie Brema, Olive Fremstad and Margarethe Matzenauer all began their careers as contraltos before achieving their goal of Brünnhilde. Such efforts were surely partly inspired by the poor wages paid throughout this era to the contralto; during the 1896–97 season at the Metropolitan Opera, Eugenia Mantelli was performing leading roles four times a week for a paltry $48 for an evening's work, as against the soprano Nellie Melba's fee of $1,600 per performance.[74] (A rare exception to this general rule was Alboni, whose success in London in the 1840s rivalled that of Jenny Lind, with a salary that rose accordingly.) But the contralto's lowly position in the opera house was not always reflected on the concert stage. Ernestine Schumann-Heink, an enormously popular performer in Germany and America, celebrated a fifty-year-long career that combined opera, operetta, oratorio and concert work. A contralto she may have been, but her public status undoubtedly afforded her the title of a 'prima donna' – even though she claimed she detested the term.[75]

No quality is more essential in a singer than his power of *dramatic expression.*

Stendhal, *Life of Rossini* (1824)

At the beginning of the nineteenth century, there was a clear division between the singers of *opera buffa* and those of *opera seria*, not only in the sense of social status but also with regard to performance modes. *Opera seria* required an elevated, pictorial style – an idealisation of sentiment. *Opera buffa* demanded a much freer, more 'realistic' approach, whose reliance on improvisation and mimicry sometimes produced (as in Stendhal's description of the *buffo* bass Luigi Pacini in Rossini's *Il turco in Italia*) theatrical representations recognisably similar to some modern comedy.[1] The separation between these two modes was rigidly maintained. As late as 1829, Marietta Brambilla was criticised by *Il censore universale dei teatri* for her attempt to perform Mayr's *Che originali* alongside Paisiello's *Nina*:

> Signora Brambilla cannot be a *prima buffa*, because not having been born in the theatre, and not having applied herself particularly to this genre, she would have to be a magician to possess suddenly a wholly particular art, that requires long study and long exercise. The attractiveness of her figure, the grace of her singing will please, but these prerogatives will not be enough to sustain a character wholly comic and ridiculous, to make the jokes and witticisms take off, to represent to us in parody a fantasy warmed by a bizarre heroism.[2]

It is interesting to note that *opera buffa* was regarded by Prividali (the critic in question) to be the more difficult medium, requiring a very special and distinct knowledge of stage practices that could only be acquired as a *figlia dell'arte*. But serious opera also demanded particular qualities. In an era in which the fictional heroine of most *opera seria* was usually high-born but the singer herself came from a much lower social class, a frequent concern about female performance was the display of aristocratic attributes in the roles. Critics and journals either applauded the proficiency of the singer in this respect (as Stendhal did in his review of Colbran) or advised on more appropriate 'gentlewomanly' behaviour. In 1804, the *Corriere delle dame* praised Madame Correa for the intelligence and passion of her performance, but required something more: 'In order to sustain better her majestic character and royal dignity here and in all her roles, we advise her to leave and re-enter the stage with greater elevation of carriage and gravity of step.'[3]

Opera itself made in structural and narrative terms a similar distinction between tragedy and comedy during the early decades. But over the course of the century, this separation would gradually diminish. In Puccini's *La bohème* (1896), high tragedy and low comedy function in harmony to create an opera whose poignancy is made all the more intense by its use of humour. In performance modes, too, the sharply defined styles of serious and comic roles would similarly merge, as the new generation of singers sought to play everything, and the idealism of the early years was increasingly stained with ever-deepening tints of realism. Change was brought about through a number of factors: the singers' own individuality and artistry; their contact with other artists; the interventions of theorists and teachers; and certain operatic roles, which for one reason or another provided defining moments in the development of stage practices. Various questions arise from an attempt to investigate the shape of this development – did singers give the same performances in every country and every *piazza*? What adjustments were made for particular conventions? We know that in the early, pre-copyright period there was no such thing as a stable score: additions and alterations were made, some with the composer's consent; some without. We also know that certain aspects of stage business were less acceptable in particular theatres than in others; for example, Cenerentola's slipper was forbidden in Rome;[4] so too in London was Alfredo's purse of money, flung at Violetta in the second act of *La traviata*.

Trying to determine precise performance modes also presents other problems: in part because reception of this ephemeral art is so subjective (each spectator notes the details that most interested him or her, that most confirmed or contrasted with their own ideas),[5] and in part because in Italy especially critics rarely discussed the histrionic aspects of the lyric stage. Nonetheless, there is a body of evidence that offers some vital clues to this complex area.

The most significant developments in operatic performance between 1820 and 1840 were led by three brilliantly innovative *attrici cantanti*: Giuditta Pasta, Wilhelmine Schröder-Devrient, and Maria Malibran, each of whom had a lasting influence on the operatic stage. Pasta's career began in 1816, her initial performances provoking only a subdued response; by the early 1820s, however, she had established a reputation for a combination of dramatic and vocal expertise that endured for the next twenty years. Even more, she had redefined the meaning of dramatic performance in opera. In 1829 Carlo Ritorni dubbed Pasta as a singer 'delle passioni', because her voice was directed 'towards expressing the most intense passions, accompanying it with expressions of physical action, unknown before her in the lyric theatre'.[6] He later expanded on her contribution to the histrionic development of the operatic stage:

> The principal talent of Pasta is . . . in having invented with shrewd intelligence the proper dramatic action and expression of the *melodramma*: that anti-dramatic work she found on the stage when she began her career, to which she not only adapted her sublime histrionic gifts by rendering them more finely as she had learnt in France, but directed them towards hiding its defects.[7]

Opera was deemed 'anti-dramatic' because of the difficulties it presented for the singing actor – particularly in terms of the gestural codes of the early nineteenth-century stage. Ritorni cited no less a personage than the famous French actor François-Joseph Talma (1763–1826), who had tried his hand at an operatic performance one day and said later that it had been very hard work trying 'to fill so many long gaps with mute action, tied nevertheless to circumscribed periods, and to the meaning of the accompanying music'. The timing of gesture was possibly the greatest problem. *The Censore universale dei teatri* made the point that in spoken theatre, the speed of the dialogue ensured a constant and rapid flow of gesture; music, however, demanded a much slower pace of delivery, with commensurately more emphasis on the gestures.[8] Some less than expert singers found themselves running out of gestures before they had reached the end of the aria, as in this criticism of one young soprano in the *Journal de Paris* in 1827: 'her gestures are too numerous and too rapid, which often produces some difficulty; the singing still continues, but the singer has no more gestures to complete the depiction of the sentiments that she expresses'.[9] Pasta, however, managed to resolve these difficulties, as Ritorni described:

> Pasta, not with gestures and pantomime, but with the action of a living
> picture, herself composes in the opera a second part of mute
> representation, sometimes better than that which the poet and the
> composer have written to be declaimed. Then, extracting a jewel of art
> from the flaw of the [operatic artform], she assumes the physical
> immobility that a *largo*, a *canon*, a *solo* requires; and meanwhile she
> transports all the dramatic situation to her face, to which the mobility of
> its ample lineaments, conceded to her by the singular favour of nature,
> wholly addresses itself, with instantaneous changes to the expression of
> the most minute passages and gradations of passion.[10]

If Ritorni is right, then Pasta reserved movement primarily for recitative passages, whilst using only very limited gesture during arias or passages requiring sustained singing. Her moments of stillness echoed the statuary approaches of earlier operatic performance: other singers of the era such as Tacchinardi admitted to seeking inspiration from sculptors for their gestural poses.[11] But then, like Hermione in *A Winter's Tale*, Pasta seems to have stepped off the pedestal and into living movement. The gestures she made were not the elegant, rhetorical poses of the classical stage; rather, her gestures had *meaning*, arising (whether as Medea, or Norma, or Amina) from the drama. Certain gestures were clearly stylised – such as the much-reported flinging up of her arms in *Medea* – and rhythmically rooted to the music. But she also supposedly used 'nature' as a mirror; Stendhal claimed that her 'genius as a tragic actress is made up of a thousand-and-one little casual *observations*' from real life.[12] In 1826, the *Harmonicon* described her as the love-maddened Nina in Paisiello's opera in words that foreshadow the acting styles of a later era. 'It is all nature', the magazine proclaimed, before citing from another review: 'she does not act the character – she *is* it, looks it, breathes it. She does not study for an effect, but strives to possess herself of the feeling which would dictate what she is to do, and which gives birth to the proper degree of grace, dignity, ease, or force.'[13] This emphasis on 'nature', however, was not always well received or regarded as appropriate within the musical framework. In 1829, the *Censore universale dei teatri* argued that the authenticity of her representation of Nina's madness (in which Pasta assumed 'the semblance of an imbecile, who moved clumsily with heavy small steps, hunched shoulders, fixed eyes, vulgar gestures, a bizarre manner, and a childish expression weeping and laughing') was in fact wholly imagined by Pasta without being the least analogous to the role as conceived musically by the composer. If Paisiello had wished to portray the character in this fashion, the *Censore* continued, then in the libretto there would have been some 'disconnections, childishness, nonsense, blunders', and in the music 'an artificial misalignment of rhythm and musical sense, capricious fits and starts, irritating dissonances, in short, a poetic and musical language truly irrational'. The proper way to perform this role was very different: Nina's 'deplorable situation must render her tender, languid, desolate, but noble in her behaviour, decorous in her gesture, true in grief, distracted in pleasure, conforming always to the plaintive delicacy of her music, to the moving affection of her words'.[14] Such comments illustrate that at times Pasta's new absorption in the reality of the moment outpaced the developments in music as well as the philosophical context surrounding opera. Given that she would subsequently create the title role of perhaps the most influential opera in establishing ideas of declamatory singing – *Norma* – one might speculate to what extent Bellini's compositional approach was influenced by this increased dramatic passion on the operatic stage, and sought to express it more fully within the music.

Pasta's contribution to the development of the operatic stage lay therefore in creating a style of performance in which the dramatic element of the role was at least as important as the singing – and in which the nature of acting was redesigned to fit with the needs of the operatic artform. She had a number of rivals during the 1820s, including Joséphine Fodor-Mainvielle and Henrietta Sontag, but only one whose influence on opera composition and performance was comparable, albeit in a different repertoire: the German soprano Wilhelmine Schröder-Devrient (1804–60), whose career began in Vienna in 1821. If Wagner was dismayed by the acting he saw in Paris in the 1830s, the 'glorious' Schröder-Devrient provided him with a quite different paradigm for his efforts to revolutionise operatic staging and realise the 'art of the sublime Illusion'. He was not alone in his admiration: Clara Schumann regarded Schröder-Devrient as 'my ideal among dramatic singers';[15] Goethe applauded her private performance of Schubert's *Erlkönig* as a 'magnificent piece of artistry';[16] Weber claimed she was 'the best Agathe [*Der Freischütz*] in the world, and surpassed anything that I had conceived for the role'.[17] But it was Wagner who paid her perhaps the most remarkable tribute by a nineteenth-century male composer to a female singer, in dedicating his essay 'On Actors and Singers' (1872) to her, and declaring that 'all my knowledge of mimetic art [*des mimischen Wesens*] I owe to this grand woman; and through that teaching can I point to truthfulness as that art's foundation'.[18]

Schröder-Devrient's 'truthfulness' lay in her 'self-divestment', as Wagner termed it, leading him to describe acting as this 'wondrous playing with the Self, wherein the player clean forgets himself'.[19] Her absorption in every moment of her role was an aspect much noted by critics, as in these comments of Ludwig Rellstab on her interpretation of Leonore:

> Her part does not begin when she first speaks or sings, or has business to do; it never ceases so long as elements of the poem concern the

character. Thus, her pantomime, in particular, establishes a chain of subtle devices which, when closely examined, are distinguished equally by organic homogeneity and imaginative variety. Every reference to the fate of the prisoner, every innocent utterance of the adoring Marzelline, finds a softly awakened echo in Leonore's features.[20]

Schröder-Devrient's ability to transcend emotionally the borders of number opera to create a sustained, cohesive performance was regarded as something exceptional. Her more rounded approach to operatic acting was almost certainly a product of her family connections to the legitimate stage. Daughter of the actress Sophie Burger and the operatic baritone Friedrich Schröder, she also married into one of the most influential theatrical dynasties in Germany, led by her father-in-law, the actor Ludwig Devrient (1784–1832). Devrient was part of a movement opposed to the stylisation of Goethe and the Weimar school, eschewing the 'mosaic of single, carefully prepared movements' (or 'points') that were so much a part of eighteenth- and nineteenth-century dramatic performance; his nephew Eduard recalls that his 'performance issued solely from the nature and the inherent necessity of his characters as he had created them. He lived his parts, he did not act them.'[21] Something of that approach is also visible in Schröder-Devrient's methodology:

When I was studying the character of Fidelio at Vienna . . . I could not attain that which appeared to me to be the desired and natural expression at the moment when Leonora [sic], throwing herself before her husband, holds out a pistol to the Governor, with the words 'Kill first his wife!' I studied and studied in vain, though I did all I could to place myself mentally in the situation of Leonora. I had pictured to myself that situation, but I felt that it was incomplete, without knowing why or wherefore. Well, the evening arrived; the audience knows not with what feelings an artiste, who enters seriously into a part, dresses for the representation. The nearer the moment approached, the greater was my alarm. When it did arrive, and as I ought to have sung the ominous words, and pointed the pistol at the Governor, I fell into such utter tremor at the thought of not being perfect in my character, that my whole frame trembled, and I thought I should have fallen. Now, only fancy how I felt when the whole house broke forth into enthusiastic shouts of applause, and what I thought when, after the curtain fell, I was told that this moment was the most effective and powerful of my whole representation. So that which I could not attain with every effort of mind and imagination, was produced at this decisive moment by my unaffected terror and anxiety. This result, and the effect it had upon the public, taught me how to seize and comprehend the incident, so that which at the first representation I had hit upon unconsciously, I adopted in full consciousness ever afterwards in this part.[22]

But perhaps the most telling impact of Schröder-Devrient's perform-ances lay in the way she sang – or rather, the way she did *not* sing. Chorley claimed that she had never even learnt to sing: 'Her tones were delivered without any care, save to give them due force. There was an air of strain and spasm throughout her performances – of that struggle for victory which never conquers.'[23] Wagner, too, was emphatic that she 'had no "voice" at all', but her lack of a con-ventionally beautiful instrument or technique did not hinder her capacity to move her audience: 'she knew how to use her breath so beautifully, and to let a true womanly soul stream forth in such wondrous sounds, that we never thought of either voice or sing-ing!'[24] For Wagner, Schröder-Devrient's vocalising was merely part of her performance *as a whole*, and he viewed her concentration on the total effect of her operatic representations as something towards which every singer should strive. The most startling effect of this effortful voice, however, emerged in her combination of music and the spoken word, as Wagner described:

> She had often previously demonstrated what overwhelming effect can be produced by tones approaching pure speech in Fidelio, carrying the public away whenever, at the words 'One more step and you are dead!' she brought out the word "dead" in her speaking rather than singing voice. The tremendous effect, to which I, of all people, was particularly sensitive, was derived from the strange shock, like the blow of an executioner's axe, which I received at being abruptly brought down from the exalted sphere into which music lifts even the most gruesome situations to the bedrock of harshest reality. This gave a direct sensation

of the peak of sublimity which, in recalling this feeling, I can only describe as the instant like a flash of lightning which, at the moment when two utterly different worlds touch and yet are completely separate, illuminates them both for us simultaneously.[25]

I have argued elsewhere that for Wagner Schröder-Devrient possessed what Barthes defines as the 'grain of the voice'. Her sudden, unlooked-for use of the spoken word transcended the literal meaning of the text ('the message') and revealed multiple meanings: in Barthes' words, 'meaning in its potential voluptuousness'.[26] Its effect on Wagner, the shattering of his 'cultural identity'[27] (his expectations as a nineteenth-century opera spectator) in a 'sensation of the peak of sublimity' equally accords with Barthes' definition of the action of *signifiance* in promoting *jouissance*. To other ears, however, this splintering of vocal conventions did not open up similar strata of understanding. Berlioz, one of Schröder-Devrient's chief detractors, found her transgressions of prevailing musical style exasperating; he declared her singing to be 'often wanting in exactness and taste',[28] and disliked her spoken interjections intensely: 'She never sings such words as O God; yes; no; impossible! They are always spoken, or rather shouted in the loudest voice. I cannot express my aversion for this anti-musical declamation. To my mind it is a hundred times worse to speak in an opera than to sing in a tragedy.'[29] And yet, as we have already seen, some aspects of declamation (although not always so extreme) became an accepted part of operatic composition in all major European repertoires.

If Schröder-Devrient in some sense challenged received ideas about the musicality of the operatic artform, so too did Maria Malibran. The daughter of the opera singers Manuel Garcia and Joaquina Briones, she spent her childhood in the proverbial trunk; the theatre was the 'only nursery and school' for her and her siblings.[30] A sincere admirer of Pasta, she sang many of the same roles during the early part of her career. But her performance style, although equally impassioned, was rather different. Where Pasta's judicious mixture of stillness and movement suggests an acting style on the cusp of change between classicism and romanticism, Malibran's greater spontaneity, physical restlessness and emotional abandonment make her firmly a child of the new age. Whilst this brought her many plaudits, she was also frequently accused of exaggeration. The *Musical World*, although acknowledging the 'delirium' created by 'this extraordinary woman', took issue with her attention to detail in performances of *La sonnambula* and *Fidelio* in 1836:

> If Madame de Beriot [Malibran's married name] have any fault in her acting, it is that she manifests a tendency to bring every point into equally high relief. The unwearied activity of her mind leads her to make even the minutiae of her part over-important . . . she does not always leave well alone; but having made a point, she is determined you shall feel she has made it.[31]

Were such complaints justified? The focus on the 'minutiae' of a role is suggestive of an early naturalistic style, and prefigures Pirandello's description of Eleonora Duse;[32] but if Malibran had accorded the smaller moments the weight applicable to more intense crises within the libretto, then it is possible her performance would indeed have appeared 'busy' and self-conscious by any standards. Her own defence of her art implies that she was deliberately challenging the idealised, choreographic performance styles of her era. On being told she moved too much and too wildly on stage, she answered: 'You're right, it isn't beautiful, but once I'm in my part I no longer think about what effect I make. At that moment I am really afraid, and I behave as I would if pursued by a murderer.'[33] Her sense of realism or, at least, of abandonment to the moment also led to a quite different and contentious approach to the relationship of gesture and music. Dispensing with the concordance between sound and image practised by Pasta and other singers, Malibran made her gestures freely, regardless of the rhythm of the music. To one Italian critic in 1835, the effect was of a 'monstrous combination' of two opposing forms of imitation: 'one, that of the music, wholly composed and conventional; the other, that of the gesture, wholly capricious and free'.[34] If for Pasta, the music was a fabric on which she wove her gestures, movement and melody becoming a single, unified expression, for Malibran, it was thus rather a backcloth against which she moved on impulse.

But another noted aspect of Malibran was her ideas of historical accuracy. Throughout much of the period, women singers were often required to supply their own costumes (except within the larger opera houses); their choice of dress therefore reflected their individual concept of a role, as well as broader ideas about dramatic representation. Theatrical costuming had occasioned much debate in the previous century, with innovative performers such as the French actress Hippolyte Clairon (1723–1803) arguing for an increased emphasis on authenticity.[35] Some of the subsequent generation of prima donnas betrayed an equal interest. Malibran's efforts to achieve greater historical accuracy in her costume for *Fidelio* in 1835 won praise from William Macready ('Her costume was admirable – will our actors never learn? – *Never.*' he wrote in his diary).[36] For the premiere of Donizetti's *Maria Stuarda* at La Scala in 1835 she prepared sketches of the costumes for principals and chorus from the tombs at Westminster Abbey;[37] in *La sonnambula* she eschewed the customary muslin négligée for the sleepwalking scene in favour of the peasant's more usual garb of 'coarse gown, woollen stockings, and night cap'.[38] Her younger sister Pauline Viardot later had a similar reputation for undertaking historical research.[39] But how accurate was such research? Clairon had earlier warned that 'costume exactly copied, however, is not practicable: it would be indecent and ridiculous';[40] and attempts at authenticity during nineteenth century show a judicious employment of broadly historical features rather than absolute imitation of the original. The drawings left by Malibran of her *Maria Stuarda* production show a reasonably convincing depiction of sixteenth-century dress, in the main details at least. But without an overall design concept that embraced similar notions in costumes for the entire cast (as Malibran attempted to achieve in *Maria Stuarda*), the efforts of individual singers must have seemed sadly isolated.[41] Attempts at historical accuracy were also often sacrificed to accord with off-stage stylistic modes of dress. Clairon

Figure 5. Adelina Patti as Amina in *La sonnambula*

and certain other eighteenth-century actresses had abandoned their hoop skirts in the interests of realism, and were praised by Diderot for doing so.[42] But the re-emergence of the hoop skirt in mid-nineteenth century fashion led to its use once again in theatrical costume, regardless of the fictional period being presented. Clara Louise Kellogg's dramatic training in the 1860s included proper management of this troublesome fashion item, especially 'how to fall gracefully in a hoop skirt' – of particular importance given the frequency with which operatic heroines expire on stage, collapse in a faint, or even simply go to bed. This last feat Kellogg recalled Anna de Lagrange achieving during a performance of *La sonnambula*;[43] a postcard photograph of Adelina Patti in the same sleepwalking scene, complete with candle, shows her too wearing a hoop beneath her nightdress. (see fig. 5). Malibran's plainer outfit for the same role some thirty years earlier obviously had had little lasting influence.

En travesti

Pasta, Schröder-Devrient and Malibran exerted a powerful impact on the opera stage, affecting compositional practices as well as setting trends followed by others. They shared a willingness to be daring, a commitment as much to dramatic as to musical performance, a wide repertoire of both soprano and contralto parts – and also both female and trousered roles. Indeed, they did not simply sing *en travesti* those roles intentionally conceived as such, but on occasion deliberately assumed male roles in preference to female ones, as Chorley claims Pasta did in her performance of the title role of Rossini's *Otello* in 1828:

> In 'Otello', finding the part of *Desdemona*, throughout two thirds of the opera, somewhat pale, she was driven by her instincts towards what is terrible and impassioned in art – 'to attempt' (her own modest phrase) the stormy and vindictive character of the Moor married 'to the gentle lady'; and, unsatisfactory as all such assumptions must be, her personation printed deep on the minds of those who saw it an impression of something fierce, masterful, Oriental, the like of which had hardly, till she came, been expressed in music.[44]

Given that Pasta had already played Rossini's *musico* lead in *Tancredi* (written for a contralto), there must have seemed little reason why she should not expand her repertoire by assuming roles specifically written for male voices. The *Harmonicon* did not agree, finding her characterisation too brutal: 'Shall we hazard the declaration that we witnessed, with a feeling little short of horror, the noble *Otello* twist his hand in the tresses of the woman he still loved (with the ferocity of a savage attacking his deadly enemy) for the purpose of rendering his butchery more effectual?'[45] In 1831 Malibran (ever Pasta's imitator, at least in the early years) followed in her footsteps and played Otello opposite the 'huge German Desdemona' of Wilhelmine Schröder-Devrient.[46]

Such practices were not exceptional when female access to similar roles was often due to the unavailability or unsuitability of male singers. Benedetta Rosmunda Pisaroni was hired by one theatre in 1831 to sing the leading tenor role of Arnold in Rossini's *Guillaume Tell*, the *tessitura* of which lay so high that two of its arias were cut by its creator Adolphe Nourrit within two performances of its premiere in Paris in 1829. (In fact, Pisaroni was then abruptly dropped by the management after her poor reception in Milan, and the part fell to Duprez instead, who thereby found his *ut de poitrine*[47] – the rest, as they say, is history.) In the first Covent Garden production of Verdi's *Ernani* in 1848, Marietta Alboni undertook the important baritone role of Carlo after the part had been rejected by both Giorgio Ronconi and Antonio Tamburini; in 1854, the *Gazzetta musicale di Firenze* mentioned a performance of *La sonnambula* at the Teatro Nuovo in which Elvino was played by a woman 'in travesti'.[48] Even later in the century, the opera critic Hermann Klein stated that the 'beautiful and fascinating' mezzo-soprano Zélia Trebelli (1834–92) was such a consummate performer of male roles ('She had the art of striking the attitudes characteristic of a boy, and of moving about the stage and making gestures like one') that she was 'more completely at home' in this aspect of her repertoire than in female characters, and sang both Tamino and Almaviva.[49] Nevertheless, these raids by female singers on the male repertoire all concern operas written before 1850: *Ernani* was the most recent role attempted. Women did not explore scores written for the new *tenore di forza*. Furthermore, such forays into male performance territory were taking place against a wider theatrical background in which a number of actresses – including well-known figures such as Sarah Bernhardt – were assuming male characters onstage.[50]

There are contradictions here about the performance of such roles. Trebelli, towards the end of the century, was obviously engaging in a substantial degree of male impersonation. But at the beginning of the period, things were rather different. Costuming was one factor. Elizabeth Howe makes the point that when actresses first emerged in the seventeenth century, breeches roles were an erotic device to expose the actress's body; male costume was therefore specifically designed to emphasise the female form rather than detract from it with realistically masculine garb.[51] Similar practices are visible on the operatic stage during this later period – at least at first glance. A review of *Abenamet e Zoraide* at La Scala in 1806, in which Augusta Schmalz played Abenamet, Generale d'Armata, complained that she lacked 'martial virile courage': 'Whether a man transforming himself into a woman, or a woman transforming herself into man, he or she must take care to hide the physical configuration of their own intrinsic sex.' The *Corriere delle dame* urged Schmalz to change her costume to Turkish pantaloons (*braghesse alla turca*), not only because this would have accurately reflected North African dress and corresponded to the costume of the rest of the cast, but also because 'it would have avoided the criticism of those who know that in all the history of the Moors there is not a single example of their generals wearing from waist to toes taut and tight-fitting chainmail'.[52] In pictures of the costumes worn some years later by Malibran and Schröder-Devrient in *Fidelio*, both women, though ostensibly disguised as men, wear not breeches but short skirts that carry a distinctly feminine flavour (see fig. 6).[53]

But an examination of the costumes worn by men playing male roles on the operatic stage sometimes exhibited great similarity: for example, Gilbert-Louis Duprez is depicted in a costume for *Guillaume Tell* reminiscent of Malibran's and Schröder-Devrient's short dresses, with an equally pinched waist (see fig. 7). And there are even rare pictures of both Pasta and Schröder-Devrient wearing a moustache.[54]

Ways of playing the breeches roles in this early period also demonstrate some inconsistencies. We have already seen that the unexpected ferocity of Pasta's Otello was criticised; nevertheless, the *Harmonicon* makes it plain that her 'undisguisable form and voice are anything but masculine'. *En travesti*, Pasta did not 'give herself masculine airs' or connect her gestures with the 'ring of her spurs', as Henri Blaze de Bury remarked.[55] Such practices, however, were according to convention. In 1833, Nicola Tacchinardi declared that women playing operatic heroes 'never take the character and the semblance' of the role; rather, 'the walk is always feminine', as was

Figure 6. Wilhelmine Schröder-Devrient as Leonore in *Fidelio*

the costume, the dressing of the hair in ringlets, and so on. 'How ever will we illude ourselves into seeing these figures represent a conqueror, a feared warrior, a husband who has already become a father, a competitor of kings and queens?'[56]

From such comments, and our modern prejudice for naturalism, we might assume that there was something faintly ridiculous about Pasta's performance in such roles. But her eschewal of an overtly 'realistic' representation in the externals of the character did not mean an equal absence of emotional substance. After all, Blaze de Bury had continued, 'what does the illusion of costume matter when one wishes to convey the passion and the dramatic accent of a role? In so perilous an enterprise, it is only through the ideal that one can save oneself. Was it a woman, this Pasta singing Tancredi's aria

Figure 7. Gilbert-Louis Duprez as Arnold in *Guillaume Tell*

"Di tanti palpiti"? Was it a man? Whoever thought to ask? It was Tancredi.'[57]

Not all singers embraced the *travesti* roles with as much confidence as Pasta or as much enthusiasm as Trebelli. Rossini's attempts to contract Rosa Morandi in the 1820s always contained the assurance that she would not have to sing male roles, although she might be required to sing female roles that involved some element of cross-dressing.[58] Blanche Roosevelt's much later fictionalised account of her experiences of operatic life depicted her young heroine ogled by impresarios with the intention of making her play *travesti* roles (she resisted indignantly).[59] In an era that emphasised female modesty, many women felt embarrassed about the physical display male dress required. Some singers actively detested such roles, and found ways of circumventing the exposure of legs: for a performance of Verdi's *Rigoletto* at La Scala in the early 1850s, Clara Novello wore a 'huge cloak, long tunic, Turkish trousers and high boots with leather frills [which] concealed all but her face and hands', with the result that she felt 'more elegant and decent than in many evening gowns'.[60] Other singers were less inventive. The baritone Charles Santley recalled Christine Nilsson as Cherubino wearing 'a nondescript dress which spoiled her figure; instead of the sprightly page, she looked exactly what she was, a woman dressed in male attire, and very unhappy without her petticoats'.[61] In contrast, Pauline Viardot's garb as Orphée included a floor-length cloak that protected her legs from at least one perspective; in this and other photographs from the same sitting, she seems quietly secure in a costume that acknowledges Greek classical male dress but does not make especial capital out of her own sexuality (see fig. 8).

Other prima donnas relished the opportunity to provoke erotic interest whilst playing breeches roles, providing it accorded with their own ideas of physical attractiveness and gave them the illusion that such display remained within their control. In 1808 the London critic Henry Robertson was scandalised that Angelica Catalani had had 'a new opera composed by Sebastiano Nasolini for the express purpose of her appearing in male attire'.[62] A century later, Bianca Stagno-Bellincioni also 'loved trouser roles' because 'I liked to show my shapely legs.'[63] For those singers less sure of shapeliness, artificial aids were available. As a young singer in her first performance as Cherubino at the Théâtre de la Monnaie in Brussels in 1882, Emma Calvé attempted to hide the unflattering (as she saw it)

Figure 8. Pauline Viardot as Orphée

Figure 9. Katharina Klafsky as Leonore in *Fidelio*

appearance of her 'thin legs, spider's legs as my mother called them' by inserting 'enormous calves of cotton' underneath her tights, and at first felt confident she had achieved the desired effect: 'The old gentlemen in the front rows trained their opera glasses on these superb affairs. I was conscious of their attention and proud of my success.' When she left the stage at the end of her first scene, she encountered the wrath of the stage director who declared that every one was laughing at her and demanded that she remove the 'hideous lumps' immediately. For her next scene, Calvé was forced to go onstage minus the padding: 'My mortification was intense. I tried to cover my legs with my cloak, but it was impossible. The audience saw the change instantly, and was highly amused. I was applauded and cheered uproariously.'[64]

By the end of the century, costumes used for breeches roles appear to have become more masculinised with a reduced element of titillation – presumably because of the growing influence of naturalism. The rather stout Hungarian soprano Katharina Klafsky (1855–96) is shown wearing baggy knee-length shorts accompanied by knee-high boots, with only a few inches of white stockinged knee visible (see fig. 9): a costume that (with some variations) is visible in many other representations of Leonore at the end of the period.[65] If ostensibly more modest, the increased masculinity of such costumes might have signalled other complex erotic messages, as is demonstrated by the sexologist Richard von Krafft-Ebing's assessment of lesbian dress code in 1886: 'Uranism may nearly always be suspected in females wearing their hair short, or who dress in the fashion of men, or pursue the sports and pastimes of their male acquaintances; also in opera singers and actresses who appear in male attire on the stage by preference.'[66] It seems that any assumption of male attire, whether realistic or non-realistic, was fraught with difficulty.

THE MIDDLE PERIOD

If Pasta, Malibran and Schröder-Devrient each, in their own way, substantially aided the histrionic development of the operatic stage, the initiative for similar innovation during the middle period arguably shifted away from the performers. The dominant *attrice cantante* in the Italian and French repertoire between 1840 and 1860 was Malibran's younger sister, Pauline Viardot, who represented a culmination of a particular style rather than something new. By now, the stage was in the fullest flowering of its 'pictorial' mode, the proscenium arch acting as a frame for precisely executed tableaux based on gestural language.

Determining the exact nature of historical operatic gesture is virtually impossible.[67] True, many nineteenth-century manuals of acting provide demonstrations of various poses and attitudes (as evident in works by or on Engel, Gilbert Austin, Antonio Morrocchesi, François Delsarte, Gustave Garcia, Henry Neville and others),[68] and there are obvious traces in theatrical reviews and memoirs of their use onstage.[69] But these fixed, statuary poses are inadequate descriptors of fluid, live performance. Moreover, it is uncertain how far these manuals governed onstage practice in opera. But if precise details of movement are often unavailable to us, we can nevertheless identify broad principles governing notions of 'good' and 'bad' gestural language. With regard to the latter, the most common factors were inappropriateness of gesture, meaningless repetition, a lack of invention, and graceless or irregular delivery. Some singers (perhaps many) seemed unsure of the purpose of their gestural display. A review in *La Revue des deux-mondes* in 1840 found fault with the erratic 'pantomime' of Rosine Stoltz: 'you see her pass in an instant from the delirium of a bacchante to the immobility of a marble statue. Never a glance, a gesture, an intention in her that suggest intelligence or the least concern for the character she is impersonating.'[70] This description (if accurate) suggests Stoltz simply stitched together a series of ill-chosen attitudes, with little coherent linkage to the fabric of the *fabula*. But at least there was some variety in her performance; other singers were more parsimonious in their effects. Kellogg, eager to acquire as much dramatic knowledge as possible, learnt much of her stagecraft by watching other artists, and recalled a performance by the tenor Pasquale Brignoli in *I puritani* in the 1850s that jarred with her theatrical sensibilities. During his first act aria, Brignoli 'stood still in one spot and thrust first one arm out, and then the other, at right angles from his body, twenty-three consecutive times . . . "Heavens!" I said, "that's one thing not to do, anyway!"'[71] In contrast, the reviews of Pauline Viardot provide an example of the pictorial style at its most effective. The most acknowledged *attrice cantante* of her generation, Viardot provoked praise even from legitimate actors: Sarah Bernhardt cited her as 'the finest actress she had ever seen', and claimed that watching her perform had been 'her greatest experience as a spectator in the theatre'.[72] An account of her appearance in *Le Prophète* in 1854 by one theatre critic delineates perhaps the most pertinent features of her performance style:

> Daguerreotype Madame Viardot suddenly at any moment during her personation of Fidès, and though she be only passing at that moment from one gesture to another, you will fix upon the plate a picturesque and expressive figure, which is moreover a figure indicating in its face and in its attitude that precise feeling which belonged to the story at the moment chosen.[73]

The fluidity and multiplicity of Viardot's attitudes, the concentration that imbued her performance, the construction of the images she presented in terms of both their appropriateness to the dramatic action and their imaginative content all encapsulated the gestural style so favoured by the nineteenth-century stage (both legitimate and lyric) before the advent of naturalism.

That the era was already giving way to new approaches in dramatic performance, however, is borne out by an article by one F. Pelzet in the *Gazzetta musicale di Firenze* in 1853.[74] Almost certainly, the author was Ferdinando Pelzet (1791–1885), husband of the acclaimed actress Maddalena Pelzet (1801–54); of lesser talent himself, Pelzet turned to teaching and in 1850 published a work especially designed for the lyric stage, *Discorso sulla mimica applicata al canto*. His primary (and not altogether disinterested) concern was that singers were now being advised to abandon the taught principles of gesture in favour of their own 'instinct'; at a time when 'the dramatic concept is the essential part of operatic singing', he argued, how could one imagine that the study of carefully conceived and proven patterns of physical expression was 'no longer necessary' or that 'in matters of sentiment *it is enough to consult only nature*?' At risk of such a strategy was the very 'illusion' of opera itself: instead of 'the expressive, simple, easy, complete gesture made at the same time with truth and frugality, and accommodated to the needs of the music', there was now only a 'confusion of signs and sounds' imperilling the spectator's comprehension of 'the interest, the emotion, and the effect of the dramatic situation'.

Pelzet's comments were made in a marketplace that had begun to show marked signs of change. The earlier reliance on set gestures as a code depicting 'universal human properties' had become unstable;[75] despite the fixed templates in the manuals, the reception – in periodicals, journals, memoirs and letters – of operatic performance makes it plain that the most prized quality of dramatic expression from Pasta onwards was originality. By the middle of the century, increasing emphasis was given to the production of gestural signs more indicative of psychological and emotional specificity. A clutch of reviews of the Italian soprano Marietta Piccolomini as Violetta in New York in 1858 remark on this innovative aspect: 'Her entire performance is, in fact, a protest against conventionality', declared the *New York Times*; whilst *Dwight's Boston Journal* found that 'Every phrase of the *libretto* she utters is accompanied by some singularly appropriate gesture or motion, that seems so perfectly natural, you at once wonder no other representative of the part has ever made use of it.'[76] As cultural and scientific ideas about individuality impacted on theatrical display as the century progressed, such unconventionality in interpretation became a prerequisite for success. During Boito and Verdi's search for the perfect Desdemona for their forthcoming *Otello*, the librettist witnessed a performance by a young singer destined to become one of the most feted artists of the *verismo* school, Gemma Bellincioni. But she failed to make much impression upon Boito in 1886: 'I don't think she possesses true dramatic feeling, true spontaneity, or power of accentuation; her gestures have evidently been taught her by an acting coach . . . Everything she does on stage seems borrowed from someone else.'[77] Blind imitation of existing conventions was thus rarely regarded as sufficiently effective; it was necessary to make one's own stamp as an interpretative artist.

Another impetus for change during the middle period was the emergence of a new type of performer. Malibran, Viardot and Schröder-Devrient had all been born into the profession, like the majority of stage artists before them. But now, with the influx of entrants from outside the profession, dramatic skills had to be taught rather than simply imbued. In 1830, at the age of ten, Jenny Lind was fortunate in being awarded a place at the state-subsidised school of the Royal Theatre, Stockholm. There she served a kind of apprenticeship, receiving tuition in acting, dancing and singing as well as performing regularly in plays staged by the company. She was provided with an allowance, and in return was bound to the theatre for a period of ten years. By her late adolescence, she was an experienced stage artist.[78] But for many other singers – particularly those from middle- and upper-class families – the only route to acquiring histrionic skills was from private teachers.

PRIVATE TUITION

Few singers relate in detail their dramatic education. One exception is Lillie de Hegermann-Lindencrone, who in the 1860s took classes in Paris with François Delsarte (1811–71).[79] One of the most prominent teachers of gesture straddling the divide between the old ways and the new, Delsarte's influence was primarily within the operatic world, teaching Jenny Lind and Henrietta Sontag amongst others; his students also included famous actors such as Coquelin and Rachel. His ideas (transmitted through his 'disciples') later also had a noticeable impact on the classic French mime of Decroux and the development of American modern dance.[80] His methodology resulted from an attempt to construct a 'semiotics' (as so described by Moses True Brown in 1888) of performance: a code of physical signs that would express accurately the full range of human emotional experience.[81] Briefly, he saw the body as a map on which could be charted the separate regions of the triumvirate that ruled human action: the intellect (the Mind), the heart (the Soul) and the flesh (the Body). By analysing a particular state of being (such as 'exaltation') in the light of this triumvirate, Delsarte developed a parallel physical 'attitude' that was supposed to convey this state to the spectator. The system was immensely detailed, including facial expressions and individual poses for hands and feet, and its approach to the weight and rhythm of gesture prefigures that of Laban. Its advantage for singers was that it allowed them to *display* emotion without necessarily having simultaneously to *feel* emotion, thus protecting the vocal need for inner 'repose' and sustained, even breathing.[82] (One of Delsarte's later acolytes, Genevieve Stebbins, nevertheless declared that the playing of the gesture actually provokes the feeling inside the actor, a theory Michael Chekhov propounded in more detail in the twentieth century.[83])

De Hegermann-Lindencrone provides a rare description of a lesson with Delsarte. Although her first impression was that she was 'in the presence of a *concierge* in a second-class establishment' (owing to his well-worn slippers, dilapidated clothing, and the stench of bad tobacco), she soon came to see him as 'a great master':

> He is not a real singing teacher, for he does not think the voice worth speaking of; he has a theory that one can express more by the features and all the tricks he teaches, and especially by the manner of enunciation, than by the voice . . .
>
> On the walls were hung some awful diagrams to illustrate the master's method of teaching. These diagrams are crayon-drawings of life-sized faces depicting every emotion that the human face is capable of expressing, such as love, sorrow, murder, terror, joy, surprise, etc.
>
> It is Delsarte's way, when he wants you to express one of these emotions in your voice, to point with a soiled forefinger to the picture in question which he expects you to imitate. The result lends expression to your voice.[84]

As far as timbre was concerned, Delsarte was more interested in dramatic truth than conventional notions of beauty – a challenging and innovative idea in the operatic world, but one (as we have seen) that Verdi had already explored in *Macbeth*. Something of his approach is illustrated by de Hegermann-Lindencrone's account of her rendition of Gounod's 'Medjé':

When I came to 'Prends cette lame et plonges-la dans mon coeur', he stopped me short, and pointing to a horrible picture on the wall indicating bloody murder and terror (No. 6), he cried, 'Voilà l'expression qu'il faut avoir.' I sang the phrase over again, trying to imagine what Medjé's lover must have felt; but I could not satisfy Delsarte. He said my voice ought to tremble; and, in fact, I ought to sing false when I say, 'Ton image encore vivante dans mon coeur qui ne bat plus.' 'No one,' he said, 'in such a moment of emotion could keep on the right note.' I tried again, in vain! If I had had a dagger in my hand and a brigand before me, I might perhaps have been more successful. However, he let it pass; but to show that it could be done he sang it for me, and actually did sing it false. Curiously enough, it sounded quite right, tremolo and all. There can be no doubt that he is a *great artist*.[85]

De Hegermann-Lindencrone was convinced enough to implement Delsarte's ideas in performance, and claimed they noticeably improved her presentation of arias.[86] Other singers, especially as the new currency of naturalism grew stronger toward the end of the century, disagreed with his theories. Emily Soldene was one such sceptic, contrasting the 'natural and impressionist school' of acting with 'the Delsartian and wooden cult formed on the semaphore signal basis, and the presumed entire absence of impulse and emotion.'[87] Delsarte's ideas nevertheless continued to influence teaching in various conservatoires well into the late twentieth century.

PROFESSIONAL EDUCATION

Whatever lessons might be absorbed within the studio, it was on the stage that the real learning took place for many singers. If some developments in performance were led by theorists and teachers, others emerged more vitally from within the opera house itself. In 1842, Nicolò Cattaneo wrote an article for the *Gazzetta musicale di Milano* entitled 'Operatic Composers Should Be Actors', in which he criticised the state of acting on the operatic stage: 'in truth, one would have to lack good sense not to laugh at [the singers'] telegraphic gesturing, their movement and attitudes on the stage that have as much to do with the sense of the poetry and the dramatic situation as the swinging of a pendulum has with the rhythmic and graceful dancing of la Cerrito'. He argued that there were five reasons for this state of affairs: the singers' ignorance of dramatic art; an undeveloped concept of the singer as dramatic artist and too great an emphasis on singing; the difficulty of acting on the operatic stage; and the lack of informed spectators to encourage a different reception of operatic performance. The fifth and final reason, absorbing the greater part of his article, was the composers themselves, and their own lack of knowledge and understanding of dramatic art. Not only should they acquire through study the requisite skills to 'embellish, reinforce, unify' text with music, they should be themselves *attori* – 'or at least have the force of imagination necessary to know how to transport themselves into the clothes of those who must sing their operas; and to imagine the attitudes, the movements, the gestures, in short the mime with which the *attori cantanti* should perform the Opera'. And when those *veri artisti* amongst the singers found themselves faced with an unplayable piece, they should say to the composer: 'Do me the kindness of ascending on to the stage for a moment and teach me the *scena muta* I should do during this *passo*, this *ritornello*, so that the *dramatic action* does not come to a stop, does not interrupt itself, languish, and destroy the illusion.'[88]

In the following years, the two most prominent composers of the latter half of the century – Verdi and Wagner – did precisely this. Not only did they privilege dramatic concept within their music, they also both engaged actively in matters of staging. Their work arguably dominated ideas about dramatic presentation on the lyric stage – albeit in different ways – for much of the period. It marked an early example of the arrival of the director, and the passing of responsibility for the stage picture from the performer to a non-executant.

We have already seen that Verdi's *Macbeth* in 1847 represented a new development in terms of vocal performance; but it was equally important for dramatic representation in opera.[89] Marianna Barbieri-Nini, the first interpreter of Lady Macbeth, left a much-cited account of Verdi's rehearsals, including his thorough coaching of the sleep-walking scene: 'for three months, morning and evening, I tried to imitate those people who talk in their sleep, who utter words (as Verdi assured me) almost without moving their lips, and keeping other parts of their face, eyes included, motionless'.[90] This early attempt of Verdi's to seek a greater authenticity of gesture infused all his later productions. In the rehearsals for *Otello* in 1887, Ugo Pesci claimed that Verdi 'would insist upon the greatest degree of natural-ness, and with a keen eye he studied every movement, every gesture to discover what seemed to him most natural and true'.[91]

Wagner was similarly concerned with breaking with the stylised theatrical conventions of the past. He perceived bodily gesture as the means by which to deliver precisely 'that which speech was incompetent to express', and as a vital component in the communi-cation of feeling: 'eye and ear must mutually assure each other of a higher-pitched message, before they can transmit it convincingly to the feeling'.[92] His ideas of *Gesamtkunstwerk* led logically to a unified production concept;[93] and like Verdi, he was concerned with a greater authenticity of histrionic expression. Neither composer, how-ever, would have regarded his efforts at 'authenticity' within drama as consonant with 'realism'; both men sought to create convincing imaginary worlds, not actual reproductions of life. Their engage-ments with authenticity were thus rather a means of enhancing a notion of art imbued with the 'ideal'.

IDEALISM AND THE PERFORMING MODES OF FEMININITY

Throughout the late eighteenth and nineteenth centuries, idealism affected not only philosophical discourses on and means of theatrical representation but also performance methodologies. The latter was most evident in the *modèle idéal*: a concept of building a dramatic performance originally formulated by Diderot in his *Paradoxe sur le comédien* (1773). It required the actor to construct a detailed 'inner model' of the character, which was then reproduced exactly in performance. Its purpose was to achieve a controlled, considered, *repeatable* recitation, free from the vagaries of sudden impulse: in Joseph Roach's words, 'The creation of the inner model is an art; performing it is a métier.'[94] Diderot's work was published only in 1830, but there are signs of the influence of this idea – or something similar – throughout the period. According to Chorley, Pasta 'never changed her readings, her effects, her ornaments. What was to her true, when once arrived at, remained with her true for ever.' Such a technique might seem rigid to modern perceptions, but Chorley argued that 'the impression made on me was that of my being always subdued and surprised, for the first time. Though I knew what was coming – when the passion broke out, or when the phrase was sung, it seemed as if they were something new, electrical, immediate.'[95] Pasta clearly lost nothing of her capacity to amaze and delight her audience; the 'mechanical' aspect of thorough preparation was converted into inspiring energy during the actual performance.

Just as the control of impulse in the act of creation was regarded as laudable in the early period, so too was idealism considered superior to mere 'imitation' of nature. In 1838 the *Musical World* claimed that a realistic depiction of Amina in *La sonnambula*, 'singing as a rustic, with no more command of the science than a peasant could be supposed to possess' would have little effect: 'Our feelings must be excited by notions of ideal beauty.'[96] Almost forty years later, Verdi stated that realism was 'photography, not painting': 'To copy truth may be a good thing, but to *invent truth* is better, much better.'[97] Idealism thus shaped the *mise en scène* of many *attrici cantanti*, even well into the twentieth century – especially amongst rather old-fashioned singers.

Rather different approaches are visible between singers at opposite ends of the period towards such notions of the 'ideal': both in terms of performance techniques and also with regard to characterisation and interpretation. This is not to suggest that such differences were always marked and distinct. On the contrary, if Pasta's unchanging use of ornamentation and effect accorded with the concept of the *modèle idéal* in the 1820s and 1830s, so did that of Marie Gutheil-Schoder in the early 1900s; if Lind idealised her roles in the 1840s, so too did Emma Eames and Amelita Galli-Curci in the early twentieth century; if Malibran and Schröder-Devrient claimed their performances arose from an innate instinct for what was 'truthful' on the stage, so too did those notable singing actresses Calvé and Garden some sixty or more years later. Nonetheless, in broad terms there was a perceptible shifting from idealism's position as the agreed centre of operatic performativity at the beginning of the period towards a greater acceptance of realism at the end – not only with regard to gestural codes, but also with regard to the methodology of constructing a performance.

However, the debate between idealism and realism also had a particular effect on modes of female performance, in terms of both representation and reception. Even in the 1920s, Amelita Galli-Curci claimed that 'in fashioning my interpretations I never gave in to what one might call the naturalistic school of acting but always idealized wherever possible', in case the audience were distracted from the 'beauty of the voice' by 'ugly stage business'.[98] But Galli-Curci was perhaps not worried about realism detracting only from her voice. The singers were often acutely aware of the performative constraints of gender. At times, they deliberately enhanced the femininity of their roles: if the early prima donnas were criticised for being insufficiently genteel, those of the late 1830s and 1840s were sometimes reproved for being too ladylike and reluctant to engage with the drama;[99] or, like Erminia Frezzolini in a performance of *Lucrezia Borgia* in Italy in 1843, for failing to perform the more unpleasant parts of the role with sufficient strength and commitment.[100] And yet it is plain that in general a good review depended on the degree of 'womanliness' displayed by the prima donna. An overtly strong presentation in the role of the heroine was often derided – particularly if it conflicted with representations of the masculine. Berlioz complained that in a performance of *Les Huguenots* in Berlin in 1843, the 'exaggeration' of Schröder-Devrient's acting as Valentine undermined her supposed father (Saint-Bris) and husband (Nevers) in the conspiracy scene: 'instead of masking her agitation and remaining almost passive, like other sensible tragediennes in this scene, Madame Devrient approaches Nevers, forces him to follow her to the back of the stage, and there, striding along beside him, appears to dictate to him both his line of conduct and his reply to Saint-Bris'. The result, Berlioz argued, was that Nevers 'only looks like a submissive husband repeating the lesson his wife has taught him'.[101] Schröder-Devrient evidently had a rather different conception of Valentine than the 'timid woman' desired by Berlioz – or, indeed, by Meyerbeer. But even when the text might justify such action, it was wise to be cautious. The further a libretto strayed from conventional notions of womanhood, the more idealised the singer's performance needed to be. In a performance of *Fidelio* at Covent Garden in 1860, Rosa Czillag was praised by Henry Morley for her feminine interpretation of the 'heroic wife':

> She is true woman in every situation; most of all when clinging within her husband's arms she braves his assassin, and following him, pistol in hand, with excited firmness to the door, half swoons at the threshold, to be revived directly by her husband's voice and the new stir of a love suddenly released from its constraints.

This Leonore employed the stage business of femininity to its full – the sheltering in strong male arms, the physical collapse, the hint of hysteria – to alleviate any possible impropriety in the enactment of a breeches role. None of this is implied in the actual text; on the contrary, Leonore is admirably controlled and resourceful. Czillag also appears to have been especially successful in avoiding any lesbian connotations in the scene with Marzelline: 'Very refined is the delicacy with which Mlle. Czillag shadows the relation between herself, as a supposed boy, and the gaoler's daughter.'[102] We must assume that Czillag made little or no attempt to assume any male characteristics properly belonging to the role in this production at least.

An effective depiction of femininity depended primarily on a carefully cultivated quality of innocence – an innocence so complete that it was often allied to distraction or even stupefaction. Hermann Klein described Rosa Sucher's performance of Elsa in *Lohengrin* in 1882 as the 'ideal histrionic realization of Wagner's conception'. This Elsa was 'under a hypnotic spell', her beautiful 'expression of maiden-like innocence' enhancing the specator's pity at her anguished humiliation: when she entered the stage, 'advancing without perceptible bodily movement, she almost gave the impression of being a somnambulist in a dream'.[103] In texts where the heroine strayed from the path of righteousness, a dream-like performance was the surest method of softening undesirable elements in the plot. Singers used this device consciously, as Eames demonstrated in her interpretation of Marguerite in *Faust*: 'The story is a sordid one unless idealized, and I preferred to see Marguerite as chaste, truly innocent and therefore unsuspecting, and that is why I made her fearlessly and directly look at Faust when he accosted her, aware of no evil, but wrapped in poetic dreams.'[104] Christine Nilsson was similarly applauded as a 'dreamy, poetic' Marguerite.[105]

This mode of demonstrating femininity through distraction emphasised the vulnerability and indeed the irresponsibility of women as they were then perceived by the dominant society. Such qualities were written into the operas themselves, appearing at their most extreme in the composition of the *bel canto* mad scenes. The virginity of Amina in Bellini's *La sonnambula* is nowhere more clearly proved than when she appears in her somnabulistic trance before the whole community, indicating not only the practical explanation for her seeming infidelity but also her status as a true innocent, unconscious of the world and all its temptations; in Donizetti's *Lucia di Lammermoor*, the unwomanly effect of Lucia's murderous assault on her bridegroom is assuaged by the heroine's complete rejection of the knowledge of her deed, and the refuge she takes instead in her delirious imaginings of a union with her lover Edgardo. Simon Maguire writes that 'What lies at the heart of such scenes is not madness, but the conjuring up of an alternative reality, through the device of mental distraction.'[106] I would add that this 'alternative reality' essentially signifies a state of feminine innocence, a haven sought earnestly by these heroines whose femininity has been questioned in some way and who have a need to re-establish their claims to maidenly demeanour, which can only be attained through various forms of unconsciousness.

But aspects of 'unknowing' also figure in the singers' own descriptions of their performances. Sometimes this reads as little more than the customary language of the stage: for example, Kellogg studied Gilda in Verdi's *Rigoletto* for 'nine months', by which time she 'was so imbued with the part as to be thoroughly at ease. Present-day actors call this condition "getting inside the skin" of a *rôle*. I simply could not make a mistake, and could do everything connected with the characterisation with entire unconsciousness.'[107] But on other occasions, the business of 'unknowing' has different connotations. We have already seen that Malibran claimed her total immersion in her role led her beyond her conscious awareness to supposedly 'natural' rather than stylised stage actions. In contrast, Schröder-Devrient's crisis of 'unknowing' in her triumphant debut in *Fidelio* occurred usefully at the most unwomanly part of the plot; her fearful ignorance (either real or assumed) at this juncture earned her numerous plaudits as constituting a 'thorough womanly personation'.[108] (Malibran was often compared unfavourably with Schröder-Devrient in this role, partly because of her more aggressive enactment of the same scene: an experienced and able shot herself, Malibran purportedly flourished two pistols at Pizarro – not merely the one.[109])

This emphasis on the 'unconscious' of course reflects something of the era's debate on whether a performance should be governed by the free improvisatory quality of 'inspiration' or by the 'conscious imitation' of the *modèle idéal*.[110] Nevertheless, the search for 'unconsciousness' by women performers is perhaps disturbing in the context of male-written fiction which constructed the 'ideal' prima donna as a figure sublimely unaware: for example, Hoffmann's automated doll, Olympia; or Du Maurier's mesmerised Trilby; or Leroux's uneasily enchanted Christine Danae. Did some female performers feel more comfortable in presenting their work as the product of instinct rather than reason – thus avoiding accusations of 'unwomanly' intellectual endeavour? Or were they perhaps also more genuinely open to exploiting elements of their 'unconscious' on stage than their male colleagues?

Despite its restrictive aspects, idealism in operatic performance sometimes facilitated the emergence of operatic heroines who did not accord with strict notions of morality. I have explored elsewhere the arrival of La traviata (an opera feared for its potential to contaminate the female audience) in London in 1856, and how two Italian prima donnas – Marietta Piccolomini and Angiolina Bosio – offered contrasting interpretations of Violetta. Piccolomini, the first female aristocrat (daughter of a wealthy Italian family and niece of a cardinal) to enter the profession, was praised by one critic for having conquered the 'detestable' libretto: her interpretation provided a heroine 'far different' from that of Dumas' 'immoral drama', and 'engages all our sympathies'. But despite her evident popularity with the female audience, she was also criticised by some for the overt realism of her performance as a courtesan. Chorley (who similarly regarded Verdi's opera as 'distasteful and feeble')[111] compared her unfavourably with London's next Violetta, Angelina Bosio. A figlia dell'arte, she was once described by Chorley as 'the most lady-like person' he had ever seen on the operatic stage (with the exception of Henrietta Sontag).[112] And only Bosio, he wrote, played Violetta with 'that half-elegance, half-distraction of manner, which alone could make such a heroine supportable'; if Piccolomini was 'the willing grisette', Bosio was the 'woman whom bad chances had driven into fitful recklessness'.[113] Another reviewer in The Musical World, commenting on Bosio's performance in St Petersburg, thought likewise:

> A low-minded realist might object in Madame Bosio's performance of the part to her lady-like demeanour. She in fact looks like a young girl accidentally living in the region of the Dames [sic] aux Camélias, where she appears quite depaysée. But it seems to me that the Dame aux Camélias – on stage as in real life – is tolerable under no other circumstances, and that in order not to be offensive, it is necessary, in the first instance, that she should not look like what she is.[114]

Bosio, it seems, had rendered the 'prostitute' invisible: Violetta was no longer magdalen and madonna in equal measure, both pleasure-seeking and self-sacrificing, both liberated and domesticated – she had become 'unknowing', unconscious even to herself of her own desires and actions. But there were other dimensions to such portrayals. In presenting a Violetta onstage who (unlike the prostitutes ranging the streets around the Haymarket) was recognisable in gesture, mannerism and dress as belonging to the same class as the spectators, singers such as Bosio and Piccolomini created a subversive bond between the character and its female audience: Violetta's plight became one projected through the empathic imagination of the woman spectator, one which she could herself partake in and re-enact through her own private music-making.

We might note too that the contrasing approaches of Bosio and Piccolomini were influenced by factors beyond aesthetic taste. If Violetta's aim in the opera is partly to achieve acceptance by society, so too was the mid-nineteenth-century prima donna engaged on a similar quest. Bosio belonged to a generation of artists from professional or humble backgrounds whose need to conform rigorously to onstage codes of femininity was part of the rising gentrification of the stage artist. Piccolomini, however, as a forerunner of those upper- and middle-class women who increasingly sought a theatrical career, needed to establish not social but professional credentials: to demonstrate that the *dilettante* singer was as fearless and inventive an actress as any of her colleagues trained in stagecraft from their infancy. As the century progressed, other singers began to experiment with ever more risqué performances that contravened notions of the 'feminine ideal'.

THE ARRIVAL OF REALISM

If distracted innocence represented absolute femininity, 'knowingness' in female performance was regarded as unwomanly and an implicit sign of the whore. Pauline Lucca's interpretation of Marguerite in Gounod's *Faust* in London, 1864, was universally frowned upon as 'too coquettish': one critic commented that she was 'far too "knowing" to have captivated so refined and gentlemanly a Faust as Signor Mario'. To her credit, Lucca refused to alter her performance, 'declared that she knew a great deal more about the character of the German Gretchen than did either French artists or English critics', and promptly left town.[115] Even in Germany her interpretation of Marguerite was controversial; Lilli Lehmann recalls an incident in Berlin during the 1871–72 season where after a production of *Faust* Lucca was publicly denounced as 'a street-walker or some similar epithet' whilst leaving the theatre in her carriage.[116] But 'knowingness' was not always so easily determined; whilst Morley thought Piccolomini's Violetta demonstrated 'all that is noblest in woman', Chorley condemned her as betraying her aristocratic background:

> Never did any young lady, whose private claims to modest respect were so great as hers are known to be – with such self-denial, fling off their protection, in her resolution to lay hold of her public, at all risks. – Her performances at times approached offence against maidenly reticence and delicacy. – They were the *slang* of the musical theatre; – no other word will characterize them: – and *slang* has no place in opera, be it the broadest *opera buffa*. – When she played *Zerlina*, in 'Don Giovanni', such virtue as there was between the two seemed absolutely on the side of the libertine hero, – so much invitation was thrown into the peasant girl's rusticity.[117]

'Knowingness' in female performance thus signified not only the possession of sensual knowledge, but (in an obvious echo of the siren) the conscious use of such knowledge to seduce or entrap men. If mid-nineteenth-century roles such as Violetta or Marguerite allowed a certain room for manoeuvre in this area, characters emerging in the later period – Carmen, Dalila, Nedda, Manon, Thaïs, Louise, Zazà, Tosca, Salome, Lulu – did not. The first of these, Carmen, exerted a powerful influence on later performance modes. After the premiere in 1875, a French critic castigated Célestine Galli-Marié for not doing more to alleviate the impact of this new imprint of female 'licentiousness':

This distinguished artist could have corrected what was shocking and antipathetic in the character of this heartless, faithless, lawless gypsy. She has, on the contrary, exaggerated Carmen's vices by a realism that would at best be bearable in an operetta in a small theatre. At the Opéra-Comique, a subsidized theatre, a decent theatre if ever there was one, Mlle Carmen should temper her passions.[118]

It is plain that realism was associated with rebellion. Galli-Marié's efforts in this direction were probably fairly mild; but a later pairing of Carmen and Emma Calvé (1858–1942) created even more controversy.

Calvé made her debut in 1882, and for a while had an unremarkable career. But she then radically changed her performance style, inspired, she wrote, by the work of the doyenne of naturalistic acting, Eleonora Duse: 'Her art, simple, human, passionately sincere, was a revelation to me. It broke down the false and conventional standards of lyric expression [sic] to which I had become accustomed.'[119] Calvé too began to subsume something of this approach in her own acting. Her first real success occurred in *Cavalleria rusticana* at the Opéra-Comique in Paris, where although her 'spontaneous and apparently unstudied gestures' alarmed her colleagues at rehearsals, and her costume (that of a 'real peasant woman') was 'considered eccentric and ugly', the actual performance was a 'triumph'. She was regarded as even more effective in her next role, Carmen, claiming she used 'the same sincerity, the same courage and disregard for tradition' with which she had approached Santuzza. She refused to wear the conventional bolero and short skirt, and instead adopted authentic Spanish garb. Having spent part of her childhood in Spain, she also elected to dance the 'true dance of the *gitanas*, with its special use of arms and hands' rather than the dainty steps performed by Galli-Marié. But Calvé's emphasis on realism extended beyond these attempts at authenticity into the heart of her performance. A review by Shaw in 1894 illustrates the impact of her new style of acting on an unsuspecting audience. Declaring that the success of Bizet's opera relied on the attraction 'of seeing a pretty and respectable middle-class young lady, expensively dressed, harmlessly pretending to be a wicked person', Shaw proclaimed himself to be 'shocked beyond measure' by Calvé's interpretation:

> Her Carmen is a superstitious, pleasure-loving good-for-nothing, caught by the outside of anything glittering, with no power but the power of seduction, which she exercises without sense or decency. There is no suggestion of any fine quality about her, not a spark of honesty, courage, or even of the sort of honor supposed to prevail among thieves.

That Calvé achieved this by dispensing with all notions of idealism is apparent from Shaw's comment that she has divested 'her beauty and grace of the nobility . . . which seems inseparable from them in other parts'. Her stage business was frank and explicit, full of 'indescribable allurements'. But it was in the opera's final moments that Calvé most startled Shaw:

> Her death scene, too, is horribly real. The young lady Carmen is never so effectively alive as when she falls, stage dead, beneath José's cruel knife. But to see Calvé's Carmen changing from a live creature, with properly coordinated movements, into a reeling, staggering, flopping, disorganized thing, and finally tumble down a mere heap of carrion, is to get much the same sensation as might be given by the reality of a brutal murder. It is perhaps just as well that a great artist should, once in a way, give our opera-goers a glimpse of the truth about the things they play with so light-heartedly.[120]

There could be no clearer rebuttal of Engel's strictures about giving the audience an image of the kind of death they might wish for, than this 'reeling, staggering, flopping, disorganized thing'. Importantly, too, Shaw makes particular note that Calvé (as Malibran had done sixty years previously) acted 'out of time': that her gestures were no longer tied to the music, but followed their own rhythmic logic according to the drama. The previous unifying of the musical sphere with dramatic action through the medium of a 'musicalised' gestural language was split; now, increasingly, the search for a 'realistic' *mise en scène* would be pursued as a visual counterpoint to the music, in a foreshadowing of the kind of relationship common today between film music and cinematic image.

Calvé's representation of Carmen constituted a criticism of the role, for it was developed from her own sense of dislike for Bizet's incarnation. Finding little to admire about the character, she acted what she saw.[121] Later she claimed that her enthusiasm for realism had led her to extremes, and that she subsequently toned down her interpretations.[122] But other singers seized on the possibilities of some roles to challenge perceived and outmoded thinking. In 1899 at the Teatro Costanzi in Rome, the soprano Emma Carelli sang Margherita in *Mefistofele*, in a striking and controversial interpretation. The baritone Delfino Menotti criticised her 'repugnant poses' in the mad-scene, arguing that such a performance might be 'true' but it was 'inartistic, because art is only the representation of the beautiful'. Carelli responded that such criticisms were her greatest triumph: Menotti's incomprehension was merely the 'protesting cry of a form of art that is dying: Conventionalism. For you, to act means to dress well, it means to be beautiful, serene – not to feel agitated, tormented, desperate. For you there are no cripples, nor do the blind and the malnourished exist: all must be idealised. Instead, I wanted Margherita to experience her life of damned madness, and I made her a wretched creature, as the beautiful Margherita of "Martha's garden" must be after having poisoned her mother with narcotics, killed the fruit of her guilt and been thrown onto the litter of a foul prison.'[123] An equally questioning approach was brought to Carelli's other roles: her performance of Desdemona at La Scala in 1899 was praised in the *Perseveranza* for its spirit of rebellion, in contrast to the 'passivity to which the tragedy consigns [the role]'.[124]

One of the most influential of the young, modern singers was Mary Garden, who developed her own highly distinctive style. Reportedly influenced by her study of the *café-concert* singer Yvette Guilbert, Bernhardt and Duse,[125] Garden's effects were novel and memorable. Kathleen Howard contrasted the stuffy, old-fashioned modes of operatic acting promulgated by the French studios with the 'inspiration' of Garden's 'new order of sung performance': 'Her power of suggestion in those days was capable of conveying any shade of thought or delicate mood to the spectator.'[126]

What differentiated this 'new order' from the old traditions? It was, perhaps, Garden's particular combination of aspects both of naturalism and symbolism that perfectly suited the 'New Opera' of the *fin-de-siècle*. First, there was her ability to colour her voice imaginatively according to the needs of each individual role: Huneker wrote that she 'paints with her voice' using a palette of the 'entire gamut of tones, from passionate purple to the iridescent delicacies of iris-grey'.[127] This prioritising of the voice of the character above that of the singer was an innovative departure. Secondly, Garden declared that 'improvisation' was the most appropriate word to apply to her performances, because each rendition varied according to how she 'caught the moods' of the characters: one night, she might play Thaïs in 'a very suave mood. Then the next time I'd make her very arrogant, very Thaïs, very powerful. And the time after that she might be very *amoureuse* and *câline*.'[128] Garden attributed this flexibility to the fact that she 'lived' her roles onstage, utterly submerging herself in the characters, in contrast to those singers who 'never lost their identities': 'I was never myself on the stage. I was always the woman I was singing.'[129] Her subjectivity is apparent in the way she talks about her roles in the first person: for example, 'I, Thaïs, was tired of life. All my lovers had ceased to interest me'; or as Salome: 'I was just a child of fifteen, born in vice, and I saw Jokanaan and I said to myself, "I want that man!"'[130] This use of 'I' rather than 'she' when speaking of a character is a fundamental element in Stanislavskian technique. She disclaimed any conscious responsibility for the development of her characters, declaring that she never 'studied' her roles in the conventional sense: 'I didn't go to books and I didn't go to museums, as many people say they do, and I didn't go to see what death was like.' Instead, Garden claimed the characters were simply 'inside' her: 'I just *knew* them . . . I just had it *in* me, all of it. I *was* Thaïs, I *was* Mélisande, I *was* Salome. That was all there was to it. I put on the clothes and the wigs and I became Salome.'[131] Should we believe her? Did she truly experience a kind of mystical union with her roles (so intense on occasion that she said she '*really died*' as Mélisande)? Or was her ability to assume different roles presented as akin to reincarnation in order to promote the mystique of the artist herself? Or was she simply incapable of articulating her histrionic skills in any other terms?

Certainly, Garden's trance-like immersion in the roles again raises the matter of 'unknowingness' in female performance; yet in other matters she seems to have been perfectly aware. Her body, for example, was an important tool in her performances. Instead of perceiving a performance in the old manner of a continually changing series of gestures, Garden chose absolute stillness coupled with occasional telling movements – hints of a Wagnerian approach, perhaps? She also freely employed elements of physical eroticism. In at least three of her roles (Salome, Thaïs and Chrysis) she willingly colluded in creating the illusion of nudity, dressing in flimsy material that clung to her body leaving her arms and shoulders bare. Her aim was a kind of classical beauty rather than the 'coarseness' she supposedly despised. One photograph in her autobiography, however, belies this. As Salome, she sometimes wore a costume that gave the impression that one breast was left unclothed – a standard image of many theatrical drawings and posters dating from Restoration times, but one that presumably found no actual reflection on the legitimate stage itself – and she adopts a pose more commonly found in Victorian erotica: one hand clutches at the exposed breast, whilst the other arm is thrown above her head in apparent sexual abandonment. We do not know whether such a pose was staged by the photographer or suggested by Garden herself; nor is it clear that this pose was used by Garden at the moment of Salome's *jouissance* in actual productions of the opera.

The successes of prima donnas such as Calvé, Bellincioni and Garden meant that a whole generation of young singers strived to become 'singing actresses' in their wake. Geraldine Farrar handed out advice to the novice: 'You must sing, not from the outside, in; but from the inside, out';[132] Rosa Ponselle advocated that if the singer 'thoroughly identifies herself with the role', then 'spontaneous interpretation' produced far more natural effects than 'the most painstaking study'.[133] Such theories brought new difficulties. The critics, complained Garden and Farrar, were too unsophisticated to recognise that certain vocal qualities displayed in performance were purely a result of 'colorization' and not (as was frequently implied) due to any failings of technique. (It wasn't only the critics who were unimpressed by such arguments. The formidably talented soprano Zinka Milanov declared: 'Acting is all very well, but it does not take the place of the voice. When they say "a great actress", beware. It usually means that there is not much voice.'[134]) Another consequence was a heightened emphasis on physical image, which took on a new urgency at the *fin-de-siècle*. Farrar urged young singers to remember that the 'world of opera is one of illusion': 'it is hard to nurse poetic and fantastic illusions, no matter how fine a voice is trying to convey them, when the eye is oppressed by the sight of some three hundred pounds of human avoirdupois, ill-fitting costumes, wigs, awkward stage deportment or ill-timed mannerisms'.[135] Such remarks make it apparent that idealism had not been banished from the twentieth-century operatic stage – rather, it had merely been moulded to suit the requirements of a different era.

In 1920, Huneker could confidently claim that 'every year the space that separates the lyric from the dramatic stage is shrinking'.[136] Stanislavski's introduction of an Opera Studio in Moscow in 1918 provided for novice singers a full training in his techniques of psychological realism – a perhaps unsurprising move, given that an opera-singer had been one of the most influential figures in the development of his theories of performance ('I have copied my system from Shalyapin . . . When I told him my views on the art of acting, Shalyapin yelled, "Help! I've been robbed!"').[137] The reputation of the singing actresses as histrionic artists of stature (and their commercial viability at the box office) was also underlined by the appearance of many singers in silent films in North America and Europe: Cavalieri, Farrar, Garden, Stagno-Bellincioni and Novotna all participated in such projects. But with the introduction of talking films in 1927, ideas about acting were set to change radically. From then on, the singers were less likely to be regarded as equals to the new generation of 'naturalistic' actors.

But if the drive for onstage coherence had created new divas, there was too the sense that something had been lost. The arrival of the stage director and the conductor undoubtedly disrupted the prima donna's former autonomy over her performances; the economic ties between composer and publisher bound ever tighter. No longer, Tito Ricordi proclaimed, was opera dependent on 'the virtuosity of the throat' and the star performer; now a 'homogeneous ensemble' was required, because it was 'not the artist that makes the opera please, but the opera itself!'[138] Bellincioni complained of how this new autocracy within the opera house hampered young artists 'by suffocating every germ of creativity and expressive strength' in them, and stifling every artistic individuality.[139] At the beginning of the period, Pasta had impressed by her stamp on a role, by adapting each part to her own artistic supremacy and authority; now, at the end, Garden sought to submerge her identity completely within the fictional casing. Another era had ended.

Postscript

I wrote part of this book in a hotel in northern Italy, sometimes accompanied by the desultory voices of fellow guests – singers appearing at the local opera house. Even as I write now, a soprano is teasing out the upper notes of her register: slow, delicate flexings, like a cat stretching its paws, tenderly done. Such sounds are a fitting reminder of the long tradition of artistry that marks the lives recorded in these pages – and of the realities that shaped their experiences. Outside it is foggy and growing dark, and the singer worries away at her voice, mindful, perhaps, of the performance in three days' time. Am I listening to a siren? a songbird? a superwoman? Rather, I think, I am listening to Giuditta Pasta writing to her mother in a dressing-room before a performance she was dreading; Kathleen Howard on a train journey to Glasgow from Germany; Virginia Boccabadati, alone and anxious. I am listening to the sounds that ordinary women with an extraordinary gift can make.

I began this book with the words of one singer; it should end with those of another. Almost a hundred years after Giorgi Righetti set pen to paper, Emma Calvé attempted to define the singer's primary aim:

> Finally, there is one thing every student should remember, whether her objective be the opera or the concert stage – she must remember to be herself . . . But to be yourself in your art is sometimes very difficult. It is hard to know where to draw the line between tradition and precept and your own artistic instinct. In such a case, when you are driven to choose, rely upon yourself. For only the artist who radiates a personality of her own, who expresses her own self, her own mind, her own soul, instead of the traditions of others, wins greater achievement and success.[1]

Perhaps it is here, in the notion of originality and self-determination, of learning to think for oneself, of the importance of challenging tradition, that the singers' true legacy to their era – and our own – lies. The prima donna's 'voice of freedom' liberated only a few exceptionally gifted and dedicated women. But it signalled to many others the possibilities of 'voice' in every sense.

NOTES

INTRODUCTION

1 Geltrude Maria Giorgi Righetti, *Cenni di una donna già cantante sopra di maestro Rossini* (Bologna: Sassi, 1823), pp. 3–4.

2 Attilio Favorini, quoted in Bruce A. McConachie, 'Towards a Postpositivist Theatre History', *Theatre Journal*, 37/4 (December 1985), 465.

3 Ellen Rosand addresses the need to employ 'a flexible and varied arsenal of hermeneutical/interpretive instruments' in the investigation of opera. 'Criticism and the Undoing of Opera', *19th-century Music*, 14 (1990), 77.

4 See Carlotta Sorba, *Teatri: l'Italia del melodramma nell'età del Risorgimento* (Bologna: Il Mulino, 2001), pp. 227–58. On the closure of La Scala, see Giuseppe Barigazzi, *La Scala racconta* (Milan: Biblioteca Universale Rizzoli, 1998), pp. 412–21.

5 See John Rosselli, *Singers of Italian Opera: The History of a Profession* (Cambridge: Cambridge University Press, 1992), p. 117.

6 Gilbert-Louis Duprez, *Souvenirs d'un chanteur* (1880), in Thierry de la Croix (ed.), *Voix d'opéra: écrits de chanteurs du XIXe siècle* (Paris: Michel de Maule, 1988), pp. 78–9. Sergio Durante places Duprez's use of this effect in a wider context of contemporaneous developments in the tenor voice. 'The Opera Singer', in Lorenzo Bianconi and Giorgio Pestelli (eds.), *Opera Production and Its Resources*, trans. L. G. Cochrane (Chicago: University of Chicago Press, 1998), pp. 400–1.

7 Foreword to Hermann Klein's *Great Women Singers of My Time* (London: Routledge & Sons, Ltd, 1931), pp. 2–3.

8 On the change from 'star' to 'musician' from 1920 onwards, see John Barry Steane, *The Grand Tradition: Seventy Years of Singing On Record* (London: Duckworth, 1974), p. 6.

9 Elizabeth K. Helsinger, Robin Lauterbach Sheets, and William Veeder (eds.), *The Woman Question: Society and Literature in Britain and America,*

1837–1883, 3 vols. (Manchester: Manchester University Press, 1983). Simone de Beauvoir, *The Second Sex* (1949), trans. H. M. Parshley (London: Jonathan Cape, 1953).

10 Jean-Jacques Rousseau, *Emile, ou de l'éducation*, Book V (1762), in *Œuvres complètes de Jean-Jacques Rousseau*, vol. IV (Paris: Gallimard, 1969).

11 George Eliot noted this on her visit to the opera house in Weimar in 1855: 'The ladies come alone, and slip quietly into their places without need of "protection" – a proof of civilisation perhaps more than equivalent to our pre-eminence in patent locks and carriage springs'. Thomas Pinney (ed.), *Essays of George Eliot* (London: Routledge & Kegan Paul, 1963), p. 117.

12 Peter Gay, *The Bourgeois Experience from Victoria to Freud*, 2 vols. (Oxford: Oxford University Press, 1984), vol. I, p. 430.

13 Coventry Patmore, *The Angel in the House* (1854; 4th edn, London: Macmillan, 1866).

14 For a discussion of all these images, see Helsinger, Sheets, and Veeder (eds.), *The Woman Question*.

15 Richard Evans, *The Feminists: Women's Emancipation Movements in Europe, America and Australasia 1840–1920* (London: Croom Helm, 1977), p. 239. On Italy, see also Camilla Ravera, *Breve storia del movimento femminile in Italia* (Rome: Riuniti, 1978), p. 72. Similar concerns about women's conservatism were also expressed in Britain.

16 Evans, *The Feminists*, p. 199.

17 *Ibid.*, p. 212.

18 *Ibid.*, p. 232.

19 Rosselli, *Singers of Italian Opera*, p. 259.

20 Bonnie S. Anderson and Judith P. Zinsser, *A History of their Own: Women in Europe from Prehistory to the Present*, 2 vols. (London: Penguin Books, 1990), vol. I, p. xv.

21 See Ellen Rosand, 'Criticism and the Undoing of Opera', 78–81; Katherine Bergeron, 'Clément's Opera, or One Woman's Undoing', *Cambridge Opera Journal*, 2/1 (March 1990), 93–8; Anthony Arblaster, *Viva la Libertà! Politics in Opera* (London and New York: Verso, 1992), pp. 227–9; Ralph P. Locke, 'What Are These Women Doing in Opera?', and Mary Ann Smart, 'The Lost Voice of Rosine Stoltz', in Corinne E. Blackmer and Patricia Juliana Smith (eds.), *En Travesti: Women, Gender Subversion, Opera* (New York: Columbia University Press, 1995), pp. 59–98

and 169–89; Carolyn Abbate, 'Opera; or, the Envoicing of Women', in Ruth Solie (ed.), *Musicology and Difference: Gender and Sexuality in Music Scholarship* (Berkeley: University of California Press, 1993), pp. 253–5.

22 Catherine Clément, *Opera, or the Undoing of Women*, trans. Betsy Wing (London: Virago Press, 1989), p. 6.

23 On Louise Bertin, see Anselm Gerhard, *The Urbanization of Opera: Music Theater in Paris in the Nineteenth Century*, trans. Mary Whittall (Chicago and London: University of Chicago Press, 1998), pp. 215–46; on Augusta Holmès, see Karen Henson, 'In the House of Disillusion: Augusta Holmès and *La Montagne noire*', *Cambridge Opera Journal*, 9/3 (November 1997), 233–62; on Ethel Smyth, see Elizabeth Wood, 'Performing Rights: A Sonography of Women's Suffrage', *The Musical Quarterly*, 79/4 (Winter 1995), 606–43. Contextualisation on the difficulties faced by female composers is provided by (amongst others) Marcia Citron, *Gender and the Musical Canon* (Cambridge: Cambridge University Press, 1993); Roswitha Sperber (ed.), *Women Composers in Germany* (Bonn: Inter Nationes, 1996); Jill Halstead, *The Woman Composer: Creativity and the Gendered Politics of Musical Composition* (Aldershot: Ashgate, 1997); Jacqueline Letzer and Robert Adelson, *Women Writing Opera: Creativity and Controversy in the Age of the French Revolution* (London and Berkeley: University of California Press, 2001).

24 See Jürgen Kühnel, 'The Prose Writings', in Ulrich Müller and Peter Wapnewski (eds.), *The Wagner Handbook*, trans. John Deathridge (London and Cambridge, Mass.: Harvard University Press, 1992), p. 618.

25 Rimsky-Korsakov claims that Borodin was prominent in the 1870s in the Russian movement to enable women to enter the medical profession, and participated in 'various societies for the aid and support' of women. *My Musical Life* (London: Faber and Faber, 1989), pp. 194–5.

26 Letter to Michele Accursi, Paris, late January 1842, *Studi donizettiani*, 1/1 (1962), 79–80.

27 Willliam Ashbrook, *Donizetti and His Operas* (Cambridge: Cambridge University Press, 1982), p. 153.

28 Scribe's libretto had been written for Halévy in 1838, but the composer withdrew. Only then was it offered to Donizetti. His version was completed by Matteo Salvi, and was staged in 1882 in Rome.

29 Rebecca Meitlis, 'The Adjusted Woman', in Nicholas John (ed.), *Violetta and Her Sisters* (London: Faber and Faber, 1994), p. 288.

30 Peter le Huray and James Day, *Music and Aesthetics in the Eighteenth and Early Nineteenth Centuries* (Cambridge: Cambridge University Press, 1988), p. 288.

31 Richard Wagner, *My Life*, trans. Andrew Gray (Cambridge: Cambridge University Press, 1983), p. 337.

32 Ashbrook comments on Moriani's performance: 'In the tomb scene from *Lucia* his "sighs, laments, contortions, grasping his throat, falling and re-falling, his convulsive and labored effort to get up again" moved Roman audiences to delirium in 1838.' *Donizetti and His Operas*, p. 642. Averil Mackenzie-Grieve, *Clara Novello 1818–1908* (London: Geoffrey Bles, 1955), p. 114.

33 Philippe Ariès, 'The Reversal of Death: Changes in Attitudes Toward Death in Western Societies', *American Quarterly*, 26/5, Special Issue (December 1974), 536–60; p. 560.

34 Marie Bashkirtseff, *The Journal of Marie Bashkirtseff*, trans. Mathilde Blind (1891; repr. London: Virago, 1985), p. 303.

35 Ralph Locke remarks on Clément's neglect of comic opera in 'What Are These Women Doing in Opera?', in Blackmer and Smith (eds.), *En Travesti: Women, Gender, Subversion, Opera*, pp. 62–3.

36 Rupert Christiansen, *Prima Donna: A History* (London: Penguin Books, 1986), p. 53.

37 Gerhard describes the 'submissive' women in Meyerbeer's operas in *The Urbanization of Opera*, pp. 177–81.

38 *The Musical World*, 6/62, 28 July 1837, p. 110.

39 Sue Rickard, 'Movies in Disguise: Negotiating Censorship and Patriarchy Through the Dances of Fred Astaire and Ginger Rogers', in Robert Lawson-Peebles (ed.), *Approaches to the American Musical* (Exeter: University of Exeter Press, 1996), pp. 81–8. See also Susan Rutherford, 'La traviata, or the "Willing Grisette": Male Critics and Female Performance in the 1850s', in Fabrizio Della Seta, Roberta Montemorra Marvin and Marco Marica (eds.), *Verdi 2001. Atti del convegno internazionale di studi, Parma, New York, New Haven 24 gennaio–1° febbraio 2001*, 2 vols. (Florence: Olschki, 2003), vol. II, pp. 597–8.

40 Brigid Brophy, *Mozart the Dramatist* (London: Faber and Faber, 1964), p. 58.

41 Tom Sutcliffe, *Believing in Opera* (London: Faber and Faber, 1996), pp. 134–5.

42 Hélène Cixous and Catherine Clément, *The Newly Born Woman*, trans. Betsy Wing (Manchester: Manchester University Press, 1986), p. 92.

43 *Ibid.*, p. 107.

44 Abbate, 'Opera; or, the Envoicing of Women', p. 258.

45 *Ibid.*, pp. 253–4; see also Abbate's *Unsung Voices: Opera and Musical Narrative in the Nineteenth Century* (Princeton: Princeton University Press, 1991), p. ix.

46 Lynda Nead, 'Traviata-ism and the Great Social Evil', in John (ed.), *Violetta and Her Sisters*, p. 250.

47 Jane Fulcher, *The Nation's Image: French Grand Opera as Politics and Politicized Art* (Cambridge: Cambridge University Press, 1987), pp. 201–3. Gerhard, however, urges caution in attributing the Belgian rebellion to a wholly spontaneous reaction to the opera, and stresses that the uprising was actually planned to coincide with the opera's premiere. *The Urbanization of Opera*, pp. 127–8.

48 Roger Parker, *Leonora's Last Act: Essays in Verdian Discourse* (Princeton: Princeton University Press, 1997), p. 37.

49 John Rosselli, *The Opera Industry in Italy from Cimarosa to Verdi* (Cambridge: Cambridge University Press, 1984), p. 82.

50 On Mayr, see the review of the *Gazzetta di Genova*, 22 June 1814 in Emilia Branca, *Felice Romani* (Turin, Florence and Rome, 1882), pp. 120–1; Branca also relates the furore created by a performance of *Norma* in Milan during the late 1840s (pp. 172–5). In 1859 at the Teatro Regio in Parma, the baritone's rendition of 'Viva Italia' provoked a political demonstration in the audience – see Marco Capra, 'Il secondo Ottocento', in Claudio Del Monte and Vincenzo Raffaele Segreto (eds.), *La civiltà musicale di Parma* (Parma: Grafiche STEP, 1989), p. 104. Roger Parker has discussed at length the exaggeration of the links between Verdi's operas and the *risorgimento* movement in *Leonora's Last Act*, pp. 20–41.

51 Wagner, *My Life*, p. 369. First performed at the Deutsches Theater in Prague, 19 February 1848.

52 Herbert Lindenberger, *Opera: The Extravagant Art* (Ithaca and London: Cornell University Press, 1984), p. 274.

53 Lesley Blanch (ed.), *Harriette Wilson's Memoirs* (1825; repr. London: Century, 1985), pp. 40–1; see also pp. 66, 264–70 and 303.

54 Henry Fothergill Chorley, *Thirty Years Musical Recollections*, 2 vols. (London: Hurst & Blackett, 1862), vol. I, pp. 80–1.

55 Emma Eames, *Some Memories and Reflections* (1927; repr. New York: Arno Press, 1977).

56 'In a word, the Opera is to a certain and dubious extent fashionable – but it has long ceased to be exclusive.' *The Musical World*, 13/177, n.s. 5/84, 8 August 1839, p. 228.

57 Fulcher, *The Nation's Image*, pp. 113–21.

58 Gerhard, *The Urbanization of Opera*, p. 30. See also Steven Huebner, 'Opera Audiences in Paris 1830–1870', *Music and Letters*, 70/2 (May 1989), 206–25; pp. 223–4.

59 Parker, *Leonora's Last Act*, p. 37; Rosselli, *The Opera Industry*, p. 45; Sorba offers an extended discussion of the Italian audience in *Teatri*, pp. 93–153.

60 Fabio Mariano (ed.), *Il teatro nelle Marche* (Fiesole: Nardini, 1997), p. 48.

61 Arthur Symons, 'The Ideas of Richard Wagner', in Eric Bentley (ed.), *Theories of the Modern Stage* (London: Penguin, 1976), pp. 306–7.

62 Frederic Spotts, *Bayreuth: A History of the Wagner Festival* (New Haven and London: Yale University Press, 1994), p. 25.

63 Sergei Levik, *The Levik Memoirs: An Opera Singer's Notes*, trans. Edward Morgan (London: Symposium Records, 1995), p. 135.

64 Katherine K. Preston, *Opera on the Road: Traveling Opera Troupes in the United States, 1825–60* (Urbana and Chicago: University of Illinois Press, 1993), pp. 116–28.

65 Emily Soldene, *My Theatrical and Musical Recollections* (London: Downey & Co. Ltd., 1897), p. 304.

66 Max Maretzek, *Revelations of an Opera Manager in 19th Century America* (1855 and 1890; repr. New York: Dover Publications Inc., 1968), vol. I, pp. 219–301; vol. II, pp. 26–36.

67 Col. J. H. Mapleson, *The Mapleson Memoirs: The Career of an Operatic Impresario 1858–1888*, ed. Harold Rosenthal (London: Putnam, 1966).

68 Soldene, *My Theatrical and Musical Recollections*, pp. 236–8. Derek Hyde, *New Found Voices: Women in Nineteenth-century Music* (Kent: Tritone Music Publications, 1991), p. 23.

69 Lanfranco Rasponi, *The Last Prima Donnas* (New York: Limelight Editions, 1990), p. 531.

70 Frances Alda, *Men, Women and Tenors* (Boston: Houghton Mifflin, 1937), p. 35.

71 David Kimbell, *Verdi in the Age of Italian Romanticism* (Cambridge: Cambridge University Press, 1981), p. 22.

72 'Throwing light on the "Ring"', *The Observer*, 17 April 1994, p. 14.

73 Wilfrid Mellers, *The Masks of Orpheus: Seven Stages in the Story of European Music* (Manchester: Manchester University Press, 1987), p. 128.

74 See Soldene's account of her early years in music-hall in *My Theatrical and Musical Recollections*.

75 *The Musical World*, 13/178, n.s. 5/85, 15 August 1839, p. 237.

76 Letter to Princess Frederick William, 20 April 1859, in Christopher Hibbert, *Queen Victoria in her Letters and Journals* (London: John Murray, 1984), p. 111.

77 See my essay, 'The Voice of Freedom: the Image of the Prima Donna', in Viv Gardner and Susan Rutherford (eds.), *The New Woman and Her Sisters: Feminism and Theatre 1850–1914* (London: Harvester Wheatsheaf, 1992). Various other studies on this theme by a number of scholars are cited in the notes to Chapter 2.

78 For Italy, see Durante, 'The Opera Singer', in Bianconi and Pestelli (eds.), *Opera Production and Its Resources*, pp. 396–7; also Rosselli, *The Opera Industry in Italy*, pp. 145–6. For France, see Maurice Descotes, *Histoire de la critique dramatique en France* (Tübingen: Gunter Narr Verlag, 1980), pp. 213–15. For the USA and Britain, see, for example, the accounts in the *Musical World* of a row between Henrietta Sontag and the press concerning accusations of bribery in 1853: 31/41, 8 October 1853, pp. 640–2, and 31/42, 15 October 1853, pp. 653–4.

79 As Jeffrey Weeks states, 'the relationship between symbol and symbolised is not only referential, does not simply describe, but is productive, that is it creates'. *Sex, Politics and Society: The Regulation of Sexuality Since 1800* (London: Longman, 1981), p. 7.

80 Tracy C. Davis, 'Questions for a Feminist Methodology in Theatre History', in Thomas Postlewait and Bruce McConachie (eds.), *Interpreting the Theatrical Past: Essays in the Historiography of Performance* (Iowa City: Iowa University Press, 1989), pp. 59–77.

81 Jackie Stacey, *Star Gazing: Hollywood Cinema and Female Spectatorship* (London and New York: Routledge, 1994), pp. 19–24; Rickard, 'Movies in Disguise', pp. 81–3; Sally Banes, *Dancing Women: Female Bodies on Stage* (London and New York: Routledge, 1998), pp. 2–5; Abbate, 'Opera; or the Envoicing of Women', p. 253.

82 Jacques Le Goff, *History and Memory*, trans. Steven Rendall and Elizabeth Claman (New York: Columbia University Press, 1992), p. 211.

83 Giorgi Righetti, *Cenni di una donna*, pp. 3–4.

I   SIRENS AND SONGBIRDS

1 Christiansen, *Prima Donna*, pp. 9–10.

2 *Strenna teatrale europea*, 7 (1844), pp. 5–6.

3 *Ibid.*, p. 7.

4 *Ibid.*, pp. 7–11.

5 *Ibid.*, pp. 105–8. The author was Ferdinando Pellegrini.

6 *Ibid.*, pp. 87–93.

7 Christiansen, *Prima Donna*, p. 46.

8 Quoted in Elizabeth Forbes, *Mario and Grisi: A Biography* (London: Victor Gollancz, 1985), p. 39.

9 *Ibid.*, p. 29.

10 April Fitzlyon, *Maria Malibran: Diva of the Romantic Age* (London: Souvenir Press, 1987), pp. 130–2 and 152–5.

11 'Madame De Beriot', *The Musical World*, 3/30, 7 October 1836, p. 49.

12 Jacques Offenbach, *Les Contes d'Hoffmann* (1881), libretto by Jules Barbier based on his own and Michel Carré's play, *Les Contes fantastiques d'Hoffmann* (1851). Incomplete at Offenbach's death, the opera has undergone numerous revisions since its first performance in 1881; the version used here is from the 1989 Deutsche Grammophon recording, which combines elements of both the traditional version performed since 1905 and Fritz Oeser's scholarly reconstruction of 1977.

13 Maretzek, *Revelations of an Opera Manager*, vol. I, p. 119.

14 Offenbach, *Les Contes d'Hoffmann*, p. 268.

15 These comments on *Les Contes d'Hoffmann* were first published as part of my essay 'The Voice of Freedom: Images of the Prima Donna', in Gardner and Rutherford (eds.), *The New Woman and Her Sisters: Feminism and Theatre 1850–1914*. Heather Hadlock makes similar use of this opera as a paradigm for representations of the prima donna with specific reference to the singer Hortense Schneider in 'Return of the repressed: The Prima Donna from Hoffmann's *Tales* to Offenbach's *Contes*', *Cambridge Opera Journal*, 6/3 (November 1994), 221–43.

16 Benedetto Marcello, *Il Teatro alla moda* (1720; repr. Rome: Castelvecchi, 1993).

17 Michel Foucault, *The History of Sexuality*, 3 vols. (1976), trans. Robert Hurley (London: Penguin, 1990), vol. I, pp. 100–1.

18 Walter Benjamin, 'The Work of Art in the Age of Mechanical Reproduction', in *Illuminations*, trans. Harry Zohn (London: Pimlico, 1999), pp. 214–18.

19 *Figaro*, 5/99, 13 December 1837, p. 396.

20 Homer, *The Odyssey*, trans. Walter Shewring (Oxford: Oxford University Press, 1980), pp. 143–4.

21 Hugo Rahner, *Greek Myths and Christian Mystery*, trans. Brian Battershaw (London: Burns & Oates, 1963). For a precise example, see Hippolytus, *The Refutation of All Heresies*, Book vii, trans. Rev. J. M. MacMahon (Edinburgh: T. & T. Clark, 1870), pp. 266–7.

22 'Let your women keep silence in the churches: for it is not permitted unto them to speak; but they are commanded to be under obedience, as also saith the law. / And if they will learn any thing, let them ask their husbands at home: for it is a shame for women to speak in the church.' St Paul, 1 Corinthians 15:34–5. According to Sophie Drinker, in AD 318 women were forbidden to sing in church, and in AD 367 the Council of Laodicea formally prohibited all congregational singing by both men and women. Male choirs, afforded a quasi-priestly function and status, henceforth undertook church singing. Drinker, *Music and Women: The Story of Women in Their Relation to Music* (New York: Coward McCann Inc., 1948), p. 179; see also Henry Chadwick, *The Early Church* (London: Penguin Books, 1967), pp. 273–4. On the emergence of women choristers in Protestant churches during the nineteenth century, see Nicholas Temperley, *The Music of the English Parish Church*, 2 vols. (Cambridge: Cambridge University Press, 1979), vol. I, p. 281; the Roman Catholic church not only continued the ban but reinforced it in the *Motu Proprio* of Pope Pius X in 1903.

23 Jerome, Letter liv: 13, *The Principal Works of St. Jerome*, trans. W. H. Fremantle (1892; repr. Grand Rapids, Mich.: Wm. B. Eerdmans, 1954), p. 106. In the third century, Hippolytus' vision of the sirens as 'beings filled with the most hideous savagery towards all who passed that way, though by the sweetness of their song they deceived the seafarers and tempted them by the enchantment of this singing to draw near'

(quoted in Rahner, *Greek Myths and Christian Mystery*, p. 363) seems echoed in his disapproval of the professional woman singer: 'A woman who attracts people by the beautiful but deluding sweetness of her voice (which is full of seduction to sin) must give up her trade and wait forty days if she is to receive communion.' Quoted in Drinker, *Music and Women*, p. 179.

24 See *Physiologus*, trans. Michael J. Curley (Austin and London: University of Texas Press, 1979), p. 23. Isidore of Seville (c. 560–636) also listed the sirens twice: in their classical sense in Book xi, and also as a species of Arabian serpent in Book XII: *Etymologiarvm Sive Orginvm Libri XI–XX* (London: Oxford University Press, 1911; repr. 1957), pp. 30–2. Other depictions of the siren appear in the works of numerous writers including Chaucer, Ariosto, Shakespeare, Daniels, Milton and Pope.

25 Dante Alighieri, *The Divine Comedy: Purgatorio*, trans. Charles S. Singleton (Princeton: Princeton University Press, 1973), p. 200.

26 Edmund Spenser, *The Faerie Queene*, ed. A. C. Hamilton (London and New York: Longman Group Ltd., 1977), Book 2, Canto xii, stanza 70.

27 For an account of the siren's influence in myths and fairy tales, see Marina Warner, *From the Beast to the Blonde: On Fairytales and Their Tellers* (London: Chatto & Windus, 1994), pp. 396–408.

28 Théophile Gautier, *Poésies complètes*, 3 vols. (Paris: A. G. Nizet, 1970), vol. III, p. 36.

29 See Ibsen's notes for this play in Michael Meyer, *Ibsen* (London: Penguin, 1985), p. 620.

30 'Tu non hai nulla e hai tutto; non sai nulla e sai tutto'. Gabriele d'Annunzio, *La Gioconda* (Milan: Arnoldo Mondadori Editore, 1940), p. 136.

31 Anton Chekhov, *Uncle Vanya*, trans. Ronald Hingley (Oxford: Oxford Paperbacks, 1998).

32 Bram Dijkstra, *Idols of Perversity: Fantasies of Feminine Evil in Fin-de-Siècle Culture* (New York and Oxford: Oxford University Press, 1986), p. 261.

33 *Ibid.*, p. 265.

34 Frank M. Turner, *The Greek Heritage in Victorian Britain* (New Haven: Yale University Press, 1981), p. 1.

35 See Gay, *The Bourgeois Experience*, vol. I, p. 207.

36 Michel Poizat, 'The Objectified Voice and the Vocal Object', in *The Angel's Cry: Beyond the Pleasure Principle in Opera*, trans. Arthur Denner (Ithaca and London: Cornell University Press, 1992), pp. 93–106.

37 Roland Barthes, *Image Music Text*, trans. S. Heath (London: Fontana Press, 1977), p. 182.

38 See Jean Jacques Barthélemy's description of initially pleasurable yet ultimately harmful music, contained in his influential essay *Entretiens sur l'etat de la musique grecque au quatrième siècle* (1777), quoted in Peter le Huray and James Day (eds.), *Music and Aesthetics in the Eighteenth and Early Nineteenth Centuries* (Cambridge: Cambridge University Press, 1988), pp. 128–9.

39 On France, see Georgina Cowart, 'Of Women, Sex and Folly: Opera under the Old Regime', *Cambridge Opera Journal*, 6/3 (November 1994), 205–20; on Germany, see Gloria Flaherty, *Opera in the Development of German Critical Thought* (Princeton: Princeton University Press, 1978), pp. 93–101; on England, see Suzanne Aspden, '"An Infinity of Factions": Opera in Eighteenth-Century Britain and the Undoing of Society', *Cambridge Opera Journal*, 9/1 (March 1997), 1–19, and Eric Walter White, *A History of English Opera* (London: Faber and Faber Ltd., 1983), pp. 151–2; on Italy, Ludovico Antonio Muratori's argument in 1706 that 'our present theatre music has become unduly effeminate. . . Spectators thus never leave the theatres feeling high-minded and nobly inspired, but only full of feminine tenderness, unworthy both of virile spirits and of wise and valourous people. . . it is a fact that modern theatre music is exceeding harmful for public mores, in that people become ever baser and prone to lasciviousness when listening to it.' Quoted in Enrico Fubini, *Music and Culture in Eighteenth-Century Europe: A Source Book*, trans. and ed. Bonnie J. Blackburn (Chicago and London: University of Chicago Press, 1994), pp. 39–41; also Apostolo Zeno's letter of 1730, where he links 'musical drama inextricably to the exploration of the "effeminate" emotion of love', quoted in Daniel E. Freeman, '*La guerriera amante*; Representation of Amazons and Warrior Queens in Venetian Baroque Opera', *The Musical Quarterly*, 80/3 (Fall 1996), 456.

40 Quoted in le Huray and Day (eds.), *Music and Aesthetics in the Eighteenth and Early Nineteenth Centuries*, p. 184.

41 Quoted in Theodore Fenner, *Leigh Hunt and Opera Criticism* (Lawrence, Manhattan and Wichita: University of Kansas Press, 1972), p. 179.

42 William Hazlitt, *The Complete Works of William Hazlitt* (London and Toronto: J. M. Dent & Sons Ltd., 1934), vol. xx, pp. 92–3. In 1898, Tolstoy similarly described opera as a 'nasty folly' full of 'gigantic absurdities': 'The man of culture is heartily sick of them, while to a real working-man they are utterly incomprehensible.' Quoted in Jacques Barzun (ed.), *Pleasures of Music* (London: Cassell, 1977), pp. 206–7.

43 Hazlitt, *Complete Works*, vol. xx, p. 94. Other anti-opera British critics include Thomas Carlyle, who argued that behind the 'glitter' of the opera-house 'stalks the shadow of Eternal Death' leading to 'Falsity, Vacuity, and the dwelling-place of Everlasting Despair'. *The Works of Thomas Carlyle* (London: Chapman and Hall, 1899), vol. xxix, p. 402. John Ruskin presented similar ideas in his Rede Lecture given in 1867; in 1877 he attacked opera again for its 'sirenic blasphemy' in *Fors Clavigera*, no. 83; quoted in William J. Gatens, 'Ruskin and Music', in Nicholas Temperley (ed.), *The Lost Chord: Essays in Victorian Music* (Bloomington and Indianapolis: Indiana University Press, 1989), pp. 82–3. On older linkages between music and effeminacy in Britain, see Linda Phyllis Austern, '"Alluring the Auditorie to Effeminacie": Music and the Idea of the Feminine in Early Modern England', *Music and Letters*, 74/3 (August 1993), 343–54.

44 Quoted in George Rowell (ed.), *Victorian Dramatic Criticism* (London: Methuen & Co. Ltd, 1971), p. 170.

45 Giuseppe Barigazzi, *La Scala racconta* (Milan: Rizzoli, 1998), pp. 145–55. On the reception of Liszt's comments, see Regli's vigorous rebuttal in *Il pirata*, 4/5, 17 July 1838, p. 17; also Kenneth Hamilton, 'Reminiscences of a Scandal – Reminiscences of La Scala: Liszt's Fantasy on Mercadante's *Il giuramento*', in *Cambridge Opera Journal*, 5/3 (1993), 187–90.

46 Ugo Foscolo, *Lacrime d'amore: Lettere a Antonietta Fagnani Arese*, ed. Giovanni Pacchiano (Milan: Serra e Riva, 1981), pp. 44–8.

47 Stendhal, *Rome, Naples et Florence* (1817; Paris: Le Divan, 1927), p. 27.

48 Leo Tolstoy, *War and Peace* (1869), trans. Constance Garnett (London: Pan Books Ltd., 1972), pp. 604–14.

49 H. G. Wells, *Ann Veronica* (1909; repr. London: Virago, 1980), pp. 155–9.

50 This practice was evident from opera's beginnings. Marcello Buttigli in 1628 describes Settimia Romano Caccini as 'una celeste Sirena'; Gustavo Marchesi, *Canto e cantanti* (Milan: Casa Ricordi, 1996), p. 21. Milton wrote Latin epigrams comparing Leonora Baroni to the sirens, after

hearing her sing in Rome in 1638. Walter MacKellar (ed.), *The Latin Poems of John Milton* (New Haven: Yale University Press, 1930), pp. 110–13. Jean Millet made similar allusions in his dedication of his treatise on singing to Madame la Baronne de Soye, *La Belle Méthode, ou l'art de bien chanter* (1666; repr. New York: Da Capo Press, 1973).

51 Sergio Ragni, 'Isabella Colbran: appunti per una biografia', *Bollettino del Centro Rossiniano di Studi*, 37 (1998), 33.

52 Kenneth A. Stern, 'A Documentary Study of Giuditta Pasta on the Opera Stage (Italy)', Ph.D. dissertation, City University of New York, 1983, p. 123.

53 Charles E. Pearce, *Madame Vestris and Her Times* (London: Stanley Paul & Co., 1923), p. 146.

54 Giovanni Pacini, *Le mie memorie artistiche* (Florence: Ferdinando Magnani, 1875), p. 185.

55 *Strenna teatrale europea*, 8 (1845), p. 179.

56 *Gazzetta musicale di Milano*, 8/33, 18 August 1859, p. 141.

57 *El Comercio*, 31 October 1857, in Lima, Peru; quoted in Richard Davis, *Anna Bishop: The Adventures of an Intrepid Prima Donna* (Sydney: Currency Press, 1997), p. 199.

58 *Teatro illustrato*, 4/42, June 1884, p. 82.

59 Norman Davies, *Europe: A History* (London: Pimlico, 1997), p. 759.

60 Stendhal, *The Life of Rossini*, trans. Richard Coe (2nd edn, 1824; repr. London: John Calder, 1985), p. 374.

61 On the connections between 'actress' and 'whore' see Tracy C. Davis, *Actresses as Working Women: Their Social Identity in Victorian Culture* (London and New York: Routledge, 1991), pp. 69–101, and Lesley Ferris, *Acting Women: Images of Women in Theatre* (London: Macmillan, 1990), p. 95.

62 Rosselli examines courtesan-singers such as Giulia Ciulla (1646–97) in *Singers of Italian Opera*, pp. 56–70; see also Beth L. Glixon, 'Private Lives of Public Women: Prima Donnas in Mid-Seventeenth-Century Venice', *Music and Letters*, 76/4 (November 1995), 509–31; 523–4.

63 Henry Mayhew, *London Labour and the London Poor*, 4 vols. (1861), vol. IV, p. 217.

64 Benedetto Croce, *I teatri di Napoli* (Bari: Gius, Laterza & Figli, 1966).

65 For Schröder-Devrient, see *Aus den Memoiren einer Sängerin* (1862), abridged and translated as *Pauline, the Prima Donna* (London and New York: Erotika Biblion Society, 1898); Guillaume Apollinaire also

translated the German original into French, *Les Mémoires d'une chanteuse allemande* (Paris, 1913); other editions in various languages are still in print. For Vestris, see *Confessions of Madame Vestris* (London and New York: Erotic Biblion Society, 1899).

66 Letter to Florimo, February 1835; quoted in Herbert Weinstock, *Vincenzo Bellini: His Life and His Operas* (London: Weidenfeld & Nicolson, 1971), p. 177.

67 Maretzek, *Revelations of an Opera Manager*, vol. ii, p. 33.

68 Charles Neilson Gattey, *Luisa Tetrazzini: The Florentine Nightingale* (Aldershot: Scolar Press, 1995), p. 56.

69 Jonathan Keates, *Handel: The Man and his Music* (London: Hamish Hamilton, 1986), p. 102.

70 E. T. A. Hoffmann, 'Councillor Krespel', in *Tales of Hoffmann*, trans. R. J. Hollingdale (Harmondsworth, Middlesex: Penguin Books, 1982), p. 176.

71 George Moore, *Evelyn Innes* (London: T. Fisher Unwin, 1898), p. 269.

72 James Huneker, *Painted Veils* (1920; repr. New York: Horace Liveright, 1928), p. 305.

73 George Du Maurier, *Trilby* (1894; repr. London: Dent, 1931), p. 40.

74 Moore, *Evelyn Innes*, p. 233.

75 George Moore, *Sister Theresa* (London: T. Fisher Unwin, 1901), p. 40.

76 See George Moore, *Memoirs of My Dead Life* (1906; rev. edn London: Heinemann Ltd), p. 216; and Josephine Huneker (ed.), *Intimate Letters of James Gibbons Huneker* (New York: Liverwright Publishers, 1924), pp. 248–9.

77 For more information on these and other vocal tutors, see Chapter 3.

78 Gaston Leroux, *The Phantom of the Opera* (1910; Cambridge: Dedalus, 1990), p. 24.

79 *Ibid.*, p. 103.

80 Hoffmann, 'Councillor Krespel', p. 180.

81 Du Maurier, *Trilby*, p. 253.

82 *Ibid.*, p. 248.

83 *Ibid.*, p. 357.

84 Pausanias and Homer; quoted in Robert Graves, *The Greek Myths*, 2 vols. (London: Penguin, 1955), vol. ii, p. 245.

85 William Weber, *Music and the Middle Class* (London: Croom Helm, 1975), p. 6. See also Arthur Loesser, *Men, Women and Pianos* (New York: Simon and Schuster, 1954).

86 *The Musical World*, 8/109, n.s. 1/15, 12 April 1838, p. 244. In the same
year, *Strenna teatrale europea* declared: 'music refines the souls, and we
in society have more need of tender souls than strong souls; music
refines our sensibilities, awakens ingenuity, educates the heart, it is a
sweet comfort of life, it is the balsam of grief . . . and required by
lovers' (1838, p. 125). In 1853 the music critic Abramo Basevi wrote a
series of articles for the *Gazzetta musicale di Firenze* entitled 'Potenza
della Musica', 1/24, 24 November 1853, p. 97: 'Music has the virtue of
rendering more lively and permanent the affections, serving as a
marvellous auxiliary to the imagination.' See also the description of
music as 'a moralising agent' in the *Napoli musicale*, 3/13 and 14, 10 July
1870, p. 1; and the discussion in the *Gazzetta teatrale italiana*, 34/5, 20
February 1905, p. 1: 'Music sharpens our mental faculties; it is a
powerful means for the moral education of the populace, because it
exerts in our souls an irresistible fascination and stirs the fibres of our
hearts.'

87 Weber, *Music and the Middle Class*, p. 30.

88 For example, see Fanny Trollope, *Paris and the Parisians* (1836; repr.
Gloucester: Alan Sutton Publising Ltd., 1985), p. 128.

89 Richard Leppert, *Music and Image: Domesticity, Ideology and Sociocultural
Formation in Eighteenth-century England* (Cambridge: Cambridge
University Press, 1988), pp. 28–50; Judith Tick, *American Women
Composers Before 1870* (Ann Arbor: UMI Research Press), pp. 13–31.

90 *Allgemeine musikalische Zeitung*, 22 October, 1800; quoted in Loesser,
Men, Women and Pianos, pp. 137–8.

91 Maria Coldwell, in Jane Bowers and Judith Tick (eds.), *Women Making
Music: the Western Art Tradition 1150–1950* (Urbana: University of Illinois
Press, 1986), p. 41.

92 Cyril Ehrlich, *The Music Profession in Britain Since the Eighteenth Century:
A Social History* (Oxford: Clarendon Press, 1985), pp. 100–7.

93 *Strenna teatrale europea*, 1 (1838), p. 124.

94 Again, this concept was hardly new: Greek legend reports that the
goddess Athene abandoned her playing of the double-flute because
although 'her music seemed to delight the other deities', Hera and
Aphrodite laughed at her as the effort of playing resulted in a 'bluish
face and swollen cheeks', and made her look 'ludicrous'. Graves, *The
Greek Myths*, vol. I, p. 77.

95 George Sand, *Histoire de ma vie* (1855; repr. Paris: Editions Stock, 1945), p. 246.

96 Werner Juker, *Musikschule und Konservatorium für Musik in Bern 1858–1958*; quoted in Reich, 'Women as Musicians: A Question of Class', in Solie (ed.), *Musicology and Difference*, p. 135. Of the 335 female students admitted to the newly opened Royal College of Music in London in 1883, there were 185 pianists, 124 singers, 16 violinists, 1 harpist, and 1 organist. Ehrlich, *The Music Profession in Britain*, p. 110.

97 Francesco Florimo, *Cenno storico sulla scuola musicale di Napoli*, 2 vols. (Naples: Lorenzo Bocco, 1869), vol. I, p. 83.

98 Quoted in Carol Neuls-Bates, *Women in Music: An Anthology of Source Readings from the Middle Ages to the Present* (Boston: Northeastern University Press, 1996), p. 200. An anonymous article in *The Musical World* in 1839 made a radical plea for women to be accepted as violinists, despite the 'common objection . . . that it is ungraceful': 12/166, n.s. 5/72, 16 May 1839, pp. 34–7. The Milanollo sisters, Domenica (1827–1904) and Maria (1832–48), were touring Europe in the 1840s; the concerts of the later Ferni sisters, Carolina (1839–1926) and Virginia (1837–1926), are recorded in the periodicals from 1851 onwards.

99 An advertisement for a concert given by the fifteen-year-old Laudelia Giuseppina Rachelle on 24 March 1820 at the Teatro Ducale in Parma is a rare indication of the presence of female cellists playing in public; Archivio Storico del Teatro Regio, Manifesti A137. The British actress Fanny Kemble recalled her surprise around the early 1840s on seeing Mrs George Grote (an eccentric society hostess, keen amateur musician and wife of a respected banker and MP) order her manservant to bring her 'the big fiddle', and then proceed to play music by Gluck with 'excellent taste and expression'. Frances Anne Kemble, *Records of Later Life*, 3 vols. (London: R. Bentley, 1882), vol. II, p. 54.

100 Ethel Smyth wrote sardonically of the female harpist's lonely existence as 'an immemorial concession, I imagine, to aesthetic promptings. . . this solitary, daintily clad, white-armed sample of womanhood among the black coats, as it might be a flower on a coal dump'. *The Memoirs of Ethel Smyth* (Harmondsworth: Viking, 1987), p. 340. In Britain, women were first employed by a male orchestra in 1913; various all-women orchestras existed in the latter years of the century in Europe and the USA.

101 Loesser, *Men, Women and Pianos*, p. 66; see also Weber, *Music and the Middle Class*, p. 30.

102 Quoted in Loesser, *Men, Women and Pianos*, p. 217. At a hotel in Cologne in 1844 Marianne Lincoln was entertained by two such performers in the coffee-room after dinner: 'two little girls came in, and sang several Duets, each accompanying on a Guitar. Then they came round to collect money.' *Debut at the Gewandhaus and After: A 19th-Century Singer's Diary* (New Malden, Surrey: F. M. Harper, 1980), p. 2.

103 Pietro Lichtenthal, *Trattato dell'influenza della musica sul corpo umano e del suo uso in certe malattie con alcuni cenni come si abbia ad intendere una buona musica, tradotto dal tedesco e ricorretto dall'autore medesimo* (Milan: Giuseppe Maspero, 1811), p. 28.

104 Baldassarre Gamucci in *Boccherini*, 12/12, 31 December 1874, pp. 45–6.

105 Lowell Mason, 'General Observations on Vocal Music', *The Musical World*, 6/66, 16 June 1837, p. 5.

106 See the reviews in Hector Berlioz, *Critique Musicale 1823–1863*, vol. III ed. Yves Gérard, Anne Bongrain and Marie-Hélène Coudroy-Saghai (Paris: Buchet/Chastel, 2001), pp. 25–6 (January 1837), and 459–62 (May 1838).

107 Kerry Murphy, 'Joseph Mainzer's "Sacred and Beautiful Mission": An Aspect of Parisian Musical Life of the 1830s', *Music and Letters*, 75 (February 1994), p. 34.

108 Founded in 1842, appearing twice monthly. Bought by J. Alfred Novello in 1844 (who altered the original title to 'The Musical Times and Singing Class etc.'), it was then produced once a month.

109 Joseph Mainzer, *Singing for the Million* (London, 1841; repr. Kilkenny, Ireland: Boethius Press, 1984), p. x. For other ways in which these ideas were reinforced, see also the *Musical Times*, 1/12, 1 May 1845, which cites at length Luther's dictums on music.

110 Mainzer, *Singing for the Million*, p. iv; also p. xiii.

111 *Ibid.*, p. vii.

112 Mainzer had a significant influence on the emergence of the 'singing class' in this era (supposedly around one hundred thousand pupils took part); other practitioners such as John Hullah started similar classes, which served to encourage working-class singers to further participation in music-making through local choirs. *Ibid.*, introduction.

113 See, for example, a description of a Mainzer-style school for Italian workers in Florence run by a priest, Don Pirro Palazzeschi. *Gazzetta musicale di Milano*, 4/9, 2 March 1845, pp. 39–40.

114 John Ruskin, *Sesame and Lilies* (1865; new edn, London: George Allen, 1893), p. 109.

115 *Ibid.*, p. xviii.

116 *Ibid.*, pp. 122–3. Leppert makes the point that the 'connection between song texts and female morality' was an old one even by the eighteenth century. *Music and Image*, p. 30.

117 George Bernard Shaw, *Music in London 1890–1894*, 3 vols. (London: Constable & Co., 1932), vol. III, pp. 203–4.

118 Hugh Reginald Haweis, *Music and Morals* (London: W. H. Allen, 1874), p. 110.

119 *Ibid.*, pp. 111–12.

120 In the church, Haweis' understanding of the restrictions imposed on womanhood apparently resulted in more positive action: despite opposition from members of his parish, he introduced female membership of the traditionally male church choir. Drinker, *Music and Women*, p. 268; see also Hyde, *New Found Voices*, p. 20.

121 Quoted in Reginald Nettel, *Sing A Song of England: A Social History of Traditional Song* (London: Phoenix House Ltd., 1969), p. 184.

122 J. F. Reichardt, 'The Physiognomy of the Voice', *The Musical World*, 8/107, n.s. 1/13, 29 March 1838, p. 211.

123 Sir Walter Scott, *The Bride of Lammermoor* (1819; repr. London: Dent, 1985), p. 39.

124 Victor Hugo, *Notre Dame* (1831; London: Thomas Nelson & Sons Ltd., n.d.), p. 78.

125 *The Musical World*, 6/81, 21 July 1837, pp. 93–4.

126 Hermann Hesse, *Gertrude* (1910), trans. Hilda Rosner (Harmondsworth: Penguin Books, 1986), p. 72.

127 Jane Austen, *Emma* (1816; repr. London: Dent, 1964), p. 200.

128 Tolstoy, *War and Peace*, p. 564.

129 Marguerite Blessington, *The Two Friends*, in *The Works of Lady Blessington*, 2 vols. (1838; repr. New York: AMS Press Inc., 1975), vol. I, p. 22.

130 *Ibid.*, p. 27.

131 *Ibid.*, p. 22.

132 *Ibid.*, p. 28.

133 *Ibid.*, p. 22.

134 Thos. Henderson, 'The Place of the Singing Class in Education', *The Music Student*, 4/3, December 1911, p. 89.

135 James Huneker, *Bedouins* (1920; London: T. Werner Laurie, n.d.), p. 108.

2 SUPERDIVAS AND SUPERWOMEN

1 George Eliot, 'Armgart', in *The Legend of Jubal and Other Poems, Old and New* (1871; London: Blackwood, 1879), p. 98. This chapter is partly based on my earlier essay, 'The Voice of Freedom: the Image of the Prima Donna', in Viv Gardner and Susan Rutherford (eds.), *The New Woman and Her Sisters: Feminism and Theatre 1850–1914*. Some of this ground was later covered by Susan Leonardi and Rebecca A. Pope in *The Diva's Mouth: Body, Voice, Prima Donna Politics* (New Brunswick, NJ: Rutgers University Press, 1996).

2 See Ellen Moers, 'Performing Heroinisim: The Myth of Corinne', *Literary Women* (London: The Women's Press, 1978), pp. 173–210. Also Renate Mohrmann, 'Women's Work as Portrayed in Women's Literature', in Ellen B. Joeres and Mary Jo Maynes (eds.), *German Women in the Eighteenth and Nineteenth Centuries* (Bloomington: Indiana University Press, 1986), pp. 70–73.

3 Arthur Schopenhauer, 'Ueber die Weiber,' *Werke in zehn Bänden*, 10 vols. (Zurich: Diogenes, 1977), vol. x, p. 674.

4 Charles De Boigne, *Petits mémoires de l'Opéra* (Paris: Librairie Nouvelle, 1857), p. 339.

5 *Ibid.*, p. 81.

6 Letter to Mlle Leroyer de Chantapie, 30 March 1860; quoted in G. Jean-Aubry, 'Gustave Flaubert and Music', *Music and Letters*, 31/1 (January 1950), 17.

7 Christiansen, *Prima Donna*, p. 78.

8 Letter to Pauline Viardot, 25–28 June 1842. *Correspondance de George Sand*, 25 vols. (Paris: Garnier Frères, 1969), vol. v, pp. 705–6. On Viardot, see April Fitzlyon, *The Price of Genius: A Life of Pauline Viardot* (London: John Calder, 1964).

9 Balzac reportedly told Sand: 'Vous cherchez l'homme tel qu'il devrait être; moi, je prends tel qu'il est.' Sand, *Histoire de ma vie*, p. 302.

10 See A. Rea, 'Towards a Definition of Women's Voice in Sand's
   Novels: The Siren and the Witch', in Janis Glasgow (ed.), *George Sand:
   Collected Essays* (New York: Whitson Publishing Company, 1985),
   pp. 227–38.

11 George Sand, *Consuelo: A Romance of Venice* (1842; repr. New York:
   Da Capo Press, 1979), pp. 335–7 (all citations from the top of the page
   to this point); and *The Countess of Rudolstadt* (London: A. & F. Denny,
   n.d.).

12 *Ibid.*, p. 200.

13 *Ibid.*, p. 599.

14 *Ibid.*, p. 504.

15 First performed at the Hoftheater, Vienna in 1740; libretto by
   Metastasio.

16 Sand, *Consuelo*, p. 709.

17 *Ibid.*, p. 616.

18 Letter to Charles Lee Lewes, 26 April 1871; Gordon S. Haight (ed.), *The
   George Eliot Letters*, 9 vols. (London: Oxford University Press, 1954),
   vol. v, pp. 143–4.

19 Eliot first saw a performance of this opera in Berlin on 2 January 1855,
   with Johanna Wagner in the title role. *Ibid.*, vol. ii, p. 191.

20 Eliot, 'Armgart', p. 105.

21 *Ibid.*, p. 126.

22 *Ibid.*, p. 75.

23 *Ibid.*, pp. 95–6.

24 *Ibid.*, p. 96.

25 *Ibid.*, p. 97.

26 *Ibid.*, p. 105.

27 *Ibid.*, p. 76.

28 *Ibid.*, pp. 102–3.

29 George Eliot, 'Liszt, Wagner, and Weimar', in Pinney (ed.), *Essays of
   George Eliot*, pp. 98–9.

30 Eliot, 'Armgart', p. 113.

31 *Ibid.*, p. 119.

32 *Ibid.*, p. 124.

33 Shirley Foster, *Victorian Women's Fiction: Marriage, Freedom and the
   Individual* (London and Sydney: Croom Helm, 1986), pp. 198–201.

34 Eliot, 'Armgart', p. 93.

35 *Ibid.*, p. 138.
36 *Ibid.*, p. 140.
37 George Eliot, *Daniel Deronda* (1876; repr. London: Penguin Classics, 1986), p. 295.
38 *Ibid.*, p. 729.
39 *Ibid.*, p. 256.
40 *Ibid.*, pp. 253–4.
41 *Ibid.*, p. 728.
42 *Ibid.*, p. 256.
43 *Ibid.*, pp. 693–4.
44 *Ibid.*, p. 730.
45 *Ibid.*, p. 689.
46 *Ibid.*, p. 691.
47 *Ibid.*, p. 702.
48 *Ibid.*, p. 727.
49 *Ibid.*, p. 730.
50 Willa Cather, *The Song of the Lark* (1915; repr. London: Virago, 1982), p. 571.
51 *Ibid.*, p. 266.
52 *Ibid.*, p. 91.
53 *Ibid.*, p. 237.
54 *Ibid.*, p. 544.
55 *Ibid.*, p. 550.
56 *Ibid.*, p. 571.
57 *Ibid.*, p. 274.
58 *Ibid.*, p. 378.
59 *Ibid.*, p. 510.
60 In a letter of 4 January 1859, Viardot advises Julius Rietz to 'read over the first part of *Consuelo*; I shall see if you can discover the other similiarity with me'. In 'Pauline Viardot-Garcia to Julius Rietz (Letters of Friendship)', *The Musical Quarterly*, 1/3 (July 1915), 350–80; p. 374; see also Fitzlyon, *The Price of Genius*, p. 118.
61 Clara Louise Kellogg, *Memoirs of an American Prima Donna* (New York and London: G. P. Putnam, 1913), p. 314.
62 Mary Watkins Cushing, *The Rainbow Bridge* (New York: Putnam, 1954), p. 244.
63 Moers, *Literary Women*, p. 191.

64 The Association for the Advancement of Women, founded in 1873 by the astronomer Maria Mitchell, and part of the wider US feminist movement. Evans, *The Feminists*, p. 51.

65 Fanny Raymond Ritter, *Woman as a Musician: An Art-Historical Study* (London: William Reeves, n.d.), pp. 8–12.

66 *Ibid.*, p. 4.

67 See also Hyde, *New Found Voices*, pp. 40–72.

68 Ritter, *Woman as a Musician*, pp. 11–12.

69 *Ibid.*, p. 10.

70 *The Musical Times*, 1/18, 1 November 1845, p. 134; 'Della decadenza delle voci', *Gazzetta musicale di Milano*, 13/11, 18 March 1855, pp. 81–2.

71 See Ira Glackens, *Yankee Diva: Lillian Nordica and the Golden Days of Opera* (New York: Coleridge Press, 1963), p. 340.

72 H. Ernest Hunt, 'Singing and the General Health', *The Music Student*, 5/12, August 1913, p. 343.

73 Carlo Ritorni, *Annali del teatro della città di Reggio* (Bologna: Nobili e Comp., 1829), vol. VI, p. 174.

74 'In the head. Headaches, dizziness, tendency towards fainting, complaints of the eyes, pain and ringing in the ears, nose-bleeds.
   In the thorax. Beyond dislocation of the bones, tight-lacing produces laboured breathing, spitting of blood, consumption, acceleration in the pulse rate, palpitations of the heart and hydropsy of the chest. In the abdomen. Loss of appetite, nausea, expectoration of blood, poor digestion, flatulence, diarrhoea, colicky pains, hardening of the liver, hydropsy and hernia. There follows also hypochondria, hysteria and a quantity of illnesses particular to women, illnesses that it is superfluous to number here.' *Ibid.*, pp. 179–80.

75 Michael Aspinall, 'Adelina Patti' (London: EMI Records Ltd, 1973), p. 5.

76 *The Musical World*, 31/41, 8 October 1853, p. 649.

77 'Madame Bessie Cox', *The Musical Herald*, 623, 1 February 1900, pp. 35–6.

78 Enrico Caruso and Luisa Tetrazzini, *Caruso and Tetrazzini on the Art of Singing* (1909; repr. New York: Dover Publications Inc., 1975), p. 11.

79 Quoted in Glackens, *Yankee Diva: Lillian Nordica and the Golden Days of Opera*, p. 334.

80 On the history of amateur music-making, see Tick, *American Women Composers Before 1870*; Ehrlich, *The Music Professsion in Britain Since the Eighteenth Century*; and Loesser, *Men, Women and Pianos*. On repertoire,

see also David Gramit, *Cultivating Music: The Aspirations, Interests, and Limits of German Musical Culture, 1770–1848* (Berkeley and London: University of California Press, 2002), and David Tunley, *Salons, Singers and Songs: A Background to Romantic French Song 1830–1870* (Aldershot: Ashgate, 2002).

81 J. A. V. Chapple, *Elizabeth Gaskell: A Portrait in Letters* (Manchester: Manchester University Press, 1980), p. 2.

82 Lady Mary Monkswell, *A Victorian Diarist 1873–1895* (London: John Murray, 1944), p. 2.

83 *Ibid.*, pp. 210–11.

84 Smyth, *The Memoirs of Ethel Smyth*, p. 44.

85 Tierl Thompson (ed.), *Dear Girl: The Diaries and Letters of Two Working Women 1897–1917* (London: The Women's Press, 1987), p. 36.

86 Letter from Queen Victoria to King Leopold, 1 August 1837; quoted in Hibbert, *Queen Victoria*, p. 17.

87 R. D. Smith (ed.), *The Writings of Anna Wickham: Free Woman and Poet* (London: Virago, 1984), p. 95.

88 George Bernard Shaw, *London Music in 1888–89* (London: Constable & Co. Ltd., 1937), p. 9.

89 *Ibid.*, p. 15.

90 Quoted in Chapple, *Elizabeth Gaskell*, p. 59.

91 *Ibid.*, Letter to Lady Kay Shuttleworth, 12 November 1850, p. 50.

92 Gertrude Atherton, *Adventures of a Novelist* (London: Cape, 1932), p. 118.

93 Marie Bashkirtseff, *The Journal of Marie Bashkirtseff*, p. xi.

94 *Ibid.*, p. vii.

95 George Bernard Shaw, *Major Critical Essays* (London: Penguin, 1986), pp. 54–5.

96 Bashkirtseff claimed to be only twelve – an alteration almost certainly made by her mother prior to the publication of the diary.

97 *Ibid.*, p. 2.

98 *Ibid.*, p. 51.

99 *Ibid.*, p. 28.

100 Bashkirtseff, *Journal*, p. 416.

101 Pacini, *Le mie memorie*, pp. 52–3.

102 *Ibid.*, pp. 63–4.

103 Letter from Mendelssohn to his mother, 1842; *The Musical Times and Singing-Class Circular*, 38/652, 1 June 1897, p. 391.

104 Wagner, *My Life*, p. 651.

105 Charles Villiers Stanford, *Pages from an Unwritten Diary* (London: Edward Arnold, 1914), p. 25.

106 Pacini, *Le mie memorie*, p. 73. Further details of this singer, Bartolini, have so far not been traced.

107 Tunley, *Salons, Singers and Songs*, pp. 1–17.

108 *The Musical Times*, 38/652, 1 June 1897, pp. 369–71.

109 Tina Whitaker Scalia (1858–1957) had reportedly turned down an approach to audition for La Scala in favour of marriage and domesticity. Consuelo Giglio, 'Tina Whitaker e la musica a Palermo nella belle epoque', in Rosario Lentini and Pietro Silvestri (eds.), *I Whitaker di villa Malfitano: atti del seminario di studi, Palermo, 16–18 marzo 1995* (Palermo: Fondazione Giuseppe Whitaker, Regione Siciliana, 1995), pp. 339–64.

110 Eames, *Some Memories and Reflections*, p. 121. Clara Louise Kellogg heard May Callender sing, and wrote that she 'could easily have been an opera singer, and a distinguished one, if she had so chosen'. Kellogg, *Memoirs*, p. 277. Fremstad was also well acquainted with these two women. Cushing, *The Rainbow Bridge*, p. 37.

111 Hector Berlioz, *Mémoires de Hector Berlioz, comprenant ses voyages en Italie, en Allemagne, en Russie et en Angleterre 1803–1865*, 2 vols. (Paris: Calmann Lévy, 1897), vol. II, p. 119. The singers identified here were the tenor Eduard Mantius (1806–74) and the soprano Amalie Hähnel (1807–49); the bass was probably 'Hr. Bötticher', first bass at the Hoftheater in Berlin in 1841 (see the index of *Allgemeine Wiener Musik-Zeitung*, 1, p. 38).

112 This was almost certainly Josephine Clarke, the niece of Lady Morgan, who in her youth in 1833 had sung Act I of *Norma* with Pasta and Bellini in London at her aunt's house; Bellini was supposedly 'charmed' with her voice. See Weinstock, *Vincenzo Bellini*, p. 146.

113 Stanford, *Pages from an Unwritten Diary*, p. 26.

114 Wagner, *My Life*, pp. 705–6.

115 See, for example, 'La musica in famiglia', *Euterpe*, 1/24, 24 June 1869, p. 5.

116 Alda, *Men, Women and Tenors*, p. 300.

117 For further information about Delsarte, see Chapter 6.

118 Lillian de Hegermann-Lindencrone, *In the Courts of Memory 1858–1875* (New York and London: Harper & Bros., 1911), p. 62.

119 *Ibid.*, pp. 57–8.

120 *Ibid.*, p. 190.

121 *Ibid.*, pp. 66–8.

122 *Ibid.*, p. 65.

123 *Ibid.*, pp. 52–3.

124 *Ibid.*, p. 87.

125 *Ibid.*, p. 160.

126 *L'Art Musical*, 3/11, 12 February 1863, p. 95. Although de Hegermann-Lindencrone is not named directly, this passage undoubtedly refers to her: it mentions her concert in the Tuileries as well as Auber's *Benedictus*.

127 *Ibid.*, p. 16.

128 *Ibid.*, p. 73.

129 *Ibid.*, pp. 74–5.

130 *Ibid.*, pp. 336–7.

131 *Ibid.*, pp. 339–40.

132 On Piccolomini, see my essay '*La traviata*, or the "Willing Grisette"': Male Critics and Female Performance in the 1850s', in Della Seta, Marvin and Marica (eds.), *Verdi 2001*, vol. II, pp. 585–600. Mario was the pseudonym of Giovanni Matteo, Cavaliere de Candia (1810–83).

133 From *The Enchantress*, an operetta by Victor Herbert (1859–1924), with a libretto by Fred de Gresac (wife of the operatic baritone Victor Maurel). It was first produced in New York on 19 October 1911.

134 April Fitzlyon, *Maria Malibran*, p. 129.

135 Harold Rosenthal records Edvina's Covent Garden debut: 'The press and gossip writers made great publicity for her, and Society turned out in full force to hear "their" own prima donna, who made her debut on 15 July as Marguérite in *Faust*. In actual fact Edvina was a serious artist and a good singer, and her Louise the following year firmly established her as an artist of Covent Garden stature.' Rosenthal, *Two Hundred Years at Covent Garden* (London: Putnam & Co., 1958), p. 333.

136 Eames, *Some Memories and Reflections*, p. 149.

137 Mary Lawton, *Schumann-Heink: The Last of the Titans* (New York: J. J. Little & Ives, 1928), pp. 337–8.

138 Mathilde Marchesi, *Marchesi and Music: Passages from the Life of a Famous Singing Teacher* (London and New York: Harper & Bros., 1897), pp. 202–3.

139 *Ibid.*, p. 224.

140 *Ibid.*, pp. 150–1.

141 Alda, *Men, Women and Tenors*, p. 46.

142 *Ibid.*, p. 151.

143 Document 70 (VI: 148–56): 'Illinois Campaign 1910–1913', in Mario Jo and Paul Buhle (eds.), *The Concise History of Women's Suffrage* (Chicago: University of Illinois Press, 1978).

144 *Ibid.*, pp. 404–5.

145 Inez Haynes Irwin, *Angels and Amazons* (New York: Doubleday, 1933), pp. 339–40.

146 Nordica arrived in London in May 1908, and sang at the Queen's Hall on 29 May. A second concert followed. She was then married to George Washington Young in Grosvenor Square on 29 July, and left on a honeymoon to France. She arrived back in the States in September, an 'ardent suffragette'. Glackens, *Yankee Diva*, pp. 239–40.

147 *Ibid.*, p. 241.

148 *Ibid.*, p. 258.

149 In an article for *The World Magazine*, 11 November 1917, Garden wrote: 'I am one of the few women in the world who can lay claim to being genuinely modern and yet opposed to all the various invasive tendencies which have come upon women in recent years. I consider that suffrage will do women no good.' Quoted in Michael Turnbull, *Mary Garden* (Aldershot: Scolar Press, 1997), p. 129.

150 For more information about the AFL, see Viv Gardner (ed.), *Sketches from the Actresses' Franchise League* (Nottingham: Nottingham Drama Texts, 1985).

151 Educational methods included propaganda meetings, the sale of propaganda material, plays and lectures.

152 *The Musical World*, 8/76, 17 February 1908, pp. 29–30.

153 Glackens, *Yankee Diva*, pp. 170 and 174.

154 Robert Tuggle, *The Golden Age of Opera* (New York: Holt, Rinehart & Winston, 1983), p. 39.

155 *Ibid.*, p. 144.

156 Smyth, *Memoirs*, p. 293.

157 Evans, *The Feminists*, p. 246. See also Ravera's comments on the
connections between Italian feminist groups and international
associations, *Breve storia*, p. 72.

158 Graves, *The Greek Myths*, vol. II, p. 245.

3 TUTORS AND TUITION

1 Quoted in Frederick Martens, *The Art of the Prima Donna* (London:
D. Appleton & Co., 1922), p. 239.

2 In 1867, Panofka claimed that sopranos had had to 'increase considerably
the volume of their voice and their breathing in order to wrestle with [*per
lottare contro*] the *tenore di forza*'; and that similarly dangerous
consequences were experienced by the other voices. Enrico Panofka,
*Voci e cantanti: ventotto capitoli di considerazioni generali sulla voce e
sull'altare del canto* (Florence, 1871: repr. Bologna: Arnaldo Forni, 1984),
pp. 87–8.

3 For a full discussion of *bel canto*, see Rodolfo Celletti, *A History of Bel
Canto*, trans. Frederick Fuller (Oxford: Clarendon Press, 1991).

4 As described by Pier Francesco Tosi, *Observations on the Florid Song*,
trans. J. E. Galliard (1743; repr. London: William Reeves, 1967).

5 *Gazzetta musicale di Milano*, 5/9, 1 March 1846, pp. 69–70.

6 On the García family and their influence on ideas and methods of singing,
see Harold Bruder, 'Manuel García the Elder: His School and His Legacy',
Opera Quarterly, 13/4 (Summer 1997), 19–47. The tenor Manuel García
(1775–1832) led a remarkable dynasty: his children included not only
Malibran and Viardot but also their half-brother Manuel Garcia II (1805–
1906), one of the most important vocal tutors of the period. The family
name was anglicised owing to Garcia II's residence in London.

7 See Percy Scholes, *The Mirror of Music 1844–1944*, 2 vols. (London:
Oxford University Press and Novello & Co., 1947), vol. I, pp. 289–91.

8 For example, *Gazzetta musicale di Milano*, 12/36, 3 September 1854,
pp. 285–6; *Gazzetta musicale di Napoli*, 4/4, 27 January 1855, pp. 25–6;
Euterpe, 1/2, 2 July 1869, p. 2; *Boccherini*, 12/12, 31 December 1874, pp. 45–6.

9 See also F. Campanella, *Sulla decadenza del canto in Italia* (Naples, 1885),
L. Vivarelli, *Ancora della decadenza dell'arte del canto* (Milan, 1889),
L. Leonesi, *La decadenza dell'arte del canto: causa e rimedio* (Bologna,
1894), L. Mastrigli, *La decadenza del canto in Italia: cause e rimedi*
(Rome, 1897).

10 Quoted in Francesco Florimo, *Cenno storico sulla scuola musicale di Napoli* (Naples: Lorenzo Rocco, 1869), p. 85. *Rondoncini* and *canonetti* are Italian diminutives for popular, canonic songs of a light, pleasing and tuneful nature.

11 Fubini, *Music and Culture*, p. 269.

12 *L'Art musical*, 1/5, 3 January 1861, p. 36.

13 Alda, *Men, Women and Tenors*, p. 294.

14 Lotte Lehmann, *My Many Lives* (1948: repr. Westport, Conn.: Greenwood Press, 1974), p. 56.

15 Alda, *Men, Women and Tenors*, pp. 295–6.

16 Emma Calvé, *My Life*, trans. Rosamond Gilder (New York: D. Appleton & Co., 1922), p. 229.

17 Shaw, *Music in London*, vol. I, p. 40.

18 Reynaldo Hahn, *On Singers and Singing*, trans. Leopold Simoneau (1913–14; Portland, Ore.: Amadeus Press, 1990), p. 93.

19 *Ibid.*, p. 77.

20 *The Musical Times*, June 1923; Quoted in Scholes, *The Mirror of Music*, vol. I, p. 287.

21 Quoted in Michael Holroyd, *Bernard Shaw: Volume I, 1856–1898* (London: Penguin, 1990), p. 22. It is probable that Lee was also the anonymous London 'Svengali' who claimed he could 'make a voice in six weeks', mentioned by Blanche Marchesi, *A Singer's Pilgrimage* (London: Grant Richards, 1923), pp. 296–7.

22 Shaw, *Music in London*, vol. I, pp. 40–1. See also Holroyd, *Bernard Shaw*, p. 64.

23 Rosselli, *Singers of Italian Opera*, pp. 106–13.

24 Clara Kathleen Rogers, *The Philosophy of Singing* (London: Osgood, McIlvaine & Co., 1893), pp. 185–6.

25 Nicola Tacchinardi, *Dell'opera in musica sul teatro italiano e de' suoi difetti* (1833), in Paola Ciarlantini, 'Una testimonianza sul teatro musicale degli inizi dell'ottocento: il saggio "Dell'opera in musica" di Nicola Tacchinardi', *Bollettino del Centro Rossiniano di Studi*, 29 (1989), p. 95.

26 María de las Mercedes Santa Cruz y Montalvo, comtesse de Merlin, *Memoirs of Madame Malibran, by the countess of Merlin, and other intimate friends* (London: H. Colburn, 1840), pp. 21–2.

27 Garry O'Connor, *The Pursuit of Perfection: A Life of Maggie Teyte* (London: Victor Gollancz Ltd., 1979), p. 46.

28 Rosselli, *Singers of Italian Opera*, p. 109.

29 See Cornelius L. Reid, *Bel Canto: Principles and Practices* (1950; repr. New York: Joseph Patelson Music House, 1971), p. 165.

30 *Ibid.*, pp. 145–7.

31 For example, see 'Nouvelles recherches sur la phonation', *L'Art musical*, 36, 8 August 1861, p. 281: an article about the new *larynthoscop* invented by Charles Battaille, which he claimed demonstrated 'la supériorité de ce mode de respiration'.

32 Durante, 'The Opera Singer', in Bianconi and Pestelli (eds.), *Opera and its Resources*, p. 403.

33 Lilli Lehmann, *How To Sing* (1902), trans. Richard Aldrich (New York: Dover Publications Inc., 1933), p. 13.

34 *The Musical World*, 70/20, 17 May 1890, p. 387.

35 Hahn, *On Singers and Singing*, p. 53.

36 Letter from Verdi to Giuseppe Piroli, 20 February 1871; quoted in Charles Osborne (ed.), *Letters of Giuseppe Verdi* (New York, Chicago, San Francisco: Holt, Rinehart and Winston, 1971), pp. 175–6.

37 Almost certainly the former singer and popular teacher Anna de Lagrange (1824–1905).

38 The French tenor Pierre-François Wartel (1806–82).

39 'Singing Lessons in Paris', *The Musical World*, 70/1, 4 January 1890, pp. 9–10.

40 Letter from Garden to Florence Mayer, 1 June 1896.

41 Mary Garden and Louis Biancolli, *Mary Garden's Story* (London: Michael Joseph, 1952), p. 23. A bill from Sbriglia to Garden dated 27 June 1896 for 250 francs shows that she took at least nine lessons from this tutor.

42 Jacques Bouhy (1848–1929), a Belgian baritone who created the role of Escamillo in Bizet's *Carmen* in 1875. Director of the New York Conservatory 1885–9, he later taught in Paris. The contralto Kathleen Howard studied with him in the early 1900s.

43 One of the most sought-after teachers in Europe in the late nineteenth century, the German mezzo-soprano Mathilde Marchesi (1821–1913) had studied with the legendary Manuel Garcia and mostly produced coloratura sopranos, including Emma Calvé, Irma Di Murska, Emma Eames, Etelka Gerster, Nellie Melba and Sibyl Sanderson.

44 Marchesi had three levels of classes: First Class, Second Class and the Opera Class. Garden does not seem to have been asked to participate

actively in the Opera Class (comprising the most senior pupils) and was allowed there solely as a spectator.

45 Alda writes that Marchesi 'advised daily lessons of twenty minutes each, and no more. But her pupils were assembled in a class, and each pupil, though she actually sang no more than the twenty minutes Marchesi heard her, heard the lessons of the other pupils in the class, and benefited by the criticism and instruction.' *Men, Women and Tenors*, p. 298.

46 The American soprano Emma Eames (1865–1952) also studied with Marchesi in Paris, making her operatic debut in 1889.

47 Marchesi was widely known as a martinet. Melba recalls that 'her word was law', but that 'her sense of humour' alleviated many of the petty cruelties she inflicted on her pupils. Nellie Melba, *Melodies and Memories* (1925; repr. London: Hamish Hamilton, 1980), p. 20.

48 Alda comments that 'Marchesi's exercises were little more than scales, sung very slowly. Single, sustained tones, repeated time and time again, until her critical ear was entirely satisfied. Then came arpeggios. After these came a more complicated technical drill to prepare the pupil for fioritura work in the more florid operas.' *Men, Women and Tenors*, p. 299.

49 Letter No. 6, Mary Garden to Florence Mayer, summer 1896.

50 Garden and Biancolli, *Mary Garden's Story*, pp. 23–4.

51 Alda, *Men, Women and Tenors*, p. 44.

52 Letter No. 11, Mary Garden to Florence Mayer, 26 September 1896.

53 A marquis and composer, Trabadelo was also the former teacher of Geraldine Farrar.

54 Garden and Biancolli, *Mary Garden's Story*, p. 25. Garden does not describe Trabadelo's methodology in any depth: she implies that he relied on 'simple scales and exercises', and kept a watchful eye on 'breathing and the quality of the voice'.

55 Enrico Caruso and Luisa Tetrazzini, *Caruso and Tetrazzini on the Art of Singing*, p. 36.

56 *Ibid.*, p. 65.

57 'Singing Lessons in Paris', *The Musical World*, 70/1, 4 January 1890, pp. 9–10.

58 De Hegermann-Lindencrone, *In the Courts of Memory*, p. 12.

59 Rasponi, *The Last Prima Donnas*, p. 310.

60 *Ibid.*, p. 222.

61 Maretzek, *Revelations of an Opera Manager*, vol. II, p. 1.

62 Jerome Hines, *Great Singers on Great Singing* (London: Victor Gollancz Ltd., 1983), p. 164.

63 Reid argues that we underestimate the significance of innate talent in the development of the voice: singers are 'seldom successful in that they have been taught to sing but because they had naturally well-placed voices before training'. *Bel Canto*, pp. 120–1.

64 For the fullest account of the myths that surrounded Ponselle's debut, see James A. Drake, *Rosa Ponselle: A Centenary Biography* (Portland, Ore.: Amadeus Press, 1997), pp. 11–42.

65 Reich, 'Women as Musicians', in Solie (ed.), *Musicology and Difference*, pp. 134–5.

66 Marie-Claire Le Moigne-Mussat, *Musique et société à Rennes aux XVIIIe et XIXe siècles* (Geneva: Minkoff, 1988), p. 319.

67 Florimo, *Cenno storico* (1869), p. 82.

68 *Ibid.*, p. 82.

69 *Instituzione e regolamenti pel conservatorio di musica in Milano* (Milan: Imperiale Regia Stamperia, 1816), p. 12.

70 *Ibid.*, p. 14.

71 Lodovico Melzi, *Cenni storici sul R. Conservatorio di Musica di Milano*, 2 vols. (Milan: R. Stabilmento Ricordi, 1873), vol. II, p. 33: The teacher in question was Paolina Filippi-Vaneri. 'This is the first time that a woman assumes a teaching role of so much importance in the Conservatorio, but the excellent technique and the refined taste that we have all admired in signora Filippi in the several concerts given at our conservatorio is guarantee of the outcome of the trial.'

72 Giusto Dacci, *Cenni storici e statistici intorno alla Reale Scuola di Musica a Parma: dal giorno 2 maggio 1818 (epoca della sua origine) a tutto l'anno scolastico 1886–87* (Parma: Luigi Battei, 1888), p. 19.

73 Florimo, *Cenno storico* (1869), p. 83.

74 *Ibid.*, 2nd rev. edn (1872), p. 57.

75 *Regolamenti per il Liceo Comunale di Musica in Bologna* (Bologna: Governativa Sassi, 1833), p. 8.

76 Dacci, *Cenni storici*, p. 165.

77 *L'Art musical*, 1/34, 25 July 1861, p. 267.

78 Le Moigne-Mussat, *Musique et société*, p. 322.

79 Dacci, *Cenni storici*, pp. 254–5.

80 *Ibid.*, pp. 254–7.

81 Giulietta and Elena Zoboli. *Ibid.*, pp. 282–3.

82 *Ibid.*, p. 295.

83 *Ibid.*, pp. 296–7.

84 Reich, in Solie (ed.), *Musicology and Difference*, p. 137.

85 Ehrlich, *Music Professsion in Britain*, p. 110.

86 See Hyde, *New Found Voices*, pp. 40–1.

87 Charles Villiers Stanford, *Studies and Memories* (London: Archibald Constable, 1908), p. 5.

88 Quoted in Harriette Brewer and James Francis Cooke, *Great Singers on the Art of Singing* (New York: Dover Publications Inc., 1996), p. 17.

89 See, for example, *Regolamenti per il Liceo comunale di musica in Bologna*, p. 10.

90 *Gazzetta musicale di Milano*, 4/6, 9 February 1845, p. 23. Francesco Regli gives this name as 'Sannazzaro' in his *Dizionario biografico dei più celebri poeti ed artisti melodrammatici, tragici e comici, maestri, concertisti, coreografi, mimi, ballerini, scenografi, giornalisti, impresarii, ecc. ecc. che fiorirono in Italia dal 1800 al 1860* (Turin: E. Dalmazzo, 1860).

91 Quoted in Frédérique Patureau, *Le Palais Garnier dans la société parisienne 1875–1914* (Liège: Mardaga, 1991), p. 122.

92 Georges Bizet, *Lettres de Georges Bizet: Impressions de Rome (1857–1860), La Comune (1871)* (Paris: Calmann Lévy, n.d.), pp. 291–2.

93 Shaw, *Music in London*, vol. II, p. 213. See also vol. III, pp. 120–1; and vol. I, pp. 40–1.

94 Lilli Lehmann, *How to Sing*, p. 2.

95 Quoted in Martens, *The Art of the Prima Donna*, p. 154.

96 *Ibid.*, p. 89.

97 Alda, *Men, Women and Tenors*, p. 305.

98 Lilli Lehmann, *How To Sing*, p. 6.

99 *Musical Standard*, 4/82, 25 July 1914, p. 66.

100 Kathleen Howard, *Confessions of an Opera Singer* (London: Kegan Paul & Co., 1920), pp. 57–8.

101 Marguerite D'Alvarez, *Forsaken Altars* (London: Rupert Hart-Davis, 1954).

102 Rosselli, *Singers of Italian Opera*, pp. 102–3.

103 Calvé, *My Life*, p. 235. See also Caruso, *On the Art of Singing*, pp. 70–1.

104 Blanche Marchesi, *A Singer's Pilgrimage*, p. 286.

105 Félia Litvinne, *Ma vie et mon art* (Paris: Librairie Plon, 1933), pp. 21–3.

106 Kellogg, *Memoirs of an American Prima Donna*, p. 323.

107 *Ibid.*, p. 320.

108 Eleonora Cisneros, interview in *New York Herald Tribune*, 29 December 1907.

109 R. D. Smith (ed.), *The Writings of Anna Wickham*, pp. 122–7.

110 *Ibid.*, p. 134.

111 *Ibid.*, p. xx.

112 *Ibid.*, p. 118.

113 Quoted by Charles Neider (ed.), in his introduction to *Papa: An Intimate Biography of Mark Twain by His Thirteen-year-old Daughter Susy* (New York: Doubleday, 1985), p. 12.

114 Blanche Marchesi described Susy as 'a case of voluntary self-starvation'. *A Singer's Pilgrimage*, p. 241.

115 Quoted by Neider, *Papa*, p. 19.

116 *Ibid.*, p. 44.

117 *Ibid.*, pp. 48–50.

118 Edith Colgate Salsbury, *Susy and Mark Twain: Family Dialogues* (New York: Harper & Row, 1965), pp. 344–5, 374–5 and 378–9.

119 *Ibid.*, pp. 381–3.

120 *Ibid.*, p. 345.

121 Viola Tree, *Castles in the Air: A Story of My Singing Days* (New York: George H. Doran Company, 1926), pp. 11–12.

122 *Ibid.*, p. 22.

123 *Ibid.*, p. 31.

124 *Ibid.*, p. 41.

125 *Ibid.*, pp. 288–9.

126 The reference to the 'Australian' is probably Nellie Melba (although it might also be Frances Alda); the relevant teacher was Marchesi. The 'Liverpudlian' singer was possibly Marie Brema, who made a very late professional debut in her mid-thirties having studied briefly with Henschel.

127 Tree, *Castles in the Air*, pp. 193–4.

4 THE SUPPORTING CAST

1 Gerd Nauhaus (ed.), *The Marriage Diaries of Robert and Clara Schumann*, trans. Peter Ostwald (London: Robson Books, 1994), pp. 15–17. Translation modified.

2 Ragni, 'Isabella Colbran: appunti per una biografia', pp. 22–35 passim.

3 Archivio Storico del Teatro Regio Carteggio A104, 24 November 1819: a poster for Tacchinardi's concert featuring his two daughters, aged eleven and thirteen, singing and playing the piano.

4 Merlin, *Memoirs of Madame Malibran*, vol. i, pp. 9–10.

5 See 'La cantante' in *Cosmorama pittorico*, 21/87, 25 November 1857, pp. 345–6 (and subsequent issues nos. 90, 91, 94, 96, 97); also Meini's 'Eleonora' in *Boccherini*.

6 Willert Beale, *The Light of Other Days*, 2 vols. (London: Richard Bentley & Son, 1890), vol. i, pp. 64–5.

7 Marcello, 'Alle madri delle virtuose', in *Il Teatro alla moda*, pp. 90–4.

8 Haydn, *La canterina* (1766; Bryn Mawr, PA: Theodore Presser, 1980).

9 Ashbrook, *Donizetti*, p. 543. The work was first performed as *Le convenienze teatrali* in 1827; it was later revised in 1831 to include Sografi's second *farsa* and performed as *Le convenienze e inconvenienze teatrali*.

10 Beale, *Light of Other Days*, pp. 73–4.

11 'Le madri dell'attrici', *Il pirata*, 3/49, 19 December 1837, pp. 203–4.

12 *Corriere delle dame*, 49/5, 3 February 1852, pp. 35–36.

13 Ashbrook, *Donizetti*, p. 102.

14 *New Grove Dictionary of Opera*, ed. Stanley Sadie (London & New York: Macmillan, 1992), vol. i, p. 389.

15 *Strenna teatrale europea*, 7 (1844), pp. 7–8.

16 Maretzek, *Revelations*, vol. ii, p. 2.

17 Marchesi, *Marchesi and Music*, p. 3. Perhaps the strangest treatment of a stage mother is Geraldine Farrar's bizarre depiction in *Such Sweet Compulsion* (New York: Greystone, 1938): her deceased mother is the book's narrator, and recounts (as imagined by Farrar) her daughter's life and career.

18 Frieda Hempel, *My Golden Age of Singing* (Portland, Ore.: Amadeus Press, 1998), p. 25. See also Frances Alda's description of her family in *Men, Women and Tenors*, pp. 22–3.

19 Lawton, *Schumann-Heink*, p. 22.

20 *Ibid.*, p. 19.

21 Alessandro Belardinelli, *Documenti Spontini inediti*, 2 vols. (Florence: Edizioni Sansoni Antiquariato, 1955), vol. ii, p. 288.

22 Benjamin Lumley, *Reminiscences of the Opera* (London: Hurst and Blackett, 1864), pp. 422–3.

23 Marchesi, *Marchesi and Music*, pp. 185–6.

24 This singer was possibly Felice Lyne (1891–1935), who on 25 November 1911 had appeared in her first major role as Gilda at the London Opera House to great acclaim. See Vincent Sheehan, *The Amazing Oscar Hammerstein* (London: Weidenfeld & Nicolson, 1956), pp. 318–26; and Oscar Thompson, *The American Singer* (New York: Dial Press, 1937), p. 321.

25 Henry Wood, *My Life of Music* (London: Victor Gollancz, 1938), p. 266.

26 Letter to Mr Beyland, 1 March 1826; quoted in Jean-Louis Tamvaco, *Les Cancans de l'Opéra: Le Journal d'une habilleuse 1836–1848*, 2 vols. (Paris: CNRS Editions, 2000), vol. II, p. 1024.

27 Mackenzie-Grieve, *Clara Novello*, p. 10.

28 A family friend, Hunt penned the following rhyme: 'Mary Novello / I know not your fellow / For having your way / Both by night and by day.' *Ibid.*, p. 4.

29 *Ibid.*, p. 160.

30 Eames, *Some Memories and Reflections*, p. 110.

31 *Ibid.*, p. 111.

32 *Ibid.*, pp. 127–8.

33 See Chapter 5.

34 Letter from Amanda Norton to her brother, November, 1882, quoted in Glackens, *Yankee Diva*, p. 103.

35 Kellogg, *Memoirs*, p. 365.

36 *Ibid.*, pp. 30–1.

37 Rasponi, *Last Prima Donnas*, p. 199.

38 *Ibid.*, pp. 467–71.

39 De Hegermann-Lindencrone, *In the Courts of Memory*, pp. 72–3. Some singers' claims to propriety are inaccurate: Luisa Tetrazzini, for example, wrote in her autobiography that during her trip to Buenos Aires in 1892 she was accompanied by a chaperone; this companion was in fact her lover, the bass-baritone Pietro Cesari. Gattey, *Luisa Tetrazzini*, p. 7.

40 Mapleson, *The Mapleson Memoirs*, p. 22. Male singers could also benefit from the counsel of quasi-stage mothers. The singing teacher Madame Puzzi (described by Rosenthal as a 'most judicious adviser on vocal matters' to Lumley during his management of Her Majesty's Theatre) figures in Mapleson's memoirs largely as the fearless and resourceful protector of the tenor Giuglini, rescuing him both from the

importunings of 'enterprising young women' and also from the manipulations of impresarios like Mapleson himself. Madame Puzzi (the former soprano Giacinta Toso and wife of the horn-player and conductor Giovanni Puzzi) was almost certainly also the model for Beale's caricature. *Ibid.*, pp. 40–5.

41 Gemma Bellincioni, *Io e il palcoscenico: trenta e un anno di vita artistica* (Milan: Società Anonima Editoriale, 1920), p. 5.

42 *Ibid.*, p. 22.

43 *Ibid.*, p. 67.

44 *Ibid.*, pp. 39–41.

45 Bianca Stagno-Bellincioni, *Roberto Stagno e Gemma Bellincioni intimi* (Florence: Monsalvato, 1943), pp. 11–12.

46 *Ibid.*, p. 12

47 Bellincioni, *Io e il palcoscenico*, pp. 80–1.

48 Stagno-Bellincioni, *Roberto Stagno e Gemma Bellincioni intimi*, p. 29.

49 Bellincioni, *Io e il palcoscenico*, p. 72.

50 Glackens, *Yankee Diva*, p. 17.

51 *Ibid.*, p. 49.

52 Letter, 28 March 1880; *ibid.*, p. 67.

53 *Ibid.*, p. 89.

54 *The Herald*, 14 August 1882; *ibid.*, p. 93.

55 1 October 1882; *ibid.*, pp. 95–6.

56 *Ibid.*, p. 79.

57 *Ibid.*, pp. 348–9.

58 Stendhal provides an interesting if typically flamboyant account of Micheroux (dubbed Michevaux) in *Souvenirs d'egotisme* (1832; Paris: Le Divan, 1927), pp. 115–31.

59 Letter, 21–22 October 1826, Paris; in Bruno Cagli and Sergio Ragni (eds.), *Gioachino Rossini: Lettere e documenti*, vol. III (Pesaro: Fondazione Rossini, 1996), pp. 16–17.

60 *Ibid.*, p. 14.

61 See Paolo Russo, 'Giuditta Pasta: cantante pantomimica', *Musica e storia*, 10/2 (2002), 497–528.

62 Cagli and Ragni (eds.), *Gioachino Rossini*, vol. III, p. 55.

63 Gaia Servadio, *The Real Traviata: The life of Giuseppina Strepponi, wife of Giuseppe Verdi* (London: Hodder & Stoughton, 1994), pp. 41–2.

64 Litvinne, *Ma vie et mon art*, p. 30.

65 Lawton, *Schumann-Heink*, pp. 39–41.

66 *Ibid.*, p. 55.

67 Melba, *Melodies and Memories*, p. 37.

68 Ralph P. Locke, 'Paradossi nel mecenatismo musicale delle donne in America', *Musica/Realtà*, 28/54 (November 1997), 37–64.

69 Ritter, *Woman as a Musician*, pp. 16–17.

70 Kellogg, *Memoirs*, pp. 319–20.

71 See Chapter 3.

72 *Gazzetta musicale di Firenze*, 1/18, 18 October 1853, p. 71.

73 Sister M. W. McCarthy (ed.), *More Letters of Amy Fay: The American Years, 1879–1916* (Detroit: Information Co-ordinators, 1986).

74 Amy Fay, *Music-Study in Germany* (1880; repr. New York: Dover, 1965), p. 35.

75 *Ibid.*, p. 117.

76 *Ibid.*, p. 28.

77 Eleanora de Cisneros, *New York Herald Tribune*, 29 December 1907.

78 Elaine Brody, *Paris: The Musical Kaleidoscope 1870–1925* (London: Robson Books, 1988), p. 226.

79 Winifred Ponder, *Clara Butt: Her Life-Story* (London: George G. Harrap & Co. Ltd., 1928), p. 103.

80 O'Connor, *Pursuit of Perfection*, p. 42.

81 Geraldine Farrar, *The Story of an American Singer, by Herself* (Boston & New York: Houghton Mifflin Company, 1916), p. 44.

82 Howard, *Confessions of an Opera Singer*, pp. 28–31.

83 *Ibid.*, p. 245.

84 *Ibid.*, p. 257.

85 O'Connor, *Pursuit of Perfection*, p. 123.

86 *New York Herald Tribune*, 3 December 1907, p. 4.

87 Garden and Biancolli, *Mary Garden's Story*, p. 271.

88 *Ibid.*, pp. 11–12.

89 Louis C. Elson, 'The Story of A Prima Donna', *Musical World*, 70/1, 17 May 1890, pp. 386–7.

90 Kellogg, *Memoirs*, p. 320.

91 Garden and Biancolli, *Mary Garden's Story*, p. 18.

92 This correspondence was discovered by Professor Mayer (Florence Mayer's grandson) in the 1950s. Transcribing it has presented various problems. Most of the letters are undated; many are incomplete; and

Garden's idiosyncratic handwriting has made deciphering their contents occasionally impossible. My transcriptions are therefore a tentative step towards establishing some kind of order and coherence. Wherever possible, I have suggested possible dates according to the factual information contained in the letters. In certain cases, no such information exists and my dating must obviously be regarded as highly suspect. The letters and my transcriptions are now lodged with the Chicago Historical Society.

93 Garden and Biancolli, *Mary Garden's Story*, p. 18.

94 Letter No. 14, December 1896[?].

95 *Ibid.*

96 Letter No. 25, 7 May 1899.

97 e.g. Letter No. 18, autumn 1897[?]; Letter No. 24, December 1898[?].

98 Garden and Biancolli, *Mary Garden's Story*, p. 137.

99 *Ibid.*, p. 271.

100 Letter No. 4, 10 June 1896.

101 *Ibid.*; also Letter No. 10, 20 July 1896. Garden was a mere two years younger than Florence Mayer, but was regarded (being unmarried) as a 'young American girl'.

102 Letter No. 6, summer 1896[?].

103 Garden and Biancolli, *Mary Garden's Story*, p. 19.

104 *Ibid.*, pp. 26–8.

105 Letter No. 27, summer 1899[?].

106 Letter No. 15, spring or early summer 1897[?]. See also Letter No. 16 (from Mina Adelaide to Florence Mayer), July 1897[?].

107 The evidence suggests that the M. Lée who with his sister accompanied Garden on this holiday was in fact the 'young doctor' with whom Garden later claimed she had had a passionate affair, and which ended in his unsuccessful suicide attempt. Garden and Biancolli, *Mary Garden's Story*, pp. 44–7.

108 Letter No. 25, 7 May 1899.

109 Garden claimed that Grehier had said it was no longer necessary to provide receipts, and had then changed his mind; *ibid.*

110 Letter No. 27, summer 1899[?].

111 *Philadelphia Inquirer*, 29 May 1909.

112 See Chapter 3.

113 The money paid to Clara Butt was to be regarded 'entirely as a gift of admiration', but some years later Butt discovered the identity of her sponsor (Lord Royston) and repaid the sum. Ponder, *Clara Butt*, p. 103. See also Farrar, *Geraldine Farrar*, p. 44.

114 *Philadelphia Inquirer*, 29 May 1909.

115 *The Evening World*, 27 March 1909.

116 Letter No. 2, May 1896.

117 Willa Cather, 'Scandal', in *Youth and the Bright Medusa* (New York: Alfred A. Knopf, 1920).

118 Cather based *The Song of the Lark* on the Swedish soprano Olive Fremstad, and *The Diamond Mine* on Lillian Nordica.

119 Quoted in Henry Scott Holland and W. S. Rockstro, *Memoir of Madame Jenny Lind-Goldschmidt: Her Early Art-life and Dramatic Career, 1820–1851*, 2 vols. (London: John Murry, 1891), vol. I, p. 317.

120 Quoted in Glackens, *Yankee Diva*, pp. 103.

121 *La moda*, 22, 14 March 1836, pp. 85–6. Other prima donnas, such as Christine Nilsson and Mary Garden, were plagued by stalkers (male and female): so too was Grisi's second husband, the tenor Mario.

122 Forbes, *Mario and Grisi*, p. 31.

123 Maretzek, *Revelations*, vol. I, pp. 160–2.

124 Piotr Ilyich Tchaikovsky, *Letters to His Family: An Autobiography*, trans. Galina Von Meck (New York: Stein & Day, 1981), pp. 45–6.

125 Mackenzie-Grieve, *Clara Novello*, pp. 176–81.

126 Rasponi, *Last Prima Donnas*, p. 195.

127 This was in marked contrast to the previous century, when singers in Italy (such as Marianna Monti at Naples in 1760) could be imprisoned or banished because of their associations with members of the aristocracy. Croce, *I teatri di Napoli*, pp. 177–80.

128 *The Musical World*, 18/48, 30 November 1843, p. 399.

129 Chorley, *Thirty Years*, vol. I, p. 73.

130 *Ibid.*, p. 78.

131 Lilli Lehmann, *My Path Through Life* (New York and London: G. P. Putnam's Sons, 1914), p. 114.

132 Holland and Rockstro, *Memoir*, vol. II, pp. 345–6.

133 Rasponi, *Last Prima Donnas*, p. 131. Finding supportive husbands is a perennial difficulty for opera singers: Clare Watson had similar problems with her marriage in the 1950s (*ibid.*, pp. 394–8 passim.)

134 Quoted in Glackens, *Yankee Diva*, p. 336.

135 Reforms of these laws varied: e.g. Married Women's Property acts were passed in New York State in 1848, in New Zealand in 1860 and 1870, and in Britain in 1882. In contrast, Germany rejected reform until after the First World War, whilst in France married women did not become 'independent legal persons' until 1938. See Evans, *The Feminists*, pp. 47, 61, 111 and 125–8.

136 Forbes, *Mario and Grisi*, p. 58.

137 See Chapter 3; also Holland and Rockstro, *Memoir*, vol. II, pp. 345–6.

138 Christiansen, *Prima Donna*, p. 296.

139 Enrico Rosmini, *La legislazione e la giurisprudenza dei teatri e dei diritti d'autore*, 2 vols. (Milan: F. Manini, 1876), vol. I, p. 363.

140 *Ibid.*, p. 361. See also Maura Palazzi, *Donne sole. Storia dell'altra faccia dell'Italia tra antico regime e società contemporanea* (Milan: Bruno Mondadori, 1997), pp. 116–18.

141 Quoted in Davis, *Anna Bishop*, p. 45.

142 A letter from Anna's father rather belies her assertion that he had given her his full support – at least, with regard to her decision to leave the marital home; *ibid.*, p. 43.

143 *The Times*, 25 July 1839, p. 5.

144 *The Times*, 26 July 1839, p. 7.

145 Davis, *Anna Bishop*, p. 105.

146 The separation agreement stipulated that Anna and Henry were each 'restrained from interfering or attempting to control the other', and 'gave each the right to live with whomever they chose'. Anna was also protected against any action for divorce on Bishop's side. She was given custody of the children, providing £95. 5s. annually for their support; in practice, however, the children remained with their father until her return. Bishop also 'relinquished all claim on Anna's earnings and property acquired since her departure'. *Ibid.*, pp. 109–10.

147 *Ibid.*, p. 81.

148 *Ibid.*, pp. 110–11.

149 Maretzek, *Revelations*, vol. I, pp. 160–2. Maretzek lists the kind of men who might marry a prima donna, including a 'green fish, recently caught in the army or navy', a waiter, an orchestra player, a 'desperate *maestro di canto*' who weds a singer 'as the last resort against suicide or

starvation', or even the valet of the prima donna's 'titled lover' in the case of inconvenient pregnancy. Whatever their former position, however, 'the first object in the life of a *prima donna*'s husband is to impress his wife with a vivid sense of his own importance to her'. He beats time when she is singing, turns the pages of her music, carries the poodle, fetches the carriage, closes all the windows and doors, and quarrels with the impresario. (Perhaps it was the last activity that most aroused Maretzek's antagonism.)

150 See, for example, 'Il marito della prima donna', *Gazzetta musicale di Milano*, 1/3, 16 January 1842, pp. 9–10; and 'Gli anni d'un procolo', in *Strenna teatrale europea*, 7 (1844), pp. 39–44.

151 Paola Colombo, 'Alcuni inediti di Giuditta Pasta', in *'Son regina, son guerriera': Giuditta Pasta: donna italiana, artista europea tra età neoclassica e romantica* (Saronno: Comune di Saronno, 1997), pp. 92–6.

152 Glackens, *Yankee Diva*, pp. 123–4.

153 *Ibid.*, p. 222.

154 *Ibid.*, pp. 264–5.

155 Tamvaco, *Les Cancans*, vol. I, p. 117. He was possibly referring to Jean Schneitzhoeffer, a timpanist at the Opéra.

156 Rasponi, *Last Prima Donnas*, p. 92.

157 *Ibid.*, p. 445.

158 Garden and Biancolli, *Mary Garden's Story*, p. 146.

159 *Ibid.*, p. 137.

5 PROFESSIONAL LIFE

1 Davies, *Europe: A History*, p. 1293.

2 The structure of 'number' opera argues against the notion of fluidity, but in fact within this particular structure there was a greater sense of 'interchangeability' of content, as different items were added by singers, and also within the area of decoration.

3 For example, the mutability of pitch, the access of women to heroic male roles, and so forth.

4 Including alterations to libretti (enforced by different censors according to individual political situations) and the addition or exchange of arias (particularly with regard to benefit performances).

5 Thomas Carlyle declared that in the opera house 'Music has, for a
long time past, been avowedly mad, divorced from sense and the
reality of things; and runs about now as an open Bedlamite . . .
bragging that she has nothing to do with sense and reality, but with
fiction and delirium only. . .' Thomas Carlyle, 'The Opera' (1852), in
The Works of Thomas Carlyle, Vol. xxix, p. 398. The accusation of
insanity has particular interest in this context, given that madness is
arguably both an innate quality of opera and a condition that in the
nineteenth century was ascribed predominantly to women. On the
former see Rosand: 'If madness is a peculiarly operatic condition
because it licenses the suspension of verisimilitude, so opera itself can
be said to be generically mad, for its double language provides a
perfect model for the splitting or fragmentation of character. The
opposition between text and music naturally embodies the conflicting
forces that disturb or undermine equilibrium.' Rosand, 'Operatic
Madness: A Challenge to Convention', in Steven Paul Scher (ed.),
Music and Text: Critical Inquiries (Cambridge: Cambridge University
Press, 1992), p. 287. On the latter, Elaine Showalter comments that the
era perceived madness as being a 'female malady': 'Women were
believed to be more vulnerable to insanity than men, to experience it
in specifically feminine ways, and to be differently affected by it in the
conduct of their lives.' *The Female Malady: Women, Madness and Culture
1830–1980* (London: Virago Press, 1987), p. 7.

6 Kimbell, *Verdi*, pp. 33–4.

7 B. Cassinelli, A. Maltempi and M. Pozzoni, *Rubini: l'uomo e l'artista*, 2
vols. (Comune di Romano di Lombardia: Cassa Rurale ed Artigiano di
Calcio e di Covo, 1993), vol. i, p. 153.

8 Berlioz, *Memoirs*, p. 372.

9 Lydia Goehr discusses the emergence of the work-concept in the early
nineteenth century, and how it came to shape philosophical
understanding of music as 'productive art' rather than 'performance'.
*The Imaginary Museum of Musical Works: An Essay in the Philosophy of
Music* (Oxford: Clarendon Press, 1992), p. 160.

10 See also texts by Metastasio and Algarotti.

11 Tacchinardi, *Dell'opera in musica sul teatro italiano e de' suoi difetti* (1833),
reprinted in Ciarlantini, 'Una testimonianza', p. 106.

12 *Ibid.*, p. 106.

13 *Ibid.*, p. 107.

14 One such example is William Holmes's account of the dispute between Margherita Gualandi and the Teatro San Bartolomeo in Naples in 1726, where he states that 'ego' was the 'motivating factor' behind Gualandi's actions. *Opera Observed: Views of a Florentine Impresario* (Chicago: University of Chicago Press, 1993), pp. 105–17.

15 Tacchinardi, *Dell'opera in musica*, p. 107.

16 *Ibid.*, p. 108.

17 Rosselli, *Opera Industry*, p. 65.

18 Velluti was also paid £2,300 the same season, but held the additional position of music director.

19 John Ebers, *Seven Years of the King's Theatre* (1828; repr. New York and London: Benjamin Blom, Inc., 1969), pp. 387–90. Pasta's season appears to have gone remarkably well, with no obvious disputes; Ebers commented that 'no performer has owed less to caprice or fashion; her reputation has been earned, and, what is more, deserved'.

20 *Ibid.*, pp. 283–5.

21 Sutherland Edwards, *History of the Opera, from Monteverdi to Donizetti*, 2 vols. (London: Wm. H. Allen & Co., 1862), vol. II, p. 23.

22 Cassinelli, Maltempi and Pozzoni, *Rubini*, vol. II, pp. 854–6. Interestingly, Comelli's salary was almost twice that of Rubini at this stage in his career; she was also given one benefit a year, whilst he was permitted only one during the whole of the three-year contract. The 'ridotti imperiali' were the two royal Viennese houses, the Kärntnertortheater and the Theater an der Wien.

23 Musi claimed that this contract had been signed 30 October 1831, and that it stated that Roser would perform 'tutte le recite e rappresentazioni' ordered by him. Interestingly, Musi does not address directly any of the points raised by Roser: he merely insists that the contract said 'tutte', and suggests that her only reason for refusing is that she can't sing the role. Letter from Musi to Sanvitale, 21 February 1832; Archivio Storico del Teatro Regio 1832, Fasc. III. Roser was probably not Musi's first choice as prima donna; his earlier correspondence with the theatre management (dated 3 May 1831) suggests that he had initially offered the contract to a Signora Melas; Archivio Storico del Teatro Regio 1831.

24 Letter from Lina Roser Balfe to Count Sanvitale, 19 February 1832; Archivio Storico del Teatro Regio 1832, Fasc. III.

25 See letter from Musi to Sanvitale, 10 February 1832; Archivio Storico del Teatro Regio 1832, Fasc. III; also Paolo-Emilio Ferrari, *Spettacoli drammatico-musicali e coreografici in Parma dall'anno 1628 all'anno 1883* (Parma 1884; repr. Bologna: Forni, 1969).

26 Letter to Sanvitale, 19 February 1832; Archivio Storico del Teatro Regio 1832, Fasc. III.

27 Letter to Sanvitale, 12 March 1832; Archivio Storico del Teatro Regio 1832, Fasc. III.

28 Letter from Johann Grünbaum to Spontini, 23 January 1834; Belardinelli, *Documenti Spontini inediti*, vol. II, pp. 221–2.

29 Spontini to the Intendant, 27 April 1834; *ibid.*, vol. II, p. 227.

30 Carlo Ritorni, *Ammaestramenti alla composizione d'ogni poema e d'ogni opera appartenente alla musica* (Milan: Giacomo Pirolo, 1841), pp. 49–50.

31 Kimbell, *Verdi*, p. 74.

32 Ashbrook, *Donizetti*, p. 252.

33 *Ibid.*, p. 678.

34 Letter, 21 May 1836, addressed to Alessandro Lanari: 'Lo scrivere colla Sig.ra Tacchinardi è reso oggi un imbarazzo, e ciò non per colpa sua: quando questa brava cantante non fà il suo dovere, tutto il mondo dice, è per favorire le opere di suo marito; e tu stesso in Firenze ne hai veduto prova. Nella *Lucia* io fui vittima, poichè essa non era al certo il migliore astro, quando aveva una scena che alle prove faceva tremare Duprez, ed io stesso sentia molte volte dirmi, *si calerà il Telone doppo* [*sic*] *l'aria della Persiani*. La cosa fu all'opposto. . . io non ne so il perchè, ma certo è però, che per schivare ogni diceria conviene che quella buona *Fanny* si sfiati, se non più, almeno al pari di quello che fà nelle opere di suo marito: Da ciò avviene, che prima di sottoscrivere le tue scritture vorrei sapere definitivamente quali opere, e prima, e dopo di me si daranno, acciò io non abbia il dispiacere di sentirmi dire, *quella non canta la vostra come quella dello sposo*, oppure *ella non abbia la pena di soffrir dispiaceri.*' Quoted in Guido Zavadini, *Donizetti: vita – musiche – epistolario* (Bergamo: Istituto Italiano d'Arti Grafiche, 1948), p. 410.

35 Quoted in Henry Pleasants, *The Great Singers* (London: Victor Gollancz Ltd., 1967), pp. 125–6.

36 Herbert Weinstock, Appendix A, *Rossini: A Biography* (1968; repr. New York: Limelight Editions, 1987), pp. 377–8.

37 Letter, Berlin, 19 December 1854; quoted in Heinz and Gudrun Becker, *Giacomo Meyerbeer: A Life in Letters*, trans. Mark Violette (London: Christopher Helm, 1989), p. 151.

38 Roger Parker, *Studies in Early Verdi 1832–1844: New Information and Perspectives on the Milanese Musical Milieu and the Operas from Oberto to Ernani* (New York and London: Garland, 1989), p. 157.

39 Susan Rutherford, 'Wilhelmine Schröder-Devrient: Wagner's Tragic Muse', in Maggie Gale and Viv Gardner (eds.), *Women, Theatre and Performance: New Histories, New Historiographies* (Manchester: Manchester University Press, 2000).

40 Richard Wagner, *Actors and Singers*, trans. William Ashton Ellis (Lincoln and London: University of Nebraska Press, 1995), p. 219.

41 23 March 1878; quoted in Dieter Borchmeyer, *Richard Wagner: Theory and Theatre*, trans. Stewart Spencer (Oxford: Clarendon Press, 1991), p. 328.

42 Leslie Orrey, *Bellini* (London: Dent, 1969), p. 24; Francesco Pastura, *Le lettere di Bellini 1819–1835* (Catania: Totalità, 1935), pp. 67–8.

43 Marcello Conati, *La bottega della musica: Verdi e La Fenice* (Milan: Il Saggiatore, 1983), p. 219; see also pp. 123–4.

44 Rimsky-Korsakov wrote of his battles in 1872 during the production of *The Maid of Pskov* with Petrov, who had complained about certain 'long-drawn passages and stage mistakes which it was difficult to overcome in the acting. He was right in many ways, but youth made me fly into a passion; I therefore yielded nothing, would not allow cuts, and naturally and obviously irritated both him and Napravnik exceedingly.' *My Musical Life*, p. 131.

45 Conati, *Bottega*, pp. 123–4.

46 Letter, 10 March 1853; *ibid.*, pp. 327–8.

47 Letter, 23 February 1827; Cagli and Ragni (eds.), *Gioachino Rossini*, vol. III, pp. 168–71.

48 On the question of interpolated arias see Hilary Poriss, 'Making Their Way Through the World: Italian One-Hit Wonders', *19th-Century Music*, 24/3 (Spring 2001), 197–224.

49 Becker, *Giacomo Meyerbeer*, pp. 116–17.

50 Letter to Ferrarini, 20 November 1829, Bologna; Archivio Storico del Teatro Regio Carteggio 22. The other singer was Elisa Orlandi (1811–c. 1833), whose promising career was cut short by her early death.

51 Bellincioni, *Io e il palcoscenico*, pp. 35–7. On the topic of cadenze and other embellishments, see Austin Caswell, 'Mme Cinti-Damoreau and the Embellishment of Italian Opera in Paris: 1820–1845', *Journal of the American Musicological Society*, 28 (Autumn 1975), 459–92.

52 Antonio Simone Sografi, *Le convenienze e le inconvenienze teatrali* (Florence: Felice Le Monnier, 1972), p. 106.

53 Joseph Kerman, *Opera as Drama* (London and Boston: Faber and Faber, 1988), pp. 13–16. See, for example, Luigi Prividali's criticisms in *Il censore universale dei teatri*, 94, 25 November 1829, p. 374.

54 Merlin, *Memoirs of Madame Malibran*, vol. II, pp. 48–51.

55 Hilary Poriss summarises various causes, including copyright legislation, publication of operatic scores, changes in the singer's status and aspects of formal operatic structure, and also adds 'that the act of recognizing a substitute aria underwent a subtle shift during the first half of the nineteenth century, and this shift affected how spectators, critics and others perceived these numbers within the context of individual productions'. Poriss, 'Verdi Meets Bellini', in Della Seta, Marvin and Marica (eds.), *Verdi 2001*, pp. 71–2.

56 Exceptions to this practice remained. Rimsky-Korsakov wrote a 'special aria' for Syekar-Rozhansky at his request for Mamontov's production of *The Tsar's Bride* in 1899: 'I had never composed special arias for anybody, but this time I could not help agreeing with him, as his remark about the more than inopportune brevity and incompleteness of Lykov's part was quite correct.' *My Musical Life*, p. 385.

57 See the letters to the mid-nineteenth-century *primo violino* and conductor Giulio Cesare Ferrarini.

58 Rimsky-Korsakov bewailed the chaos surrounding the production of *Mlada* at the Mariinsky Theatre in 1892, and the lack of a single person to 'unify' the different aspects of the production process. *My Musical Life*, p. 319.

59 Giulio Ricordi's *disposizione scenica* for the Italian premiere of *Aida* at La Scala in 1872: 'The stage director will, under no circumstances and under no pretext whatsoever, permit any artist, chorister, dancer, etc., etc., to make even the slightest changes in his or her costumes, wigs,

and jewelry, which were so scrupulously executed in accordance with the costume designs. These were studied with every possible care and executed by famous artists with scrupulous historical precision.' Hans Busch (ed.), *Verdi's* Aida: *The History of an Opera in Letters and Documents* (Minneapolis: University of Minnesota Press, 1978), p. 617.

60 Tree, *Castles in the Air*, p. 68.

61 One important dimension of the prima donna not considered here owing to lack of space is her own engagement in theatre management. See, for example, the careers of Angelica Catalani at the Théâtre-Italien in Paris (1815–18), Lucia Vestris at Covent Garden in London (1839–42), Emma Carelli at the Teatro Costanzi in Rome (1912–26), and Mary Garden for the Chicago Opera Association, USA (1912–22). A number of singers found opportunities as an impresario in smaller theatres (such as Emma Romer at the Surrey Theatre, 1852–5; Inez Fabbri at the California Theatre, San Francisco in the 1870s, Sofia Maslovskaya in Russia in the 1920s); or managing touring companies (for example, Clara Louise Kellogg in the US; Emily Soldene in Britain; Blanche Arral in south-east Asia). The topic of women managers in opera and operetta has been so far largely neglected by scholars, and is deserving of much greater attention.

62 Letter to Romani; quoted in Branca, *Felice Romani*, p. 168.

63 Letter to Minna Meyerbeer, 24 June 1832; Becker, *Giacomo Meyerbeer*, p. 55.

64 See, for example, the influence of the ministre des Beaux-Arts in Paris, described by Patureau, *Le Palais Garnier*, pp. 136–7.

65 Letter to Giulio Ricordi, 5 September 1835; Zavadini, *Donizetti*, p. 383.

66 Cagli and Ragni (eds.), *Gioachino Rossini*, vol. II, p. 416.

67 Josefine Schulz, 1790–1880. Her surname is also often given as 'Schulze'.

68 Letter, 27 March 1824; Belardinelli, *Documenti Spontini inediti*, vol. I, p. 163.

69 Letter to Verdi, 7 January 1871; Alessandro Luzio (ed.), *Carteggi verdiani*, 4 vols. (Rome: Reale Accademia d'Italia, 1935–47), vol. IV, p. 190.

70 Letter from Stolz to Ricordi, 6 January 1871; *ibid*, pp. 190–1.

71 Letter from Ricordi to Stolz, 7 January 1871; *ibid.*, p. 191.

72 Letter from Ricordi to Verdi, n.d.; *ibid.*, p. 192. Obviously, Stolz's lover Mariani was a factor in this business – or at least, Ricordi thought so.

73 Letter, 4 January 1833; Belardinelli, *Documenti Spontini inediti*, vol. II, pp. 196–7.

74 Christiansen, *Prima Donna*, p. 55. See the review from the *Examiner*, 24 September 1809 in Rowell, *Victorian Dramatic Criticism*, pp. 165–9.

75 De Boigne, *Petits mémoires de l'Opéra*, pp. 339–40.

76 *Harmonicon*, 8/12, December 1830, p. 504.

77 *Corriere dei teatri*, 19, 7 March 1838, pp. 74–5.

78 *Gazzetta musicale di Milano*, 9/40, 5 October 1851, pp. 185–6.

79 *Truth*; quoted in Mapleson, *The Mapleson Memoirs*, pp. 270–1.

80 Belardinelli, *Documenti Spontini inediti*, vol. I, p. 68.

81 Colombo, 'Alcuni inediti di Giuditta Pasta', p. 98.

82 Luzio (ed.), *Carteggi verdiani*, vol. IV, p. 195

83 *Memorie di un impresario di Maurizio Strakosch*, in Eugenio Gara (ed.), *L'impresario in angustie: Adelina Patti e altre stelle fuori leggenda (1886–1893) di Strakosch e Schürman* (Milan: Valentino Bompiani, 1940), p. 149.

84 Ebers, *Seven Years*, p. 298.

85 *Figaro*, 6/74, 15 September 1838, p. 296.

86 *Cosmorama pittorico*, 21/57, 14 August 1837, p. 250.

87 Rosselli, *Opera Impresario*, pp. 63–5; also p. 129.

88 Letter, 29 September 1829; Cagli and Ragni (eds.), *Gioachino Rossini*, vol. III, pp. 560–3.

89 Letter, 30 September 1829; *ibid.*, vol. III, pp. 564–71.

90 Letter, 16 February 1827; *ibid.*, vol. III, pp. 156–9.

91 *I teatri*, 3/2/32, 2 December 1829, p. 531.

92 Ebers, *Seven Years*, pp. 48–9.

93 Letter, 1 January 1825; Belardinelli, *Documenti Spontini inediti*, vol. I, p. 217.

94 Letter, 1 December 1840, written in St Petersburg; quoted in Colombo, 'Alcuni inediti di Giuditta Pasta', p. 100.

95 Ragni, 'Isabella Colbran', pp. 22–3.

96 Escudier Frères, *Etudes biographiques sur les chanteurs contemporains, précédées d'une esquisse sur l'art du chant* (Paris: Just Tessier, 1840), pp. 154–65.

97 Litvinne, *Ma vie et mon art*, p. 33.

98 Rosselli, *Opera Industry*, p. 21.

99 Cagli and Ragni (eds.), *Gioachino Rossini*, vol. III, p. 680.

100 Although no letters from Florence Mayer to Garden have survived, it is possible on occasions such as the above to glean some idea of the type of questions she asked Garden.

101 Letter No. 24, from Garden to Florence Mayer, December 1898[?]

102 Christiansen, *Prima Donna*, p. 281.

103 Letter No. 27, from Garden to D. Mayer, early summer, 1899[?]

104 Sheehan, *The Amazing Oscar Hammerstein*, p. 287. Also Kathleen Howard, *Confessions of an Opera Singer*, pp. 51 and 80.

105 O'Connor, *Pursuit of Perfection*, p. 67.

106 Litvinne, *Ma vie et mon art*, p. 36.

107 Blanche Arral, *The Extraordinary Operatic Adventures of Blanche Arral*, trans. Ira Glackens, ed. William Moran (Portland, Ore. and Cambridge: Amadeus Press, 2002), pp. 230–3.

108 *Memorie di un impresario di Maurizio Strakosch*, in Gara (ed.), *L'impresario in angustie*, p. 147.

109 Ciarlanti, 'Una testimonianza', p. 66. Théophile Gautier claimed that if 'feminine imagination' wished for a 'charming young man' as a tenor, nature often dispensed voices according to the configuration of the larynx rather than the purity of a profile or physical elegance; thus Napoleone Moriani's thick neck and gloomy appearance and his advanced age – over forty – belied his stature as 'a great artist'. *Histoire de l'art dramatique en France*, 4 vols. (Paris: Hetzel, 1858), vol. IV, pp. 123–5.

110 Ebers, *Seven Years*, p. 281.

111 Lorenzo Da Ponte, *Memoirs*, trans. Elisabeth Abbott (New York: New York Review of Books, 2000), p. 266.

112 Comte Armand De Pontmartin, *Souvenirs d'un vieux mélomane* (Paris: Calmann Lévy, 1879), p. 19.

113 Luigi Francesco Valdrighi and Giorgio Ferrari-Morena, *Cronistoria dei teatri di Modena dal 1539 al 1871 del maestro Alessandro Gandini arrichita d'interessanti notizie e continuata fino al presente da Luigi Francesco Valdrighi & Giorgio Ferrari-Morena* (Modena: Tipografia Sociale, 1873), p. 95.

114 Letter to Ferrarini; Archivio Storico del Teatro Regio Carteggio 22.

115 However, Shalyapin also points out that 'in Italy censure of the artist was never considered a disgrace. In reproving him, there was no personal attack. The censure lay somewhere within the framework of aesthetic evaluation.' Nina Froud and James Hanley (eds.), *Chaliapin: An Autobiography as Told to Maxim Gorky* (London: Macdonald & Co., 1967), p. 152.

116 Valerio Cervetti (ed.), *Dietro il sipario: 1881–1898: memorie e appunti del Segretario della Commissione Teatrale Giulio Ferrarini* (Parma: Grafiche STEP, 1986), p. 16.

117 *Ibid.*, p. 19.
118 Letter, 3 May 1835; Zavadini, *Donizetti*, p. 372.
119 Letter to Ferrarini; Archivio Storico del Teatro Regio Carteggio 22.
120 *Memorie di un impresario di Maurizio Strakosch*, in Gara (ed.), *L'impresario in angustie*, p. 147.
121 Tree, *Castles in the Air*, p. 113.
122 Marcello De Angelis, *Le carte dell'Impresario: Melodramma e costume teatrale nell'Ottocento* (Florence: G. C. Sansoni, 1982), p. 149.
123 Rosmini, *La legislazione e la giurisprudenza dei teatri*, p. 513.
124 Letter, 24 May [1833?]; Belardinelli, *Documenti Spontini inediti*, vol. II, p. 202.
125 Letter from Grünbaum to Spontini, 26 January 1834; *ibid.*, vol. II, p. 222.
126 Cervetti (ed.), *Dietro il sipario*, p. 11.
127 Rosmini, *La legislazione e la giurisprudenza dei teatri*, p. 513.
128 Quoted in Mario Rinaldi, *Due secoli di musica al Teatro Argentina*, 3 vols. (Florence: Leo S. Olschki, 1978), vol. I, p. 363.
129 See Nicola Tabanelli, *Le 'scritture teatrali' degli artisti lirici e drammatici* (Padua: A. Milani, 1938), pp. 203–4.
130 De Angelis, *Le carte dell'Impresario*, p. 149.
131 O'Connor, *Pursuit of Perfection*, p. 104.
132 Colombo, 'Alcuni inediti di Giuditta Pasta', p. 98.
133 Bellincioni, *Io e il palcoscenico*, pp. 61–2.
134 Letter to Giulio Cesare Ferrarini at Ferrara, 21 [?] 1854, sent from Rovigo; Archivio Storico del Teatro Regio Carteggio 22.
135 Letter to the Presidenza of the Teatro La Fenice, 30 January 1853; quoted in Conati, *La bottega della musica*, p. 312. Writing also to the Presidenza some days later regarding Verdi's proposed three singers (Penco, Piccolomini and Boccabadati), Lasina claimed that Boccabadati 'was not a competent woman and *di convenienza* in any respect': a phrase that might refer either to her professionalism or her moral conduct, or both. Given that a year later Boccabadati was caring for a small child, this statement might be a veiled reference to an illegitimate pregnancy.
136 *Italia musicale*, 4/8, 28 January 1852, p. 31: a review of *Giuramento* at the Pergola in Firenze.
137 Letter to Ferrarini, 30 June 1854, Bologna; Archivio Storico del Teatro Regio Carteggio 22.

138 Letter to Ferrarini, 20 July 1854, Rimini; Archivio Storico del Teatro Regio Carteggio 22.

139 Letter to Ferrarini, 18 October 1854, Rovigo; Archivio Storico del Teatro Regio Carteggio 22.

140 Letter to Ferrarini, undated (suggested date 19 October 1854), Rovigo; Archivio Storico del Teatro Regio Carteggio 22.

141 Letter, 20 October, 1854, Rovigo; Archivio Storico del Teatro Regio Carteggio 22.

142 Letter, 10 [..bre], 1855, Viterbo; Archivio Storico del Teatro Regio Carteggio 22.

143 The tenor was Bernardo Massimigliani; the baritone was Mazzanti. *L'armonia*, 1/41, 31 December 1856, p. 164.

144 Ferrari, *Spettacoli drammatico-musicali*, p. 246; also see Torregiani's review in *L'armonia*, 4/2, 30 January 1857, p. 170.

145 Letter to Ferrarini, 28 February, no year, no place; Archivio Storico del Teatro Regio Carteggio 22.

146 Letter from Virginia Boccabadati Carignani, 16 December 1861, Turin; Archivio Storico del Teatro Regio Carteggio 22.

147 Gino Monaldi, *Cantanti celebri 1829–1929* (Rome: Tiber, 1929).

148 Bellincioni, *Io e il palcoscenico*, pp. 130–7.

149 Toti Dal Monte, *Una voce nel mondo* (Milan: Longanesi, 1985).

150 Anna Maria Pellegrini Celoni, *Grammatica o siano regole per ben cantare* (Rome: Francesco Bourlie, 1817), p. vii.

151 On the emergence of the theatrical autobiography, its common narrative elements and its usefulness (or otherwise) to an understanding of stage life and practice, see Thomas Postlewait, 'Autobiography and Theatre History', in Postlewait and McConachie (eds.), *Interpreting the Theatrical Past*.

152 Eames, *Some Memories and Reflections*, p. 301.

6 VOCAL AND THEATRICAL LANDSCAPES

1 *The Diaries of William Charles Macready: 1833–1851*, ed. W. Toynbee (London: Chapman & Hall Ltd., 1912), vol. I, pp. 29–30.

2 Gautier, *Histoire de l'art dramatique*, p. 184.

3 Wagner, 'On Actors and Singers', p. 203.

4 Robert L. Jacobs and Geoffrey Skelton (eds.), *Wagner Writes from Paris* (London: George Allen & Unwin Ltd., 1973), p. 58.

5 Stendhal, *Life of Rossini*, p. 157.

6 *Ibid.*, pp. 164–6. Simon Maguire claims that Stendhal did not witness the *prima* of *Elisabetta* himself, but either saw Colbran on a later occasion on was citing the opinions of others. *Vincenzo Bellini and the Aesthetics of Early Nineteenth-Century Italian Opera*, Ph.D. Diss. (New York and London: Garland Publishing Inc., 1989), pp. 64–5.

7 See Celletti: '*verismo* created the mythology of the actor-singer, and still more of the actress-singer', *A History of Bel Canto*, p. 200.

8 George Brandt (ed.), *German and Dutch Theatre, 1600–1848* (Cambridge: Cambridge University Press, 1993); George Taylor, *Players and Performances in the Victorian Theatre* (Manchester: Manchester University Press, 1989).

9 Denis Diderot, 'Observations sur Garrick', *Œuvres complètes*, vol. xx (Paris: Hermann, 1995), p. 33.

10 Engel's work was translated into French in 1795, into English in 1807 by Henry Siddons, and then into Italian in 1818–19 by Giovanni Rasori.

11 Henry Siddons, *Practical Illustrations of Rhetorical Gesture and Action, adapted to the English Drama, from a work on the same subject by M. Engel* (London: Richard Phillips, 1807), pp. 15–16.

12 Hans Busch (ed.), *Verdi's* Otello *and* Simon Boccanegra *in Letters and Documents*, 2 vols. (Oxford: Clarendon Press, 1988), vol. ii, p. 616.

13 Taylor, *Players and Performances*, pp. 30–3.

14 *Ibid.*, pp. 33 and 45.

15 Susanne K. Langer, *Philosophy in a New Key* (Cambridge, Mass.: Harvard University Press, 1942), p. 235.

16 Letter from Bellini to Count Pepoli in 1834; quoted in Fitzlyon, *Maria Malibran*, p. 188.

17 Quoted in Budden, *The Operas of Verdi*, vol. iii, p. 309.

18 G. Grant, *The Science of Acting* (1838); quoted in Taylor, *Players and Performances*, p. 38. The connection between the singer and actor in this respect owed much to melodrama's use of music which necessitated particular vocal techniques; *ibid.*, pp. 125–9.

19 Constantin Stanislavski, *Building a Character* (London: Methuen, 1950), pp. 82–108.

20 Lehmann, *My Path Through Life*, pp. 176–7.

21 Rasponi, *Last Prima Donnas*, p. 199; see also Bidú Sayão's description of her debut at the Teatro Costanzi minus rehearsals in 1926 on p. 509. Rosselli describes other instances of rehearsal practice in Italian opera houses, *Singers of Italian Opera*, pp. 162–3.

22 Calvé, *My Life*, pp. 183–4. At Covent Garden in the 1850s, Patti actually had a 'clause inserted in her contract excusing her from attending rehearsals'. Rosenthal, *Two Hundred Years at Covent Garden*, p. 86.

23 Howard, *Confessions*, pp. 222–4.

24 Quoted in Martens, *Art of the Prima Donna*, p. 70.

25 Lehmann, *My Path Through Life*, p. 63.

26 Kellogg, *Memoirs*, p. 34.

27 Quoted in Kimbell, *Italian Opera*, p. 562.

28 Quoted in Martens, *Art of the Prima Donna*, p. 70.

29 Gabriele Baldini, *Abitare la battaglia: La storia di Giuseppe Verdi*, ed. Fedele Amico (Milan: Garzanti, 2001), pp. 56–8.

30 Anderson and Zinsser, *A History of their Own*, vol. II, pp. 145–7.

31 See, for example, Lichtenthal, *Trattato dell'influenza della musica sul corpo umano*, pp. 29–31.

32 *Ibid.*

33 Budden argues that 'the ideal of an even vocal quality from top to bottom of a singer's compass was unknown to Verdi's contemporaries. A sharp break, like a change of gear, between registers, so objectionable today, was tolerated then and indeed this yodelling effect can still be heard in some pre-electric recordings' (*The Operas of Verdi*, vol. II, pp. 68–9). Earlier voice teachers such as Tosi and Giovanni Battista Mancini had advocated a very different method. In 1776, Mancini wrote that 'The great art of the singer consists in acquiring the ability to render imperceptible to the ear the passing from one register to the other' (quoted in Reid, *Bel canto*, p. 68). The continuation of such ideas well into the nineteenth century is demonstrated not only by the writings of other tutors such as Giacomo Ferrari, but also by reviews of Rubini that comment on his ability to bridge the registers 'so marvellously that it is impossible to seize the moment of transition' (*ibid.*, p. 70).

34 On Pasta, see Stendhal, *Life of Rossini*, p. 374; on Malibran, see Fitzlyon, *Maria Malibran*, p. 32; on Viardot, see Chorley, *Thirty Years Musical Recollections*, vol. II, p. 42.

35 *Gazzetta musicale di Milano*, 18/22, 27 May 1860, pp. 169–71.

36 Duprez, *Souvenir d'un chanteur*, p. 79.

37 *Gazzetta musicale di Milano*, 18/23, 3 June 1860, pp. 177–9.

38 Robert Rushmore, *The Singing Voice* (London: Hamish Hamilton, 1971), pp. 31–6.

39 Rasponi, *Last Prima Donnas*, p. 192.

40 *Ibid.*, p. 470.

41 Gaetano Cesari and Alessandro Luzio (eds.), *I copialettere di Giuseppe Verdi* (1913; repr. Bologna: Forni, 1987), p. 61.

42 Blanche Marchesi, *A Singer's Pilgrimage*, p. 223.

43 Panofka, *Voci e cantanti*, pp. 86–8.

44 In contrast, the *Heldentenor* and the *tenore di forza* more closely conformed to nineteenth-century concepts of masculinity – or at least, despite their theatrical costume and make-up, could be made to seem so, as James Huneker's account of the popular De Reszke brothers and the baritone Jean Lasalle, published in the *Musical Courier* in 1899, revealed: 'Someone hums, and instantly the room is flooded with tone, the Great Trio from *William Tell*, perhaps. Jean sings C-sharp without effort. Then that rapturous breakdown known as the can-can is indulged in and suddenly a fierce dispute about the psychic possibilities of Hamlet arise, and is ended only by a call for fresh beverages. These big fellows are men, men. They play billiards, run, wrestle, smoke, and possibly swear, too.' Quoted in Eaton, *The Miracle of the Met* (Westport, Conn.: Greenwood Press, 1968), p. 92.

45 Quoted in Glackens, *Yankee Diva*, p. 344.

46 Olive Schreiner, *Woman and Labour* (1911; repr. London: Virago, 1978), pp. 145–6.

47 Raisa, in Martens, *Art of the Prima Donna*, p. 245.

48 Christiansen, *Prima Donna*, p. 176.

49 Melba, *Melodies and Memories*, p. 110.

50 Quoted in Weinstock, *Rossini*, p. 253.

51 'Non più contralti', in the *Gazzetta musicale di Firenze*, 1/17, 6 October 1853, pp. 65–6, and 1/19, 20 October 1853, pp. 73–4.

52 Poizat, *The Angel's Cry*, p. 105.

53 Gautier, *Poésies complètes*, vol. III, pp. 31–4.

54 For example, Leigh Hunt admired the contralto voice of Ann Tree because her low notes were 'deep enough without being masculine'.

Review in the *Examiner*, 26 December 1819; quoted in Fenner, *Leigh Hunt*, p. 93.

55 *The Harmonicon*, 10/6, June 1832, p. 144.

56 Dr Edouard Toulouse; quoted in Gay, *The Bourgeois Experience*, vol. I, p. 193.

57 Lichtenthal, *Trattato dell'influenza della musica sul corpo umano*, p. 29.

58 Hahn, *On Singers and Singing*, pp. 223–8.

59 Quoted in Martens, *Art of the Prima Donna*, pp. 270–1.

60 Letter from G. Brenna to Marzari, Busseto, 24 April 1852. Marcello Conati, *La bottega della musica: Verdi e La Fenice* (Milan: Saggiatore, 1983), pp. 285–6. See also Budden, *Operas of Verdi*, vol. II, p. 115.

61 Budden, *Operas of Verdi*, vol. I, p. 7. Rossini's *musico* roles included Silveno in *Demetrio e Polibio* (1812), the title role of *Tancredi*; Malcolm, *La donna del lago*, and Arsace, *Semiramide* (amongst others). Celletti claims that Rossini's use of a tenor rather than a contralto in *Elisabetta, regina d'Inghilterra* in 1815 was due to the influence of Isabella Colbran, 'who would not have tolerated being flanked by a great contralto'. 'L'arte vocale', in *Il Teatro di San Carlo*, 2 vols., ed. Raffaele Ajello and Carlo Marinelli (Naples: Guida, 1987), vol. I, pp. 290–1. But Colbran later partnered both Pisaroni (as Malcolm) *and* Mariani (as Arsace). Roles by Donizetti include the title role of *Enrico di Borgogna* (1818); Abenamet, *Zoraide di Grenata* (1822); Muley-Hassan, *Alahor in Granata* (1826); Zeidar, *Elvida* (1826); Raoul, *Gabriella di Vergy* (comp. 1826); Camillo, *Olivo e Pasquale* (1827); Smeton, *Anna Bolena* (1830); Luigi V, *Ugo conte di Parigi* (1832); Garzia, *Sancia di Castiglia* (1832); Aurelio, *L'assedio di Calais* (1836); Rodrigo, *Pia de' Tolomei* (1837); and Gondì in the revised version of *Maria di Rohan* (1843).

62 Berlioz, *Memoirs*, p. 134.

63 Berlioz also disliked this performance, complaining that a breeches role was 'a costume scarcely suited to the somewhat motherly outlines of [Schröder-Devrient's] figure'. *Ibid.*, p. 290.

64 Ritorni, *Ammaestramenti*, p. 185.

65 Letter from Guglielmo Brenna to Marzari, Busseto, 24 April 1852, in Conati, *La bottega*, pp. 285–6. See also Budden, *Operas of Verdi*, vol. II, p. 115.

66 Panofka, *Voci e cantanti*, pp. 121–2.

67 Chorley, *Thirty Years*, vol. II, p. 43.

68 *Ibid.*, p. 93.

69 Letter to Cammarano, 2 January 1851; quoted in Kimbell, *Verdi*, p. 282.
70 Letter to Cammarano, 9 April 1851; *ibid.*, p. 284.
71 Quoted in Fabrizio Della Seta, 'The Librettist', in Bianconi and Pestelli (eds.), *Opera Production and Its Resources*, p. 263.
72 Quoted in Martens, *Art of the Prima Donna*, p. 158.
73 *Ibid.*, p. 20.
74 Rosselli, *Singers of Italian Opera*, p. 138.
75 Martens, *Art of the Prima Donna*, p. 272.

7 THE SINGING ACTRESS

1 Stendhal, *Life of Rossini*, pp. 144–6.
2 *Il censore universale dei teatri*, 54, 8 July 1829, p. 213.
3 Performance at the Teatro Carcano, Milan; *Corriere delle dame*, 15, 14 October 1804, pp. 20–1. The singer in question was probably the Spanish Soprano Lorenza Correa (1777 – post 1831).
4 Giorgi Righetti, *Risposta a un giornale*, p. 38.
5 Claudio Meldolesi and Ferdinando Taviani, *Teatro e spettacolo nel primo Ottocento* (Rome and Bari: Laterza, 1998), p. 148.
6 Ritorni, *Annali*, p. 192. Pasta was compared favourably with the French actress Mlle Marguerite Georges (1787–1867) and Sarah Siddons (1755–1831).
7 Ritorni, *Ammaestramenti*, p. 176.
8 Quoted in Russo, 'Giuditta Pasta: cantante pantomimica', p. 518.
9 Cagli and Ragni (eds.), *Gioachino Rossini*, vol. III, p. 113.
10 Ritorni, *Ammaestramenti*, p. 176.
11 Ciarlantini, 'Una testimonianza sul teatro musicale', p. 66.
12 Stendhal, *Life of Rossini*, p. 385.
13 *The Harmonicon*, 3/41 June 1826, p. 132.
14 *Il censore universale dei teatri*, 54, 8 July 1829, pp. 213–14.
15 Diary entry dated 11 February 1841, in Nauhaus (ed.), *The Marriage Diaries of Robert and Clara Schumann*, p. 61.
16 David Luke and Robert Pick (trans. and eds.), *Goethe: Conversations and Encounters* (London: Oswald Wolff, 1966), p. 218.
17 Quoted in Pleasants, *Great Singers*, p. 155.
18 Wagner, *Actors and Singers*, pp. 217–19.
19 *Ibid.*, p. 219.

20 Quoted in Pleasants, *Great Singers*, pp. 152–3. Chorley also refers to this trait when he describes Schröder-Devrient's 'passion of by-play' in the same opera. *Thirty Years*, vol. I, p. 57.

21 Eduard Devrient, *Geschichte der deutschen Schauspielkunst* (1848), quoted in Brandt (ed.), *German and Dutch Theatre*, p. 305.

22 Ellen Creathorne Clayton, *Queens of Song* (London: Smith, Elder & Co., 1863), pp. 70–1.

23 Chorley, *Thirty Years*, vol. I, p. 56.

24 Wagner, *Actors and Singers*, p. 219.

25 Wagner, *My Life*, p. 285.

26 Barthes, *Image Music Text*, p. 184.

27 Heath, 'Translator's Note'; *ibid.*, p. 9.

28 Berlioz, *Memoirs*, pp. 311–17. The fact that Berlioz and Chorley found much to complain about in Schröder-Devrient's performances is read by some commentators such as Newman as proof that Wagner's own critical faculties were blinded by the singer. But in his autobiography he acknowledges the limitations of her vocal technique and the mannerisms that pervaded her acting by 1842. Nevertheless, such 'weaknesses' did not obscure for him the 'grand and incomparable element' in her performances that continued to bring him 'profound delight'. Wagner, *My Life*, p. 227.

29 Berlioz, *Memoirs*, p. 317.

30 Fitzlyon, *Maria Malibran*, p. 29.

31 *The Musical World*, 1/9, 13 May 1836, p. 140.

32 Pirandello on Duse (1924): 'For her art is wholly and always an art of movement. It is a continuous, restless, momentary flow, which has neither time nor power to stop and fix itself in any given attitude, even for the pleasure of showing for a moment the beauty that a pose may have in the truth of its expression.' Bentley (ed.), *Theory of the Modern Stage*, p. 165.

33 Fitzlyon, *Maria Malibran*, p. 96.

34 *Figaro*, 3/14, 18 February 1835, pp. 53–4.

35 Quoted in A. M. Nagler (ed.), *A Source Book in Theatrical History* (New York: Dover Publications, 1952), p. 302.

36 Macready, *Diaries*, vol. I, p. 236.

37 Fitzlyon, *Maria Malibran*, pp. 205–6.

38 Christiansen, *Prima Donna*, p. 73.

39 *The Musical World*, 13/196, n.s. 5/103, 19 December 1839, p. 527.

40 Nagler, *Source Book*, p. 302.

41 Commenting on a poor production of Rossi's *Amelia* at the Teatro di San Carlo in Naples in 1835, Guillaume Cottrau wrote that the costumes were 'completely disparate, anachronistic, like some impromptu charade'; quoted in Ashbrook, *Donizetti*, p. 94.

42 See Nagler, *Source Book*, pp. 301–5.

43 Kellogg, *Memoir*, p. 38.

44 Chorley, *Thirty Years*, vol. I, pp. 40–41.

45 *The Harmonicon*, 6/7, July 1828, p. 172.

46 Fitzlyon, *Maria Malibran*, p. 115.

47 Duprez in *Voix d'opéra*, pp. 74–5.

48 *Gazzetta musicale di Firenze*, 2/9, 10 August 1854, p. 36.

49 Klein, *Great Women Singers*, pp. 89–90. See also Monaldi, *Cantanti celebri*, p. 135.

50 See, for example, Jill Edmonds, 'Princess Hamlet', in Gardner and Rutherford (eds.), *The New Woman and Her Sisters*, pp. 59–76. On earlier operatic examples of *travesti* roles, see Nina Treadwell, 'Female Operatic Cross-Dressing: Bernardo Saddumene's Libretto for Leonardo Vinci's *Li zite 'n galera* (1722)', *Cambridge Opera Journal*, 10/2 (July 1998), 131-56.

51 Elizabeth Howe, *The First English Actresses: Women and Drama 1660–1700* (Cambridge: Cambridge University Press, 1992), p. 56.

52 *Corriere delle dame*, 1, 5 January 1806, pp. 433–4.

53 This illustration of Maria Malibran as Leonore can be found in *Fidelio*, *English National Opera Guide No. 4*, (London: John Calder, 1980) p. 12.

54 On Pasta, see the illustration of her in Michin's *Maleck-Adel* in 1831, in Beniamino Gutierrez, *Il Teatro Carcano (1803–1913). Glorie artistiche e patriottiche, decadenza e resurrezione* (Bologna: Arnaldo Forni, 1916), p. 71; on Schröder-Devrient as Romeo, see figures 22 and 23, drawings by Carl Heidelhof, in Herbert Barth, Dietrich Mack and Egon Voss, *Wagner: A Documentary Study*, trans. P. R. J. Ford and Mary Whittall (New York: Oxford University Press, 1975); on Henriette Kriete as Adriano, see figure 49, von Leyser's watercolour of *Rienzi*, in the same volume.

55 Henri Blaze de Bury, *Musiciens contemporains* (Paris: Michel Lévy Frères, 1856), p. 287.

56 Tacchinardi, *Dell'opera in musica*, in Ciarlantini, 'Una testimonianza', p. 99.

57 Blaze de Bury, *Musiciens contemporains*, p. 287.

58 Cagli and Ragni (eds.), *Gioachino Rossini*, vol. I, pp. 566 and 573.

59 Blanche Roosevelt, *Stage-struck, or, She would be an opera-singer* (London: S. Low, Marston, Searle & Rivington, 1884), pp. 347–53.

60 Quoted in MacKenzie-Grieve, *Clara Novello*, p. 237. Rosselli cites other examples of singers' antipathy for the breeches roles: see *Singers of Italian Opera*, pp. 58–9. See also Victorian actress Nelly Ternan's distress in a similar situation in Claire Tomalin, *The Invisible Woman* (London: Penguin, 1991), p. 64.

61 Quoted in Klein, *Great Women Singers*, p. 76.

62 Fenner, *Leigh Hunt*, p. 60.

63 Rasponi, *Last Prima Donnas*, p. 456.

64 Calvé, *My Life*, pp. 32–3.

65 See, for example, photographs of Cicely Gleeson White prior to 1910, and Lotte Lehmann in the 1920s.

66 Richard von Krafft-Ebing, *Psychopathia sexualis* (1886); quoted in Elaine Showalter, *Sexual Anarchy: Gender and Culture at the Fin de Siècle* (London: Bloomsbury, 1991), p. 23.

67 Isabelle Moindrot, 'Le geste et l'idéologie dans le "grand opéra" "La Juive" de Fromental Halévy', *Romantisme*, 102 (1998), 63–79, p. 65.

68 On Engel, see Chapter 6; also Gilbert Austin, *Chironomia* (London, 1806); Antonio Morrocchesi, *Lezioni di declamazione e d'arte teatrale* (1832; repr. Rome: Gremese, 1991); Gustave Garcia, *The Actor's Art: A Practical Treatise* (London: Simpkin, Marshall & Co., 1888); Henry Neville in *Voice, Speech and Gesture: A Practical Handbook to the Elocutionary Art*, ed. R. D. Blackman (London: C. W. Deacon and Co., 1895). Mary Ann Smart has explored the relevance of gestural language to the composition of opera in *Mimomania: Music and Gesture in Nineteenth-Century Opera* (Berkeley and Los Angeles: University of California Press, 2004).

69 The use of such gestures is further evidenced by early cinema; see, for example, Roberta Pearson, *Eloquent Gestures: The Transformation of Performance Style in the Griffith Biograph Films* (Oxford and Berkeley: University of California Press, 1992).

70 Quoted in Mary Ann Smart, 'The Lost Voice of Rosine Stoltz', in Blackmer and Smith (eds.), *En Travesti*, p. 183.

71 Kellogg, *Memoir*, p. 29.

72 May Agate, *Madame Sarah* (London, 1946), p. 108. Charles Dickens, who saw Viardot as Orfeo in Paris in 1862, was moved to tears by her 'extraordinary performance' and 'sublime acting': 'It is worth a journey to Paris to see, for there is no such Art to be otherwise looked upon.' Quoted in Victor Gollancz, *Journey Towards Music: A Memoir* (London: Victor Gollancz Ltd., 1965), p. 163.

73 Henry Morley, *Journal of a London Playgoer* (1866; repr. Leicester: Leicester University Press, 1974), p. 77.

74 *Gazzetta musicale di Firenze*, 1/4, 7 July 1853, pp. 14–15.

75 Erika Fischer-Lichte, *The Semiotics of Theater*, trans. Jeremy Gaines and Doris L. Jones (Bloomington and Indianapolis: Indiana University Press, 1992), p. 168.

76 All these reviews were reprinted on 20 November 1858 in *The Musical World*, 36/47, pp. 747–8.

77 Letter to Verdi, 20 January 1886; quoted in Busch (ed.), *Verdi's* Otello *and* Simon Boccanegra *in Letters and Documents*, p. 199.

78 Holland and Rockstro, *Memoir*, pp. 23–9.

79 In his account of Lillian Nordica's period of training in Paris in 1878, Glackens confuses François Delsarte (who died in 1871) with his son Gustave. Nordica studied for several months with Gustave Delsarte, who continued his father's teaching in gesture and singing, until he had a heart attack in November 1878. He died shortly afterwards, aged only forty-two. See Glackens, *Yankee Diva*, p. 47.

80 Taylor, *Players and Performance*, p. 149.

81 *Ibid.*, p. 150.

82 Nordica described this method of performance: 'It is not possible to be entirely natural. But as Delsarte used to say, the thing is *to know* what would be natural and *do it* whether you *feel* like it or not – and also to know *what not to do.*' Nordica's emphasis; quoted in Glackens, *Yankee Diva*, p. 304.

83 Genevieve Stebbins, *Delsarte System of Expression* (1902; repr. New York: Dance Horizons, 1977), p. 141. See also Michael Chekhov, 'The Psychological Gesture', in *To the Actor: On the Technique of Acting* (New York: Harper, 1953), pp. 63–84.

84 De Hegermann-Lindencrone, *Court of Memory*, p. 77.

85 *Ibid.*, p. 79. Callas was a modern example of this sacrifice of the 'voice beautiful' for dramatic realism.

86 *Ibid.*, pp. 143–5.

87 Soldene, *Theatrical and Musical Recollections*, p. 113.

88 *Gazzetta musicale di Milano*, 1/18, 1 May 1842, pp. 79–80.

89 Marco Capra, 'Aspetti della ricezione del *Macbeth* di Verdi', in Giovanna Silvani and Claudio Gallico (eds.), *Shakespeare e Verdi* (Parma: Università degli Studi di Parma, Facoltà di Lettere e Filosofia, 2000), p. 9.

90 Quoted in Marcello Conati, *Interviews and Encounters with Verdi*, trans. Richard Stokes (London: Victor Gollancz, 1984), p. 26.

91 *Ibid.*, p. 185.

92 Wagner, 'Orchestra's Power of Speech: Analogy with Gesture', in Albert Goldman and Evert Sprinchorn (eds.), *Wagner on Music and Drama* (1964; repr. New York: Da Capo Press, 1988), p. 218.

93 *Ibid.*, pp. 329–35.

94 Joseph R. Roach, *A Player's Passion: Studies in the Science of Acting* (London and Toronto: Associated University Presses, 1985), pp. 133–4. Diderot's treatise was not published until 1830.

95 Chorley, *Thirty Years*, vol. I. pp. 131–2.

96 *The Musical World*, 8/108, n.s. 1/14, 5 April 1838, p. 226.

97 Letter to Clarina Maffei; quoted in Osborne, *Letters of Giuseppe Verdi*, p. 201.

98 C. E. Massena, *Galli-Curci's Life of Song* (Beverley Hills: Monitor Book Co. Inc., 1978), p. 253.

99 *The Musical World*, 10/139, n.s. 3/45, 8 November 1838, pp. 141–3; also 11/159, n.s. 4/65, 28 March 1839, pp. 189–92.

100 *Gazzetta musicale di Milano*, 2/3, 15 January 1843, pp. 9–10.

101 Berlioz, *Memoirs*, p. 316.

102 Morley, *Journal*, p. 210.

103 Klein, *Great Women Singers*, p. 201.

104 Eames, *Some Memories*, pp. 146–7.

105 Hermann Klein, *The Golden Age of Opera* (London: George Routledge & Sons, 1933), p. 13. In his comments on the Jewel scene in *An Actor's Art*, Gustave Garcia stresses that the singer 'must not forget for a single instant that Marguerite is an innocent loving girl, not a Medea or a

Lady Macbeth' and that she should avoid 'in the last bar, especially, any aiming at effect, by attitudes and action incompatible with the simple and graceful manner of Marguerite. *The Actor's Art*, pp. 218–19.

106 Simon Maguire, 'The Mad Scene in *Lucia di Lammermoor* and Other Italian Operas', Opera North programme, Autumn 1988, p. 30. For a full account of the period's perception and treatment of the 'madwoman', see Elaine Showalter, *The Female Malady: Women, Madness and English Culture, 1830–1980* (London: Virago Press, 1987).

107 Kellogg, *Memoirs*, p. 33.

108 *The Musical World*, 1/9, 13 May 1836, p. 140.

109 Howard Bushnell, *Maria Malibran: A Biography of the Singer* (University Park and London: Pennsylvania State University Press, 1979), p. 196.

110 Taylor, *Players and Performance*, p. 179.

111 Chorley, *Thirty Years*, vol. II, p. 276.

112 *Ibid.*, p. 191. Not everyone agreed. Bosio was known for her snuff-taking habit, whilst Marie d'Agoult (a countess and mistress of Liszt) regarded Sontag quite differently: 'Spoiled by adulation in Germany, obsessed by aristocracy and fine manners, avid for praise, even more avid for money, and with very little wit, she tried to play the great lady, and she set about it badly.' Quoted in Fitzlyon, *Maria Malibran*, p. 131.

113 Chorley, *Thirty Years*, vol. II, p. 276.

114 *The Musical World*, 35/12, 21 March 1857, p. 190.

115 Klein, *Great Women Singers*, p. 61.

116 Lilli Lehmann, *My Path Through Life*, p. 159.

117 Chorley, *Thirty Years*, vol. II, pp. 236–7.

118 Jean-Pierre-Oscar Comettant, critic of *Le Siècle*; quoted in Mina Curtis, *Bizet and His World* (London: Secker & Warburg, 1959), pp. 402–4.

119 Calvé, *My Life*, p. 60.

120 Shaw, *Music in London*, vol. III, pp. 227–8.

121 Calvé, *My Life*, p. 83.

122 *Ibid.*, pp. 80–1.

123 Carelli, Augusto, *Emma Carelli: trent'anni di vita del teatro lirico* (Rome: P. Maglione, 1932), p. 51.

124 *Ibid.*, p. 53.

125 Huneker, *Bedouins*, p. 10. See also Garden and Biancolli, *Mary Garden's Story*, p. 105; pp. 145 and 268.

126 Howard, *Confessions*, pp. 53–4.

127 Huneker, *Bedouins*, pp. 7 and 17. Garden (or perhaps Biancolli) was eager to claim this image for herself; see Garden and Biancolli, *Mary Garden's Story*, p. 156.

128 *Ibid.*, p. 233.

129 *Ibid.*, p. 232.

130 *Ibid.*, p. 233.

131 *Ibid.*, p. 119.

132 Quoted in Martens, *Art of the Prima Donna*, p. 98.

133 *Ibid.*, p. 236.

134 Rasponi, *Last Prima Donnas*, p. 222.

135 *Ibid.*, p. 92. Alda agreed: 'We have left behind us the days when the public expected all opera singers to be fat. Audiences today are more critical of a singer's appearance than they used to be. They demand not only that the singer shall sing well, but that she shall look lovely and be an actress, too. No more beefy Isoldes and pudgy Carmens and bovine Violettas. Who wouldn't rather look at a slim and virginal Elsa than one who bulges unromantically?' *Men, Women and Tenors*, p. 299; see also Lotte Lehmann, *My Many Lives*, p. 10.

136 Huneker, *Bedouins*, p. 8.

137 David Magarshack, *Stanislavski: A Life* (London: Faber and Faber, 1986), p. 351.

138 Letter to Puccini, October 1895; in Eugenio Gara (ed.), *Carteggi Pucciniani* (Milan: Ricordi, 1958), p. 129.

139 Bellincioni, *Io e il palcoscenico*, p. 86.

POSTSCRIPT

1 Calvé, in Martens, *Art of the Prima Donna*, pp. 42–3.

BIBLIOGRAPHY

PERIODICALS AND NEWSPAPERS

Boccherini
Corriere delle dame
Corriere dei teatri
Cosmorama pittorico
Euterpe
Figaro
Gazzetta musicale di Firenze
Gazzetta musicale di Milano
Gazzetta musicale di Napoli
Gazzetta teatrale italiana
Harmonicon
Il mondo artistico
Il pirata
I teatri
La moda
L'armonia
L'Art musical
Napoli musicale
New York Herald Tribune
Revue musicale
Strenna teatrale europea
Teatro illustrato
The Music Student
The Musical Herald
The Musical Standard
The Musical Times and Singing-Class Circular
The Musical World

UNPUBLISHED MATERIAL

Letters of Mary Garden to Florence Mayer (Chicago Historical Society)
Miscellany of documents relating to the career of Cicely Gleeson-White (in possession of Myles Gleeson-White)
Miscellany of documents relating to the career of Susan Sunderland (in possession of Judith Sherratt)
The Enchantress, by Fred De Gresac and Victor Herbert, 1911 (MS housed in the Lord Chamberlain's Collection, British Library).

BOOKS AND ARTICLES

Abbate, Carolyn, *Unsung Voices: Opera and Musical Narrative in the Nineteenth Century* (Princeton: Princeton University Press, 1991).
'Opera; or, the Envoicing of Women', in Solie (ed.), *Musicology and Difference*.
Agate, May, *Madame Sarah* (London: Home & Van Thal Ltd., 1946).
Ajello, Raffaele and Carlo Marinelli (eds.), *Il Teatro di San Carlo*, 2 vols. (Naples: Guida, 1987).
Alda, Frances, *Men, Women and Tenors* (Boston: Houghton Mifflin, 1937).
Anderson, Bonnie S. and Judith P. Zinsser, *A History of their Own: Women in Europe from Prehistory to the Present*, 2 vols. (London: Penguin Books, 1988-90).
Anon., *Confessions of Madame Vestris* (London and New York: Erotic Biblion Society, 1899).
Giuditta Pasta: i suoi tempi e Saronno (Biblioteca di Saronno, 1977).
Instituzione [sic] e regolamenti pel conservatorio di musica in Milano (Milan: Dall'Imperiale Regia Stamperia, 1816).
'Pauline Viardot-Garcia to Julius Rietz (Letters of Friendship)', *The Musical Quarterly*, 1/3 (July 1915), 350–80.
Physiologus, trans. Michael J. Curley (Austin and London: University of Texas Press, 1979).
Regolamenti per il Liceo comunale di musica in Bologna (Tipografia Governativa Sassi, 1833).
'*Son regina, son guerriera': Giuditta Pasta: donna italiana, artista europea tra età neoclassica e romantica* (Saronno: Comune di Saronno, 1997).
Appollonia, Giorgio, *Giuditta Pasta: Gloria del bel canto* (Turin: EDA, 2000).

Arblaster, Anthony, *Viva la Libertà! Politics in Opera* (London and New York: Verso, 1992).

Ariès, Philippe, 'The Reversal of Death: Changes in Attitudes Toward Death in Western Societies', *American Quarterly*, 26/5, Special Issue (December 1974), 536–60.

Arral, Blanche, *The Extraordinary Operatic Adventures of Blanche Arral*, trans. Ira Glackens, ed. William Moran (Portland, Ore. and Cambridge: Amadeus Press, 2002).

Ashbrook, William, *Donizetti and His Operas* (Cambridge: Cambridge University Press, 1982).

Aspden, Suzanne, '"An Infinity of Factions": Opera in Eighteenth-Century Britain and the Undoing of Society', *Cambridge Opera Journal*, 9/1 (March 1997), 1–19.

Aspinall, Michael, 'Adelina Patti' (London: EMI Records Ltd, 1973).

Atherton, Gertrude, *A Tower of Ivory* (London: John Murray, 1910).

Adventures of a Novelist (London: Cape, 1932).

Austern, Linda Phyllis, '"Alluring the Auditorie to Effeminacie": Music and the Idea of the Feminine in Early Modern England', *Music and Letters*, 74/3 (August 1993), 343–54.

Austen, Jane, *Emma* (1816; repr. London: J. M. Dent & Sons Ltd, 1964).

Baldini, Gabriele, *Abitare la battaglia: La storia di Giuseppe Verdi*, ed. Fedele Amico (Milan: Garzanti, 2001).

Banes, Sally, *Dancing Women: Female Bodies on Stage* (London and New York: Routledge, 1998).

Barigazzi, Giuseppe, *La Scala racconta* (Milan: Rizzoli, 1998).

Barth, Herbert, Dietrich Mack and Egon Voss, *Wagner: A Documentary Study*, trans. P. R. J. Ford and Mary Whittall (New York: Oxford University Press, 1975).

Barthes, Roland, *Image Music Text*, trans. S. Heath (London: Fontana Press, 1977).

Barzun, Jacques (ed.), *Pleasures of Music* (London: Cassell, 1977).

Bashkirtseff, Marie, *The Journal of Marie Bashkirtseff*, trans. Mathilde Blind (1891; repr. London: Virago, 1985).

Beale, Willert, *The Light of Other Days: Seen Through the Wrong End of an Opera Glass* (London: Richard Bentley & Son, 1890).

Becker, Heinz and Gudrun, *Giacomo Meyerbeer: A Life in Letters*, trans. Mark Violette (London: Christopher Helm, 1989).

Beghelli, Marco, 'Il "do di petto": dissacrazione di un mito', *Il saggiatore musicale*, 3 (1996), pp. 105–49.

Belardinelli, Alessandro, *Documenti Spontini inediti*, 2 vols. (Florence: Edizioni Sansoni Antiquariato, 1955).

Bellincioni, Gemma, *Io e il palcoscenico: trenta e un anno di vita artistica* (Milan: Società Anonima, 1920).

Benjamin, Walter, 'The Work of Art in the Age of Mechanical Reproduction', in *Illuminations*, trans. Harry Zohn (London: Pimlico, 1999).

Bentley, Eric (ed.), *The Theory of the Modern Stage* (London: Penguin, 1976).

Bergeron, Katherine, 'Clément's Opera, or One Woman's Undoing', *Cambridge Opera Journal*, 2/1 (March 1990), 93–8.

Berlioz, Hector, *Mémoires de Hector Berlioz, comprenant ses voyages en Italie, en Allemagne, en Russie et en Angleterre 1803–1865* (Paris: Calmann Lévy, Editeur, Michel Lévy Frères, 1897).

  Critique Musicale 1823–1863, ed. H. Robert Cohen and Yves Gérard, 5 vols. (Paris: Buchet/Chastel, 1996-2003).

Bianconi, Lorenzo and Giorgio Pestelli (eds.), *Storia dell'opera italiana*, 3 vols. [vols. IV–VI] (Turin: EDT/Musica, 1987-8).

  Opera Production and Its Resources (1987), trans. L. G. Cochrane (Chicago: University of Chicago Press, 1998).

Bizet, Georges, *Lettres de Georges Bizet: Impressions de Rome (1857–1860), La Comune (1871)* (Paris: Calmann Lévy, Editeurs, n.d.).

Blackmer, Corinne E. and Patricia Juliana Smith (eds.), *En Travesti: Women, Gender Subversion, Opera* (New York: Columbia University Press, 1995).

Blanch, Lesley (ed.), *Harriette Wilson's Memoirs* (1825; London: Century, 1985).

Blanchard, Roger and Roland de Candé, *Dieux et divas de l'Opéra: Des origines au Romantisme* (Paris: Plon, 1986).

Blaze de Bury, Henri, *Musiciens contemporains* (Paris: Michel Lévy Frères, 1856).

Blessington, Lady Marguerite, 'The Two Friends', in *The Works of Lady Blessington*, vol. I (1838; repr. New York: AMS Press Inc., 1975).

Borchmeyer, Dieter, *Richard Wagner: Theory and Theatre*, trans. Stewart Spencer (Oxford: Clarendon Press, 1991).

Bowers, Jane and Judith Tick (eds.), *Women Making Music: The Western Art Tradition 1150–1950* (Urbana: University of Illinois Press, 1986).

Branca, Emilia, *Felice Romani* (Turin, Florence and Rome: Ermanno Loescher, 1882).

Brandt, George (ed.), *German and Dutch Theatre, 1600–1848* (Cambridge: Cambridge University Press, 1993).

Brewer, Harriette and James Francis Cooke, *Great Singers on the Art of Singing* (New York: Dover Publications, 1996).

Brody, Elaine, *Paris: The Musical Kaleidoscope 1870–1925* (London: Robson Books Ltd., 1988).

Brophy, Brigid, *Mozart the Dramatist* (London: Faber and Faber, 1964).

Bruder, Harold, 'Manuel García the Elder: His School and His Legacy', *Opera Quarterly*, 13/4 (Summer 1997), 19–46.

Budden, Julian, *The Operas of Verdi*, 3 vols. (London: Cassell & Co. Ltd., 1973, 1978, 1981).

Verdi (London and Melbourne; J. M. Dent & Sons Ltd., 1985).

Burgan, Mary, 'Heroines at the Piano: Women and Music in Nineteenth-century Fiction', *Victorian Studies*, 30/1 (1986), 51–76.

Busch, Hans (ed.), *Verdi's Aida: the History of an Opera in Letters and Documents* (Minneapolis: University of Minnesota Press, 1978).

Verdi's Otello and Simon Boccanegra in Letters and Documents, 2 vols. (Oxford: Clarendon Press, 1988).

Bushnell, Howard, *Maria Malibran: A Biography of the Singer* (University Park and London: Pennsylvania State University Press, 1979).

Cagli, Bruno and Sergio Ragni (eds.), *Gioachino Rossini: Lettere e documenti. Vol I: 29 febbraio 1892–17 marzo 1822* (Pesaro: Fondazione Rossini, 1992); *Vol. II: 21 marzo 1822–11 ottobre 1826* (1996); *Vol. III: 17 ottobre 1826–31 dicembre 1830* (2000).

Caswell, Austin, 'Mme Cinti-Damoreau and the Embellishment of Italian Opera in Paris: 1820–1845', *Journal of the American Musicological Society*, 28 (Autumn 1975), 459–92.

Calvé, Emma, *My Life*, trans. Rosamond Gilder (New York: D. Appleton & Co., 1922).

Capra, Marco, 'Il secondo Ottocento', in Del Monte and Segreto (eds.), *La civiltà musicale di Parma*.

'Aspetti della ricezione del *Macbeth* di Verdi', in Giovanna Silvani and Claudio Gallico (eds.), *Shakespeare e Verdi* (Parma: Università degli Studi di Parma, Facoltà di Lettere e Filosofia, 2000).

Carlyle, Sir Thomas, *The Works of Thomas Carlyle*, vol. XXIX (London: Chapman and Hall, 1899).

Carelli, Augusto, *Emma Carelli: trent'anni di vita del teatro lirico* (Rome: P. Maglione, 1932).

Caruso, Enrico, and Tetrazzini, Luisa, *On the Art of Singing* (1909; repr. New York: Dover Publications Inc., 1975).

Cassinelli, B., A. Maltempi and M. Pozzoni, *Rubini: l'uomo e l'artista*, 2 vols. (Comune di Romano di Lombardia: Cassa Rurale ed Artigiano di Calcio e di Covo, 1993).

Cather, Willa, *The Song of the Lark* (1915; repr. London: Virago, 1986).

Youth and the Bright Medusa (New York: Alfred A. Knopf, 1920).

Celletti, Rodolfo, *A History of Bel Canto*, trans. Frederick Fuller (Oxford: Clarendon Press, 1991).

Cervetti, Valerio (ed.), *Dietro il sipario: 1881–1898: memorie e appunti del Segretario della Commissione Teatrale Giulio Ferrarini* (Parma: Grafiche STEP, 1986).

Cesari, Gaetano and Alessandro Luzio (eds.), *I copialettere di Giuseppe Verdi* (1913; repr. Bologna: Forni, 1987).

Chadwick, Henry, *The Early Church* (London: Penguin Books, 1967).

Chapple, J. A. V., *Elizabeth Gaskell: A Portrait in Letters* (Manchester: Manchester University Press, 1980).

Chekhov, Anton, *Five Plays*, trans. Ronald Hingley (Oxford: Oxford University Press, 1998).

Chekhov, Michael, *To the Actor: On the Technique of Acting* (New York: Harper, 1953).

Chorley, Henry Fothergill, *Thirty Years Musical Recollections*, 2 vols. (London: Hurst & Blackett, 1862).

Christiansen, Rupert, *Prima Donna: A History* (London: Penguin Books, 1986).

The Grand Obsession (London: Collins, 1988).

Ciarlantini, Paola, 'Una testimonianza sul teatro musicale degli inizi dell'ottocento: il saggio "Dell'opera in musica" di Nicola Tacchinardi', *Bollettino del Centro Rossiniano di Studi*, 29 (1989), pp. 65–111.

Giuseppe Persiani e Fanny Tacchinardi: Due protagonisti del melodramma romantico (Bologna: Il Lavoro Editoriale, 1988).

Citron, Marcia, *Gender and the Musical Canon* (Cambridge: Cambridge University Press, 1993).

Cixous, Hélène and Catherine Clément, *The Newly Born Woman*, trans. Betsy Wing (1975; Manchester: Manchester University Press, 1986).

Clayton, Ellen Creathorne, *Queens of Song* (London: Smith, Elder & Co., 1863).

Clément, Catherine, *Opera, or the Undoing of Women*, trans. Betsy Wing (London: Virago Press, 1989).

Cohen, H. Robert, *Les Gravures musicales dans 'L'Illustration' 1843–1899*, 2 vols. (Quebec: Les Presses de l'Université Laval, 1982–3).

Colombo, Paola, 'Alcuni inediti di Giuditta Pasta', in *'Son regina, son guerriera': Giuditta Pasta: donna italiana, artista europea tra età neoclassica e romantica* (Saronno: Comune di Saronno, 1997).

Conati, Marcello, *La bottega della musica: Verdi e La Fenice* (Milan: Il Saggiatore, 1983).

Interviews and Encounters with Verdi, trans. Richard Stokes (London: Victor Gollancz, 1984).

Cowart, Georgina, 'Of Women, Sex and Folly: Opera under the Old Regime', *Cambridge Opera Journal*, 6/3 (November 1994), 205–20.

Croce, Benedetto, *I teatri di Napoli: dal Rinascimento alla fine del secolo decimottavo* (Bari: Laterza & Figli, 1966).

Curtis, Mina, *Bizet and His World* (London: Secker & Warburg, 1959).

Cushing, Mary Watkins, *The Rainbow Bridge* (New York: Putnam, 1954).

Dacci, Giusto, *Cenni Storici e Statistici intorno alla Reale Scuola di Musica in Parma: dal giorno 2 maggio 1818 (epoca della sua origine) a tutto l'anno scolastico 1886–87* (Parma: Luigi Battei, 1888).

Dahlhaus, Carl, 'Drammaturgia dell'opera italiana', in Bianconi and Pestelli (eds.), *Storia dell'opera italiana*, vol. VI.

D'Alvarez, Marguerite, *Forsaken Altars* (London: Rupert Hart-Davis Ltd., 1954).

D'Agoult, Marie, *Mes souvenirs 1806–1833, par Daniel Stern* (Paris: Calmann Lévy, 1880).

Dall'Olio, Cesare, *La musica e la civiltà: pensieri di un musicista* (Bologna: G. Cenerelli, 1897).

Dal Monte, Toti, *Una voce nel mondo* (Milan: Longanesi, 1985).

d'Annunzio, Gabriele, *La Gioconda* (Milan: Arnoldo Mondadori, 1940).

Dante Alighieri, *The Divine Comedy: Purgatorio*, trans. Charles S. Singleton (Princeton: Princeton University Press, 1973).

Da Ponte, Lorenzo, *Memoirs*, trans. Elisabeth Abbott (New York: New York Review of Books, 2000).

Davies, Norman, *Europe: A History* (London: Pimlico, 1997).

Davis, Richard, *Anna Bishop: The Adventures of an Intrepid Prima Donna* (Sydney: Currency Press, 1997).

Davis, Tracy C., *Actresses as Working Women: Their Social Identity in Victorian Culture* (London and New York: Routledge, 1991).

'Questions for a Feminist Methodology in Theatre History', in Postlewait and McConachie (eds.), *Interpreting the Theatrical Past*.

De Angelis, Marcello, *Le carte dell'Impresario: Melodramma e costume teatrale nell'Ottocento* (Florence: G. C. Sansoni, 1982).

De Beauvoir, Simone, *The Second Sex* (1949), trans. H. M. Parshley (London: Jonathan Cape, 1953).

De Boigne, Charles, *Petits mémoires de l'Opéra* (Paris: Librairie Nouvelle, 1857).

De Filippis, F. and M. Mangini: *Il Teatro Nuovo di Napoli* (Naples: Arturo Berisio, 1967).

De Pontmartin, Armand, comte de, *Souvenirs d'un vieux mélomane* (Paris: Calmann Lévy, 1879).

Del Monte, Claudio and Vincenzo Raffaele Segreto (eds.), *La civiltà musicale di Parma* (Parma: Grafiche STEP, 1989).

Descotes, Maurice, *Histoire de la critique dramatique en France* (Tübingen: Gunter Narr Verlag, 1980).

Diderot, Denis, 'Observations sur Garrick', *Œuvres complètes*, vol. XX (Paris: Hermann, 1995).

Dizikes, John, *Opera in America: A Cultural History* (New Haven and London: Yale University Press, 1993).

Dijkstra, Bram, *Idols of Perversity: Fantasies of Feminine Evil in the Fin-de-Siècle* (New York and Oxford: Oxford University Press, 1986).

Drake, James A., *Rosa Ponselle: A Centenary Biography* (Portland, Ore.: Amadeus Press, 1997).

Drinker, Sophie, *Music and Women: The Story of Women in Their Relation to Music* (New York: Coward–McCann, 1948).

Du Maurier, George, *Trilby* (1894; repr. London: Dent, 1931).

Duprez, Gilbert-Louis, *Souvenirs d'un chanteur* (1880), in Thierry de la Croix (ed.), *Voix d'opéra. Ecrits de chanteurs du XIXe siècle* (Paris: Michel de Maule, 1988).

Durante, Sergio, 'The Opera Singer', in Bianconi and Pestelli (eds.), *Opera Production and Its Resources*.

Eames, Emma, *Some Memories and Reflections* (1927; repr. New York: Arno, 1977).

Eaton, Quaintance, *The Miracle of the Met: An Informal History of the Metropolitan Opera 1883–1967* (1968; repr. Westport, Conn.: Greenwood Press, 1976).

Ebers, John, *Seven Years of the King's Theatre* (1828; repr. New York and London: Benjamin Blom, Inc., 1969).

Edwards, Sutherland, *History of the Opera, from Monteverdi to Donizetti*, 2 vols. (London: Wm. H. Allen & Co., 1862).

Ehrlich, Cyril, *The Music Professsion in Britain Since the Eighteenth Century: A Social History* (Oxford: Clarendon Press, 1985).

Eliot, George, *The Legend of Jubal and Other Poems, Old and New* (1871; London: Blackwood, 1879).

Daniel Deronda (1876; repr. London: Penguin Classics, 1986).

Escudier, Léon, *Vie et aventures des cantatrices célèbres* (Paris: E. Dentu, 1856).

Escudier Frères, *Etudes biographiques sur les chanteurs contemporains, précédées d'une esquisse sur l'art du chant* (Paris: Just Tessier, 1840).

Evans, Richard, *The Feminists* (London: Croom Helm, 1977).

Farrar, Geraldine, *The Story of An American Singer, by Herself* (Boston and New York: Houghton Mifflin Company, 1916).

Such Sweet Compulsion (New York: Greystone Press, 1938).

Fay, Amy, *Music-Study in Germany* (1880; repr. New York: Dover, 1965).

More Letters of Amy Fay: The American Years, 1879–1916, ed. Sister M. W. McCarthy (Detroit: Information Co-Ordinators, 1986).

Fenner, Theodore, *Leigh Hunt and Opera Criticism* (Lawrence, Manhattan and Wichita: University of Kansas, 1972).

Ferrari, Paolo-Emilio, *Spettacoli drammatico-musicali e coreografici in Parma dall'anno 1628 all'anno 1883* (Parma 1884; repr. Bologna: Forni, 1969).

Fétis, F. G., *La Musica accommodata alla intelligenza di tutti*, trans. Eriberto Predari (Turin: Unione tipografico-editrice, 1858).

Fischer-Lichte, Erika, *The Semiotics of Theater*, trans. Jeremy Gaines and Doris L. Jones (Bloomington and Indianapolis: Indiana University Press, 1992).

Fitzlyon, April, *The Price of Genius: A Life of Pauline Viardot* (London: John Calder, 1964).

Maria Malibran: Diva of the Romantic Age (London: Souvenir Press, 1987).

Flaherty, Gloria, *Opera in the Development of German Critical Thought* (Princeton: Princeton University Press, 1978).

Florimo, Francesco, *Cenno storico sulla scuola musicale di Napoli*, 2 vols. (Naples: Lorenzo Rocco, 1869; rev. edn 1872).

Forbes, Elizabeth, *Mario and Grisi: A Biography* (London: Victor Gollancz, 1985).

Foscolo, Ugo, *Lacrime d'amore: lettere a Antonietta Fagnani Arese*, ed. Giovanni Pacchiano (Milan: Serra e Riva, 1981).

Foster, Shirley, *Victorian Women's Fiction: Marriage, Freedom and the Individual* (London and Sydney: Croom Helm, 1986).

Foucault, Michel, *The History of Sexuality*, 3 vols. (1976), trans. Robert Hurley (London: Penguin, 1990).

Freeman, Daniel E., '*La guerriera amante*: Representations of Amazons and Warrior Queens in Venetian Baroque Opera', *The Musical Quarterly*, 80/3 (Fall 1996), 431–60.

Froud, Nina, and James Hanley (eds.), *Chaliapin: An Autobiography as Told to Maxim Gorky* (London: Macdonald & Co., 1967).

Fubini, Enrico, *Music and Culture in Eighteenth-Century Europe: A Source Book*, trans. and ed. Bonnie J. Blackburn (Chicago and London: University of Chicago Press, 1994).

Fulcher, Jane F., *The Nation's Image: French Grand Opera as Politics and Politicized Art* (Cambridge: Cambridge University Press, 1987).

Gara, Eugenio (ed.), *L'impresario in angustie: Adelina Patti e altre stelle fuori della leggenda (1886–1893) di Strakosch e Schürman* (Milan: Valentino Bompiani, 1940).

Carteggi Pucciniani (Milan: Ricordi, 1958).

Garcia, Gustave, *The Actor's Art: A Practical Treatise* (London: Simpkin, Marshall & Co., 1888).

Garden, Mary, and Louis Biancolli, *Mary Garden's Story* (London: Michael Joseph, 1952).

Gardner, Viv (ed.), *Sketches from the Actresses' Franchise League* (Nottingham: Nottingham Drama Texts, 1985).

Gardner, Viv, and Susan Rutherford (eds.), *The New Woman and Her Sisters: Feminism and Theatre 1850–1914* (London: Harvester Wheatsheaf, 1992).

Gattey, Charles Neilson, *Luisa Tetrazzini: The Florentine Nightingale* (Aldershot: Scolar Press, 1995).

Gatti-Casazza, Giulio, *Memories of the Opera* (1941; repr. London: John Calder, 1977).

Gautier, Théophile, *Histoire de l'art dramatique en France*, 4 vols. (Paris: Edition Hetzel, 1858).

Poésies complètes, 3 vols. (Paris: A. G Nizet, 1970).

Gay, Peter, *The Bourgeois Experience: Victoria to Freud*, 2 vols. (Oxford: Oxford University Press, 1984).

Gerhard, Anselm, *The Urbanization of Opera: Music Theater in Paris in the Nineteenth Century*, trans. Mary Whittall (Chicago and London: University of Chicago Press, 1998).

Giorgi Righetti, Geltrude Maria, *Cenni di una donna già cantante sopra il maestro Rossini* (Bologna: Sassi, 1823).

Gissing, George, *Thyrza* (1887; repr. Brighton: Harvester Press, 1984).

Glackens, Ira, *Yankee Diva: Lillian Nordica and the Golden Days of Opera* (New York: Coleridge Press, 1963).

Glasgow, Janis (ed.), *George Sand: Collected Essays* (New York: Whitson Publishing Company, 1985).

Glixon, Beth L. 'Private Lives of Public Women: Prima Donnas in Mid-Seventeenth-Century Venice', *Music and Letters*, 76/4 (November 1995), 509–31.

Goehr, Lydia, *The Imaginary Museum of Musical Works: An Essay in the Philosophy of Music* (Oxford: Clarendon Press, 1992).

Goldman, Albert and Evert Sprinchorn (eds.), *Wagner on Music and Drama* (1964; repr. New York: Da Capo Press, 1988).

Gollancz, Victor, *Journey Towards Music: A Memoir* (London: Victor Gollancz Ltd., 1965).

Gramit, David, *Cultivating Music: The Aspirations, Interests, and Limits of German Musical Culture, 1770–1848* (Berkeley and London: University of California Press, 2002).

Graves, Robert, *The Greek Myths*, 2 vols. (London: Penguin, 1955).

The White Goddess (London: Faber and Faber, 1961).

Gregor-Dellin, Martin and Dietrich Mack (eds.), *Cosima Wagner's Diaries*, vol. I, 1869–1877, trans. Geoffrey Skelton (London: Collins, 1978).

Groos, Arthur and Roger Parker (eds.), *Reading Opera* (Princeton: Princeton University Press, 1988).

Hadlock, Heather, 'Return of the Repressed: The Prima Donna from Hoffmann's *Tales* to Offenbach's *Contes*', *Cambridge Opera Journal*, 6/3 (November 1994), 221–43.

Hahn, Reynaldo, *On Singers and Singing*, trans. Leopold Simoneau (1913–14; Portland, Ore.: Amadeus Press, 1990).

Haight, Gordon S., (ed.), *The George Eliot Letters*, 9 vols. (London: Oxford University Press, 1954).

Halstead, Jill, *The Woman Composer: Creativity and the Gendered Politics of Musical Composition* (Aldershot: Ashgate, 1997).

Hamilton, Kenneth, 'Reminiscences of a Scandal–Reminiscences of La Scala: Liszt's Fantasy on Mercadante's *Il giuramento*', *Cambridge Opera Journal*, 5/3 (1993), 187–98.

Haweis, H. Reginald, *Music and Morals* (London: W. H. Allen, 1874).

Hazlitt, William, *The Complete Works of William Hazlitt*, 20 vols., ed. P. P. Howe (London and Toronto: J. M. Dent & Sons Ltd., 1934).

Hegermann-Lindencrone, Lillian de, *In the Courts of Memory 1858–1875* (New York and London: Harper & Bros. Publishers, 1911).

Helsinger, Elizabeth K., Robin Lauterbach Sheets and William Veeder (eds.), *The Woman Question*, 3 vols. (Manchester: Manchester University Press, 1983).

Hempel, Frieda, *My Golden Age of Singing* (Portland, Ore.: Amadeus Press, 1998).

Henson, Karen, 'In the House of Disillusion: Augusta Holmès and *La Montagne noire*', *Cambridge Opera Journal*, 9/3 (November 1997), 233–62.

Heriot, Angus, *The Castrati in Opera* (London: Calder & Boyars, 1956; repr. 1975).

Hesse, Hermann, *Gertrude*, trans. Hilda Rosner (Harmondsworth: Penguin Books, 1986).

Hibbert, Christopher, *Queen Victoria in her Letters and Journals* (London: John Murray, 1984).

Hines, Jerome, *Great Singers on Great Singing* (London: Victor Gollancz Ltd., 1983).

Hippolytus, *The Refutation of All Heresies*, Book VII, trans. Rev. J. M. MacMahon (Edinburgh: T. & T. Clark, 1870).

Hoffmann, E. T. A., *Tales of Hoffmann*, trans. R. J. Hollingdale (London: Penguin, 1982).

Holland, Henry Scott and Rockstro, W. S., *Memoir of Madame Jenny Lind-Goldschmidt: Her Early Life and Dramatic Career 1820–1851*, 2 vols. (London: John Murray, 1891).

Holmes, William C., *Opera Observed: Views of a Florentine Impresario* (Chicago: University of Chicago Press, 1993).

Holroyd, Michael, *Bernard Shaw: Volume I, 1856–1898* (London: Penguin, 1990).

Homer, *The Odyssey*, trans. Walter Shewring (Oxford: Oxford University Press, 1980).

Honolka, Kurt, *Die grossen Primadonnen von der Bordoni bis zur Callas* (Stuttgart: Cotta-Verlag, 1960).

Howard, Kathleen, *Confessions of an Opera Singer* (London: Kegan Paul & Co., 1920).

Howe, Elizabeth, *The First English Actresses: Women and Drama 1660–1700* (Cambridge: Cambridge University Press, 1992).

Huebner, Steven, 'Opera Audiences in Paris 1830–1870', *Music and Letters*, 70/2 (May 1989), 206–25.

Hugo, Victor, *Notre Dame* (1831; London: Thomas Nelson & Sons Ltd., n.d.).

Huneker, James, *Bedouins* (1920; London: T. Werner Laurie, n.d.).
  Painted Veils (1920; repr. New York: Horace Liveright, 1928).

Huneker, Josephine (ed.), *Intimate Letters of James Gibbons Huneker* (New York: Liveright Publishers, 1924).

Hyde, Derek, *New Found Voices: Women in Nineteenth-Century Music* (Kent: Tritone Music Publications, 1991).

Irwin, Inez Haynes, *Angels and Amazons* (New York: Doubleday, 1933).

Isidore of Seville, *Etymologiarvm Sive Orginvm Libri XI–XX* (London: Oxford University Press, 1911; repr. 1957).

Jacobs, Robert L. and Geoffrey Skelton (eds.), *Wagner Writes from Paris* (London: George Allen & Unwin Ltd., 1973).

Jean-Aubry, Georges, 'Gustave Flaubert and Music', *Music and Letters*, 31/1 (January 1950), 13–39.

Jerome, *The Principal Works of St. Jerome*, trans. W. H. Fremantle (1892; repr. Grand Rapids, Mich.: Wm. B. Eerdmans, 1954).

Jo, Mario and Paul Buhle (eds.), *The Concise History of Women's Suffrage* (Chicago: University of Illinois Press, 1978).

Joeres, Ellen B. and Mary Jo Maynes (eds.), *German Women in the Eighteenth and Nineteenth Centuries* (Bloomington: Indiana University Press, 1986).

John, Nicholas (ed.), *Violetta and Her Sisters, The Lady of the Camellias: Responses to the Myth* (London: Faber and Faber, 1994).

Keates, Jonathan, *Handel: The Man and his Music* (London: Hamish Hamilton, 1986).

Kelly, Michael, *Reminscences* (1825; repr. London: Oxford University Press, 1975).

Kellogg, Clara Louise, *Memoirs of an American Prima Donna* (New York and London: G. P. Putnam, 1913).

Kemble, Frances Anne, *Records of Later Life*, 3 vols. (London: R. Bentley, 1882).

Kerman, Joseph, *Opera as Drama* (London and Boston: Faber and Faber, 1988).

Kimbell, David R. B., *Verdi in the Age of Italian Romanticism* (Cambridge: Cambridge University Press, 1981).

Italian Opera (Cambridge: Cambridge University Press, 1991).

Klein, Hermann, *Great Women Singers of My Time* (London: Routledge & Sons, 1931).

The Golden Age of Opera (London: Routledge & Sons, 1933).

Lacombe, Hervé, *Les Voies de l'opéra français au XIXe siècle* (Paris: Fayard, 1997).

Langer, Susanne K., *Philosophy in a New Key: A Study in the Symbolism of Reason, Rite and Art* (Cambridge, Mass.: Harvard University Press, 1942).

Lawson-Peebles, Robert (ed.), *Approaches to the American Musical* (Exeter: University of Exeter Press, 1996).

Lawton, Mary, *Schumann-Heink: The Last of the Titans* (New York: J. J. Little & Ives, 1928).

Le Goff, Jacques, *History and Memory*, trans. Steven Rendall and Elizabeth Claman (New York: Columbia University Press, 1992).

Lehmann, Lilli, *My Path Through Life*, trans. Alice Benedict Seligman (New York and London: G. P. Putnam's Sons, 1914).

How To Sing (1902), trans. Richard Aldrich (New York: Dover Publications Inc., 1993).

Lehmann, Liza, *The Life of Liza Lehmann* (London: T. Fisher Unwin, 1919).

Lehmann, Lotte, *My Many Lives*, trans. Frances Holden (1948; repr. Westport, Conn.: Greenwood Press, 1974).

le Huray, Peter and James Day, *Music and Aesthetics in the Eighteenth and Early-Nineteenth Centuries* (Cambridge: Cambridge University Press, 1988).

Le Massena, C. E, *Galli-Curci's Life of Song* (California: Monitor Book Co. Inc., 1978).

Le Moigne-Mussat, Marie-Claire, *Musique et société à Rennes aux XVIIIe et XIXe siècles* (Geneva: Minkoff, 1988).

Leonardi, Susan J., and Rebecca A. Pope, *The Diva's Mouth: Body, Voice, Prima Donna Politics* (New Brunswick, NJ: Rutgers University Press, 1996).

Leppert, Richard, *Music and Image: Domesticity, Ideology and Socio-cultural Formation in Eighteenth-century England* (Cambridge: Cambridge University Press, 1988).

Leroux, Gaston, *The Phantom of the Opera* (1910; Cambridge: Dedalus, 1990).

Letzer, Jacqueline and Robert Adelson, *Women Writing Opera: Creativity and Controversy in the Age of the French Revolution* (London and Berkeley: University of California Press, 2001).

Levik, Sergei, *The Levik Memoirs: An Opera Singer's Notes*, trans. Edward Morgan (London: Symposium Records, 1995).

Lichtenthal, Peter, *Trattato dell'influenza della musica sul corpo umano e del suo uso in certe malattie con alcuni cenni come si abbia ad intendere una buona musica, tradotto dal tedesco e ricorretto dall'autore medesimo* (Milan: Giuseppe Maspero, 1811).

Lincoln, Marianne, *Debut at the Gewandhaus and After: A 19th-Century Singer's Diary,* ed. F. M. Harper (New Malden, Surrey: F. M. Harper, 1980).

Lindenberger, Herbert, *Opera: The Extravagant Art* (Ithaca and London: Cornell University Press, 1984).

Litvinne, Félia, *Ma vie et mon art* (Paris: Librairie Plon, 1933).

Locke, Ralph P., 'Paradossi nel mecenatismo musicale delle donne in America', *Musica/Realtà*, 18 (November 1997), 54.

'What Are These Women Doing in Opera?', in Blackmer and Smith (eds.), *En Travesti.*

Loesser, Arthur, *Men, Women and Pianos* (New York: Simon and Schuster, 1954).

Lumley, Benjamin, *Reminiscences of the Opera* (London: Hurst and Blackett, 1864).

Luke, David and Robert Pick (trans. and eds.), *Goethe: Conversations and Encounters* (London: Oswald Wolff, 1966).

Luzio, Alessandro (ed.), *Carteggi Verdiani*, 4 vols. (Rome: Reale Accademia d'Italia, 1935–47).

MacKellar, Walter (ed.), *The Latin Poems of John Milton* (New Haven: Yale University Press, 1930).

Mackenzie-Grieve, Averil, *Clara Novello: 1818–1908* (London: Geoffrey Bles, 1955).

Magarshack, David, *Stanislavski: A Life* (London: Faber and Faber, 1986).

Maguire, Simon, 'The Mad Scene in *Lucia di Lammermoor* and Other Italian Operas', Opera North programme, Autumn 1988.

'Vincenzo Bellini and the Aesthetics of Early Nineteenth-Century Italian Opera', D. Phil. dissertation, University of Oxford, 1984.

Mainzer, Joseph, *Singing for the Million*, ed. Bernarr Rainbow (1841; repr. Kilkenny, Eire: Boethius Press, 1984).

Mapleson, Col. J. H., *The Mapleson Memoirs: The Career of an Operatic Impresario 1858–1888*, ed. Harold Rosenthal (London: Putnam, 1966).

Marcello, Benedetto, *Il Teatro alla moda* (1720; repr. Rome: Castelvecchi, 1993).

Marchesi, Blanche, *A Singer's Pilgrimage* (London: Grant Richards, 1923).

The Singer's Catechism and Creed (London: J. M. Dent & Sons Ltd., 1932).

Marchesi, Gustavo, *Canto e cantanti* (Milan: Casa Ricordi, 1996).

Marchesi, Mathilde, *Marchesi and Music: Passages from the Life of a Famous Singing Teacher* (London and New York: Harper and Brothers, 1897).

Maretzek, Max, *Revelations of an Opera Manager* (1855 and 1890; repr. New York: Dover, 1968).

Mariano, Fabio (ed.), *Il teatro nelle Marche* (Fiesole: Nardini, 1997).

Martens, Frederick, *The Art of the Prima Donna* (London: D. Appleton & Co., 1922).

Mayhew, Henry, *London Labour and the London Poor*, 4 vols. (1861–62; repr. New York: Dover Publications Inc., 1968).

McConachie, Bruce A., 'Towards a Postpositivist Theatre History', *Theatre Journal*, 37/4 (December 1985), 465–86.

Melba, Nellie, *Melodies and Memories* (1925; repr. London: Hamish Hamilton, 1980).

Mellers, Wilfrid, *The Masks of Orpheus: Seven Stages in the Story of European Music* (Manchester: Manchester University Press, 1987).

Melzi, Lodovico, *Cenni storici sul R. Conservatorio di Musica di Milano* (Milan: R. Stabilmento Ricordi, 1873).

Meredith, George, *Emilia in England* (1864; repr. as *Sandra Belloni*, Westminster: Archibald Constable, 1902).

Vittoria (1866; repr. London: Constable, 1924).

Merlin, María de las Mercedes Santa Cruz y Montalvo, comtesse de, *Memoirs of Madame Malibran, by the countess of Merlin, and other intimate friends* (London: H. Colburn, 1840).

Meyer, Michael, *Ibsen* (London: Penguin Books, 1985).

Millet, Jean, *La Belle Méthode, ou l'art de bien chanter* (1666; repr. New York: Da Capo Press, 1973).

Moers, Ellen, *Literary Women* (London: The Women's Press, 1978).

Moindrot, Isabelle, 'Le geste et l'idéologie dans le "grand opéra" "La Juive" de Fromental Halévy', *Romantisme*, 102 (1998), 63–79.

Monaldi, Gino, *Cantanti celebri 1829–1929* (Rome: Edizioni Tiber, 1929).

Monkswell, Lady Mary, *A Victorian Diarist 1873–1895* (London: John Murray, 1944).

Moore, George, *Evelyn Innes* and *Sister Theresa* (1898 and 1901: repr. New York and London: Garland Publishing Inc., 1975).

Memoirs of My Dead Life (1906; rev. edn London: William Heinemann Ltd).

Morley, Henry, *Journal of a London Play-goer* (1866; repr. Leicester: Leicester University Press, 1974).

Müller, Ulrich and Peter Wapnewski (eds.), *The Wagner Handbook*, trans. John Deathridge (London and Cambridge, Mass.: Harvard University Press, 1992).

Murphy, Kerry, 'Joseph Mainzer's "Sacred and Beautiful Mission": An Aspect of Parisian Musical Life of the 1830s', *Music and Letters*, 75/1 (February 1994), 33–46.

Nagler (ed.), A. M., *A Source Book in Theatrical History* (New York: Dover Publications, 1952).

Nauhaus, Gerd (ed.), *The Marriage Diaries of Robert and Clara Schumann*, trans. Peter Ostwald (London: Robson Books, 1994).

Nead, Lynda, *Myths of Sexuality: Representations of Women in Victorian Britain* (Oxford: Basil Blackwell, 1988).

Neider, Charles (ed.), *Papa: An Intimate Biography of Mark Twain by his thirteen-year-old daughter Susy* (New York: Doubleday, 1985).

Nettel, Reginald, *Sing a Song of England: A Social History of Traditional Song* (London: Phoenix House Ltd., 1969).

Neuls-Bates, Carol (ed.), *Women in Music: An Anthology of Source Readings from the Middle Ages to the Present* (Boston: Northeastern University Press, 1996).

O'Connor, Garry, *The Pursuit of Perfection: A Life of Maggie Teyte* (London: Victor Gollancz Ltd., 1979).

Orrey, Leslie, *Bellini* (London: Dent, 1969).

Osborne, Charles (ed.), *Letters of Giuseppe Verdi* (New York: Holt, Rinehart & Winston, 1971).

Pacini, Giovanni, *Le mie memorie artistiche* (Florence: Ferdinando Magnani, 1875).

Palazzi, Maura, *Donne sole. Storia dell'altra faccia dell'Italia tra antico regime e società contemporanea* (Milan: Bruno Mondadori, 1997).

Panofka, Enrico, *Voci e cantanti: ventotto capitoli di considerazioni generali sulla voce e sull'altare del canto* (Florence, 1871; repr. Arnaldo Forni, 1984).

Parker, Roger, *Studies in Early Verdi 1832–1844: New Information and Perspectives on the Milanese Musical Milieu and the Operas from Oberto to Ernani* (New York and London: Garland, 1989).

Leonora's Last Act: Essays in Verdian Discourse (Princeton, NJ: Princeton University Press, 1997).

Pastura, Francesco, *Le lettere di Bellini 1819–1835* (Catania: Totalità, 1935).

Patmore, Coventry, *The Angel in the House* (1854; 4th edn, London: Macmillan, 1866).

Patureau, Frédérique, *Le Palais Garnier dans la société parisienne 1875–1914* (Liège: Mardaga, 1991).

Pearce, Charles E., *Madame Vestris and Her Times* (London: Stanley Paul & Co., 1923).

Pellegrini Celoni, Anna Maria, *Grammatica o siano regole per ben cantare* (Rome: Francesco Bourlie, 1817).

Petrobelli, Pierluigi, Marisa Di Gregorio Casati and Carlo Matteo Mossa (eds.), *Carteggio Verdi-Ricordi 1880–1881* (Parma: Istituto di Studi Verdiani, 1988).

Pinney, Thomas (ed.), *Essays of George Eliot* (London: Routledge & Kegan Paul, 1963).

Pleasants, Henry, *The Great Singers* (New York: Simon & Schuster, 1966).

Poizat, Michel, *The Angel's Cry: Beyond the Pleasure Principle in Opera*, trans. Arthur Denner (Ithaca and London: Cornell University Press, 1992).

Pollard, John, *Seers, Shrines and Sirens: The Greek Religious Experience in the Sixth Century B.C.* (London: George Allen & Unwin Ltd., 1965).

Ponder, Winifred, *Clara Butt: Her Life-Story* (London: George G. Harrap & Co., 1928).

Pope, Rebecca A., 'The Diva Doesn't Die: George Eliot's *Armgart*', in Leslie C. Dunn and Nancy A. Jones (eds.), *Embodied Voices: Representing Female Vocality in Western Culture* (Cambridge: Cambridge University Press, 1994).

Poriss, Hilary, 'Making Their Way Through the World: Italian One-Hit Wonders', *19th-Century Music*, 24/3 (Spring 2001), 197–224.

'Verdi Meets Bellini', in Fabrizio Della Seta, Roberta Montemorra Marvin and Marco Marica (eds.), *Verdi 2001. Atti del convegno internazionale di studi, Parma, New York, New Haven 24 gennaio-1° febbraio 2001*, 2 vols. (Florence: Olschki, 2003).

Postlewait, Thomas and McConachie, Bruce A. (eds.), *Interpreting the Theatrical Past: Essays in the Historiography of Performance* (Iowa City: University of Iowa Press, 1989).

Preston, Katherine K., *Opera on the Road: Traveling Opera Troupes in the United States, 1825–60* (Urbana and Chicago: University of Illinois Press, 1993).

Rahner, Hugo, *Greek Myths and Christian Mystery*, trans. Brian Battershaw (London: Burns & Oates, 1963).

Ragni, Sergio, 'Isabella Colbran: appunti per una biografia', *Bollettino del Centro Rossiniano di Studi*, 38 (1998), 17–55.

Rasponi, Lanfranco, *The Last Prima Donnas* (New York: Limelight Editions, 1990).

Ravera, Camilla, *Breve storia del movimento femminile in Italia* (Rome: Riuniti, 1978).

Reggioli, Aldo, *Carolina Ungher: virtuosa di Camera e Cappella di S. A. R. il Granduca di Toscano* (Florence: Polistampa, 1995).

Reich, Nancy B., 'Women as Musicians: A Question of Class', in Solie (ed.), *Musicology and Difference*.

Reid, Cornelius L., *Bel Canto: Principles and Practices* (1950; repr. New York: Joseph Patelson Music House, 1971).

Ricci, Corrado, *I teatri di Bologna nei secoli XVII e XVIII* (Bologna: Arnaldo Forni, 1888).

Rickard, Sue, 'Movies in Disguise: Negotiating Censorship and Patriarchy Through the Dances of Fred Astaire and Ginger Rogers', in Lawson-Peebles (ed.), *Approaches to the American Musical*.

Rimsky-Korsakov, Nicolay Andreyevich, *My Musical Life*, trans. Judah A. Joffe (London: Faber and Faber, 1989).

Rinaldi, Mario, *Due secoli di musica al Teatro Argentina*, 3 vols. (Florence: Olschki, 1978).

Ritorni, Carlo, *Annali del teatro della città di Reggio* (Bologna: coi tipi del Nobili e Comp., 1829).

Ammaestramenti alla composizione d'ogni poema e d'ogni opera appartenente alla musica (Milan: Giacomo Pirola, 1841).

Ritter, Fanny Raymond, *Woman as a Musician: An Art-Historical Study* (London: William Reeves, n.d.).

Roach, Joseph R., *The Player's Passion: Studies in the Science of Acting* (London and Toronto: Associated University Presses, 1985).

Rogers, Clara Kathleen, *The Philosophy of Singing* (London: Osgood, McIlvaine & Co., 1893).

Roosevelt, Blanche, *Stage-struck, or, She Would Be An Opera-singer* (London: S. Low, Marston, Searle & Rivington, 1884).

Rosand, Ellen, 'Criticism and the Undoing of Opera', *19th Century Music*, 14/1 (Summer 1990), 75–83.

'Operatic Madness: A Challenge to Convention', in Steven Paul Scher (ed.), *Music and Text: Critical Inquiries* (Cambridge: Cambridge University Press, 1992).

Rosenthal, Harold, *Two Hundred Years at Covent Garden* (London: Putnam & Co., 1958).

Rosmini, Enrico, *La legislazione e la giurisprudenza dei teatri e dei diritti d'autore*, 2 vols. (Milan: F. Manini, 1876).

Rosselli, John, *The Opera Industry in Italy from Cimarosa to Verdi* (Cambridge: Cambridge University Press, 1984).

Singers in Italian Opera: The History of a Profession (Cambridge: Cambridge University Press, 1992).

Music and Musicians in Nineteenth-Century Italy (London: B. T. Batsford Ltd., 1991).

Rousseau, Jean-Jacques, *Emile, ou de l'éducation*, Book V (1762), in *Œuvres complètes de Jean-Jacques Rousseau*, vol. IV (Paris: Gallimard, 1969).

Rowell, George (ed.), *Victorian Dramatic Criticism* (London: Methuen & Co. Ltd, 1971).

Ruffo, Titta, *La mia parabola: memorie* (Rome: Staderini S. P. A., 1977).

Ruskin, John, *Sesame and Lilies* (London: George Allen, 1893).

Russo, Paolo, 'Giuditta Pasta: cantante pantomimica', *Musica e Storia*, 10/2 (2002), 497–534.

Rutherford, Susan, 'The Voice of Freedom: Images of the Prima Donna', in Gardner and Rutherford (eds.), *The New Woman and Her Sisters*.

'Wilhelmine Schröder-Devrient: Wagner's Tragic Muse', in Maggie Gale and Viv Gardner (eds.), *Women, Theatre and Performance: New Histories, New Historiographies* (Manchester: Manchester University Press, 2000).

'"Unnatural Gesticulation" or "*un geste sublime*": Dramatic Performance in Opera', *Arcadia*, 36/2 (2001), 236–55.

'*La traviata*, or the "Willing Grisette": Male Critics and Female Performance in the 1850s', in Fabrizio Della Seta, Roberta Montemorra Marrin and Marco Marica (eds.), *Verdi 2001. Atti del convegno internazionale di studi, Parma, New York, New Haven 24 gennaio–1° febbraio 2001*, 2 vols. (Florence: Olschki, 2003).

Salazar, Philippe-Joseph, *Idéologies de l'opéra* (Paris: Presses Universitaires de France, 1980).

Salsbury, Edith Colgate, *Susy and Mark Twain: Family Dialogues* (New York: Harper & Row, 1965).

Sand, George, *Consuelo: A Romance of Venice* (1842; repr. New York: Da Capo Press, 1979).

Countess of Rudolstadt (London: A. & F. Denny, n.d.).

Correspondance de George Sand, 25 vols., ed. Georges Lubin (Paris: Garnier Frères, 1969).

Histoire de ma vie (1855; repr. Paris: Stock, 1945).

Saracino, Egidio, 'Le convenienze e inconvenienze teatrali (1827)', in *Tutti i libretti di Donizetti* (Milan: Garzanti, 1993).

Scholes, Percy A., *The Mirror of Music 1844–1944*, 2 vols. (London: Novello & Co., and Oxford University Press, 1947).

Scholes, Percy A. (ed.), *The Oxford Companion to Music* (London: Oxford University Press, 1970).

Schopenhauer, Arthur, 'Ueber die Weiber', *Werke in zehn Bänden*, 10 vols. (Zürich: Diogenes, 1977).

Schreiner, Olive, *Woman and Labour* (1911; repr. London: Virago, 1978).

Scott, Sir Walter, *The Bride of Lammermoor* (1819; London: J. M. Dent & Sons, 1985).

Servadio, Gaia, *The Real Traviata: The Life of Giuseppina Strepponi, Wife of Giuseppe Verdi* (London: Hodder & Stoughton, 1994).

Shaw, George Bernard, *London Music in 1888–89* (London: Constable & Co. Ltd., 1937).

Music in London: 1890–1894, 3 vols. (London: Constable & Co., Ltd., 1932).

Shaw's Music: 1893–1950 (London: Bodley Head, 1981).

Major Critical Essays (London: Penguin, 1986).

Sheehan, Vincent, *The Amazing Oscar Hammerstein: The Life and Exploits of an Impresario* (London: Weidenfeld & Nicolson, 1956).

Showalter, Elaine, *The Female Malady: Women, Madness and English Culture, 1830–1980* (London: Virago Press, 1987).

Sexual Anarchy: Gender and Culture at the Fin de Siècle (London: Bloomsbury, 1991).

Siddons, Henry, *Practical Illustrations of Rhetorical Gesture and Action, adapted to the English Drama, from a work on the same subject by M. Engel* (London: Richard Phillips, 1807).

Skelton, Geoffrey, *Wagner in Thought and Practice* (London: Lime Tree, 1991).

Smart, Mary Ann, 'The Lost Voice of Rosine Stoltz', in Blackmer and Smith (eds.), *En Travesti.*

Mimomania: Music and Gesture in Nineteenth-Century Opera (Berkeley and Los Angeles: University of California Press, 2004).

Smith, Patrick J., *The Tenth Muse: A Historical Study of the Opera Libretto* (London: Victor Gollancz, 1971).

Smith, R. D. (ed.), *The Writings of Anna Wickham: Free Woman and Poet* (London: Virago, 1984).

Smyth, Ethel, *The Memoirs of Ethel Smyth* (Harmondsworth: Viking, 1987).

Sografi, Antonio Simone, *Le convenienze e le inconvenienze teatrali* (Florence: Felice Le Monnier, 1972).

Soldene, Emily, *My Theatrical and Musical Recollections* (London: Downey & Co., 1897).

Solie, Ruth (ed.), *Musicology and Difference: Gender and Sexuality in Music Scholarship* (Berkeley: University of California Press, 1993).

Sorba, Carlotta, *Teatri: l'Italia del melodramma nell'età del Risorgimento* (Bologna: Il Mulino, 2001).

Spotts, Frederic, *Bayreuth: A History of the Wagner Festival* (New Haven and London: Yale University Press, 1994).

Stacey, Jackie, *Star Gazing: Hollywood Cinema and Female Spectatorship* (London and New York: Routledge, 1994).

Stagno Bellincioni, Bianca, *Roberto Stagno e Gemma Bellincioni intimi* (Florence: Monsalvato, 1943).

Stanford, Charles Villiers, *Studies and Memories* (London: Archibald Constable, 1908).

Pages from an Unwritten Diary (London: Edward Arnold, 1914).

Stanislavski, Constantin, *My Life in Art*, trans. J. J. Robbins (1924: repr. London: Methuen, 1980).

Building a Character (London: Methuen, 1950).

Steane, John Barry, *The Grand Tradition: Seventy Years of Singing On Record* (London: Duckworth, 1974).

Stebbins, Genevieve, *Delsarte System of Expression* (1902; repr. New York: Dance Horizons, 1977).

Stendhal [Marie Henri Beyle], *Rome, Naples et Florence* (1817; Paris: Le Divan, 1927).

The Life of Rossini, trans. Richard Coe (2nd edn, 1824; repr. London: John Calder, 1985).

Souvenirs d'egotisme (1832; Paris: Le Divan, 1927).

Stern, Kenneth A., 'A Documentary Study of Giuditta Pasta on the Opera Stage (Italy)', Ph.D. dissertation, City University of New York, 1983.

Stocchi, Alessandro, *Diario del Teatro Ducale di Parma dall'anno 1829 al 1840, compilato del portiere al Palco Scenico Alessandro Stocchi* (Parma: Giuseppe Rossetti, 1841).

Diario del Teatro Ducale di Parma dell'Anno 1841, compilato del portiere al Palco Scenico Alessandro Stocchi (Parma: Giuseppe Rossetti, 1842).

Strunk, Oliver (ed.), *Source Readings in Music History* (New York: W. W. Norton & Company, 1950).

Sutcliffe, Tom, *Believing in Opera* (London: Faber, 1996).

Tabanelli, Nicola, *Le 'Scritture Teatrali' degli artisti lirici e drammatici* (Padua: Milani, 1938).

Tacchinardi, Nicola, *Dell'opera in musica sul teatro italiano e de' suoi difetti* (Florence: Berni, 1833).

Tamvaco, Jean-Louis, *Les Cancans de l'Opéra: Le Journal d'une habilleuse 1836–1848*, 2 vols. (Paris: CNRS Editions, 2000).

Taylor, George, *Players and Performances in the Victorian Theatre* (Manchester and New York: Manchester University Press, 1989).

Tchaikovsky, Piotr Ilyich, *Letters to His Family: An Autobiography*, trans. Galina Von Meck (New York: Stein and Day, 1981).

Temperley, Nicholas, *The Music of the English Parish Church*, 2 vols. (Cambridge: Cambridge University Press, 1979).

Temperley, Nicholas (ed.), *The Lost Chord: Essays on Victorian Music* (Bloomington and Indianapolis: Indiana University Press, 1989).

Thompson, Oscar, *The American Singer* (New York: The Dial Press Inc., 1937).

Thompson, Tierl (ed.), *Dear Girl: The Diaries and Letters of Two Working Women (1897–1917)* (London: The Women's Press, 1987).

Tick, Judith, *American Women Composers Before 1870* (Ann Arbor: UMI Research Press, 1983).

Tolstoy, Leo, *War and Peace* (1869), trans. Constance Garnett (London: Pan Books Ltd., 1972).

Tosi, Pier Francesco, *Observations on the Florid Song*, trans. J. E. Galliard (1743; repr. London: William Reeves, 1967).

Toynbee, William (ed.), *The Diaries of William Charles Macready: 1833–1851*, 2 vols. (London: Chapman & Hall Ltd., 1912).

Treadwell, Nina, 'Female Operatic Cross-dressing: Bernardo Saddumene's Libretto for Leonardo Vinci's *Li zite 'n galera* (1722)', *Cambridge Opera Journal*, 10/2 (July 1998), 131–56.

Tree, Viola, *Castles in the Air: A Story of My Singing Days* (New York: George H. Doran Company, 1926).

Trezzini, Lamberto (ed.), *Due secoli di vita musicale: storia del Teatro Comunale di Bologna*, 3 vols. (Bologna: Nuova Alfa, 1987).

Trollope, Fanny, *Paris and the Parisians* (1836; repr. Gloucester: Alan Sutton Publishing Ltd., 1985).

Tuggle, Robert, *The Golden Age of Opera* (New York: Holt, Rinehart and Winston, 1983).

Tunley, David, *Salons, Singers and Songs: A Background to Romantic French Song 1830–1870* (Aldershot: Ashgate, 2002).

Turnbull, Michael, *Mary Garden* (Aldershot: Scolar Press, 1997).

Turner, Frank M., *The Greek Heritage in Victorian Britain* (New Haven and London: Yale University Press, 1981).

Valdrighi, Luigi Francesco and Giorgio Ferrari-Morena, *Cronistoria dei teatri di Modena dal 1539 al 1871 del maestro Alessandro Gandini arrichita d'interessanti notizie e continuata fino al presente da Luigi Francesco Valdrighi & Giorgio Ferrari-Morena* (Modena: Tipografia Sociale, 1873).

Wagner, Richard, *My Life*, trans. Andrew Gray (Cambridge: Cambridge University Press, 1983).

Actors and Singers, trans. William Ashton Ellis (Lincoln and London: University of Nebraska Press, 1995).

Walsh, T. J., *Monte Carlo Opera 1879–1909* (Dublin: Gill & Macmillan, 1975).

Warner, Marina, *Monuments and Maidens: The Allegory of the Female Form* (London: Pan Books Ltd., 1987).

From the Beast to the Blonde: On Fairytales and Their Tellers (London: Chatto & Windus, 1994).

Weaver, William, *The Golden Century of Italian Opera: From Rossini to Puccini* (London: Thames & Hudson, 1980).

Weber, William, *Music and the Middle Class: The Social Structure of Concert Life in London, Paris and Vienna* (London: Croom Helm, 1975).

Weeks, Jeffrey, *Sex, Politics and Society: The Regulation of Sexuality Since 1800* (2nd edn, London and New York: Longman, 1989).

Weinstock, Herbert, *Rossini* (1968; repr. New York: Limelight, 1987).

Vincenzo Bellini: His Life and His Operas (London: Weidenfeld & Nicolson, 1971).

Wells, H. G., *Ann Veronica* (1909; London: Virago, 1980).

White, Eric Walter, *A History of English Opera* (London: Faber and Faber Ltd., 1983).

Wood, Elizabeth, 'Performing Rights: A Sonography of Women's Suffrage', *The Musical Quarterly*, 79/4 (Winter 1995), 606–43.

Wood, Henry, *My Life of Music* (London: Victor Gollancz Ltd., 1938).

Zavadini, Guido, *Donizetti: vita – musiche – epistolario* (Bergamo: Istituto Italiano d'Arti Grafiche, 1948).

Zoppi, Umberto, *Angelo Mariani, Giuseppe Verdi e Teresa Stolz in un carteggio inedito* (Milan: Garzanti, 1947).

Zorn, John W., *The Essential Delsarte* (Metuchen, NJ: The Scarecrow Press, 1968).

INDEX

(Dates have been given for female singers, where possible.)

Actresses' Franchise League 87, 88

Adam, Adolphe 20

Albert, Prince 77

Alboni, Marietta (1826–94) 29, 31, 151,
    211, 225, 226, 230, 244

Alda, Frances (1879–1952) 21, 78, 85–6,
    92, 101, 109, 310, 339

Alexandra, Princess of
    Wales 138, 139–40

Amato, Pasquale 107, 109

aria di baule 175–6, 177

Arkel, Madame 116

Armida 183, 184

Arral, Blanche (1864–1945) 191

Arrieta, Emilio
  Ildegonda 108

Artôt, Désirée (1835–1907) 150, 151

Asquith, Rt. Hon. Herbert, Earl of
    Oxford 116

Atherton, Gertrude 73

Auber, Daniel-François-Esprit
    (1782–1871) 21, 79
  La Muette de Portici 19

audience 15, 16, 18, 25, 35, 41, 55, 58, 74,
    75, 78, 81, 88, 180, 192–3, 245,
    246, 248, 253, 258

Austen, Jane
  Emma 55

Austin, Gilbert 252

Auteri-Manzocchi, Salvatore
  Stella 194

autobiographies and memoirs 8, 24–5,
    31, 39, 42, 58, 70, 71, 83, 109, 111,
    114, 118, 123, 142, 196, 203

Bach, Johann Sebastian 77

Bagration, Princess 75

Bahr, Hermann 88

Bahr-Mildenburg, Anna (1872–1947) 88

Balfe, Michael 169, 170

Bandini, Andrea 175, 188

Barbaja, Domenico 137, 167, 169

Barbieri-Nini, Marianna (1818–87)
    207, 258

baritone 216, 223

Baroni, Leonora (1590–1640) 288

Barnum, Phineas Taylor 32

Barthe-Banderali, Anna (n.d.) 112

Barthes, Roland 38, 239

Bashkirtseff, Marie (1859–84) 13, 73–5, 89
  journal 73–4
  feminism 73
  purposes in singing 74

bass 214

Bassi, Madame 228

Beale, Willert 121, 122

Beerbohm Tree, Sir Herbert 116

Beethoven, Ludwig van (1770–1827)
  Fidelio 14, 62, 64, 182, 184, 205, 236, 237,
    240, 241, 244, 245, 251, 262, 264

Belgiojoso, Cristina (Trivulzio),
    Princess of 137

Bellincioni, Cesare 130, 132, 133
Bellincioni, Gemma (1864–1950) 123,
　　130–3, 176, 196, 207, 274
　relationship with mother 130–3
　retirement 202, 203
　as Salome 202
　dramatic performance 254, 272
Bellini, Vincenzo (1801–35) 42, 174, 180,
　　209, 226, 235, 300
　Beatrice di Tenda 173
　Bianca e Fernando 174
　I Capuleti e i Montecchi 12, 226
　I puritani 16, 252
　La sonnambula 21, 173, 217, 234, 240,
　　241, 242, 244, 245, 260, 263
　La straniera 12, 183, 184
　Norma 12, 16, 19, 28, 77, 173, 180, 213,
　　234, 235, 281, 300
Beltramelli, Giuditta (1834–?) 201
Berg, Alban
　Wozzeck 213
　Lulu 267
Berlioz, Hector 50, 59, 77, 163,
　　226, 239, 261
Bermani, Benedetto 27, 33, 123
Beringer, Mrs Oscar 87
Bernard, Madame 195
Bernau, Chiara (1852–1901) 194
Bernhardt, Sarah 244, 245–7,
　　253, 270
Bernini, Drusilla (n.d.) 105
Berry, Maria Carolina di Borbone,
　　Duchess of 136
Bertin, Louise (1805–77) 10
Biagioli, Carolina Herdlizka (n.d.) 190
Billington, Elizabeth (1765–1818) 31, 42
Birds of Rhiannon 36
Bishop, Anna (1810–84) 7, 40, 154–8
　touring 193
Bishop, Sir Henry 154–8

Bizet, Georges (1838–75) 21, 108
　Carmen 12, 13, 217, 218, 228,
　　229, 267–70, 339
Blaze de Bury, Henri 245, 246
Blessington, Marguerite 19, 74
　The Two Friends 55
Boccabadati, Augusta (?–1875) 197
Boccabadati, Luigia (1800–50) 197
Boccabadati, Virginia (1828–1922)
　　197–202, 275, 326
Bochsa, Nicholas 154–8
Boeticher, Herr 77
Boito, Arrigo (1842–1918) 20, 210, 254
　Mefistofele 270
Bolton, Mary Catherine
　　(Lady Thurlow) 152
Bonini, Emilia (*fl.*1813–29) 191
Bori, Lucrezia (1887–1960) 83, 160, 178
Borodin, Alexander Porfir'yevich 10
Bosio, Angiolina (1830–59) 186, 265–6
Bouhy, Jacques (1848–1929) 100, 140
Brambilla, Marietta (1807–75) 231
Braslau, Sophie (*fl.* 1913–22) 229
Brema, Marie (1856–1925) 87–8,
　　229, 309
Brenna, Guglielmo 225
Brignoli, Pasquale 252
Briones, Joaquina García (1780–1854) 239
Brühl, Karl von 181
Bülow, Hans von 139
Burger, Sophie 237
Butt, Clara (1872–1936) 140
Byron, Lord George Gordon Noel
　The Island 37

Callas, Maria (1923–77) 2
Callender, May 77
Calvé, Emma (1858–1942) 8, 14, 93,
　　112, 207, 211, 229, 275
　early performances 189

travesti roles 248–51
   dramatic performance 261,
      268–70, 272
Campo-Reale, Princess: Maria
   Anna Zoe Rosalia Beccadelli
   di Bologna 75
Camporese, Violante (also given as
   Camporesi) (1785–1839) 188
Carelli, Emma (1877–1928) 270
Caruso, Enrico (1873–1921) 4, 101, 103
Carlyle, Thomas 288, 317
Castil-Blaze, François-Henri-Joseph 180
Castlereagh, Lord 31
castrato 3–4, 59, 164, 214, 216, 225
Catalani, Angelica (1780–1849) 8, 14, 15,
      40, 56, 167, 168–9, 184, 192, 248
Cather, Willa 35, 59, 66, 67, 68, 148–9
   The Diamond Mine 314
   Scandal 148–9
   The Song of the Lark 66, 68
Cattaneo, Nicolò 257
Cavalieri, Lina (1874–1944) 192, 273
Censi, Virginia (n.d.) 193
Cerrito, Fanny 258
Cesari, Pietro 310
Chambers, Ada (n.d.) 142
Charpentier, Gustave
   Louise 146, 267
Chekhov, Anton
   Uncle Vanya 37
Chekhov, Michael 256
Chorley, Henry Fothergill 19, 152,
      227, 238, 243, 260, 265, 267
Cilea, Francesco (1866–1950)
   L'arlesiana 12
Circe 47
Cirelli, Camillo 137, 195
Cirillo, Duke of 130
Clairon, Claire Josèphe Hippolyte
   Léris de la Tude 241

Clément, Catherine 9–11, 17
Clemens, Susy 114–15, 117
Code Napoleon 214
Colbran, Isabella (1785–1845) 40, 121, 137,
      189, 190, 206–7, 215, 330, 232
Comelli, Adelaide (1796–1845)
   150, 167, 169
Commettant, Oscar 92
conductor 117, 125, 169–70, 171,
      178, 182–4, 211–12, 218
conservatoires 49, 76, 91, 92, 103, 114, 130
   female access to 103–5
   chaperonage 105
   numbers of women students 106–7
   advantages of 107–8
   standards of teaching 108–9
   student life 107, 109
contralto 29, 88, 214–15
   disappearance of 222–5
   roles 225–30
convenienze 27, 163–6, 171, 172
Coquelin, Benoit Constant 255
Corinaldesi, Orsola (n.d.) 192
Corradi Panatelli, Clorinda (n.d.) 175
Correa, Lorenza (1773–?) 232
Cortesi, Adelaide (n.d.) 200
Cortesi, Letizia (*fl.* 1822–32) 170, 171
Cox, Bessie 70
critical reception 33, 35, 38, 134, 177
Crotch, William 12
Cruvelli, Sophie (1826–1907) 140, 189
Cuzzoni, Francesca (1696–1778) 43
Czillag, Rosa (n.d.) 262

Dal Monte, Toti (1893–1975) 150, 203
D'Alvarez, Marguerite (1886–1953)
   111, 191
D'Annunzio, Gabriele
   La Gioconda 37
Dante Alighieri 36

D'Aoust, Marquis 79
Da Ponte, Lorenzo 192
David, Giovanni 215
Davies, Maggie 87
Davies, Marion 73
De Angelis, Hilda 87
De Beauvoir, Simone 4–5
De Boigne, Charles 59, 184
Debussy, Claude 116
    Pelléas et Mélisande 12, 213, 228, 271
De Cisneros, Eleanora (1878–1934)
    88, 113, 140
Decroux, Etienne 255
D'Eyrel, Francesco 90
De Forest, Carol 77
De Gresac, Fred 300
De Grey, Gladys, Marchioness
    of Ripon 19, 138
De Hegermann-Lindencrone,
    Lillie 79–81, 89, 102, 129
    early study in London 79
    marriage 79
    study in Paris 79
    as composer 79
    professional career 80
    dramatic training 255–7
De Laferté, Vicomte de 187
De Lagrange, Anna (1824–1905)
    98, 140, 242
Delle Sedie, Enrico 79, 91
De Lussan, Zélie (1861–1949) 229
De Melcy, Vicomte Gérard 32, 150
De Pontmartin, comte Armand 192
Delsarte, François 79, 252, 255–7
De Muro Lomanto, Enzo 150
De Reszke, Jean 4, 93, 97, 114,
    118, 141, 142, 330
De Staël, Madame
    (Anne-Louise-Germaine)
    Corinne, ou, L'Italie 59

Destinn, Emmy (1878–1930) 110
De Trabadelo, Ange-Pierre 101
De Valabrèque, P. 167, 169
Devrient, Eduard 237
Devrient, Ludwig 237
Diderot, Denis 208, 242, 259
Döme, Zoltan 159
domestic music-making 47, 58, 73, 74, 138
    as artistic enterprise 78
    contact with professionals 75
    drawing-room prima donnas
        64, 71–81, 89
    middle- and upper-class singers 47,
        76, 79
    reasons for singing 72
    salons and private concerts 76
Donizetti, Gaetano 10–11, 20,
    171–2, 180, 193, 226
    Anna Bolena 16, 173
    La donna del lago 184
    La Favorite 193
    La Fille du régiment 14
    Le convenienze ed inconvenienze
        teatrali 122, 123, 169–70
    Le Duc d'Albe 10
    Linda di Chamounix 226
    Lucia di Lammermoor 12, 28,
        171, 180, 210, 263
    Lucrezia Borgia 16, 28, 217, 261
    Maria Stuarda 169, 170, 241
    Pia de' Tolomei 171
Dorus-Gras, Julie (1805–1896) 11
dramatic performance 29, 35,
    65, 178, 207, 231
    costumes 142, 241–2, 244, 251, 268, 272
    criticism of 207
    declamation 238–9
    difficulties of 210–13, 258
    en travesti [cross-dressing] 61, 174,
        214, 225, 243

gesture 205, 206, 233–5, 237,
240, 244, 245, 252–4, 255,
257, 259, 268–70, 272
idealism 207–9, 260–6, 273
realism 207–9, 266–74
theories of 207–10
Duff, Sarah Robinson 99, 101, 143, 145
Dukas, Paul (1865–1935) 10
Dukes, George 113
Du Maurier, George
Trilby 44–6, 115, 116, 119, 264
Dupeget, Oliverio 149–50
Duprez, Gilbert-Louis 4, 112,
172, 216, 244, 245
Duse, Eleonora 207, 240, 268, 270
Duvéyrier, Anne-Honoré-Joseph,
pseud. Mélesville (1787–1865) 11

Eames, Emma (1865–1952) 19, 77,
83, 100, 127–8, 160, 179, 202,
203, 261, 263
Easton, Florence (1882–1955) 212–13
Ebers, John 167–9, 186, 188, 191
Edvina, Louise (1880–1948) 82
Eichendorff, Joseph Freiherr von
Waldesgespräch 37
Eliot, George 27, 59, 62–4, 67
Armgart 58, 62–5, 85
Daniel Deronda 64–6, 68, 152
Engel, Johann Jakob
Ideen zu einer Mimik 208, 252, 269
Erlanger, Camille
Aphrodite 272
Esty, Alice (1864–1935) 87
Eunicke, Johanna (1800–56) 188

Farrar, Geraldine (1882–1967) 83, 109,
141, 272, 310
Fauré, Gabriel 116
Fava, Fosca (n.d.) 106

Favelli, Stefania (n.d.) 151
Fay, Amy 138, 139–40
Ferdinand II 103
Ferrari, Giacomo 329
Ferrarini, Giulio Cesare 192, 197–201
Ferrarini, Giulio 192, 194
Festa Maffei, Francesca (1778–1835)
194–5
Fétis, François-Joseph 192
Filippini, Carolina (n.d.) 105
Flaubert, Gustave 59
Flécheux, Marie (1815–42) 160
Florimo, Francesco 104
Fodor-Mainvielle, Joséphine (1789–1870)
180, 236
Foote, Maria (Countess of
Harrington) 152
Forconi, Felicita (1819–?) 29, 31
Foscolo, Ugo 39
Frandin, Lison (1854–1911) 192
Friedrich Wilhelm II 124
Fremstad, Olive (1871–1951) 66,
68, 82, 86, 229
Frezzolini, Erminia (1818–84) 30,
31, 35, 42, 173, 261

Gabbi, Adalgisa (1857–?) 106
Gabbi, Carolina (1820–?) 105
Galletti Gianoli, Isabella (1835–1901) 202
Galli-Curci, Amelita (1882–1963)
83, 103, 261
Galli-Marié, Célestine (1840–1905)
267, 268
Galve, comtesse de 137
Garcia, Gustave (1837–1925) 252, 337
García, Manuel I (1775–1832) 96, 126, 235
Garcia, Manuel II (1805–1906) 79, 80, 91,
97, 102, 112, 121
Garden, Mary (1874–1967) 57, 87,
99–101, 178, 315

Garden, Mary (1874–1967) (cont.)
  study in Paris 99–101, 143
  sponsorship by the Mayers 142–9
  desire for independence 145, 160
  accusations of immorality 146–7
  sexual harassment 147, 190
  dispute with Mayers 146–7
  dramatic performance 261, 270–3, 274
Gaskell, Elizabeth 71, 72
Gaskell, Marianne 72, 73
Gatti-Casazza, Giulio 85
Gautier, Théophile 205, 223, 325
  Coerulei oculi 37
Gazzuoli, Antonio 197
Geale, Josephine, née Clark 77–8
Generali, Pietro
  Il voto di Jefte 175
Gentil, Louis 160
Georges, Marguerite 332
Gerster, Etelka (1855–1920) 140
Gibelli, Lorenzo 111
Giddens, Mrs George 87
Giglioli, Lucia (n.d.) 105
Gigli, Beniamino 4
Gigliucci, Count Giovanni
  Battista 126–7, 151
Giordano, Umberto (1867–1948) 10
Giorgi Righetti, Geltrude Maria
  (1793–1862) 1, 26, 275
Giovannini, Luigia (n.d.) 105
Giraldoni, Leone 97
Gissing, George
  Thyrza 44
Giuglini, Antonio 311
Gleeson-White, Cicely 82
Gluck, Christoph Willibald
  Ritter von
  Iphigénie en Aulide 12
  Orfeo ed Euridice 59, 62, 63, 66, 248
Goethe, Johann Wolfgang von 236

Goldoni, Carlo
  L'Impresario delle Smirne 163
Gomes, Carlos
  Il Guarany 77
Gonsalez, Giuseppe (*fl. c.* 1900–35) 21
Gounod, Charles-François 21, 77,
  79, 256
  Faust 13, 22, 217, 226, 263, 266,
    267, 337
  Roméo et Juliette 138–9
Gower, Fred 128, 134, 159
Grainger, Percy 116
Grassi, Maddalena (n.d.) 40
Grehier, Leon 145, 147
Grisi, Ernesta (1819–99) 223
Grisi, Giuditta (1805–40) 151
Grisi, Giulia (1811–69) 15, 16, 31,
  149–50, 153, 186, 192, 205
Grünbaum, Caroline (1814–68)
  170, 171, 194
Guadagni, Gaetano 59
Guarducci, Mlle (n.d.) 130
Guilbert, Yvette 270
Guglielmi, Pietro 203
Gunsberg, Raoul 191
Gutheil-Schoder, Marie
  (1874–1935) 261

Hahn, Reynaldo 93, 98, 224
Hähnel, Amalie (1807–49) 77
Hammerstein, Oscar 88, 125, 190
Handel, George Frideric 43
Harris, Captain 152
Haweis, H. Reginald 52, 53, 69, 72
Haydn, Joseph 62
  La canterina 121
Hazlewood, C. H. 21
Hazlitt, William 38
Heine, Heinrich
  Die Lorelei 36

Heinefetter, Clara (1816–57) 124
Hempel, Frieda (1885–1955) 109, 124
Hepburn, Patrick 114
Herbert, Victor 82
Hérold, Ferdinand
  Zampa 49
Hesse, Hermann
  Gertrude 55
Hippolytus of Rome 285
Hoffmann, E. T. A. 264
  Councillor Krespel 43, 45–6
Hoffmann, Paul 21
Holmès, Augusta (1847–1903) 279
Holmes, Vera 87
Homer, Louise (1871–1947) 229
Höngen, Elisabeth (1906–97) 82, 102
Howard, Kathleen (1880–1956) 83,
    110–11, 141–2, 211, 270, 275
Hugo, Victor
  Notre Dame 54
Huneker, James 35, 57,
    271, 273
  Bedouins 57
  Painted Veils 43–5
Hund, Alicia 139
Hunt, Ernest 71
Hunt, Leigh 39, 126
husbands 32, 43, 55, 61, 63, 81, 84, 85, 87,
    114, 118, 120–1, 124, 130, 137, 150,
    152, 166, 167, 169, 172, 194
  antagonistic towards singers'
    careers 151, 152–3, 159
  supportive of singers' careers 159
  marital authority 153–4, 157
  mockery of 158–9
Hyde, General Thomas 127

Ibsen, Henrik
  A Doll's House 158
  The Lady from the Sea 37

impresarios 28, 32, 80, 85, 116, 117,
    121, 124, 125, 130, 131, 158–9,
    164, 166, 167–70, 171, 180, 186,
    191, 197, 200
  on greed of singers 184–5
  on singers' fees 186
  negotiation 187–8
  sexual harassment 190–1
  problems with singers' health 194–5

Janáček, Leos 10
  Jenůfa 14, 228
Jason 47
Jenoure, Aida 87
Jerome, St 36
Joan of Arc, St 11
Jones, Rosalie 85

Kellogg, Clara Louise (1842–1916) 68,
    82, 113, 128–9, 138–9, 143, 149,
    212, 242, 252, 264
Kemble Sartoris, Adelaide (1814–79) 203
Kemble, Fanny [Frances Anne] 291
Kienzl, Nina 137
Kingsley, Charles
  Westward Ho! 37
Kittl, Jan Bedrich
  *Bianca und Giuseppe, oder Die
    Franzosen vor Nizza* 19
Klafsky, Katharina (1855–96) 251
Klein, Hermann 244, 245, 263
Krafft-Ebing, Richard von 251
Kyntherland, Maria Cascelli 175–6

Lablache, Luigi 72, 77, 205
Laickham, Baroness 75
Lanari, Alessandro 171, 194, 195, 197
Laporte, Pierre François 186
Larkcom, Agnes (n.d.) 87
Lasalle, Jean 330

Lavater, Johann 54
Leclerc, Jean Baptiste 38
Lee, George J. Vandeleur 94–5
Lehmann, Carl 152
Lehmann, Lilli (1848–1929) 77, 97,
    108, 109, 152, 211, 221, 267
Lehmann, Liza (1862–1918) 87, 88
Lehmann, Lotte (1888–1976) 83,
    92, 109, 212
Leonardo, Leo 62, 64
Leo, Rosa (n.d.) 87
Leoncavallo, Ruggero
    Pagliacci 267
    Zazà 267
Leroux, Gaston
    The Phantom of the Opera 43, 45, 264
Levik, Sergei 20
Lewes, G. H. 62
Lichtenthal, Peter 49, 214, 224
Lincoln, Abraham 79
Lincoln, Marianne (1822–85) 292
Lind, Jenny (1820–87) 32, 77, 78,
    79, 149, 152, 153, 175, 192,
    230, 255, 261
Lipkowska, Lydia (1882–1955) 88
List, Elise (1822–93) 120
List, Lina (n.d.) 120
Liszt, Franz 39, 139
Litvinne, Céline (n.d.) 112
Litvinne, Félia (1860–1936) 112,
    137, 189, 191
Lloyd, Marie 224
Loew, Marie (n.d.) 152
Loewe, Sofia (1812–66) 174
Lorelei *see* singers, image, sirens
Lubin, Germaine (1890–1979) 160
Lucca, Pauline (1841–1908) 266
Lumley, Benjamin 32, 35, 125, 151
Lusignani, Carolina (n.d.) 105
Lyne, Felice (1891–1935) 310

MacDonnell, Mrs Hercules (n.d.) 75
Macready, William 205, 241
Mainzer, Joseph 50–2, 53, 69
Malibran, Eugène 126
Malibran, Maria Garcia (1808–36) 2, 15,
    32, 55, 59, 60, 82, 96, 102, 115, 116,
    121, 126, 187, 193, 215, 221, 233, 251
    dramatic performance 239–43, 255,
        261, 264
    travesti roles 244, 245
Mancini, Giovanni Battista 329
Mantelli, Eugenia (1860–1926) 229
Mantius, Eduard 77
Mapleson, Colonel James Henry
    21, 22–3, 130
Marcello, Benedetto 33, 121, 163
Marchelli, Domenico 200
Marchesi, Blanche (1863–1940) 45,
    93–4, 112, 114–15, 218
Marchesi, Matilde (1821–1913) 84–5, 97,
    98, 100–1, 123, 124, 125, 140
Marchisio, Barbara (1833–1914) 203
Maretzek, Max 21, 23, 32, 42, 102, 123, 150
Maria Isabella di Borbone, Queen of
    Naples 136
Maria Luigia, Duchess of Parma 104
Mariani, Rosa (1799–1832) 224, 331
Mario, Giovanni Matteo, Cavaliere
    de Candia 82, 150, 315
Marliani, Marco Aurelio
    Ildegonda 15, 16
Mascagni, Pietro 207
    Cavalleria rusticana 268
Massenet, Jules 79, 227
    Cendrillon 227
    Esclarmonde 73
    Manon 267
    Thaïs 267, 271–2
    Werther 12
Mattei, Saverio 91

Matzenauer, Margarethe
(1881–1963) 229
Maurel, Victor 112, 137, 301
Mayer, David 143–9, 190
Mayer, Florence 99, 142–9, 190
Mayhew, Henry 42
Mayr, Simon
Atar, ossia Il seraglio d'Ormus 19
Che originali 231
Ginevra di Scozia 192
Medea in Corinto 14, 136–7, 167, 169,
173, 175, 234, 337
La rosa bianca e la rosa rossa 167, 169
Mazzarelli, Rosina (n.d.) 151
Mazzoleni, Esther (1882–1982) 151, 217
McKinlay, Jean Sterling 87
Melba, Nellie (1861–1931) 15, 83, 97, 138,
196, 202, 222, 230, 309
Mendelssohn, Felix 53, 75
Menotti, Delfino 270
Mercadante, Saverio
Il giuramento 49
Meredith, George
Vittoria 43, 44
Merlin, María de las Mercedes Santa
Cruz y Montalvo, comtesse
de 96, 177
Metastasio, Pietro 91
Meux, Mrs Thos. 87
Meyerbeer, Giacomo (1791–1864)
21, 32, 173, 180, 262
Dinorah 81
Les Huguenots 16, 72, 213, 261
Le Prophète 16, 173, 227–8, 229, 253
Robert le diable 170, 171, 180, 199
Vielka 175
mezzo-soprano 54, 72, 87, 88, 215,
221, 228
Micheroux, Alessandro 135–7, 175, 187
Milanov, Zinka (1906–89) 102, 273

Milder-Hauptmann, Anna
(1785–1838) 185
Millöcker, Carl 21
Moja, Teresa (n.d.) 123
Monkswell, Lady Mary 71, 72
Monti, Marianna (1730–1814) 315
Moore, Bertha 87
Moore, Decima (1871–1964) 87
Moore, George
Evelyn Innes 43–5
Sister Theresa 43
Morandi, Rosa (1782–1824) 247
Morgan, Lady Sydney 299
Moriani, Napoleon 13, 325
Morley, Henry 262, 267
Morrochesi, Antonio 29, 252
Moulton, Charles 79
Mozart, Wolfgang Amadeus 172
Die Zauberflöte 77, 211, 244, 245
Don Giovanni 12, 16, 267
Le nozze di Figaro 81, 227, 244,
245, 248
Mukle, May 113
Musi, Claudio 169–70, 171
music and moral influence 22, 38, 47,
63, 69, 89, 291
Musorgsky, Modest Petrovich
Boris Godunov 14, 19

Naldi, Caroline, comtesse de Sparre
(fl. 1819–23) 151
Napoleon III, 79
Nasolini, Sebastiano 248
Neville, Henry 252
Nicolai, Otto
Die lustigen Weiber von Windsor 211
Nicolini, Giuseppe 175
Abenamet e Zoraide 244, 245
Nilsson, Christine (1843–1921) 80, 98,
129, 248, 263, 315

Nordica, Lillian (1857–1914) 70, 71, 86–7,
88, 128, 133–5, 149, 153, 255, 315
marriage 159
end of career 202
on Brünnhilde 219
vocal development 221–2
dramatic performance 336
Normanby, Lady 77
Norreys, Lady 76
Norton, Amanda 128, 133–5, 149
Norton, Edwin 133, 135
Norton, Onie 134
Norton, Wilhelmina 133
Nourrit, Adolphe 4, 215, 244
Novello, Clara (1818–1908) 13, 126–8,
151, 248
Novello, Mary Sabilla 126–7
Novello, Vincent 126
Novotna, Jarmila (1907–94) 221, 273

Offenbach, Jacques 20
Les Contes d'Hoffmann 32–3, 221
Old Price riots, Covent Garden 184
opera houses
Monte Carlo Opera House 191
Théâtre de la Monnaie,
Brussels 248
Britain, theatres
Covent Garden 19, 39, 88, 138, 142,
184, 205, 244, 262
Her Majesty's Theatre 15, 16,
19, 266
[also known as] King's Theatre 167
London Opera House 310
France, theatres
Paris Opéra 108, 134
Opéra-Comique 108, 146, 268
Opéra-National 20
Théâtre-Italien 137, 149, 179, 180,
187, 199, 205

Théâtre Lyrique 59, 80
Germany, theatres
Bayreuth 20, 88, 221, 222
Hoftheater, Dresden 182
Hoftheater, Berlin 169, 170, 179,
180, 181, 184, 185–6, 211
Italy, theatres
politeami 20
Teatro Carlo Felice,
Genoa 117, 174
Teatro Comunale, Bologna 175,
179, 188
Teatro Comunale, Cormons 117
Teatro Comunale, Modena 192
Teatro della Concordia,
Cremona 186
Teatro Costanzi, Rome 20,
270, 328
Teatro La Fenice, Venice 194
Teatro Lauro Rossi,
Macerata 197–8, 199, 200, 201
Teatro Metastasio, Prato 211
Teatro Nuovo, Spoleto 193
Teatro Nuovo, Naples 244, 245
Teatro della Pergola,
Florence 20, 171
Teatro Regio, Parma 3, 164, 169,
179, 192, 200
Teatro Regio, Turin 20, 179
Teatro di San Carlo, Naples 3, 136,
180, 193, 333
Teatro alla Scala, Milan 39, 118,
129, 190, 192, 228, 241, 244,
245, 270
Teatro della Società,
Rovigo 198
Teatro di Torre Argentina,
Rome 172, 194
Teatro dell'Unione,
Viterbo 199

Russia, theatres
Bol'shoy, St Petersburg 265
Mariinsky, St Petersburg 202, 322
Narodnïy Dom, St Petersburg 20
USA, theatres
Niblo's Garden, New York 20
Palmo's Opera House,
New York 20
Manhattan Opera House 88, 147
Metropolitan Opera House,
New York 78, 86, 88, 103,
222, 229
Tivoli Opera House, San
Francisco 20
Vienna, theatres
Kärntnertortheater 318
Theater an der Wien 318
operatic marketplace 15, 2, 3–45,
57, 90, 135–7, 161, 221, 254
Orlandi, Elisa (1811–33?) 175
Orpheus 47, 55, 63, 67, 89
Oxenberry, W. H. 21

Pacetti, Iva (1898–1981) 82, 129, 211
Pacini, Giovanni 75
Pacini, Luigi 131
Paisiello, Giovanni
Nina 167, 169, 231, 235
Palgrave Turner, Mary 87
Pallerini, Antonietta 207
Palliser, Esther (1872–?) 87, 88
Pankhurst, Emmeline 85, 86
Panofka, Heinrich 79,
218, 227
Pasta, Clelia 196
Pasta, Giuditta (1797–1865) 14, 40,
55, 135–7, 159, 170, 171, 173,
175–6, 186, 187, 189, 190,
193, 203, 207, 215, 239, 260,
275, 300

contract with King's Theatre,
London 167–8, 169
in *Norma* 179, 180
dispute at Théâtre-Italien 180
fees in London 186
enjoyment in singing 189
motherhood 196
end of career 202
dramatic performance 233–6, 240,
254, 260
travesti roles 226, 243, 244
Pasta, Giuseppe 159
patrons and patronage 23, 99, 110,
114, 135–49
female patrons 137
relationships with singers 141
Patti, Adelina (1843–1919) 15, 40,
70, 71, 95, 185, 211, 229, 242
Patmore, Coventry
The Angel in the House 6
Pellegrini Celoni, Anna (n.d.) 203
Pelzet, Ferdinando 253
Pelzet, Maddalena 255
Penco, Rosina (1823–94) 326
Petrov, Osip Afanas'yevich 321
Piave, Francesco Maria 174
Picchi, Ermanno 223
Piccolomini, Marietta (1834–99) 82,
89, 125, 151, 254, 326
dramatic performance 265–6, 267
Pirandello, Luigi 240
Pisaroni, Benedetta Rosmunda
(1793–1872) 41, 191, 224,
244, 331
Poizat, Michel 37
Ponchielli, Amilcare
La Gioconda 12, 228
Ponselle, Rosa (1897–1981) 7, 90,
103, 229, 272
Potocki, Count 183, 184

Predieri, Luca Antonio
   Zenobia 61
Prividali, Luigi 231
protettore 28, 135–7
Puccini, Giacomo
   La bohème 12, 232
   La fanciulla del West 14, 15
   Madama Butterfly 12, 13, 213,
      217–18
   Manon Lescaut 267
   Tosca 11, 12, 161, 176, 217, 267
Puzzi, Giacinta Toso (1808–89) 311

Quilter, Roger 116

Raaf, Anton 172
Rachel (Elisa Felix) 255
Rachelle, Laudelia Giuseppina 291
Raisa, Rosa (1893–1963) 221
Randeggar, Madame 113
Rastrelli, Giuseppe 182–4
Ray, William 114
Reed, Fanny 144
rehearsals 28, 43, 125, 168, 172,
      180, 182–3, 194, 210–11
Reichardt, Johann Friedrich 54
Rellstab, Ludwig 236
Reynolds, Sir Joshua 31
Ricci, Federico
   Il disertore per amore 77
Richardson, Josiah 97
Richardson, Miss 129
Ricordi, Giulio 181
Ricordi, Tito 116, 118, 274
Rimsky-Korsakov, Nikolai
     321, 322
   The Maid of Pskov 321
   The Tsar's Bride 322
   Mlada 322
Ritorni, Carlo 70, 71, 170, 171, 226, 233

Riviere, Robert 155
Ritter, Fanny Raymond 68–9, 138
Robert, Edouard 187
Robertson, Henry 248
Rode, Pierre 56
Rogers, Clara Kathleen (1844–1931) 95
Ronconi, Giorgio 244
Ronzi De Begnis, Giuseppina
     (1800–53) 193
Roosevelt, Blanche (1853–98) 98, 248
Roser Balfe, Lina (1808–88) 169–70
Rosmini, Enrico 153–4, 194, 195
Rossini, Gioachino 79, 110, 112,
     121, 126, 172, 178, 190, 222–3,
     225, 226, 227, 247
   La cenerentola 225, 232
   Elisabetta, regina d'Inghilterra 206
   Guillaume Tell 19, 49, 216,
     244, 245
   Il barbiere di Siviglia 172, 175,
     225, 229
   Il turco in Italia 231
   Le Comte Ory 227
   L'italiana in Algeri 14
   Mosè in Egitto 200
   Otello 13, 167, 169, 173, 175, 182, 184,
     209, 243, 245
   Semiramide 81, 167, 169, 180
   Tancredi 167, 168–9, 173, 175–6, 179,
     225, 243, 247
Rousseau, Jean-Jacques 5
   Essai sur l'origine des langues 38
Ryley, Madeleine Lucette 87
Rubens, Victor and Mrs 142
Rubini, Giovanni Battista 4, 77,
     150, 167, 169, 185, 215, 329
Rubini, Margherita 170, 171
rusalki see singers, image, sirens
Ruskin, John 69, 74
   Sesame and Lilies 52

Salvini-Donatelli, Fanny (?1815–1891) 40
Saint-Saëns, Camille 75
  Samson et Dalila 211, 228, 267
Samoyloff, Giulia 137
Sanelli, Gualtiero
  Gusmano il prode 200
Sand, George 35, 49, 59, 60–1, 63, 67
  Consuelo 60–2, 68
Sanderson, Sybil (1865–1903) 73, 82, 146
Sandwich, Lady 76
Sannazzaro, Carlotta 108
Santley, Sir Charles 248
Sanvitale, Count Stefano 170, 171
Saxony, Queen of 138
Sayão, Bidú (1902–99) 328
Sbriglia, Giovanni 99, 100
Scalia, Tina Whitaker (1858–1957) 77
Schmalz, Augusta (n.d.) 244, 245
Schneitzhoeffer, (Jean) 160
Schopenhauer, Arthur 59
Schreiner, Olive 220
Schröder, Friedrich 237
Schröder-Devrient, Wilhelmine
    (1804–60) 42, 173–4, 207, 215,
    233, 251
  at Dresden 182–4
  moral conduct 183–4
  custody of children 196
  travesti roles 226, 243, 244, 245, 330
  dramatic performance 236–9, 261, 264
Schubert, Franz 53
Schulz, Josefine (given by Kutsch as
    'Schulze') (1790–1880) 181, 185–6
Schumann, Clara 120, 139, 236
Schumann, Robert 53
Schumann-Heink, Ernestine
    (1861–1936) 83–4, 124, 137,
    225, 230
Scott, Sir Walter
  The Bride of Lammermoor 54

Scribe, Eugène 11
Scuderi, Sara (1906–87) 103, 129, 217
Seidler, Carolina (Karolina)
    (1790–1872) 174
Severini, Carlo 187
Shalyapin, Fyodor 178, 192, 273
Shaw, Bessie 72, 73, 94
Shaw, George Bernard 52, 72, 93, 94,
    108, 118, 268–9
Shaw, Lucy Carr 87, 94
Sherwin, Amy 87
Siddons, Sarah 332
singers
  as artists 59, 61, 62, 63, 64, 66,
    67, 68, 75, 84, 85–6, 98, 112,
    179, 184, 202, 274
  as composers 59, 88
  career 67, 68, 69
    developing a 120, 124–6, 189
    as escape 73, 110, 128
    legitimisation 68
    pleasure in 140, 160, 189, 203
    temporality 64
  celebrity 40, 57, 162
  confidence 192–3
  contracts 57, 124, 132, 142, 153–4,
    167–70, 171, 180, 181–2, 194–5
  education 27, 29, 104, 111–12
  eroticism 42, 44–5, 46, 272
  figlie dell'arte 82, 116, 121, 130,
    197, 231, 239, 255
  freedom 70, 71, 83, 89, 112, 145, 160,
    162, 179
  image 4–5, 22–3, 29, 31, 58, 73
    critical reception 35, 57
    discourses on 31–3, 35, 57, 58,
      68–9, 161
    fictional 27, 32–3, 35, 58, 59,
      60, 143
    odes and sonnets 29–31, 35, 40

singers (cont.)
  pornography 31, 42, 45
  proto-feminist 34, 59
  sirens 36, 47, 55, 60, 150; Lorelei 36;
    rusalki 36; *undine* 36; nineteenth-
    century representations 36–7;
    and music 36, 37–8; and opera
    38–40; and prima donnas 32,
    40–7, 56–7, 58
  songbirds 32, 47, 57, 58, 69
  superwoman 57, 58
independence
  personal 61, 62, 63, 64, 65–6, 67,
    145, 152, 160, 162
  financial 33, 56, 69, 73, 127, 158
  sexual 33, 44, 56
influence in opera house
    management 162, 184
lack of success 113–19
lesbianism 160
as managers 168
marriage 29, 43, 63, 64, 72, 86, 114,
    120, 126–8, 130, 134, 149–60, 300
  titled marriages 151–2
  legislation 153–4
  pre-marital contracts 130, 153
  divorce 127, 196
menstruation 194
middle- and upper-class 73, 82–3, 92,
    116, 128, 139, 143, 162, 179, 255
morality 27, 29, 33, 46, 55, 56, 61, 82,
    111, 124, 128–9, 146, 183–4
as moral 'agent' 69, 89
motherhood 43, 61, 65–6, 84,
    104, 133, 154–6, 158, 195–7
political activity 86
physical appearance 191–2, 194–5, 273
pregnancy 32, 160, 170, 181, 194–6
relationship with composers 172
retirement 129, 150–2, 195, 202

salaries and fees 15, 56, 127, 153–4,
    156–7, 161, 162, 167, 168, 180,
    181–2, 184–9, 229–30
  sexual harassment 147, 190–1
  working-class 138, 140, 231
singing
  decadence in 91
  expressive possibilities 210
  theories about 49, 90
  and health 51, 69–70, 115, 193
    corsets 70–1
  and character 54
  moral influence of 50–4
  pleasure in 74–5, 202
  tuition 22, 23, 46, 47, 50–4, 76,
    79, 90–119, 139, 140
    science 91, 115, 161
    methodologies 90, 91–2, 93–103
    respiration 70–1, 97–8
    study abroad 111, 113, 126, 133,
      135, 139, 141–2, 143
    tutors 45, 64, 65, 66, 73, 92–102,
      117, 140
      charlatans 92–5, 109
      ideal tutor 95–6
      finding tutors 98
    vocal technique 29, 90–2, 117,
      122, 215
singing actress 22, 207
Slate, Daisy 72
Slate, Ruth 72
Slawson, Eva 72
Smith Jones, Frank and Mrs 142
Smyth, Ethel (1858–1944) 10, 71,
    88, 292
Smyth, Mary 71
Sodese, Camilla (n.d.) 82
Sografi, Antonio Simone 122, 176
  Le convenienze teatrali 163
  Le inconvenienze teatrali 163

Soldene, Emily (1840–1912) 20–1, 257
Sontag, Henrietta (1806–54) 151, 152, 236, 265, 281
soprano 29, 57, 75, 76, 88, 214–15, 216–22, 223, 228, 229
    coloratura 216–17, 218, 220–2
    dramatic soprano 218–22
    hochdramatischer Sopran 218–22
    lirico spinto 218–22
    lyric soprano 217–22
Soroldoni, Carlotta 130–3
Spenser, Edmund 36
Spezia, Maria Alighieri (1828–1907) 77
Spontini, Gasparo 124, 169–70, 171, 181, 185–6, 188, 194
    Olimpie 170, 171
St Cecilia, patron saint of music 31
Stabile, Gemma Bosini (1890–1982) 103
stage director 178
stage fathers 120–1, 126, 131, 132, 135, 166, 171, 178, 194
    fictional representation 121
stage mothers 23, 114, 120, 135,
    mockery of 121–3
    operatic representation 121
    singers' accounts of 123–4, 310
    contribution to daughters' careers 123, 124
    as agent 124–6, 134
    marriage 134
    chaperonage 128–30, 131, 142, 145
    as singing tutor 130, 131
Stagno, Roberto 131–2, 133
Stagno-Bellincioni, Bianca (1888–1981) 130, 131, 132, 196, 248, 273
Stanford, Sir Charles Villiers 75, 77, 78, 107
Stanislavski, Constantin 210, 273
Stendhal, Henri Beyle 39, 206–7, 231, 235
Sternberg, Josef von

The Blue Angel 224
Stevens, Catherine (Countess of Essex) 151
Stoltz, Rosine (1815–1903) 10–11, 173, 252
Stolz, Teresa (1834–1902) 181–2, 186
Strakosch, Maurice 80, 186, 191, 193
Strauss, Richard 10, 193, 218, 227
    Ariadne auf Naxos 217
    Der Rosenkavalier 14, 227
    Elektra 90
    Salome 117, 267, 271–2
Strepponi, Giuseppina (1815–97) 137, 194, 195, 201
Sucher, Rosa (1849–1927) 263
Sullivan, Arthur 20
Sunderland, Susan (1819–1905) 76
Svengali 46, 94, 115, 117, 119, 178

Tacchinardi, Nicola 96, 121, 164, 166, 167, 171, 191, 234, 245
Tacchinardi-Persiani, Fanny (1812–67) 171–2, 180, 192
Talma, François-Joseph 206, 233
Tamagno, Francesco 77
Tamberlick, Enrico 130
Tamburini, Antonio 244, 245
Tchaikovsky, Pyotr Il'yich 10, 150–1
    Eugene Onegin 14
Teck, Princess of 138
Tellini, Ines Alfani (1896–1985) 103
Ternina, Milka (1863–1941) 102
Tetrazzini, Luisa (1871–1940) 42, 70, 71, 101, 153, 311
Teyte, Maggie (1888–1976) 82, 97, 141, 142, 191, 196
Tiberini, Angiolina Ortolani-Valandris (1836–?) 40
tenor 4, 82, 90, 97, 214–15, 216, 218, 223, 225, 226
    female tenor 77

tenor (cont.)
   Heldentenor 219
   tenore di forza 15, 218, 244, 245
Tess, Giulia (1889–1976) 21, 103
Tessoni, Teresa (n.d.) 105
theatrical agent 166, 178, 195
Thérésa (1837–1913) 224
Thomas, Ambroise
   Mignon 193
   Hamlet 217
Tietjens, Therese (1831–77) 130
Tolstoy, Leo
   War and Peace 39
Toscanini, Arturo 129, 178
Tosi, Adelaide (1800–59) 151, 174
Tosi, Pier Francesco 205
Tosti, Sir Paolo 116
Tovey, Sir Donald 116
tragedy 12–14, 232
   operatic death scenes 11–14
Trebelli, Zélia (1834–92) 244, 245
Tree, Ann (1801–62) 330
Tree, Viola (1885–1938) 116, 178
   study at Royal College of
      Music 116
   study in Italy 116
   professional ambitions 116
   vocal problems 116–17
   operatic debut 117
   loss of voice 117
   audition for Strauss 193
Turner, Eva (1892–1990) 83
Twain, Mark 114

Ulysses 37, 47, 89
undines see singers, image, sirens
Ungher, Caroline (Karoline)
      (1803–77) 35, 194
Urso, Camilla (1842–1902) 49
Ursuleac, Viorica (1894–1985) 152

Valentine, Mrs Sydney 87
Valletti, Rosa (1878–1937) 224
Varesi, Felice 106, 175, 197
Velluti, Giovanni Battista 191
Verdi, Giuseppe 10, 11, 98, 173, 174, 175,
      181, 186, 196, 197, 207, 210,
      212, 213, 225, 226, 227, 254, 256,
      258–9, 260
   Aida 12, 181, 228
   Attila 14
   Don Carlos 218, 228
   Ernani 12, 174, 244
   Falstaff 228
   Giovanna d'Arco 217
   I Lombardi alla prima crociata 19, 173
   La battaglia di Legnano 19
   La forza del destino 103, 218
   La traviata 11, 12, 13, 18, 80, 117, 175,
      197, 198–9, 200, 221, 225, 226,
      232, 254, 265, 267, 339
   Les Vêpres siciliennes 11, 14
   Macbeth 193, 218, 256, 258, 337
   Otello 12, 209, 210, 254, 259, 270
   Rigoletto 103, 210, 248, 264
   Simon Boccanegra 112, 137
   Il trovatore 200, 227–8
   Un ballo in maschera 12, 226
Vernier, Rafaella (n.d.) 122
Vestris, Lucia (1797–1856) 40, 42
Viardot García, Pauline (1821–1910) 14,
      45, 59–62, 66, 68, 79, 80, 96, 99,
      101, 112, 189, 221–2, 228, 241,
      248, 255
   as 'artist' 184
   dramatic performance 251–3
Victoria, Queen of Great Britain and
      Ireland 22, 32, 54, 72, 75, 76–7
Visetti, Albert 116
vocal tuition and training
   see singing, tuition

Wagner, Cosima 173
Wagner, Richard 10, 12, 19, 20, 75, 78,
        139, 173–4, 178, 205, 207, 226, 236,
        238–9, 258, 259, 263
    heroines 67, 218, 229
    Der fliegende Holländer 12, 173
    Der Ring des Nibelungen 21, 78, 160,
        218, 219–20, 221, 229
    Lohengrin 67, 88, 160, 228, 263, 339
    Rienzi 173, 226
    Tannhäuser 160, 173
    Tristan und Isolde 12, 39, 40, 75, 160,
        173–4, 217, 218, 339
Wartel, Pierre 98
Webb, Mrs 141
Weber, Carl Maria von (1786–1826)
        21, 236
    Der Freischütz 213, 236
Weldon, Georgina (1837–1914) 81
Wells, H. G.
    Ann Veronica 39
Whiteley, John William
    A Sail! 37
Wickham, Anna 72, 73, 113–14, 117
Williamson, Lady 76
Williamson and Musgrove's Light
        Opera Company 21
Wilson, Harriette 19
Wolf-Ferrari, Ermanno
    I gioielli della Madonna 228
Wolfram, Joseph Maria 182–3, 184
    Schloss Candra 182–3

Wollstonecraft, Mary
    Vindication of the Rights of
        Women 6
women
    courtesans and prostitutes 42
    domesticity 65, 73, 83–4, 151
    education 47, 50, 52, 56
    emancipation 5, 10, 16–18, 64,
        67, 83, 84
    'Female Saviour' 6
    feminine ideal 5–6, 7, 14, 18, 33,
        43, 45, 55, 56, 162, 216–18
    femininity 32, 45, 64, 70, 71,
        216–18, 261–6
    feminism 24–5, 63, 65, 85, 113
    ideas of womanhood 16, 57, 58, 83,
        216–17, 218
    instrumentalists 49, 74, 103,
        106, 113
    'male gaze' 24–5, 55
    motherhood 63
    'New Woman' 6, 33, 37, 57, 83
    suffrage movements 33, 57, 83,
        85, 86–8, 220
    Woman Question 10, 84
Women's Musical Congress 86
Wood, Sir Henry 125

Young, George Washington 159

Zingarelli, Nicola 203
    Giulietta e Romeo 167, 169, 175